PORNOGRAPHY
AND SEXUAL AGGRESSION

PORNOGRAPHY
AND SEXUAL AGGRESSION

Edited by

NEIL M. MALAMUTH

Communication Studies
University of California, Los Angeles
Los Angeles, California

EDWARD DONNERSTEIN

Center for Communication Research
Communication Arts
University of Wisconsin—Madison
Madison, Wisconsin

1984

ACADEMIC PRESS, INC.
Harcourt Brace Jovanovich, Publishers
Orlando   San Diego   New York
Austin   London   Montreal   Sydney
Tokyo   Toronto

ACADEMIC PRESS, INC.
Orlando, Florida 32887

United Kingdom Edition published by
ACADEMIC PRESS, INC. (LONDON) LTD.
24/28 Oval Road, London NW1 7DX

Library of Congress Cataloging in Publication Data
Main entry under title:

Pornography and sexual aggression.

    Includes index.
    1. Pornography--Social aspects--Addresses, essays,
lectures. 2. Aggressiveness (Psychology)--Addresses,
essays, lectures. 3. Women--Crimes against--Addresses,
essays, lectures. 4. Violent crimes--Addresses, essays,
lectures. I. Malamuth, Neil M. II. Donnerstein, Edward.
HQ471.P646 1984   363.4'7   84-3086
ISBN 0-12-466280-3 (alk. paper)

PRINTED IN THE UNITED STATES OF AMERICA

    86 87   9 8 7 6 5 4 3 2

To a truly wonderful person,
Eldad,
Who has given me love, hope, and inspiration
N.M.

To Debbie
E.D.

Contents

Contributors

Numbers in parentheses indicate the pages on which the authors' contributions begin.

Paul R. Abramson[1] (173), Department of Psychology, University of California, Los Angeles, Los Angeles, California 90024

Larry Baron (185), Family Research Laboratory, and Department of Sociology, University of New Hampshire, Durham, New Hampshire 03824

Jennings Bryant (115), Department of Communications, University of Evansville, Evansville, Indiana 47701

Donn Byrne (1), Department of Psychology, State University of New York at Albany, Albany, New York 12222

John H. Court (143), Psychology Discipline, School of Social Sciences, The Flinders University of South Australia, Bedford Park, South Australia 5042

Edward Donnerstein (53), Center for Communication Research, Communication Arts, University of Wisconsin—Madison, Madison, Wisconsin 53706

H. J. Eysenck (305), Institute of Psychiatry, University of London, Denmark Hill, London, SE 5, United Kingdom

Jacqueline D. Goodchilds (233), Department of Psychology, University of California, Los Angeles, Los Angeles, California 90024

[1]Author's chapter was completed while he was a Visiting Professor of Psychology at Kyoto University, Kyoto, Japan.

Haruo Hayashi (173), Department of Social Psychology, Hirosaki University, Aomori, Japan 036

Bradford W. Hesse (277), Department of Psychology, University of Utah, Salt Lake City, Utah 84112

Kathryn Kelley (1), Department of Psychology, State University of New York at Albany, Albany, New York 12222

Mary P. Koss (213), Department of Psychology, Kent State University, Kent, Ohio 44242

Kenneth E. Leonard (213), Western Psychiatric Institute and Clinic, University of Pittsburgh, Pittsburgh, Pennsylvania 15260

Daniel Linz (247, 277), Department of Psychology, University of Wisconsin— Madison, Madison, Wisconsin 53706

Neil M. Malamuth (19), Communication Studies, University of California, Los Angeles, Los Angeles, California 90024

Steven Penrod (247, 277), Department of Psychology, University of Wisconsin—Madison, Madison, Wisconsin 53706

Barry S. Sapolsky (85), Communication Research Center, Florida State University, Tallahassee, Florida 32306

Murray A. Straus (185), Family Research Laboratory, and Department of Sociology, University of New Hampshire, Durham, New Hampshire 03824

Charles W. Turner (277), Department of Psychology, University of Utah, Salt Lake City, Utah 32306

Gail L. Zellman (233), The Rand Corporation, Santa Monica, California 90406

Dolf Zillmann (115), Institute for Communications Research, Indiana University, Bloomington, Indiana 47405

Preface

A very large industry exists throughout the world that produces sexually explicit media including books, magazines, videocassettes, and movies. Although reliable data regarding profits from pornography are difficult to obtain, some have estimated that the yearly profits exceed those of the general movie and record industries combined. It is clear that very large numbers of people regularly buy the products of this industry. For example, according to the Target Group Index for 1978, the adult male readership of the two most popular sexually oriented magazines, *Playboy* and *Penthouse,* exceeds the combined readership of the two most popular newsmagazines, *Time* and *Newsweek.* With recent technological developments in cable television and videocassettes, the proliferation of sexually explicit materials has dramatically increased. Not only is this industry a large and important segment of the mass media, but the production and content of sexually explicit stimuli has historically stimulated a great deal of controversy, rhetoric, and acrimonious debate. It is surprising, therefore, that there has been relatively little systematic attention to this topic among social science researchers.

Examination of the number of studies falling under the headings *pornography* or *erotica* in volumes summarizing social science research such as *Psychological Abstracts* or *Communications Abstracts* reveals a dearth of studies. When the presidential Commission on Obscenity and Pornography was created in the late 1960s, a sudden surge of research occurred for a brief period of time. The findings of this commission were given a great deal of attention among social scientists and the public at large. It appeared to some that the general conclusion of the commission—that there was no scientific basis to support contentions that pornography has antisocial effects—settled the issue. Recently, however, factors such as changes in the content of these mass media stimuli and criticisms of the commission's conclusions by some scientists and feminists rekindled researchers' interest in this topic.

This book is designed to present and integrate much of the new research in this area. Where similar measures and conditions were examined by the commission and the newer research, the data themselves are generally consistent. However, the findings of these newer studies by and large challenge the commission's general conclusions. This is because the present studies include assessment of the impact of sexually explicit stimuli under conditions not considered by the commission, such as the effects of violent pornography. The theoretical perspective in these newer studies is, in general, that the stimuli's degree of sexual explicitness per se does not necessarily determine whether prosocial or antisocial effects occur. The research has been guided instead by the view that the message communicated (e.g., that violence has positive consequences, that male dominance over women is natural, that sexuality involves mutual respect) may be crucial in determining the message's effects.

The research presented in this book analyzes various facets of pornography and sexual aggression and possible linkages between them. It is important to note that the terms *pornography* and *sexual aggression* are used in a very general sense. The terms *pornography* and *erotica* (used interchangeably in this volume) refer to many different sexually explicit stimuli, without any pejorative meaning necessarily intended. It is clear that their effects vary markedly, depending on the specific content, the consumer, the culture, and the situation. Sexual aggression is a term also used to refer to many diverse acts. Generally, it is used here to refer to the use of aggression in an attempt to engage in sexual acts or the commission of aggression in the context of sexual arousal. Some of the research in this book also focuses on the causes of male aggression against women that may or may not occur within a sexual context, as well as on possible causes of sexual aggression that are not directly related to pornography. Further, the terms *aggression* and *violence* are sometimes used interchangeably herein. While we recognize that there are often important distinctions among the various stimuli and acts subsumed within the general categories of pornography, erotica, sexual aggression, and violence, we believe it would not be advisable to get bogged down in a debate about the exact meanings of each of the various terms. Instead, the author(s) of each chapter provides the reader with the operational definitions of these terms.

In the introductory chapter, Byrne and Kelley offer a historical perspective on pornography research in general and on the research presented in this volume in particular. The parts that follow present research findings.

In Part I, the chapters by Malamuth and by Donnerstein present the findings of a series of experimental studies that primarily focused on the effects of violent (or aggressive) pornography on fantasies, attitudes, beliefs, and aggressive behavior. They stress the importance of a cultural climate in which acts of aggression against women may be relatively acceptable or unacceptable. These chapters also examine the role of such factors as individual differences in aggressive inclinations, emotional states, and situational inhibitions in mediating the impact of aggressive pornography.

Part II includes two chapters that address experimental research on the impact of pornography that is not primarily violent in content. Sapolsky considers the ability of a theoretical model based on physiological arousal and emotional reactions to account for some of the data in this area. He also discusses various individual difference variables that may affect reactions to pornography. In their chapter, Zillmann and Bryant study the impact of long-term exposure to pornography on arousal and on attitudes. While their findings generally replicate those of the Commission on Obscenity and Pornography (1970) when sexual arousal is the dependent measure, the conclusions with respect to attitudes are very different from those of the commission.

Part III presents correlational data both within the United States and other areas of the world. Court describes data suggesting that legalization of pornography has been associated with an increase in the incidence of rape in several countries. In the next chapter, however, Abramson and Hayashi provide an example of a country where pornography, including violent pornography, is relatively common but where the incidence of reported rape is relatively low. This example should alert the reader to the fact that any connection between the availability of pornography and antisocial behavior, if one indeed exists, is certainly not a simple relationship but one that may be affected by many other factors. In the third chapter of this part, Baron and Straus show a significant association between the sales of pornography magazines in the 50 states of the United States and the rates of reported crimes against women in these states. This relationship remains statistically significant even when several controls are applied.

In Part IV, some psychological and communicative factors that may cause sexual aggression are considered in the chapters by Koss and Leonard and by Goodchilds and Zellman. While the inclusion of these chapters is not meant to provide an exhaustive analysis of the diverse causes of sexual aggression, the editors believe it is crucial to include discussion of possible causes of sexual aggression other than pornography. Such discussions should alert us to the obvious fact that, if certain types of pornography are found to cause sexual aggression, there are clearly many other causal factors that may be at least as important or even more so. Yet, there may be a common thread between some of the causes described in these two chapters and pornography in that they may foster a particular cultural climate that affects attitudes and behavior.

In Part V, two chapters describe the implications for legal change of some of the research in this volume, particularly research on violent pornography. The focus shifts from constitutional law in Chapter 10 by Penrod and Linz to civil, or tort, law in Chapter 11 by Linz, Turner, Hesse, and Penrod. These implications are analyzed in the context of two differing legal systems, that of Great Britain and of the United States.

In the closing chapter, Eysenck considers where we stand now. He draws upon the research of this volume and on his own research and ideas to discuss such issues as difficulties in conducting systematic research on pornography, the nature of the research findings, social policy implications, theoretical issues, and directions for future research.

NEIL M. MALAMUTH
EDWARD DONNERSTEIN

Introduction

Pornography and Sex Research

Donn Byrne
Kathryn Kelley

INVESTIGATIONS OF THE EFFECTS OF PORNOGRAPHY

A major impetus for the experimental investigation of sexuality by behavioral scientists was the appointment by President Johnson of the Commission on Obscenity and Pornography in January of 1968. One of the tasks specified by Congress in Public Law 90-100 establishing the Commission was "to study the effect of obscenity and pornography upon the public, and particularly minors, and its relationship to crime and other antisocial behavior" (Commission on Obscenity and Pornography, 1970, p. 1). The nine volumes of technical reports describing the research sponsored by this group were published in 1971 and constituted the first wave of what has become a major area of research activity for psychologists and others.

Prior to the appearance of the commission's summary report in 1970, knowledge about the effects of explicit erotic stimuli on behavior was severely limited (Cairns, Paul, & Wishner, 1962, 1971). There were a few scattered studies of responses to cheesecake photographs (e.g., Clark, 1952) and to erotic passages from novels and other sources (e.g., Byrne, 1961; Byrne & Sheffield, 1965; Jakobovits, 1965; Paris & Goodstein, 1966). There was research on the effects of music on fantasy responses (Beardslee & Fogelson, 1958) and investigations of authoritarianism as a factor in judging paintings such as *September Morn* to be

PORNOGRAPHY AND
SEXUAL AGGRESSION

pornographic (Eliasberg & Stuart, 1961; Stuart & Eliasberg, 1962). In general, the behavioral effects under investigation were severely limited and involved only selected affective, evaluative, and imaginative responses.

By the latter part of the 1960s, a few bold investigators had gone beyond such research to examine various responses to pictorial stimuli that contained one or more of the three crucial elements of hard-core pornography: erection, penetration, and ejaculation. Further, in some investigations, response measures began to include assessments of subjective and physiological excitement (e.g., Freund, Sedlacek, & Knob, 1965; Jovanovic, 1971) as well as self-reports of overt sexual activity. Such studies included male medical students (Brady & Levitt, 1965; Levitt & Brady, 1965) and various groups of males and females in West Germany (Schmidt & Sigusch, 1970; Schmidt, Sigusch, & Meyberg, 1969; Schmidt, Sigusch, & Schafer, 1973; Sigusch, Schmidt, Reinfeld, & Wiedemann-Sutor, 1970). With the publication of the commission's work, this tentative trickle of research was suddenly augmented by the opening of a floodgate. Over the past few years, such research has steadily grown into one of the mainstream concerns of social, personality, and clinical psychologists.

One of several basic lines of inquiry has been the behavioral effects of erotica. Before summarizing some of the findings and the issues involved in such investigations, it may be helpful to place this phenomenon in its historical context.

SEXUAL DEPICTIONS IN HISTORY AND PREHISTORY

It is well established that sex was among the earliest subjects of art, but we can only guess at the motivations of the creators and the reactions of the viewers. Sexual anatomy (often in exaggerated proportions) and diverse sexual activities were depicted in drawings on the walls of caves, on pottery, and in statuary. Long before the establishment of the Roman Empire, every acceptable and unacceptable sexual practice that we know today (with the exception of obscene telephone calls) had been sketched, painted, carved, or sculpted countless times. In addition, verbal accounts began to be preserved, and in every part of the world sexual behavior was described in lubricious detail in works ranging from the instructional *Kama Sutra* to fictional accounts of sexual activity in China, England, France, Germany, Greece, Italy, Japan, and elsewhere (Legman, 1966). We do not know the effects, good or bad, of such material on what people thought, felt, or did, nor is there much evidence that governmental bodies believed that sexual representations fell within their purview. Erotic writings were published openly and legally, including Poggio's *Facetiarum Liber* in 1470 and Cynthio degli Fabritii's *Origine delle Volgari Proverbi* in 1526. The latter work was depicted to Pope Clement VII (Legman, 1966).

About the time of the Reformation, religious bodies *did* begin to respond to erotic works on moral grounds. The general assumption was that certain activities were intrinsically immoral. Exposure to sexual stimuli was to be avoided because of the dangers involved in inciting impure thoughts, initiating improper desires, and motivating sinful behavior. Thus, the creators of erotica were guilty of corrupting the morals of the innocent, while the consumers of erotica were victims to be protected from the weaknesses of the flesh. In diverse parts of the world those who produced the erotic words and images were prosecuted; the resulting books, paintings, and statues were destroyed; and the corruptible members of the flock were presumably safe from having the opportunity to sin.

One of the first recorded instances of the attempt to invoke secular powers in the regulation of pornography occurred in England in 1708 when action was brought against those who produced *The Fifteen Plagues of Maidenhead*. The court ruled that spiritual rather than legal punishment was appropriate for anyone who wrote "bawdy stuff." Though that skirmish was lost by the forces of censorship, they soon rallied to win the war.

In this particular war, there was, of course, no final victory. By the beginning of the present century, the counterforce of liberalism bearing the banner of free speech was strongly applied. Over and over again, legal battles were fought, and very gradually it became possible to produce books, magazines, photographs, and films that were as unrestricted in content as was true of the "pornographers" of antiquity. Such once-notorious books as Joyce's *Ulysses* (1914) and Lawrence's *Lady Chatterley's Lover* (1928) no longer had to be smuggled into the United States by furtive travelers returning from Europe. It was in 1933 that Joyce's classic work could be brought legally into the United States for the first time; on December 6 of that year, Judge Woolsey ruled that *Ulysses* was not obscene because it did not elicit "lustful thoughts" or "excite sexual impulses" (Woolsey, 1933). Censorship did not die in 1933, however. Even in the 1970s, the state of Maryland continued to spend $70,000 annually on a censorship board that made decisions as to which movies could be shown there and which scenes had to be removed as unacceptable (Carlinsky, 1978). More commonly, in the United States, as in much of the industrially developed world, current legal restrictions on erotica are aimed primarily at *who* may be exposed to sexual images rather than at *what* sexual images may be created. As one sign of the times, the Catholic Church has closed its office that once reviewed the contents of all movies (Ostling, 1980).

Despite these civil libertarian victories, most Americans strongly believe that pornography is potentially dangerous and that it should be subjected to legal restrictions (Frank, 1979; Gordon, 1980; Wallace, 1973; Wilson & Abelson, 1973). Attitudes about pornography are found to be age related. Respondents under 40 are more likely to suggest positive effects such as improving marital sex while those over 40 stress negative consequences such as a breakdown in morals (Merritt, Gerstl, & Lo Sciuto, 1975). Despite the strength of the attitudes expressed on each side of the issue for several hundred years, it must be emphasized once again that until the beginning of the 1970s essentially no information was available as to the effects of erotica. While religious concerns focused on morality and corruption, laws restricting pornography tended to be based on assumptions of behavioral effects (Lederer, 1980; Wills, 1977). These assumptions ranged from the possible encouragement of some unacceptable behavior that was depicted in the erotic material (e.g., bestiality) to less direct behavioral effects of arousal on unacceptable behavior that was not necessarily depicted (e.g., rape). The former assumption rested on an imitation model while the latter assumption involved a drive model. After over a decade of research, what do we know? The data fall into several categories.

THE EFFECTS OF EXPOSURE TO SEXUAL IMAGES

Erotica Is Sexually Arousing

A very consistent finding in a great many experimental investigations is that males and females who read explicit sexual passages, view explicit photographs or films, or listen to erotic recordings become sexually aroused as measured by self-reports of subjective arousal, self-descriptions of physiological reactions, and externally monitored assessments of erections, vaginal vasocongestion, blood pressure, and genital temperature (Kelley & Byrne, 1983). Though arousal can be affected by the subject's sex (Becker & Byrne, in press; Hatfield, Sprecher, & Traupmann, 1978; Herrel, 1975; Kelley, in press; Schmidt, 1975), sexual experience (Griffitt, 1975), and positive versus negative attitudinal orientation to sex (Abramson, Perry, Rothblatt, Seeley, & Seeley, 1979; Mosher & O'Grady, 1979), the most general effect of exposure is sexual excitement (Byrne, 1977; Fisher & Byrne, 1978b; Griffitt, 1973; Przybyla, Byrne, & Kelley, 1983).

The mechanisms underlying such arousal are not fully documented, but existing evidence suggests that cognitive and imaginative processing is necessary (Geer & Fuhr, 1976; Przybyla & Byrne, 1984). Subjective reports indicate that individuals exposed to an erotic audiotape tend to generate visual imagery that depict the scenes being enacted or described (Stock & Geer, 1982). It has been established for some time that self-generated imaginative activity (even in the absence of external erotic depictions) can elicit arousal as intense as or more intense than that based on external erotica (Byrne & Lamberth, 1971; Fuhr, 1976; Henson & Rubin, 1971; Laws & Rubin, 1969).

Societal Data: Perhaps Erotica Has Beneficial Effects

Those with the most permissive attitudes about pornography have gone a step beyond the belief that erotic stimuli are harmless. Their argument is that sex and sexual arousal are healthful, liberating, and otherwise "good for you" (Bernstein, 1982; Goleman & Bush, 1977). In addition, it is possible that even the most objectionable content is of value because those who are aroused by such material can satisfy their needs through fantasy-induced masturbation and hence avoid acting out their fantasies with innocent victims (Crepault, 1972). Even among contributors to this volume, views differ, as represented in the opinions expressed by Court in Chapter 5 in contrast to those of Abramson and Hayashi in Chapter 6.

Interestingly enough, several kinds of data are consistent with the "pro-pornography" position. Eysenck (1972) reports that sex criminals are several years older than noncriminals before they first view a picture of intercourse. Other studies of sex criminals paint a picture of individuals raised in sexually restrictive families, who hear less, see less, and know less about sexual matters than is true of other criminals or of noncriminals (Goldstein, Kant, & Hartman, 1974).

Even more impressive, perhaps, has been the experience in Denmark where laws were changed in the 1960s removing all restrictions dealing with the production and distribution of erotica. In addition to the economic boom to pornographers, the purveyors of live sex shows, and tourism, the effect on Danish behavior was dramatic and generally unexpected. Sex crimes, such as rape, Peeping Tomism, and child molestation showed an immediate *decrease,* a trend that continued in subsequent years (Ben-Veniste, 1971; Commission on Obscenity and Pornography, 1970; Kutchinsky, 1973). As indicated by Court in Chapter 5, there are controversies about Kutchinsky's data. For example, it is contended that only nonviolent sex crimes showed a decrease, and this limited effect may be attributable to a lower rate of reporting minor offenses.

Nevertheless, most arguments about the benefits of pornography plus the supporting data raised the interesting possibility that explicit erotica could serve to prevent the development and expression of antisocial sexual behavior.

The Initial Experiments: Erotica Has Minimal, Short-Term Effects

To the disappointment of both the anti-pornography majority and the pro-pornography avant-garde, the initial wave of experimental data on the behavioral effects of erotic stimulation was not very dramatic. Though there was no systematic analysis of stimulus variables (heterogeneous subject matter in several media), subject populations (married–unmarried, student–nonstudent, nationality), or response measures (an array of self-report and physiological assessment devices), investigators reported that erotica had either no effect on overt behavior or it slightly increased the probability of an individual engaging in previously established patterns of sexual activity (Amoroso, Brown, Pruesse, Ware, & Pilkey, 1971; Byrne & Lamberth, 1971; Cattell, Kawash, & De Young, 1972;

Eisenman, 1982; Kutchinsky, 1971). Such behavioral effects were relatively short lived and their primary expression was during the hours immediately following exposure. Continued exposure to such material, even when different stimuli are presented on each occasion, tends to result in less and less responsivity (Howard, Reifler, & Liptzin, 1971; Kelley, 1983; Mann, Berkowitz, Sidman, Starr, & West, 1974).

Many sexually tolerant observers reacted positively to this body of evidence that attributed only negligible or even benign effects to pornography. The conclusions were comfortably consistent with values involving free speech, civil liberties, and sexual liberalism.

Some of those directly involved in such research were also quite relieved to find that erotic presentations in the laboratory did not send sex-crazed subjects dashing into the streets to commit unspeakable sexual acts with passing strangers. Nevertheless, there was a lingering sense of disquiet about the early conclusions. The doubts were of several kinds. Berkowitz (1971) noted that the liberal values of behavioral scientists led them to look at similar data on the effects of violent and sexual stimuli and subsequently to condemn the violence and condone the sexuality. In addition, studies of modeling behavior have consistently shown that viewers tend to imitate the activities of filmed models both in interacting with previously feared animals such as snakes and dogs (Bandura, Blanchard, & Ritter, 1969; Bandura & Menlove, 1968), and in aggressing (Bandura, 1965; Bandura, Ross, & Ross, 1963a, 1963b; Leyens, Camino, Parke, & Berkowitz, 1975; Liebert & Baron, 1972; Liebert & Schwartzberg, 1977; Parke, Berkowitz, Leyens, West, & Sebastian, 1977). It seems highly unlikely that sexual behavior constitutes a unique exception to this pattern of findings.

Further, as Malamuth and Donnerstein (1982) have pointed out and as elaborated by Malamuth in Chapter 1 of this volume, individual differences would be expected in response to erotica. Consistent with such an expectation are findings that response to opposite-sex strangers following exposure to erotica involves avoidance behavior for those whose affective state is negative and approach for those who are positive about their sexual excitement (Griffitt, May, & Veitch, 1974). Interestingly, the probability of sexual activity seems to follow the opposite pattern. Fisher and Byrne (1978a) reported greater behavioral effects for erotica among individuals with a negative attitudinal orientation to sex (erotophobes) than for those with positive attitudes (erotophiles), as described by Sapolsky in Chapter 4. Because the range of personality differences in the general population is much greater than among the experimental subjects in such investigations, any dispositional effects may be of even greater importance in the society at large, as suggested in Chapter 8 by Koss and Leonard.

Finally, the effects of erotica on behavior could have been obscured in the initial body of research because two major components of the influence process were missing from the early investigations: the extended time period necessary for change to occur and the specification of the depicted behavior as well as the relationship between the interactants. How important might such components be?

Pornography Revisited: There May Be Strong Effects after All

THE TIME FACTOR

It has been argued elsewhere (Byrne, 1977; Byrne & Kelley, 1983) that brief experimental exposure to erotica is unlikely to demonstrate modeling effects. Zajonc (1968) and his colleagues (Harrison, 1969; Moreland & Zajonc, 1976; Wilson & Nakajo, 1965; Zajonc & Rajecki, 1969) have convincingly shown that *repeated exposure* to various types of stimuli results in decreased anxiety and increasingly favorable evaluations. Because of the anxieties associated with sex in our society, it seems likely that change would be brought about only following a series of contacts with erotica. By no means conclusive, but at least consistent with such a proposition, is the finding that males who are exposed to a great deal of erotica before the age of 14 are more sexually active and engage in more varied sexual behaviors as adults than is true for males not so exposed (Davis & Braucht, 1973).

Even if erotica influences behavior, the search for those influences in overt sexual behavior may yield little. Simply searching for immediate effects on sexual practices could be futile because the first changes brought about by repeated exposure tend to involve emotions, fantasies, and beliefs (Byrne, 1977). For example, when Wishnoff (1978) exposed sexually inexperienced undergraduate females to explicit erotic films, sexual anxiety decreased while expectations about engaging in intercourse in the near future revealed a sharp increase. Had this investigator simply assessed whether or not they engaged in intercourse immediately after viewing the film, he would have been forced to the erroneous conclusion that the erotica had no effect whatsoever. Using multiple exposures to erotica and assessing a variety of possible responses, Zillmann and Bryant in Chapter 4 report a series of effects that are qualitatively and quantitatively different from those in the usual experiments.

The possible influence of the context or the setting in which the exposure occurs was also suggested by Malamuth and Donnerstein (1982). An incident in a graduate seminar illustrates one aspect of situational effects. A small group of students who were interested in sex research were shown four of the Schmidt and Sigusch (1970) films (explicit depictions of masturbation, petting, and coitus) in order to determine which to use as the stimulus material in an experiment. One male student later described his reaction to the films as consisting primarily of anxiety and embarrassment without the least amount of sexual arousal. When the class was over, however, and he was back in his apartment, his memories of the movie scenes resulted in intense excitement that culminated in masturbation. Presumably, his thoughts about the films were more exciting than the actual images on the screen in part because sexual excitement and sexual activity were differentially acceptable in the two different settings.

With this student, masturbation was initiated by the delayed effects of the erotica. This brings up a second aspect of context—the availability of a cooperative partner with whom to engage in the interpersonal behavior depicted in the erotic scenes. Modeling obviously cannot take place if there are constraints on the behavior in question. Analogously, violent gunplay in movies is difficult to model in countries such as Japan and Great Britain because of legal restrictions on the possession of such weapons; the ubiquity of firearms in the United States permits simple imitation. With respect to sex, the viewer must not only have a sexual partner who is amenable to participating in a specific behavior, but there is an intervening step in which the topic must somehow be broached. In our society, it is very difficult even for couples who regularly have sexual relations to discuss alterations in their routine. In fact, it is difficult for many people to discuss sex at all (Fisher, Miller, Byrne, & White, 1980) or even to talk about contraceptive protection (Byrne, 1983). A possibly apochryphal letter to Ann Landers contained a complaint from a female about having to pay for birth control pills over the past 2 years rather than share the cost with her boyfriend. She felt that she did "not know him well enough" to discuss financial matters. Similarly, spouses may "not know each other well enough" to discuss the possibility of group sex, anal intercourse, bondage, or whatever else they might otherwise be inclined to model from pornographic sources.

Altogether, then, an extended time period for examining the effects of erotica on behavior is needed so that (1) the subject becomes desensitized to any anxiety-evoking effects; (2) informational, expectative, and intentional changes can occur; (3) the subject can experience erotica in varying settings; and (4) the individual can locate and communicate with an agreeable partner.

Such an extended framework for research seems likely to lead us to quite different conclusions about pornography from those reached in 1971. Even so, the entire enterprise tends to retain a relatively benign atmosphere. That is, lovers might utilize erotic depictions as instructional materials that add variety to their sexual interactions (e.g., the Japanese prints and paintings described by Abramson and Hayashi in Chapter 6), therapists might help dysfunctional patients to overcome their fears and inhibitions by exposing them to images of uninhibited autosexual and heterosexual activity (Anderson, 1983; Heiby & Becker, 1980; Heiman, Lo Piccolo, & Lo Piccolo, 1976; Madsen & Ullman, 1967; McMullen & Rosen, 1979; Nemetz, Craig, & Reith, 1978; Nims, 1975; Ranzani, 1972; Wincze & Caird, 1976; Wish, 1975), and those with deviant preferences could be changed for the better through experience with alternative excitatory cues (Abel & Blanchard, 1974; Lazarus, 1968; Marquis, 1970; Wolpe, 1963). Unfortunately, there are some less positive potential effects.

NEGATIVE AFFECT AND AGGRESSIVE CONTENT

Beyond the lyrical depiction of lovers in love, consider other possibilities. What if the emotional state elicited by the sexual imagery involves negative affect rather than simply sexual arousal and pleasure (White, 1979)? What if the content of the erotica includes unequal power relationships, coercion, or violence (Steinem, 1980)? What if no willing partner is available, but the viewer has been shown that unwilling partners are legitimate objects of one's sexual expression and that, deep down, women really *like* for a man to force sex on them (Burt, 1980; Mosher, 1971)? Sex differences in communicating sexual intentions are described by Goodchilds and Zellman in Chapter 9; ambiguities in interpretation might well be "resolved" by the messages contained in aggressive erotica.

When any or all of these elements—negative affect, coercive imagery, and rape myths—are integral aspects of the pornographic presentation, some very different consequences are suggested beyond arousal, sexual enhancement, and reduced anxiety and are described in the chapters by Sapolsky, by Court, and by Baron & Straus (Chapters 3, 5, and 7) and elsewhere (Cline, 1970, 1974; Eysenck & Nias, 1978). Exposure to particular kinds of erotic imagery can result in an increase in aggressive-sexual fantasies, aggressive behavior, acceptance of anti-female attitudes, and, specifically, in male aggression against females (Malamuth & Donnerstein, 1982). In the extreme case, the fusion of sex and violence is such that, among some rapists, sexual arousal is greatest in response to images of nonconsensual sex and even in response to nonsexual violent depictions (Abel, Barlow, Blanchard, & Guild, 1977). It is such aspects of pornography-induced sexual aggression that provide the theme of this book. Most of the following chapters summarize the existing theoretical and empirical knowledge about the effects of pornography on sexual aggression.

A CONCLUDING CAUTION

Prevailing attitudes about erotica have swung back and forth from acceptance to rejection over the past centuries. Empirical research in the second half of the twentieth century has led to equally mercurial conclusions as procedures and methodologies have been constantly refined, extended, and improved. To an increasing degree, however, we have firm data as to what kinds of effects to expect from what kinds of erotica on what kinds of individuals under clearly specified conditions. On the basis of such data, behavioral scientists may become inclined to place themselves on the side of selective censorship of erotica, and their research findings can serve an important evidential role as described by

Linz, Turner, Hesse, and Penrod in Chapter 10. Such a stance may be extremely uncomfortable for many of us, and the legal barriers as outlined by Penrod and Linz in Chapter 9 are as formidable as the ideological ones. Before we embrace censorship with undue enthusiasm, however, two difficulties should be recognized. First, as has been repeatedly demonstrated in attempts to forbid the creation and use of strongly desired products (e.g., alcohol, marijuana, pornography), legal bans are never totally effective. Second, there is reason to believe that the very act of censorship can induce aggressive responses while at the same time alter perceptions of the restricted material so that it appears to be even more desirable and more exciting than before the barriers were raised (Brock, 1971; Tannenbaum, 1971; Worchel & Arnold, 1973).

Perhaps a better procedure is that of federal regulations that protect consumers from ingesting potentially dangerous substances by warning of the harm attributable to a particular product. This type of data-based action seems far preferable to either shrill complaints against any and all sexual depictions or smug assumptions that no one can be harmed by any form of erotica.

Both the study of sexual behavior and the conclusions to which they lead us may be coming of age.

REFERENCES

Abel, G. G., Barlow, D. H., Blanchard, E., & Guild, D. (1977). The components of rapists' sexual arousal. *Archives of General Psychiatry, 34,* 895–903.

Abel, G., & Blanchard, E. (1974). The role of fantasy in the treatment of sexual deviation. *Archives of General Psychiatry, 30,* 467–475.

Abramson, P. R., Perry, L. B., Rothblatt, A., Seeley, T. T., & Seeley, D. M. (1979). *Negative attitudes toward masturbation and pelvic vasocongestion: A thermographic analysis.* Unpublished manuscript, University of California at Los Angeles, Department of Psychology, Los Angeles.

Amoroso, D. M., Brown, M., Pruesse, M., Ware, E. E., & Pilkey, D. W. (1971). An investigation of behavioral, psychological, and physiological reactions to pornographic stimuli. In *Technical report of the Commission on Obscenity and Pornography,* Vol. 8 (pp. 1–40). Washington, DC: U.S. Government Printing Office.

Anderson, B. L. (1983). Primary orgasmic dysfunction: Diagnostic considerations and review of treatment. *Psychological Bulletin, 93,* 105–136.

Bandura, A. (1965). Influence of models' reinforcement contingencies on the acquisition of imitative responses. *Journal of Personality and Social Psychology, 1,* 589–595.

Bandura, A., Blanchard, E., & Ritter, B. (1969). Relative efficacy of desensitization and modeling approaches for inducing behavioral, affective, and attitudinal changes. *Journal of Personality and Social Psychology, 13,* 173–199.

Bandura, A., & Menlove, F. L. (1968). Factors determining vicarious extinction of avoidance behavior through symbolic modeling. *Journal of Personality and Social Psychology, 8,* 99–108.

Bandura, A., Ross, D., & Ross, S. (1963a). Imitation of film-mediated aggressive models. *Journal of Abnormal and Social Psychology, 66,* 3–11.

Bandura, A., Ross, D., & Ross, S. (1963b). Vicarious reinforcement and imitative learning. *Journal of Abnormal and Social Psychology, 67,* 601–607.

Beardslee, D. C., & Fogelson, R. (1958). Sex differences in sexual imagery aroused by musical stimulation. In J. W. Atkinson (Ed.), *Motives in fantasy, action, and society* (pp. 132–142). Princeton, NJ: Van Nostrand.

Becker, M. A., & Byrne, D. (in press). Self-regulated exposure to erotica, recall errors, and subective reactions as a function of erotophobia and Type A coronary-prone behavior. *Journal of Personality and Social Psychology.*

Berkowitz, L. (1971, September). *Bad aggression and good (or bad) sex: Some observations on the reports of the violence and pornography commissions.* Paper presented at the meeting of the American Psychological Association, Washington, DC.

Bernstein, S. (1982). Editorial. *Puritan, 9,* 1.

Ben-Veniste, R. (1971). Pornography and sex crime: The Danish experience. In *Technical report of the Commission on Obscenity and Pornography,* Vol. 7 (pp. 245–261). Washington, DC: U.S. Government Printing Office.

Brady, J., & Levitt, E. E. (1965). The relation of sexual preferences to sexual experiences. *Psychological Record, 15,* 377–384.

Brock, T. C. (1971). Erotic materials: A commodity theory analysis of availability and desirability. In *Technical report of the Commission on Obscenity and Pornography* Vol. 1 (pp. 131–137). Washington, DC: U.S. Government Printing Office.

Burt, M. R. (1980). Cultural myths and support for rape. *Journal of Personality and Social Psychology, 38,* 217–230.

Byrne, D. (1961). Some inconsistencies in the effect of motivation arousal on humor preferences. *Journal of Abnormal and Social Psychology, 62,* 158–160.

Byrne, D. (1977). The imagery of sex. In J. Money & H. Musaph (Eds.), *Handbook of sexology* (pp. 327–350). Amsterdam: Excerpta Medica.

Byrne, D. (1983). Sex without contraception. In D. Byrne & W. A. Fisher (Eds.), *Adolescents, sex, and contraception* (pp. 3–31). Hillsdale, NJ: Lawrence Erlbaum Associates.

Byrne, D., & Kelley, K. (1983). *Internal and external imagery as determinants of individual differences in sexual expression.* Unpublished manuscript, State University of New York at Albany, Department of Psychology, Albany.

Byrne, D., & Lamberth, J. (1971). The effect of erotic stimulation on sex arousal, evaluative responses, and subsequent behavior. In *Technical report of the Commission on Obscenity and Pornography,* Vol. 8 (pp. 41–67). Washington, DC: U.S. Government Printing Office.

Byrne, D., & Sheffield, J. (1965). Response to sexually arousing stimuli as a function of repressing and sensitizing defenses. *Journal of Abnormal Psychology, 70,* 114–118.

Cairns, R. B., Paul, J. C. N., & Wishner, J. (1962). Sex censorship: The assumptions of anti-obscenity laws and the empirical evidence. *Minnesota Law Review, 46,* 1009–1041.

Cairns, R. B., Paul, J. C. N., & Wishner, J. (1971). Psychological assumptions in sex censorship: An evaluative review of recent research (1961–1968). In *Technical report of the Commission on Obscenity and Pornography,* Vol. 1 (pp. 5–21). Washington, DC: U.S. Government Printing Office.

Carlinsky, D. (1978, December). People. *Playboy,* 48.

Cattell, R. B., Kawash, G. F., & De Young, G. E. (1972). Validation of objective measures of ergic tension: Response of the sex erg to visual stimulation. *Journal of Experimental Research in Personality, 6,* 76–83.

Clark, R. A. (1952). The projective measurement of experimentally induced levels of sexual motivation. *Journal of Experimental Psychology, 44,* 391–399.

Cline, V. B. (1970). *Minority report of the U.S. Commission on Obscenity and Pornography.* New York: Bantam Books.

Cline, V. B. (1974). *Where do you draw the line?* Provo, UT: Brigham Young University Press.
Commission on Obscenity and Pornography. (1970). *The report of the Commission on Obscenity and Pornography.* Washington, DC: U.S. Government Printing Office.
Crepault, C. (1972). Sexual fantasies and visualization of "pornographic scenes." *Journal of Sex Research, 8,* 154–155.
Davis, K. E., & Braucht, G. N. (1973). Exposure to pornography, character, and sexual deviance: A retrospective survey. *Journal of Social Issues, 29* (3), 183–196.
Eisenman, R. (1982). Sexual behavior as related to sex fantasies and experimental manipulation of authoritarianism and creativity. *Journal of Personality and Social Psychology, 43,* 853–860.
Eliasberg, W. G., & Stuart, I. R. (1961). Authoritarian personality and the obscenity threshold. *Journal of Social Psychology, 55,* 143–151.
Eysenck, H. J. (1972). Obscenity—officially speaking. *Penthouse, 3* (11), 95–102.
Eysenck, H. J., & Nias, D. K. B. (1978). *Sex, violence, and the media.* New York: Harper and Row.
Fisher, W. A., & Byrne, D. (1978a). Individual differences in affective, evaluative, and behavioral responses to an erotic film. *Journal of Applied Social Psychology, 8,* 355–365.
Fisher, W. A., & Byrne, D. (1978b). Sex differences in response to erotica? Love versus lust. *Journal of Personality and Social Psychology, 36,* 119–125.
Fisher, W. A., Miller, C. T., Byrne, D., & White, L. A. (1980). Talking dirty: Responses to communicating a sexual message as a function of situational and personality factors. *Basic and Applied Social Psychology, 1,* 115–126.
Frank, A. D. (1979, January 28). The problem of pornography in cities large and small. *Family Weekly,* 5.
Freund, D., Sedlacek, F., & Knob, K. (1965). A simple transducer for mechanical plethysmography of the male genital. *Journal of the Experimental Analysis of Behavior, 8,* 169–170.
Fuhr, R. (1976). *Facilitation of sexual arousal through imagery.* Unpublished doctoral dissertation, State University of New York at Stony Brook, Stony Brook.
Geer, J. H., & Fuhr, R. (1976). Cognitive factors in sexual arousal: The role of distraction. *Journal of Consulting and Clinical Psychology, 44,* 238–243.
Goldstein, M. J., Kant, H. S., & Hartman, J. J. (1974). *Pornography and sexual deviance.* Berkeley: University of California Press.
Goleman, D., & Bush, S. (1977). The liberation of sexual fantasy. *Psychology Today, 11* (5), 48–49, 51–53, 104, 106–107.
Gordon, S. (1980). Sexual politics and the far right. *Impact '80, 1*(3), 1–2.
Griffitt, W. (1973). Response to erotica and the projection of response to erotica in the opposite sex. *Journal of Experimental Research in Personality, 6,* 330–338.
Griffitt, W. (1975). Sexual experience and sexual responsiveness: Sex differences. *Archives of Sexual Behavior, 4,* 529–540.
Griffitt, W., May, J., & Veitch, R. (1974). Sexual stimulation and interpersonal behavior: Heterosexual evaluative responses, visual behavior, and physical proximity. *Journal of Personality and Social Psychology, 30,* 367–377.
Harrison, A. A. (1969). Exposure and popularity. *Journal of Personality, 38,* 359–377.
Hatfield, E., Sprecher, S., & Traupmann, J. (1978). Men's and women's reactions to sexually explicit films: A serendipitous finding. *Archives of Sexual Behavior, 7,* 583–592.
Heiby, E., & Becker, J. D. (1980). Effect of filmed modeling on the self-reported frequency of masturbation. *Archives of Sexual Behavior, 9,* 115–121.
Heiman, J., Lo Piccolo, L., & Lo Piccolo, J. (1976). *Becoming orgasmic: A sexual growth program for women.* Englewood Cliffs, NJ: Prentice-Hall.
Henson, D., & Rubin, H. (1971). Voluntary control of eroticism. *Journal of Applied Behavior Analysis, 4,* 37–44.
Herrell, J. M. (1975). Sex differences in emotional responses to "erotic literature." *Journal of Consulting and Clinical Psychology, 43,* 921.

Howard, J. L., Reifler, C. B., & Liptzin, M. B. (1971). Effects of exposure to pornography. In *Technical report of the Commission on Obscenity and Pornography*, Vol. 8 (pp. 97–132). Washington, DC: U.S. Government Printing Office.

Jakobovits, L. A. (1965). Evaluational reactions to erotic literature. *Psychological Reports, 16*, 985–994.

Jovanovic, U. J. (1971). The recording of physiological evidence of genital arousal in human males and females. *Archives of Sexual Behavior, 1*, 309–320.

Kelley, K. (1983). *Variety is the spice of erotica: Repeated exposure, novelty, sex, and sexual attitudes.* Unpublished manuscript, State University of New York at Albany, Department of Psychology, Albany.

Kelley, K. (in press). Sex, sex guilt, and authoritarianism: Differences in responses to explicit heterosexual and masturbatory slides. *Journal of Sex Research.*

Kelley, K., & Byrne, D. (1983). Assessment of sexual responding: Arousal, affect, and behavior. In J. Cacioppo & R. Petty (Eds.), *Social psychophysiology* (pp. 467–490). New York: Guilford.

Kutchinsky, B. (1971). The effect of pornography: A pilot experiment on perception, behavior, and attitudes. In *Technical report of the Commission on Obscenity and Pornography*, Vol. 8 (pp. 133–169). Washington, DC: U.S. Government Printing Office.

Kutchinsky, B. (1973). The effect of easy availability of pornography on the incidence of sex crimes: The Danish experience. *Journal of Social Issues, 29*(3), 163–181.

Laws, D., & Rubin, H. (1969). Instructional control of an autonomic sexual response. *Journal of Applied Behavior Analysis, 2*, 93–99.

Lazarus, A. (1968). A case of pseudonecrophilia treated by behavior therapy. *Journal of Clinical Psychology, 24*, 113–115.

Lederer, L. (Ed.). (1980). *Take back the night: Women on pornography.* New York: William Morrow.

Legman, G. (1966). Introduction. In Anonymous, *My secret life* (pp. xxi–lxii). New York: Grove Press.

Levitt, E. E., & Brady, J. P. (1965). Sexual preferences in young adult males and some correlates. *Journal of Clinical Psychology, 21*, 347–354.

Leyens, J. P., Camino, L., Parke, R. D., & Berkowitz, L. (1975). Effects of movie violence on aggression in a field setting as a function of group dominance and cohesion. *Journal of Personality and Social Psychology, 32*, 346–360.

Liebert, R. M., & Baron, R. A. (1972). Some immediate effects of televised violence on children's behavior. *Developmental Psychology, 6*, 469–475.

Liebert, R. M., & Schwartzberg, N. S. (1977). Effects of mass media. *Annual Review of Psychology, 28*, 141–173.

Madsen, C., & Ullman, L. (1967). Innovations in the desensitization of frigidity. *Behavior Research and Therapy, 5*, 67–68.

Malamuth, N. M., & Donnerstein, E. (1982). The effects of aggressive-pornographic mass media stimuli. In L. Berkowitz (Ed.), *Advances in experimental social psychology*, Vol. 15 (pp. 103–136). New York: Academic Press.

Mann, J., Berkowitz, L., Sidman, J., Starr, S., & West, S. (1974). Satiation of the transient stimulating effect of erotic films. *Journal of Personality and Social Psychology, 30*, 729–735.

Marquis, J. (1970). Orgasmic reconditioning: Changing sexual object choice by controlling masturbatory fantasies. *Journal of Behavior Therapy and Experimental Psychiatry, 1*, 263–271.

McMullen, S., & Rosen, R. C. (1979). Self-administered masturbation training in the treatment of primary orgasmic dysfunction. *Journal of Consulting and Clinical Psychology, 47*, 912–918.

Merritt, C. G., Gerstl, J. E., & Lo Sciuto, L. A. (1975). Age and perceived effects of erotica-pornography: A national sample study. *Archives of Sexual Behavior, 4*, 605–621.

Moreland, R. L., & Zajonc, R. B. (1976). A strong test of exposure effects. *Journal of Experimental Social Psychology, 12*, 170–179.

Mosher, D. L. (1971). Sex callousness toward women. In *Technical report of the Commission on Obscenity and Pornography*, Vol. 8 (pp. 313–325). Washington, DC: U.S. Government Printing Office.

Mosher, D. L., & O'Grady, K. E. (1979). Sex guilt, trait anxiety, and females' subjective sexual arousal to erotica. *Motivation and Emotion, 3,* 235–249.

Nemetz, G. H., Craig, K. D., & Reith, G. (1978). Treatment of female sexual dysfunction through symbolic modeling. *Journal of Consulting and Clinical Psychology, 46,* 62–73.

Nims, I. (1975). Imagery, shaping, and orgasm. *Journal of Sex and Marriage Therapy, 1,* 198–203.

Ostling, R. N. (1980, October 6). A scrupulous monitor closes shop. *Time,* 70–71.

Paris, J., & Goodstein, L. D. (1966). Responses to death and sex stimulus materials as a function of repression-sensitization. *Psychological Reports, 19,* 1283–1291.

Parke, R. D., Berkowitz, L., Leyens, J. P., West, S. G., & Sebastian, R. J. (1977). Some effects of violent and nonviolent movies on the behavior of juvenile delinquents. In L. Berkowitz (Ed.), *Advances in experimental social psychology,* Vol. 10. New York: Academic Press.

Przybyla, D. P. J., & Byrne, D. (1984). The mediating role of cognitive processes in self-reported sexual arousal. *Journal of Research in Personality, 18,* 54–63.

Przybyla, D. P. J., Byrne, D., & Kelley, K. (1983). The role of imagery in sexual behavior. In A. A. Sheikh (Ed.), *Imagery: Current theory, research, and application* (pp. 436–467). New York: Wiley.

Ranzani, J. (1972). Ejaculatory incompetence treated by deconditioning anxiety. *Journal of Behavior Therapy and Experimental Psychiatry, 3,* 65–70.

Schmidt, G. (1975). Male–female differences in sexual arousal and behavior during and after exposure to sexually explicit stimuli. *Archives of Sexual Behavior, 4,* 353–364.

Schmidt, G., & Sigusch, V. (1970). Sex differences in response to psychosexual stimulation by films and slides. *Journal of Sex Research, 6,* 268–283.

Schmidt, G., Sigusch, V., & Meyberg, U. (1969). Psychosexual stimulation in men: Emotional reactions, changes of sex behavior, and measures of conservative attitudes. *Journal of Sex Research, 5,* 199–217.

Schmidt, G., Sigusch, V., & Shafer, S. (1973). Responses to reading erotic stories: Male–female differences. *Archives of Sexual Behavior, 2,* 181–199.

Sigusch, V., Schmidt, G., Reinfeld, A., & Wiedemann-Sutor, I. (1970). Psychosexual stimulation: Sex differences. *Journal of Sex Research, 6,* 10–24.

Steinem, G. (1980). Erotica and pornography: A clear and present difference. In L. Lederer (Ed.), *Take back the night: Women on pornography.* New York: Morrow.

Stock, W. E., & Geer, J. H. (1982). A study of fantasy-based sexual arousal in women. *Archives of Sexual Behavior, 11,* 33–47.

Stuart, I. R., & Eliasberg, W. G. (1962). Personality structures which reject the human form in art: An exploratory study of cross-cultural perceptions of the nude—Cuban vs. United States. *Journal of Social Psychology, 57,* 383–389.

Tannenbaum, P. H. (1971). Emotional arousal as a mediator of erotic communication effects. In *Technical report of the Commission on Obscenity and Pornography,* Vol. 8 (pp. 326–356). Washington, DC: U.S. Government Printing Office.

Wallace, D. H. (1973). Obscenity and contemporary community standards: A survey. *Journal of Social Issues, 29,* 53–68.

White, L. A. (1979). Erotica and aggression: The influence of sexual arousal, positive affect, and negative affect on aggressive behavior. *Journal of Personality and Social Psychology, 37,* 591–601.

Wills, G. (1977). Measuring the impact of erotica. *Psychology Today, 11,* (3), 30–31, 33–34, 74, 76.

Wilson, W. C., & Abelson, H. I. (1973). Experience with and attitudes toward explicit sexual materials. *Journal of Social Issues, 29* (3), 19–39.

Wilson, W., & Nakajo, H. (1965). Preference for photographs as a function of frequency of presentation. *Psychonomic Science, 3,* 577–578.

Wincze, J. P., & Caird, W. K. (1976). The effects of systematic desensitization in the treatment of essential sexual dysfunction in women. *Behavior Therapy, 7,* 335–342.

Wish, P. (1975). The use of imagery-based techniques in the treatment of sexual dysfunction. *Counseling Psychology, 5,* 52–54.

Wishnoff, R. (1978). Modeling effects of explicit and nonexplicit sexual stimuli on the sexual anxiety and behavior of women. *Archives of Sexual Behavior, 7,* 455–461.

Wolpe, J. (1963). Isolation of a conditioning procedure as a crucial psychotherapeutic factor: A case study. *Journal of Nervous and Mental Disease, 134,* 316–329.

Woolsey, J. M. (1933, December 6). Opinion A. 110–59 in the case of United States District Court, Southern District of New York, *United States of America* V. *One Book called "Ulysses,"* Random House, Inc.

Worchel, S., & Arnold, S. E. (1973). The effects of censorship and attractiveness of the censor on attitude change. *Journal of Experimental Social Psychology, 9,* 365–377.

Zajonc, R. B. (1968). Attitudinal effects of mere exposure. *Journal of Personality and Social Psychology Monograph Supplement, 9,* 1–27.

Zajonc, R. B., & Rajecki, D. W. (1969). Exposure and affect: A field experiment. *Psychonomic Science, 17,* 216–217.

PART I

Aggressive Pornography: Individual Differences and Aggression

The chapters in this first part present the findings of two complementary research programs carried out in the late 1970s and early 1980s. Both programs empirically studied the impact of mass media stimuli involving sexual and/or aggressive themes on the responses of normal subjects. While both male and female subjects participated in these studies, the focus has been primarily on males, since they are more likely to be consumers of pornography and to commit physical aggression in cross-gender relations. There has been some overlap in the issues addressed and methods used in these two research programs. However, by and large, Malamuth and associates have concentrated primarily on beliefs and attitudes, measures of sexual arousal, and reported likelihood of engaging in violence; Donnerstein and associates have focused mainly on behavioral measures of laboratory aggression. The findings of these two research projects have generally been highly consistent and thereby have strengthened the conclusions reached by each of these investigators independently.

In the first chapter, "Aggression against Women: Cultural and Individual Causes," Malamuth presents laboratory and field data that address a series of interrelated questions: What is the relative frequency of stimuli that fuse aggressive and sexual themes within the mass media? Does exposure to aggressive pornography and similar media affect people's sexual responsiveness, fantasies, perceptions, attitudes, beliefs, and aggressive behavior? What theoretical pro-

PORNOGRAPHY AND
SEXUAL AGGRESSION

cesses might account for the effects found? Do individual differences, such as men's propensities to aggress against women, mediate the effects of aggressive pornography? Do men with relatively high inclinations to aggress against women derive more gratification from aggressive pornography than men with lower inclinations? What factors distinguish men with higher inclinations to aggress against women from those men with lower inclinations? Do men in the general population share certain characteristics with convicted rapists that reflect a propensity to commit acts of violence against women? Can generalizations be made from conclusions reached in laboratory studies of aggression to real-world violence such as rape or wife battering? What are the influences of certain recurring themes in aggressive pornography, such as the portrayal of rape victims as becoming involuntarily aroused by the assault? What are potential strategies for counteracting the adverse effects of aggressive pornography?

In the second chapter, "Pornography: Its Effect on Violence against Women," Donnerstein presents the findings of experimental studies on the effects of nonaggressive and aggressive pornography on aggressive behavior. This research systematically addresses questions about the influence of films that brigade sexual and aggressive elements, as compared to either films portraying one of these elements only or to neutral depictions. These questions concern both the impact of differing types of films and the potential role of mediating processes that may account for the effects observed: Does the impact of exposure to various types of pornographic and nonpornographic films on male subjects differ when males as compared to females are the targets of aggression? What role do situational inhibitions regarding the expression of aggression have in mediating the effects of pornography? Does anger instigation heighten the level of aggression produced following exposure to pornography, particularly aggressive pornography? Will such exposure increase aggression without any prior anger instigation or without any physiological arousal? What is the importance of associations between characteristics of the victim portrayed in the film and those of the victim in the laboratory? What are the effects of the film victim's reactions on the viewers' aggression? In addition to addressing these and related issues, Donnerstein's research extends earlier work in demonstrating that certain forms of pornography may affect subjects' attitudes and reactions to violence against women.

1

*Aggression against Women: Cultural and Individual Causes**

Neil M. Malamuth

OVERVIEW

Analysis of the causes of male violence against women requires consideration of the interaction among three types of factors: cultural factors that affect members of the society in general, the psychological makeup of individuals who are more likely to commit such acts of violence, and situational factors that may suppress or trigger the actual expression of aggressive responses. This chapter describes data from a research program my associates and I have been conducting that is designed particularly to investigate cultural and individual causes of aggression against women, although some attention has also been given to situational factors. The primary focus of our research has been on violent inclinations in the general population rather than on individuals who were arrested for crimes such as rape. We anticipate, however, that the findings will also shed some light on the roots of aggressive acts that come to the attention of legal and mental health agencies.

*The research reported in this chapter was facilitated by grants from the Social Sciences and Humanities Research Council of Canada.

19

Individual Causes

Our research on individual differences has been geared, as a first step, to identify males within the general population who show greater inclinations to aggress against females. It is our expectation that once we have succeeded in distinguishing among those with different inclinations to aggress against women, we can proceed to investigate the factors responsible for these differences. We are also interested in the extent to which individual differences mediate the effects of cultural influences.

Cultural Causes

One of the ways we have attempted to study the role of cultural factors is by focusing on the mass media. The media, according to numerous writers (e.g., Brown, 1981; Goffman, 1979), both reflect and shape cultural images, values, social scripts, etc. Our research in this area has to date dealt primarily with sexually explicit materials, that is, pornography.[1] It is important to note, however, that the effects found are likely to occur with other types of stimuli as well and that the depiction of sexual aggression in the mass media is by no means limited to pornography. For example, a content analysis of sexual interactions in television soap operas (Lowry, Love, & Kirby, 1981) indicated that aggressive sexual contact was the second most frequent type of sexual interaction (with erotic touching among unmarried persons being the most frequent). Similarly, a cover story in *Newsweek* magazine (1981, September 28) focused on the tremendous viewer attention that soap operas have attracted. Interviews in *Newsweek* with producers and actors from these shows stressed the belief that aggression against women attracts audiences, for example, "The male population started watching us because we no longer were wimps. When a woman was wrong, we'd slap her down" (p. 65). Thus, although the discussion in this chapter concerns primarily empirical findings on the effects of aggressive pornography, we expect the conclusions also apply to many other areas of the mass media.

INDIVIDUAL DIFFERENCES: PROPENSITY TO RAPE

Research Strategy

In this section, I describe research concerning individual differences among subjects. Attention to individual differences has unfortunately frequently been neglected in psychology and sociological research in general and in mass media research in particular (Eysenck, 1978; Eysenck & Nias, 1978). As noted earlier,

[1]The terms *pornography* and *erotica* are used interchangeably in this chapter without any pejorative meaning necessarily intended.

a major part of our research in this area has been geared to identify differences among men within the general population with respect to their inclinations to aggress against women. We have placed some emphasis on this goal for two reasons. First, it is our expectation that if we can differentiate successfully among men vis-à-vis their inclinations to aggress against women, we can begin to study the background factors that may have caused these differences. These might include familial experiences with violence, male–female power relations, sex-role stereotyping, hostility toward women, sexual attitudes and experiences, sensitivity to rejection, social perceptions (or misperceptions), and the like. Second, we anticipate that the impact of mass media stimuli such as aggressive pornography may be mediated by individuals' propensity to aggress against women. This expectation was partially based on research on the effects of media violence on children (Eron, 1982; Huesmann & Eron, 1983). This research suggests a bidirectional causal relationship between aggressive tendencies and media violence (i.e., having higher aggressive inclinations causes more attraction to media violence and exposure to media violence causes increases in aggressive tendencies). We thus hypothesized similar effects, anticipating that individual differences in tendencies to aggress against women would mediate gratifications derived from and susceptibility to be influenced by media portrayals of violence against women.

To study individual characteristics related to aggression against women, we chose to focus on rape. An idea frequently suggested in feminists' writings on the subject of rape is that there are many "normal" men in the general population with a propensity to rape (e.g., Brownmiller, 1975; Russell, 1975, 1980). This perspective is at variance with the position taken by many psychotherapists that rape is a "form of sexual psychopathy" (Groth & Burgess, 1977, p. 406). These therapists, therefore, have focused their attention on treating the pathology of individual rapists. While feminists recognize the need to treat such individuals, they contend that the fundamental underlying causes for most rapes are rooted in traditional sex roles and misogynous forces within society. Such societal factors, according to feminists, cause many men to be inclined to aggress sexually against women, although only relatively few men may actually be convicted of the crime of rape. This view contends that it is essential also to "treat" societal factors in order to address the causes of rape fully.

To address empirically the contention that many men have a propensity to rape requires a more rigorous definition of the concept of "rape proclivity" than is currently available in the feminist literature. It is not readily apparent how one could test empirically the argument that all men are "real or potential rapists" (Clark & Lewis, 1977, p. 140). People have the potential to engage in virtually any behavior. From a scientific perspective, it is more meaningful to consider the relative probability of engaging in certain acts. Thus for the purposes of the present chapter, the degree of a person's "proclivity to rape" will be defined according to the *relative* likelihood to rape under various conditions that may or may not actually occur (e.g., wartime, circumstances where detection is extremely unlikely, etc.).

The following four steps were undertaken in order to determine whether a procedure could be developed to identify differences among men's inclinations to rape (Step 1) and to obtain some assessment of the construct validity (Cronbach & Meehl, 1955) of such a procedure (Steps 2 through 4, inclusive):

1. A procedure of identifying males with a *relative* propensity to rape was developed.
2. Dimensions that discriminate between rapists and nonrapists were found.
3. We determined whether men identified in Step 1 as having a relative propensity to rape were more similar to rapists on the relevant dimensions identified in Step 2.
4. We assessed whether men identified as having a relative propensity to rape were actually more aggressive against women under some conditions.

The discussion that follows presents more information regarding the procedures used in each of these steps and the data obtained.

Identifying Individuals with a Propensity to Rape

In an attempt to identify individuals who may show relatively stronger inclinations to aggress against women, males (mostly college students) were asked in a series of studies (Malamuth, 1981a; Malamuth, Haber & Feshbach, 1980; Malamuth & Check, 1980a, 1981a, 1983; Malamuth, Reisen, & Spinner, 1979; Tieger, 1981) to indicate the likelihood that they personally would rape if they could be assured of not being caught and punished. The samples were derived from varied parts of North America including the Los Angeles and Stanford areas in California and the Winnipeg area in Canada. Typically they were asked to indicate their responses on a 5-point scale ranging from not at all likely (1) to very likely (5). This question was asked under a variety of conditions, such as after viewing a videotaped interview with an actual rape victim, following the reading of a pornographic description of rape, and without any prior exposure treatment at all. While, as might be expected, there was some variability in the distribution of responses across studies, in general there was a great deal of consistency showing that a sizable percentage of the respondents indicated some likelihood of raping (LR). Across these studies, an average of about 35% of males indicated any likelihood of raping (i.e., a 2 or above on the scale) and an average of about 20% reported a 3 or above.[2]

***

[2]Recent research suggests that in addition to differentiating among men on the basis of reported LR it is useful to consider subjects' reported likelihood to use force to coerce a woman into sexual acts. It appears that some of the men who indicate no LR will indicate some likelihood of forcing a woman into sexual acts. More specifically, of approximately 350 men who participated in a study by Briere

Without additional data, the self-report and hypothetical nature of this question (i.e., if you could be assured of not being caught) makes it difficult to judge whether it reveals any socially meaningful information. One way to begin to assess its construct validity (Cronbach & Meehl, 1955) as a measure of rape proclivity is to determine whether LR reports are associated with other responses in a theoretically expected manner.

In order to specify the responses that LR reports should theoretically be associated with, it is necessary to identify responses that distinguish known rapists from the general population. If such responses can be identified reliably, then it can be determined empirically whether those who report a greater LR are more similar to rapists than those who indicate less (or no) LR. If LR reports were found to predict responses known to be associated with rapists, this would provide some empirical support for the possibility that LR reports may reflect a propensity to rape.

Ideally, research that compared the responses of known rapists to those of nonrapists would have access to similar representative samples from both populations. Samples of rapists, however, can generally be obtained only from jails or mental institutions. Since the percentage of rapes that are reported and convicted is very small and since those rapists that are actually convicted differ markedly from those who are not apprehended (Clark & Lewis, 1977; Rada, 1978), rapists samples are probably quite unrepresentative.

This conclusion is supported by a rather unusual attempt to study the responses of rapists who have not come to the attention of the law. Smithyman (1978) placed ads in Los Angeles newspapers asking, "Are you a rapist? If so, call me." He interviewed 50 anonymous callers and found that they differed considerably from samples of convicted rapists (e.g., more of these undetected rapists were college educated).

The present analysis examines whether men who indicated greater LR were more similar to actual rapists (on responses found to characterize rapists) than men who indicated lower LR. As a function of the variables that led certain rapists to be caught and convicted (e.g., low socioeconomic level, particularly brutal act), the unrepresentativeness of rapist samples is far more likely to obscure rather than accentuate similarities that may exist between men with relatively high LR ratings and rapists. If the data nonetheless showed similarities on pertinent dimensions between men who indicated a relatively high LR and con-

---

and Malamuth (1983), about 30% indicated some likelihood of both raping and using force to coerce a woman into sexual acts. About an equal number of subjects indicated some likelihood of using force but no likelihood of raping and the remaining 40% indicated no likelihood of either raping or forcing. This research also suggests that subjects who indicate some likelihood of forcing a woman but who indicate no likelihood when the label "rape" is used are intermediate in their aggressive tendencies between those indicating neither force nor rape likelihood and subjects indicating some likelihood of both.

victed rapists, then it would be likely that even greater similarities would have been found in comparisons with representative samples of rapists.

In order to determine the utility of LR reports as a means of distinguishing among men with differing inclinations to rape, the following steps of the research program were taken: (1) Dimensions were sought that discriminate between rapists and nonrapists, (2) associations between LR and dimensions characterizing rapists were investigated, and (3) associations between LR and aggressive behavior were considered.

Finding Dimensions that Discriminate between Rapists and Nonrapists

Investigators have attempted to identify differences between convicted rapists and control groups on a variety of general measures. For example, comparisons have been made on the Rorscharch Inkblot Test (e.g., Perdue & Lester, 1972), the Minnesota Multiphasic Personality Inventory (MMPI) (e.g., Carroll & Fuller, 1971), the Edwards Personal Preference Schedule (Fisher & Rivlin, 1971), the Buss-Durkee Hostility Inventory (Buss & Durkee, 1957; Rada, Laws & Kellner, 1976), and intelligence scales (Rada, 1978). As discussed by Rada (1978), these studies failed to provide reliable differences between rapists and nonrapists.

There have been, however, two types of responses that appear to discriminate between rapists and the general population. Not surprisingly, these responses seem to be more directly linked to acts of rape. It has been found that rapists are more likely than other males (1) to hold callous attitudes about rape and to believe in rape myths and (2) to show relatively high levels of sexual arousal to depictions of rape (see Malamuth, 1981b, for a more detailed description of these differences in attitudes and sexual arousal).

Likelihood of Raping and Dimensions Characterizing Rapists

LIKELIHOOD OF RAPING AND ATTITUDE

It has been found consistently that individuals with higher LR reports hold more callous attitudes toward rape and believe in rape myths to a greater degree than those with lower LR scores (Malamuth & Check, 1980a; Malamuth, Haber, & Feshbach, 1980; Malamuth et al., 1979; Tieger, 1981). For example, higher LR scores have been shown to be related to (1) the belief that other men would rape if they knew they could avoid being caught, (2) identification with rapists in depictions of rape, (3) perceptions that rape victims cause such assaults and derive pleasure from them (in fictionalized portrayals and in an actual interview with a rape victim), and (4) the belief that women in general secretly desire and enjoy such victimization. Also, higher LR scores have been related to scores on the Rape Myth acceptance scale developed by Burt (1980). The conclusion that higher LR scores are strongly associated with callous attitudes toward rape and with beliefs in rape myths thus seems well supported. The magnitude of the differences between high versus low LR subjects is illustrated in data presented later in this chapter.

LIKELIHOOD OF RAPING AND SEXUAL AROUSAL

LR ratings have been found to be positively correlated with sexual arousal to rape but not with arousal to consenting depictions (Check & Malamuth, 1983; Malamuth & Check, 1980a, 1981a, 1983; Malamuth, Heim, & Feshbach 1980). This has been particularly true of self-reported sexual arousal, although similar results have been obtained with tumescence measures (Malamuth & Check, 1980a, 1981a). The sexual arousal patterns of high LR subjects to rape as compared to consenting-sex portrayals have consistently been found to be much more similar to those of rapists (e.g., Abel, Barlow, Blanchard, & Guild, 1977) than the responses of low LR subjects (Malamuth, 1981b).

The relationship between LR ratings and sexual arousal has been shown to be significantly influenced by the content of the rape depiction. In particular, the manipulation of the rape victim's reaction (i.e., the outcome variable) has been implicated as exerting a major influence on subjects' arousal (e.g., Malamuth & Check, 1980a, 1980b; Malamuth, Heim, & Feshbach, 1980; Quinsey & Chaplin, in press). Findings in this area are well illustrated in the data of Malamuth and Check (1983). In a preliminary session, male subjects were administered questionnaires concerning their sexual attitudes and behaviors. One of the items inquired about the likelihood that the subject himself would rape if he could be assured of not being caught and punished (i.e., the LR item). On the basis of this item, 62 subjects were classified as low LR (a rating of 1 being "not at all likely" on the 5-point scale). Forty-two subjects were classified as high LR (a rating of 2 or higher).

Several days later, these subjects listened to one of eight audio tapes of an interaction involving sexual acts between a man and a woman. The content of these depictions was systematically manipulated along the dimensions of consent (woman's consent vs. nonconsent), pain (woman's pain vs. no pain), and outcome (woman's arousal vs. disgust).

The data highlighted the importance of the interaction between individual differences among subjects and variations in the depiction content in affecting sexual arousal to rape portrayals. As indicated in Figure 1.1. the pattern of the data on both self-report and tumescence measures clearly indicated that when the woman was portrayed as experiencing disgust, both low and high LR subjects were less aroused sexually by the nonconsenting as compared with consenting depictions. However, when the woman was perceived as becoming aroused sexually (the myth frequently portrayed in aggressive pornography), a very different pattern emerged: Low LR subjects were equally aroused to the consenting and the nonconsenting depictions, whereas high LR subjects showed *greater*

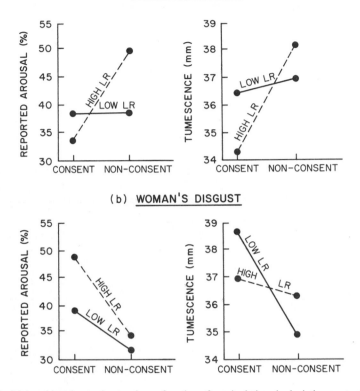

Fig. 1.1. Male subjects' sexual arousal as a function of manipulations in depiction content (consent versus nonconsent and woman's arousal versus woman's disgust) and subjects' LR classification. (From Malamuth & Check, 1983).

arousal to the nonconsenting scenes. It should also be noted that if comparisons are made between the two types of depictions employed by Abel *et al.* (1977) in their research with rapists (i.e., consenting woman's arousal vs. nonconsenting woman's disgust portrayals), the data of the high LR subjects are much more similar to those of the identified rapists than are the data for low LR subjects.

Noteworthy as well is a strong association found in several studies between LR reports and the belief that if the subject were to commit a rape he would find the experience sexually arousing (e.g., Malamuth, 1981b, 1982). These data raise the possibility that in some cases the self-perception (Bem, 1972) that one is sexually aroused by violent pornographic portrayals may result in the attribution that the actual commission of rape would be sexually stimulating. (See Malamuth, 1981b, for more detailed discussion of this issue.)

Likelihood of Raping and Aggressive Behavior

The data reviewed above indicate that LR scores are associated with rape myth acceptance and callous attitudes about rape as well as with sexual arousal to rape in a theoretically expected manner. However, it remains to be demonstrated that LR reports can predict aggressive acts. Obviously, it is impossible to examine rape within an experimental setting. An alternative is to determine whether LR ratings predict acts of aggression that can be studied within a research context. While it is not suggested that such aggression constitutes an actual analogue to the crime of rape, it is suggested that rape is an act of violence related to other acts of aggression against women (Burt, 1980; Clark & Lewis, 1977). Therefore, measures assessing rape propensity should predict other acts of aggression against women. In determining whether LR ratings are associated with aggression, we examined subjects' own self-reported acts of aggression in dating interactions, as well as a more objective measure—aggressive behavior in the laboratory.

DATE AGGRESSION

A significant association has been found consistently between LR ratings and subjects' reports that they have personally used force against females in sexual relations and may do so again in the future. This association was obtained both when subjects reported such "date aggression" on items embedded within other questions on a lengthy questionnaire (e.g., Malamuth & Check, 1981a) as well as when using a scale developed by Koss and Oros (1982) to specifically measure the incidence of sexual aggression (Malamuth, 1982).

LABORATORY AGGRESSION

In a number of recent studies (Malamuth, 1981b, 1982, 1983; Malamuth & Check, 1982), males (both students and nonstudents) were first asked how likely they would be to rape if they could not be caught (i.e., the LR report). Days later, the same subjects participated in what was ostensibly a totally different experiment; it was actually the second phase of the research. Postexperimental questionnaires verified that subjects believed they were participating in two completely unrelated experiments. In this second phase of the research, subjects were mildly rejected and insulted by a woman or by a man (confederates of the experimenter). The study used a Buss paradigm (see Buss, 1961). Subjects were allowed to choose among different levels of aversive noise and of money that they could (ostensibly) administer to the confederate as punishment for incorrect responses and rewards for correct responses. This research has generally found that higher LR ratings are associated with the delivery of higher aversive noise levels and lower rewards to the female target but not to the male target. Furthermore, self-reported likelihood of committing various violent acts (e.g., murder, armed robbery) or sexual acts (e.g., group sex, pedophilia) assessed in a similar manner as the LR report do not show similar predictive ability of male aggression against women (Malamuth, 1982). These data suggest that higher LR ratings are predictive of male aggression against women under certain conditions (such as when aggression is to some degree sanctioned within the laboratory).

Conclusions

The data show that a substantial percentage of the male subjects indicated some likelihood that they would rape if they could be assured of not being caught. These LR reports were found to be associated with attitudes, sexual arousal, and aggressive behavior in a theoretically predicted pattern based on rapists' attitudinal and arousal patterns and on the conceptualization of rape as an act of aggression linked to other aggressive acts against women. Moreover, LR reports have recently been found to be related in a theoretically predicted pattern to a variety of other responses including sex role stereotyping, personality characteristics, cognitive misperceptions of women's behavior, hostility towards women, and power as a motive for sexuality (Check & Malamuth, 1983; Malamuth, 1982, 1984; Malamuth & Check, 1983).

These data support theorizing that within the general population there are many men with inclinations to commit acts of violence against women. Such findings are consistent with the idea of a continuum of aggressive inclinations placing men with relatively no propensity to aggress at one end and those who have actually aggressed (e.g., rapists) at the other end. At differing points along this continuum between the two extremes would be other men who may have some inclinations to aggress against women but who may not actually commit acts of violence. This perspective suggests that differences along this continuum may be primarily in degree of aggressive propensity and/or the existence of other attributes, such as empathy rather than, in most cases, qualitative differences. To address problems of violence against women adequately, therefore, it is insufficient to treat those men at the extreme of the continuum who are known to have committed acts of violence. It may also be essential to ''treat'' the factors that lead many men to be inclined to aggress against women. This may necessitate basic changes in many aspects of our culture and its socialization practices. We now turn to consider the potential role of one of the many cultural factors that may reflect and contribute to acceptance of violence against women as well as, under some circumstances, cause aggressive behavior.

CULTURAL FACTORS: AGGRESSIVE PORNOGRAPHY

Defining Aggressive Pornography

Many feminist writers argue that pornography is hate literature against women: ''So we can admit that pornography is sexist propaganda, pornography is the theory and rape the practice,'' contends Robin Morgan (1980, p. 139). The content of pornography, according to these writers, is primarily intended to dehumanize and degrade women:

> The most prevalent theme in pornography is one of utter contempt for women. In movie after movie women are raped, ejaculated on, urinated on, anally penetrated, beaten, and, with the advent of snuff films, murdered in an orgy of sexual pleasure. Women are the objects of pornography, men its largest consumers, and sexual degradation its theme. (Barry, 1979; p. 175).

> Pornography, like rape, is a male invention, designed to dehumanize women, to reduce the female to an object of sexual access, not to free sensuality from moralistic or parental inhibition. The staple of porn will always be the naked female body, breasts and genitals exposed, because as man devised it, her naked body is the female's "shame," her private parts the private property of man, while his are the ancient, holy, universal, patriarchal instrument of his power, his rule by force over *her*. Pornography is the undiluted essence of anti-female propaganda. (Brownmiller, 1975, p. 443)

Feminist writers do not object to sexually explicit materials that portray men and women in humanized and positive relationships. Rather, they object to what they perceive as portrayals of unequal power relationships between men and women and the dehumanization and degradation of women (Brownmiller, 1980; Russell, 1975; 1980). They argue that as an expression of a sexist ideology such materials "promote a climate in which acts of sexual hostility directed against women are not only tolerated but ideologically encouraged" (Brownmiller, 1975, p. 444). In other words, their position is that pornography contributes, although not necessarily directly, to acts of violence against women by making such acts seem less reprehensible.

The distinction between aggressive versus "positive" types of pornography is often difficult to establish operationally and conceptually. Gloria Steinem (1980) differentiated between what she considers acceptable erotica from objectionable pornography in the following way:

> Look at any photo or film of people making love; really making love. The images may be diverse, but there is usually a sensuality and touch and warmth, an acceptance of bodies and nerve endings. There is always a spontaneous sense of people who are there because they want to be, out of shared pleasure.
>
> Now look at any depiction of sex in which there is clear force, or an unequal power that spells coercion. It may be very blatant, with weapons of torture or bondage, wounds and bruises, some clear humiliation, or an adult's sexual power being used over a child. It may be much more subtle: a physical attitude of conqueror and victim, the use of race or class difference to imply the same thing, perhaps a very unequal nudity, with one person exposed and vulnerable while the other is clothed. In either case, there is no sense of equal choice or equal power. (p. 37)

In the studies described below, aggressive pornography refers to depictions of sex that would be considered blatantly coercive by Steinem. By and large, these are portrayals in which physical force is either used or threatened to coerce a woman to engage in sexual acts (e.g., rape). At this point, therefore, conclusions and implications of the research findings concerning aggressive pornography can be applied only to such blatantly aggressive materials. Effects of materials that portray coercion more subtly have not been adequately researched as yet. However, the findings presented in this volume by Zillmann and Bryant (Chapter 4) suggest that massive exposure to some pornography that is not blatantly aggressive can have similar effects to those documented from clearly aggressive depictions.

The President's Commission

In 1967 the U.S. Congress established the Commission on Obscenity and Pornography to conduct a thorough investigation of this issue. Based on several converging lines of evidence, the commission concluded in its report (Commission on Obscenity and Pornography, 1970) that the evidence did not support contentions that pornography has antisocial effects. When the commission conducted its research studies, however, aggressive-pornographic materials were relatively infrequent. This may partially explain why the commission's studies almost without exception did not include stimuli that involved rape or other forms of coercive sexuality. The only commission studies in which more than passing attention was paid to such materials were retrospective surveys comparing the reports of sexual offenders, sexual deviants, and comparison groups from the general population regarding their previous exposure to pornography. These studies unfortunately yielded highly conflicting conclusions (Goldstein, Kant, Judd, Rice, & Geen, 1971; Davis & Braucht, 1971).

Although aggressive pornography was relatively rare in earlier years, a number of articles in the general media (e.g., *Time,* 1976, April 5; *Village Voice,* 1977, May 9) and in pornography magazines (e.g., Thistle, 1980) observed that aggression has become increasingly prevalent in sexually explicit books, magazines, and films during the 1970s. More systematic content analyses generally corroborate these observations. For example, Smith (1976a, 1976b) analyzed the content of hard-core paperback books published between 1968 and 1974. He found that, in about one-third of the episodes, force is used, almost always by a male, to coerce a female to engage in an unwanted act of sex. Furthermore, he found that the average number of acts depicting rape doubled from 1968 to 1974. Similarly, Malamuth and Spinner (1980) analyzed the pictorials and cartoons in *Playboy* and *Penthouse* magazines. While throughout this 5-year period about 10% of the cartoons were rated as sexually violent, a change occurred in pictorials, with sexual violence increasing from about 1% in 1973 to about 5% in 1977. In 1982, Dietz and Evans classified 1760 heterosexual pornographic magazines according to the imagery depicted on the cover. Whereas in 1970, when the commission on pornography had completed its research, magazine covers depicting a woman posed alone had predominated, such imagery was found to constitute a much smaller percentage by 1981. In contrast, bondage and domination imagery increased very markedly since 1970 and in 1981 constituted 17.2%

of the magazine covers, second in frequency only to the depiction of couples in sexual activity.

Theoretical Concerns

There appears to be ample reason for concern about the effects of aggressively toned pornographic stimuli. To begin with, the antisocial effects shown to result from nonsexual depictions of aggression in the mass media (e.g., Eron, 1980, 1982; Parke, Berkowitz, Leyens, West, & Sebastian, 1977; Thomas, Horton, Lippencott, & Drabman, 1977) seem likely to also occur when the aggression is presented within a sexual context. However, there are theoretical reasons for being particularly concerned about the fusion of sexuality and aggression in the media (Malamuth & Spinner, 1980). First, the coupling of sex and aggression in these portrayals may result in conditioning processes whereby aggressive acts become associated with sexual arousal, a powerful unconditioned stimulus and reinforcer. In fact, current treatments for sexual offenders using procedures such as covert sensitization or orgasmic reorientation (e.g., Abel, Blanchard, & Becker, 1978; Brownell, Hayes, & Barlow, 1977; Hayes, Brownell, & Barlow, 1978) are based on the premise that conditioning may occur by associating fantasies of socially sanctioned arousal with masturbation or other behaviors. It is also possible that the juxtaposition of media portrayals of aggression and sexuality could lead to conditioning and thereby increase sexual arousal to aggressive stimuli, possibly leading to concomitant changes in fantasies and behavior. Second, in aggressive-pornographic depictions the victim is frequently portrayed as secretly desiring the assault and as eventually deriving sexual pleasure from it (Malamuth, Heim, & Feshbach, 1980; Smith, 1976a, 1976b). In other words, the victim supposedly likes being assaulted sexually. Such information may suggest that even if a woman seems repulsed by a pursuer, she will eventually respond favorably to forceful advances, aggression, and overpowering by a male assailant (Brownmiller, 1975; Johnson & Goodchilds, 1973).

Many subjects may recognize the fictional nature of this type of information. Still, research in cognitive psychology on the "availability heuristic" (Tversky & Kahneman, 1973) and "priming" effects (Higgins, Rholes & Jones, 1977; Wyer & Srull, 1981) suggests that such depictions may nonetheless have a significant impact. (These concepts are discussed in greater detail later in this chapter in the section entitled "Conclusions and Directions for Future Research.") According to the availability heuristic and priming explanations, events that come relatively easily to mind or are more accessible in memory are apt to be regarded as more likely to occur. To the extent that the media presents images of women as responding favorably to male aggression, such images may easily come to people's minds and affect their beliefs, attitudes, and behavior. This possibility is consistent with theorizing and research on the role of the mass media in "cultivating" people's perceptions of the real world (e.g., Gerbner,

Gross, Eleey, Jackson-Beeck, Jeffries-Fox, & Signorelli, 1977; Gerbner, Gross, Morgan, & Signorielli, 1982).

In the next section I summarize the research findings concerning the effects of exposure to aggressive pornography. I examine whether the data indicate that such exposure produces *changes* in a person's sexual responsiveness to aggressive-pornographic stimuli, in fantasies, in perceptions, in attitudes, and in aggressive behavior.

CHANGES INDUCED BY EXPOSURE TO AGGRESSIVE PORNOGRAPHY

Sexual Responsiveness

Little evidence at this time indicates that exposure to aggressive pornography increases a person's sexual responsiveness to such stimuli. A nonsignificant trend in one study (Malamuth, Haber, & Feshbach, 1980) suggested that if subjects first read a sadomasochistic portrayal, their subsequent reported sexual arousal to a rape scene presented shortly afterwards tended to be heightened. Later research, however, did not confirm this finding. Failure to find a sexual arousal enhancement effect of exposure to aggressive pornography has occurred both with single presentations (Malamuth, 1981b; Malamuth & Check, 1980a; 1981a) as well as with repeated presentations over a period of several weeks with five aggressive-pornographic feature-length movies (Ceniti & Malamuth, in press).

Fantasies

Only one experiment to date has examined the effects of aggressive pornography on sexual fantasies (Malamuth, 1981a). Subjects were presented with either rape or mutually consenting-sex versions of a slide–audio show. All subjects were then exposed to the same audio description of a rape incident taken from Abel *et al.* (1977). Later in the same session, they were asked to create their own sexual fantasies and then to record them. Content analyses of subjects' self-reported fantasies indicated that those exposed to the rape version of the slide–audio show created more aggressive sexual fantasies than those exposed to the mutually consenting-sex version.

Perceptions and Attitudes

Considerable data indicate that exposure to aggressive pornography may alter observers' perceptions of rape and of rape victims. In three experiments subjects were presented first with either pornographic rape scenes in which the aggressor perceived that the assault resulted in the female victims' sexual arousal (i.e., a "positive" outcome) or with other depictions (e.g., a rape with victim abhorrence or a mutually consenting scene). Afterwards, all of these subjects were given a different depiction of rape and asked to indicate their perceptions of the experiences of the victim. In two of these experiments (Malamuth, Haber, & Feshbach, 1980; Malamuth & Check, 1980a) those exposed to the positive outcome version of the aggressive scene, in comparison to other subjects, thought the rape victim in the second portrayal had suffered less. The third experiment (Malamuth & Check, 1981b), to be elaborated upon later in this chapter, revealed effects on general perceptions about women.

In contrast to the previously cited studies, Malamuth *et al.* (1979) found no evidence of changes in perceptions or in attitudes following exposure to aggressive pornography. In this experiment, one group of male and female subjects looked at issues of *Penthouse* and *Playboy* magazines showing incidents of sadomasochism and rape. A second group examined issues of these magazines that contained only nonaggressive pornography, and a third group was given only neutral materials. Shortly afterwards, subjects watched a videotaped interview with an actual victim of rape and responded to a questionnaire assessing their perceptions of the victim and her experience. Weeks later, in what was purported to be a general survey of public attitudes, subjects indicated their views on rape. Exposure to the aggressive pornography did not affect perceptions of rape either in response to the videotaped interview with the rape victim or to the survey of attitudes.

One of the differences between this study and the three experiments that did show significant effects on perceptions of rape concerns the content of the materials used. In the three experiments in which antisocial effects were found, the aggressive-pornographic stimuli were specifically selected because they explicitly depicted violence against women as having positive consequences. Malamuth *et al.* (1979), on the other hand, used materials that generally did not show such positive outcomes. At least with respect to cognitive changes, therefore, the antisocial effects of aggressive pornography may be limited to stimuli depicting positive consequences of sexual aggression.

In a field experiment Malamuth and Check (1981a) obtained perhaps the strongest evidence to date to suggest that depictions of sexual aggression with positive consequences can affect social perceptions and attitudes. In this investigation 271 male and female students served as subjects. Some had agreed to participate in a study ostensibly focusing on movie ratings. They watched on two different evenings either (1) the movies *Swept Away* and *The Getaway,* films that portray sexual aggression and suggest that such aggression may have positive consequences, or (2) neutral feature-length movies. These films were viewed in theatres on campus, and two of the movies (i.e., one experimental and one control) were being shown by the university as part of the campus film program.

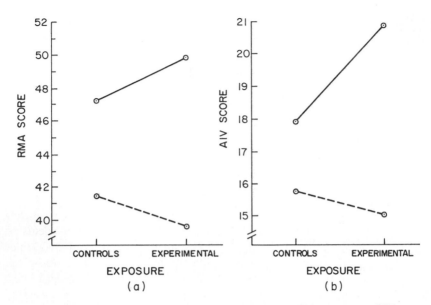

Fig. 1.2 Scores for (a) Rape Myth Acceptance (RMA) and (b) Acceptance of Interpersonal Violence (AIV) as a function of media exposure and subjects' gender. (From Malamuth & Check, 1981a.) (Broken lines represent females; solid lines represent males.)

Members of the classes from which subjects had been recruited but who had not signed up for the experiment were also used as a comparison group. The dependent measures were scales assessing Acceptance of Interpersonal Violence (AIV) against women, Rape Myth Acceptance (RMA), and beliefs in Adversarial Sexual Relations (ASB). These measures were embedded within many other items in a Sexual Attitude Survey administered to all students in classes several days after some of them (i.e., those who had signed up for the experiment) had been exposed to the movies. Subjects were not aware that there was any relationship between this survey and the movies.

Results indicated that exposure to films portraying aggressive sexuality as having positive consequences significantly increased male but not female subjects' acceptance of interpersonal violence against women and tended to increase males' acceptance of rape myths (see Figure 1.2). These data demonstrated in a nonlaboratory setting, not vulnerable to criticisms of laboratory artificiality and demand characteristics (Orne, 1962), that there can be relatively long-term antisocial effects of movies that portray sexual violence as having positive consequences.

Aggressive Behavior

A number of studies examined the effects of viewing aggressive pornography on males' aggression. In an experiment by Malamuth (1978), male subjects were assigned to one of three exposure conditions. Subjects read pictorial stories that contained aggressive pornography, nonaggressive pornography, or neutral stimuli. Both the aggressive- and nonaggressive-pornographic stimuli were taken from issues of *Penthouse* magazine and were reported by subjects to be equally sexually arousing. The aggressive-pornographic stimuli depicted a rape of a woman by a male pirate with some suggestion of a positive outcome. The nonaggressive pornography portrayed a loving interaction between a man and a woman. The neutral stimuli were taken from *National Geographic* magazine. Following exposure to these stimuli, all subjects were insulted by a female confederate and then were placed in a situation where they could aggress against her via the ostensible delivery of electric shocks under one of two assessment conditions. Half of the subjects were assigned to read a communication that suggested that it was "permissible" to behave as aggressively as they wished (disinhibitory communication); the other half were given a communication designed to make them somewhat self-conscious about aggressing (inhibitory communication). The experimental design thus consisted of a 3 (Exposure) × 2 (Communication) factorial design.

The results revealed no significant differences in aggression following the inhibitory communication. Following the disinhibitory communication, the highest level of aggression was found in the aggressive-pornography exposure ($M = 4.20$), which was significantly greater than that following the nonaggressive-pornography exposure ($M = 2.75$). However, the neutral exposure ($M = 3.44$) was not found to differ significantly from either of the other two exposure conditions. The findings, therefore, although somewhat equivocal, pointed to the possibility that aggressive-pornographic stimuli may, under certain conditions, increase aggression against women. These data highlight the important role of situational factors in affecting aggression against women and suggest that, while cultural factors such as aggressive pornography may increase some males' aggressive tendencies, the actual expression of aggressive responses may be strongly regulated by varied internal and external (i.e., situational) variables.

A series of experiments on the effects of aggressive pornography on aggression are discussed in detail by Donnerstein in Chapter 2 and are only summarized briefly here. These experiments used the Buss paradigm (Buss, 1961) in which the delivery of aversive stimuli (e.g., electric shock, noise) to the confederate of the experimenter constitutes the operational definition of aggression. The data show that exposure of male subjects to aggressive pornography increases aggressive behavior against *female* but not male targets in comparison to exposure to neutral, nonpornographic-aggressive (e.g., a man hitting a woman) and nonaggressive-pornographic (e.g., mutually consenting sex) media stimuli (Donnerstein, 1980, 1983; Donnerstein & Berkowitz, 1981). Interestingly, nonpornographic films that portrayed aggression against women were also found to increase the levels of males' aggression against female victims, although to a lesser degree than aggressive-pornographic scenes (Donnerstein, 1983).

Increased aggression against female victims following the viewing of aggressive pornography was found both with subjects who were first angered by the confederate as well as with nonangered subjects, although the increase tended to be greater for angered subjects (e.g., Donnerstein & Berkowitz, 1981). Interesting differences between the effects of aggressive pornography on angered as compared to nonangered subjects emerged when the outcome of the aggression was systematically manipulated in a manner similar to the experiments described earlier (i.e., positive vs. negative victim reaction). It was found that a negative ending to an aggressive-pornographic film increased aggression only for angered subjects. In contrast, when the victim's reaction was portrayed as positive, a very clear increase in aggression was found for both angered and nonangered male subjects (Donnerstein & Berkowitz, 1981). These data may be interpreted to suggest that positive victim reactions (those that are, as noted earlier, very common in aggressive pornography) may act to justify aggression and to reduce general inhibitions against aggression. The portrayal of negative victim reactions, on the other hand, may inhibit the aggression of nonangered subjects but may fail to restrain the increased violence of individuals in a state of anger or who are particularly inclined to aggress against women for other reasons (Donnerstein & Berkowitz, 1981).

There has been considerable controversy regarding the construct validity and generalizability of conclusions derived from laboratory investigations of behavioral aggression using procedures such as the Buss paradigm (Berkowitz & Donnerstein, 1982; Edmunds & Kendrick, 1980; Kaplan, in press). A series of studies (Malamuth, 1982, 1983; Malamuth & Check, 1982) were designed to address this issue vis-à-vis research on aggression against women. These experiments assessed whether attitudes facilitating aggression and sexual responsiveness to rape would predict male aggression against women within a laboratory setting. While laboratory aggression does not constitute an actual analogue to the crime of rape, we theorized that various acts of aggression against women may share some similar underlying causes (e.g., Brownmiller, 1975; Burt, 1980; Clark & Lewis, 1977). It was reasoned that if the measures designed to assess attitudes condoning aggression against women and sexual responsiveness to rape are valid indicators of aggressive tendencies, then such measures should predict aggressive behavior. Furthermore, to the extent that laboratory aggression is an indicator of aggressive responses in real-world settings, the laboratory provides a feasible means of assessing aggressive acts. Therefore, if a relationship were found between measures of the factors associated with rape and laboratory aggression, support would be provided for the construct validity (Cronbach & Meehl, 1955) of the following nomological network: (1) there are common factors in the varied acts of violence against women, (2) measures of sexual arousal to rape and attitudes can predict aggressive tendencies, and (3) the methodology of assessing aggression within a laboratory context can be used as a basis for testing theory in the area, for further refining the predictive measures of aggression, and for drawing implications to nonlaboratory settings.

The research by Malamuth (1983) was conducted in two phases. In the first phase, two factors theorized to cause rape and related acts of aggression against women were assessed. The subjects were males from the general population, mostly college students. The first factor was labeled Sexual Arousal to Rape, which was measured by the rape index developed by Abel *et al.* (1977) (i.e., sexual arousal to rape relative to arousal to consenting depictions). Two separate measurements of this index were taken several weeks apart using different rape and consenting depictions. Abel *et al.* (see also Abel, Becker & Skinner, 1980; Abel, Blanchard, & Becker, 1976) contend that this measure assesses a "proclivity to rape."

The second factor assessed in the first phase of the research was labeled Attitudes Facilitating Violence. This was measured by the Rape Myth Acceptance (RMA) and Acceptance of Interpersonal Violence (AIV) against women scales developed by Burt (1980). These scales were embedded within many other items so that subjects would not be aware of their specific focus. Burt (1978, 1980) theorized that attitudes about violence against women contribute to the commission of rape and similar aggressive acts.

The second phase of the research was held several days after each subject completed the first phase. In this second phase, aggression was assessed. However, subjects were completely unaware of the relationship between the two phases of the research; they believed that they were participating in two completely unrelated experiments. This procedure eliminated the possible role of demand characteristics. In this second phase, subjects were angered by a woman (a confederate) and were given the opportunity of ostensibly punishing her with aversive noise. Also, subjects were later asked about their desire to hurt the woman with the aversive noise (Baron & Eggleston, 1972).

The results show that the measures assessed in the first phase successfully predicted aggressive behavior in the second phase of the research. This was apparent both in correlational data and in the results of an analysis using "causal" modeling with latent and manifest variables (Bentler, 1978, 1980; Bentler & Bonnett, 1980; Joreskog & Sorbom, 1978) (see Figure 1.3). Using the causal modeling approach, a latent variable named Sexual Arousal to Rape was operationally defined by the two assessments of the rape index. A second latent factor, named Attitudes Facilitating Violence, was operationally defined by the RMA and AIV scales. In addition, a latent factor labeled Aggression against Women was operationally defined by the levels of aversive noise and levels of the reported desire to hurt the woman. The model constructed had causal paths from the Sexual Arousal to Rape and from the Attitudes Facilitating Violence factors to the Aggression against Women factor. This model was tested by the LISREL IV program (Joreskog & Sorbom, 1978). The model was found to represent the

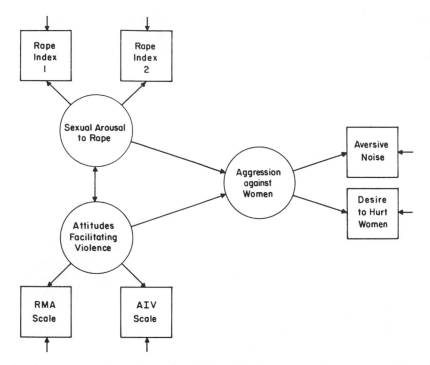

Fig. 1.3 Model of factors associated with real-world aggression against women as predictors of laboratory aggression. (From Malamuth, 1983.)

data successfully and both of the causal paths to aggression were found to be significant, indicating that better prediction of laboratory aggression could be achieved from assessing both Sexual Arousal to Rape and Attitudes Facilitating Violence than on the basis of either of these factors individually. Together, these two factors accounted for 43% of the variance of the Aggression against Women factor.

Malamuth and Check (1982) recently attempted to replicate and extend one aspect of the above findings—the prediction of aggression on the basis of scales measuring attitudes about aggression. In addition to the RMA and AIV scales, they administered to male undergraduates a scale that assessed General Acceptance of Violence (GAV) (in contrast to acceptance of violence against women). The results indicated that the RMA and AIV scales but not the GAV scale successfully predicted aggression against women. These data are in keeping with other findings in our research program suggesting that male aggression against women may be affected by processes that differ from those that affect male–male aggression, although there also are, in all likelihood, common mechanisms affecting aggression against male or female targets.

These findings provide support for the construct validity of the nomological network described above. The data may be especially pertinent to the debate concerning the external validity of laboratory assessment of aggression (e.g., Berkowitz & Donnerstein, 1982). It is hoped that these data will encourage further empirical work in this area with particular emphasis on the development of testable theoretical models of the cultural and individual factors that cause aggression against women.

THE INTERACTION BETWEEN CULTURAL AND INDIVIDUAL CAUSES

The data presented heretofore indicate (1) that cultural factors such as the mass media can affect responses associated with aggression against women and (2) that meaningful distinctions can be made empirically among men in the general population vis-à-vis their propensity to aggress against women. Now we turn to an example of research designed to relate these two lines of investigation by assessing the interaction between cultural and individual factors. We sought to determine whether the individual characteristics of men mediate the impact of mass media messages.

In this experiment (Malamuth & Check, 1981b), male undergraduates were first classified as low versus high LR on the basis of their responses to a questionnaire administered in a preliminary session. A laboratory session was held at a later date. In this session, subjects were randomly assigned to listen to audiotapes that were systematically manipulated in their content along the dimensions of consent (women's consent vs. nonconsent) and outcome (women's arousal vs. disgust). Later, subjects completed a questionnaire about their beliefs regarding the percentage of women, if any, that would "enjoy" being raped. Ethical questions may be raised concerning the use of such questions since their use may perpetuate or strengthen existing beliefs in rape myths. However, the use of a debriefing shown to be effective at counteracting such false beliefs (Malamuth & Check, in press; Check and Malamuth, in press; Donnerstein & Berkowitz, 1981) may justify these inquiries within a research context.

The results (see Figure 1.4) indicated a main effect of LR reports, with high LR subjects estimating much higher percentages of women enjoying being raped in comparison with low LR subjects ($M = 24.7\%$ and $M = 6.63\%$, respectively, $p < .0001$). In addition, an interaction effect was obtained between the consent (consenting versus nonconsenting sex) and outcome (arousal versus disgust) dimensions. Whereas the manipulation of outcome (i.e., woman's arousal vs. woman's disgust) within the consenting portrayals had no significant impact on subjects' perceptions of women's reactions to rape, manipulations of the outcome dimension within nonconsenting (i.e., rape) depictions did significantly affect subjects' perceptions. However, further analyses indicated that this impact primarily occurred with high LR subjects who had earlier been exposed to

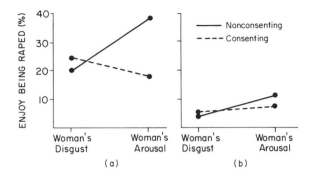

Fig. 1.4 Males' belief that women enjoy rape as a function of subjects' LR classification and exposure to manipulations in media depiction: (a) high LR subjects, (b) low LR subjects. (From Malamuth & Check, 1981b.)

the nonconsenting woman's arousal depiction. This high LR group believed that more women would enjoy being raped (mean of 36.9%) than high LR subjects presented with the other depictions (see Figure 1.4). For low LR subjects, the manipulation of outcome within the rape depictions did not have a significant effect, although the pattern of the means was in the same direction as the significant differences obtained for high LR subjects. These data suggest that men who have relatively higher inclinations to aggress against women are not only accepting of rape myths to a relatively high degree but may also be particularly susceptible to the influence of media depictions of such myths.

CONCLUSIONS AND DIRECTIONS FOR FUTURE RESEARCH

The overall pattern of the data across the various laboratory and field experiments discussed in this chapter strongly supports the assertion that the mass media can contribute to a cultural climate that is more accepting of aggression against women. This is not to suggest that the mass media is the most or even one of the most powerful influences in this area. Rather, it may be only one of the many factors that interact to affect responses. The nature of the effects and the degree of influence may depend, among other things, on the background and psychological makeup of the persons exposed to the media stimuli and the sociocultural context in which exposure takes place. The data are consistent with a bidirectional causal relationship also identified elsewhere in research on media violence (Huesmann & Eron, 1983) such that individuals with higher inclinations to aggress against women may derive more gratification from media portrayals of violence against women and may also be more susceptible to the influence of such messages. The latter conclusion, that individuals with higher aggressive tendencies are more susceptible to media influences, is consistent with the findings of other research on the effects of television violence on children's aggression (for a review of these data see Dorr & Kovaric, 1980).

If a point is reached at which we conclude that the weight of the evidence is sufficiently compelling to justify social action to bring about changes in the content of the mass media, how can this be accomplished? We should be cognizant of the reality that demonstrating scientifically the existence of negative effects is unlikely to be sufficient to prompt changes when strong economic and structural–institutional factors resist such changes. This is aptly documented in discussions of the limited success of attempts to bring about modifications in media content based on research on the negative effects of television violence (Siegel, 1980) and of children's advertising (Choate, 1980).

There are, however, some indications that the research reported herein is directly affecting social policy in some countries. For example, this research was cited as the basis for the British Board of Film Censors' decision to cut 4 minutes from the film *Death Wish II*. These 4 minutes depicted a rape scene. Moreover, this board indicated that the present research has increased the likelihood of further restrictions on violent portrayals in television and in cinemas (see *New Zealand Herald*, March 24, 1982, and *Auckland Star*, July 4, 1982). These events should not be interpreted as necessarily indicating my endorsement of censorship. Also, as discussed in Chapter 10 by Penrod and Linz, the laws relevant to censorship differ greatly in the United States as compared with countries such as Great Britain.

There are a variety of strategies that may be used to introduce changes in media content. Elsewhere, I have discussed legal, political–economic, and educational strategies (Malamuth, 1984). My intent has *not* been to advocate specific changes or particular strategies. Rather, as an investigator conducting research in an area relevant to social policy decisions, I believe that it is important to explore such policy options in order to highlight issues that merit further research. While I shall not discuss specific policy alternatives here, I briefly outline some research issues that are likely to be relevant to various social policy options. These consist of research on the type of stimulus, context of presentation, setting of exposure, and educational interventions.

Type of Stimuli

A need clearly exists to investigate systematically the type of mass media stimuli that may have antisocial effects. The aggressive-pornographic stimuli used in the research discussed in this chapter fall, as noted earlier, into the blatantly coercive category according to the distinctions suggested by Steinem (1980). Are the effects found limited to such materials or might similar effects be obtained with stimuli that more subtly or indirectly portray unequal power relationships between males and females? In other words, is there a clear distinction to be made between aggressive and nonaggressive pornography, or is it more accurate to distinguish sexually explicit stimuli that place emphasis on "shared pleasure" (Steinem, 1980) from aggressive pornography that varies on a continuum of blatancy? Future research should assess the impact of varied types of sexual materials including those that portray unequal power relations between males and females without the explicit depiction of aggression.

Context of Presentation

The increased acceptance of aggression against women found by Malamuth & Check (1981a) occurred following exposure to movies that have been shown on national television and were clearly not X-rated pornographic films. Moreover, the primary theme of the films was not aggressive sexuality. It may be that a film that is explicitly pornographic is perceived as highly unrealistic and stimulates subjects' defenses against accepting the information conveyed uncritically. In contrast, the type of film used by these investigators may communicate more subtly false information about women's reactions to sexual aggression and thus may have a more potent effect on viewers who are not "forewarned" (Freedman & Sears, 1965) by the label "X-rated" or "pornographic." Similarly, the portrayal of sexual aggression within such "legitimate" magazines as *Playboy* or *Penthouse* may have a greater impact than comparable portrayals in hard-core pornography. Research is needed that examines specifically the impact of the context within which aggressive pornography appears.

Setting

In concluding their discussion of research on the effects of mass media violence on children's aggression, Parke *et al.* (1977) stress the need to address the question "How does this influence occur in naturalistic settings?" A similar emphasis is needed in research on aggressive pornography. While laboratory experiments provide a useful framework for determining whether aggressive pornography *can* affect aggressive tendencies (Berkowitz & Donnerstein, 1982), there is a need at this point to extend the examination of influences that mass media stimuli may have to naturalistic settings. To accomplish this goal a multimethod approach including correlational analyses using statistical controls must be employed (e.g., causal modeling [Bentler, 1980]) as well as laboratory and field experiments.

We also need to obtain survey data regarding the use of aggressive and other types of pornography by differing subject populations in naturalistic settings. These data should be gathered in the context of developing theoretical models concerning the "uses and gratifications" (Katz, Blumler, & Gurevitch, 1973) of such media stimuli as well as concerning the effects of exposure. The development of models will require information not only about pornography consumption, but about other aspects of the person. The testing of these models may require experimental research to move beyond single exposures to measure impact over long time periods of differing "dosages" of aggressive pornography in the context of other media stimuli. Causal modeling may prove particularly useful in testing aspects of theoretical models not amenable to experimental manipulations (e.g., the hypothesis that childhood experiences mediate the impact of pornography).

Mediating Processes

It is important that future research analyzes the mediating processes responsible for the effects found as a result of exposure to mass media stimuli that brigade sexual and aggressive elements. One of the effects consistently found is that exposure to media depictions that suggest that women derive some pleasure from being sexually assaulted increases men's acceptance of such a myth (Malamuth & Check, 1980a; 1981a, 1981b). To consider some potential mediating processes, let us focus on the findings of Malamuth & Check (1981b) described in this chapter in the section entitled "The Interaction between Cultural and Individual Causes."

There appear to be three types of processes or explanations that may be relevant to the findings of that and similar studies. The first is that the effects found were not due to any change in subjects' beliefs or perceptions but to a greater willingness to report a belief that may be judged as socially inappropriate (e.g., that women enjoy being raped). Such a change in willingness to report may have been due to disinhibitory (Bandura, 1973) or demand characteristic (Orne, 1962) effects. The former suggests that when subjects were presented with a pornographic portrayal that implied victim arousal they became less concerned about the adverse consequences, such as the experimenter's disapproval, of expressing a rape myth. The latter explanation contends that subjects were merely responding in accordance with the experimenter's perceived expectations. The anonymity of subjects' responses (i.e., no names were indicated and questionnaires were administered in relatively large groups) argues against any fear of consequences by subjects. Similarly, the postexperimental questionnaire data indicating no subject awareness of the hypotheses weakens the demand characteristics explanation. Moreover, similar data in one of the earlier studies in this line of investigation (i.e., Malamuth & Check, 1981a) are extremely unlikely to have been caused by a demand-characteristics process.

A second type of explanation suggests that some new information contained in the nonconsenting woman's arousal depiction changed subjects' perceptions of women's reactions to sexual violence. Such an explanation appears unlikely since it is doubtful that subjects had not previously encountered the type of myth portrayed in the woman's arousal version of the rape depiction. Further, no arguments relevant to changing attitudes were presented.

A third and the most compelling explanation is not based on the acquisition of new information but on the processing of information and its retrieval from memory. Particularly relevant is the growing body of research on "priming effects" mentioned earlier (Higgins, Rholes, & Jones, 1977; Wyer & Carlston, 1979; Wyer & Srull, 1981). According to the priming theoretical framework, when subjects are faced with a judgment, they do not perform a complete search of memory for all relevant information. Instead, they sample only a subset of the relevant information that is most easily accessible in memory, and given that the implications of the information are sufficiently consistent, they may base their judgments on these implications only. One of the factors that has been shown to affect accessibility in memory is the recency with which the concept has been used in the past. Exposure to a communication may make certain cognitions more easily accessible in memory due to the activation (or priming) of these cognitions in the course of processing the information contained in the communication. The primed cognitions may then be used in making subsequent judgments to which these cognitions are relevant. Thus, in the experiment by Malamuth & Check (1981b), exposure to a portrayal of a rape resulting in the victim's arousal may have primed cognitions relevant to such a rape myth. These cognitions might have been used in subsequent inferences (e.g., in judging the frequency of women's pleasurable reactions to being raped).

The use of a priming explanation raises two important issues relevant to the significance of the present findings. The first concerns the fictitious nature of the depictions used and the second the generalizability of priming effects beyond brief durations. It may be argued that priming based on fictitious stories is unlikely to affect judgments about events in the real world. However, considerable evidence suggests that even when subjects are clearly aware of the fictional nature of ideas or information, the greater accessibility of these cognitions in memory may have a significant impact on their real-world judgments (e.g., Carroll, 1978). With respect to the question of the generalizability of priming effects, it is essential to note that while the priming of cognitions used in making judgments may be limited to a relatively short time span, the effects of the inferences affected by the primed cognitions may be of indefinite duration (Srull & Wyer, 1979; Wyer & Srull, 1980, 1981).

One aspect of the data that fits well within a priming theory is the finding that high LR subjects' judgments regarding women's reactions to rape were more affected than those of low LR subjects by exposure to the nonconsenting woman's arousal portrayal. Theory and research on priming effects (e.g., Wyer & Hartwick, 1980) suggest that a communication is more likely to affect attitudes when the audience's existing beliefs are consistent with the information contained in the communication than when the existing beliefs and the communication have inconsistent implications. The data clearly suggested that the beliefs of high LR as compared to those of low LR subjects were initially more in keeping with the myth that many women would enjoy being raped. A priming explanation would therefore predict, as found, that high LR subjects would be more susceptible than low LR individuals to the influence of the nonconsenting woman's arousal depiction.

Educational Interventions

Growing interest in educational interventions to modify the impact of the mass media on the audience is apparent (e.g., Doolittle, 1976; Feshbach, 1978; Singer, Singer, & Zuckerman, 1980). With respect to the media and aggression against women, there are varied educational endeavors that would prove effective. These may be analyzed along two dimensions: indirect versus direct and individual versus mass.

INDIRECT APPROACHES

Indirect educational interventions do not specifically address the content of media depictions but deal with topics or issues that may reduce a person's vulnerability to undesirable media influences. For example, a general sex education program may make a participant sufficiently knowledgeable that he or she would be less likely to be influenced by myths depicted in the media. Such educational programs should teach about similarities and differences in male–female responses, sex-role rigidity and role alternatives, differences in males' and females' interpretations of various "signals" (Abbey, 1982; Henley, 1977), and communication skills. The study by Malamuth and Check (1981b) discussed earlier, which suggested that certain men may be more susceptible to media portrayals of rape myths, may provide a starting point for exploring systematically differences in educational backgrounds that affect vulnerability to media influences.

Another example of indirect educational efforts is the creation of positive alternatives to aggressive pornography. Scandinavian sexologists Drs. Phyllis and Erberhard Kronhausen produced a feature-length X-rated film entitled *The Hottest Show in Town,* which was shown in regular adult theatres throughout North America. This movie was designed to portray sex in a manner much more akin to the desirable erotica advocated in the quote by Steinem (1980) cited earlier in this chapter. Ironically, this movie was sometimes shown in adult theatres as part of a double feature with such films as *Femmes de Sade,* which focused on sadomasochistic relationships between women. Nonetheless, it may be that the availability of "desirable erotica" that portrayed "shared pleasure" (Steinem, 1980) could indirectly counteract the impact of aggressive pornography by providing an alternative to those seeking sexual stimulation via media depictions.

DIRECT APPROACHES

In contrast to indirect approaches, direct educational interventions could address specifically the myths portrayed in the media. As noted earlier, some recent research in this area (Check & Malamuth, in press; Donnerstein & Berkowitz, 1981; Malamuth & Check, in press) presented subjects with information designed to dispel rape myths. This information was presented to subjects who were first exposed to aggressive pornography portraying rape myths as well as to subjects who were not first exposed to such pornography. Assessment of the effectiveness of such educational intervention was conducted as long as 4 months following research participation (Donnerstein & Berkowitz, 1981) and without subjects' awareness that this assessment was related to the earlier exposure to the educational materials (Check & Malamuth, in press; Malamuth & Check, in press). The findings of these studies indicated consistently that the educational interventions were successful in counteracting the effects of aggressive pornography and in reducing beliefs in rape myths. These studies, however, can only be construed as a first step in an area that requires considerable additional work.

INTERVENTIONS FOR INDIVIDUALS

Educational interventions may be designed for individuals judged particularly likely to benefit from such interventions. Educational programs geared to individuals who have already committed crimes such as rape (Burt, 1978) are clearly desirable. It may be ethically questionable, however, to select individuals who have not come to the attention of the law but who according to attitude surveys and self-reported inclinations to aggress against women may be particularly susceptible to media and other influences. Ethical concerns arise because such selection for educational programs may result in undesirable labels applied to the participants.

There is clearly a need, however, for the development of educational interventions that can be applied to individuals. I vividly remember my own experience as a child while waiting for my mother at a magazine counter. I became aware that some respectable-looking men were viewing magazines with aggressive pornographic images. My own confusion was not alleviated by my mother's obvious embarrassment and loss of words when I asked her about the reasons for these images. There is a need for the development of educational guidelines that would help parents to explain aggressive pornography and related media portrayals to both girls and boys. Such efforts may be somewhat facilitated by parental guidelines for dealing with violence in other areas of the media (e.g., Singer *et al.*, 1980).

MASS AUDIENCE INTERVENTIONS

Educational efforts addressing mass audiences are well exemplified by recent media programs (documentaries, docudramas, and fictional drama) concerning subjects such as rape and rape myths (e.g., *Cry Rape, Why Men Rape, A Scream of Silence*) and aggressive pornography (e.g., *Not a Love Story*). These programs were designed to raise the viewers' consciousness about these issues. Such programs may be important in affecting large segments of the population and thereby contributing to a cultural climate that is less accepting of aggression against women. However, trying to reach a large audience without tailoring the information to particular individuals may result in unintended and undesirable effects. For example, such films may include segments showing explicit sexual depictions and rape scenes. These may be sexually stimulating to some members of the audience. Such arousal may interfere with the attitude changes sought by the film's producers. Similarly, such educational films may include interviews with rapists or other men who express rape myths. In light of research that indicates that selective processing of information may lead viewers to strengthen their preexisting beliefs if any supportive information is presented (Lord, Ross, & Lepper, 1979), it is essential to investigate the impact of such media programs. In this area as well as with the other educational endeavors described previously, there is a clear need for research designed to improve the development of a program (i.e., formative evaluation) as well as for research concerned with judging the overall effectiveness of a developed program (i.e., summative evaluation).

In concluding this chapter, I reiterate that it is unlikely that social scientific research on the present topic, or for that matter on most subjects, is likely by itself to be responsible for major social changes. Nonetheless, there is an important role for the researcher in providing data that will aid those engaged in efforts to reduce and prevent violence against women.

REFERENCES

Abbey, A. (1982). Sex differences in attributions for friendly behavior: Do males misperceive females' friendliness? *Journal of Personality and Social Psychology, 42,* 830–838.

Abel, G. G., Barlow, D. H., Blanchard, E., & Guild, D. (1977). The components of rapists' sexual arousal. *Archives of General Psychiatry, 34,* 895–903.

Abel, G. G., Becker, J. V., & Skinner, L. J. (1980). Aggressive behavior and sex. *Psychiatric Clinics of North America, 3,* 133–151.

Abel, G. G., Blanchard, E. B., & Becker, J. V. (1978). An integrated treatment program for rapists. In R. Rada (Ed.), *Clinical aspects of the rapist.* New York: Grune & Stratton.

Abel, G. G., Blanchard, E. B., & Becker, J. V. (1976). Psychological treatment of rapists. In M. Walker & S. Brodsky (Eds.), *Sexual assault: The victim and the rapist.* Lexington, MA: Lexington Books.

Auckland Star, July 4, 1982.

Bandura, A. (1973). *Social learning theory.* Englewood Cliffs, NJ: Prentice-Hall.

Baron, R. A., & Eggleston, R. J. (1972). Performance on the "Aggression Machine:" Motivation to help or harm? *Psychonomic Science, 26,* 321–22.

Barry, K. (1979). *Female sexual slavery.* Englewood Cliffs, NJ: Prentice-Hall.

Bem, D. (1972). Self-perception theory. In L. Berkowitz (Ed.), *Advances in experimental social psychology* (Vol. 6). New York: Academic Press.

Bentler, P. M. (1978). The interdependence of theory, methodology and empirical data: Causal modeling as an approach to construct validation. In D. B. Kendel (Ed.), *Longitudinal research on drug use.* New York: Wiley.

Bentler, P. M. (1980). Multivariate analysis with latent variables: Causal modeling. *Annual Review of Psychology, 31,* 419–456.

Bentler, P. M., & Bonnett, D. G. (1980). Significance tests and goodness of fit in the analysis of covariance structures. *Psychological Bulletin, 88,* 588–606.

Berkowitz, L., & Donnerstein, E. (1982). External validity is more than skin deep: Some answers to criticisms of laboratory experiments (with special reference to research on aggression). *American Psychologist, 37,* 245–257.

Briere, J., & Malamuth, N. M. (1983). Self-reported likelihood of sexually aggressive behavior: Attitudinal vs. sexual explanations. *Journal of Research in Personality, 17,* 315–323.

Brown, B. C. (1981). *Images of family life in magazine advertising.* New York: Praeger.

Brownell, K. D., Hayes, S. C., & Barlow, D. H. (1977). Patterns of appropriate and deviant sexual arousal: The behavioral treatment of multiple sexual deviations. *Journal of Consulting and Clinical Psychology, 45,* 1144–1155.

Brownmiller, S. (1975). *Against our will: Men, women and rape.* New York: Simon and Schuster.

Brownmiller, S. (1980). Let's put pornography back in the closet. In L. Lederer (Ed.), *Take back the night: Women on pornography.* New York: William Morrow and Co.

Burt, M. R. (1978). Attitudes supportive of rape in American culture. *House Committee on Science and Technology, Subcommittee Domestic and International Scientific Planning Analysis and Cooperation, Research into violent behavior: Sexual Assaults* (Hearing, 95th Congress, 2nd session, January 10–12, 1978). Washington, DC: Government Printing Office, pp. 277–322.

Burt, M. R. (1980) . Cultural myths and support for rape. *Journal of Personality and Social Psychology, 38,* 217–230.

Buss, A. (1961). *The psychology of aggression.* New York: Wiley.

Buss, A. H., & Durkee, A. (1957). An inventory for assessing different kinds of hostility. *Journal of Consulting Psychology, 21,* 343–349.

Carroll, J. S. (1978). The effect of imagining an event on expectations for the event: An interpretation in terms of the availability heuristic. *Journal of Experimental Social Psychology, 14,* 88–96.

Carroll, J. L., & Fuller, G. B. (1971). An MMPI comparison of three groups of criminals. *Journal of Clinical Psychology, 27,* 240–242.

Ceniti, J. & Malamuth, N. M. (in press). Effects of repeated exposure to sexually violent or sexually nonviolent stimuli on sexual arousal to rape and nonrape depictions. *Behaviour Research and Therapy.*

Check, J. V. P., & Malamuth, N. M. (1983). Sex-role stereotyping and reactions to stranger vs. acquaintance rape. *Journal of Personality and Social Psychology, 45,* 344–356.

Check, J. V. P., & Malamuth, N. M. (in press). Can participation in pornography experiments have positive effects? *The Journal of Sex Research.*

Choate, R. B. (1980). The politics of change. In E. L. Palmer and A. Dorr (Eds.), *Children and the faces of television.* New York: Academic Press.

Clark, L., & Lewis, D. (1977). *Rape: The price of coercive sexuality.* Toronto: The Women's Press.

Commission on Obscenity and Pornography. (1970). *The report of the commission on obscenity and pornography.* New York: Bantam Books.

Cronbach, L. J., & Meehl, P. (1955). Construct validity in psychological tests. *Psychological Bulletin, 52,* 281–302.

Davis, K. E., & Braucht, G. N. (1971). Exposure to pornograpny, character and sexual deviance: A retrospective survey. *Technical reports of the Commission on Obscenity and Pornography* (Vol. 7). Washington, DC: Government Printing Office.

Dietz, P. E., & Evans, B. (1982). Pornographic imagery and prevalence of paraphilia. *American Journal of Psychiatry, 139,* 1493–1495.

Donnerstein, E. (1980). Aggressive-erotica and violence against women. *Journal of Personality and Social Psychology, 39,* 269–277.

Donnerstein, E. (1983). Erotica and human aggression. In R. Geen and E. Donnerstein (Eds.), *Aggression: Theoretical and empirical reviews* (Vol. 2). New York: Academic Press.

Donnerstein, E., & Berkowitz, L. (1981). Victim reactions in aggressive-erotic films as a factor in violence against women. *Journal of Personality and Social Psychology, 41,* 710–724.

Doolittle, J. (1976). *Immunizing children against the possible anti-social effects of viewing television violence: A curricular intervention.* Unpublished doctoral dissertation, University of Wisconsin-Madison.

Dorr, A., & Kovaric, P. (1980). Some of the people some of the time—but which people? Televised violence and its effects. In E. L. Palmer & A. Dorr (Eds.), *Children and the faces of television.* New York: Academic Press.

Edmunds, G., & Kendrick, D. C. (1980). *The measurement of human aggressiveness.* New York: Wiley.

Eron, L. D. (1980). Prescription for the reduction of aggression. *American Psychologist, 35,* 244–252.

Eron, L. D. (1982). Parent–child interaction, television violence and aggression of children. *American Psychologist, 37,* 197–211.

Eysenck, H. J. (1978). *Sex and personality.* London: Sphere Books.

Eysenck, H. J., & Nias, D. K. B. (1978). *Sex, violence and the media.* London: Granada.

Feshbach, S. (September 1978). *Television advertising and children: Policy issues and alternatives.* Paper presented at the 86th annual meeting of the American Psychological Association, Toronto, Canada.

Fisher, G., & Rivlin, E. (1971). Psychological needs of rapists. *British Journal of Criminology, 11,* 182–185.

Freedman, J., & Sears, D. (1965). Warning, distraction and resistance to influence. *Journal of Personality and Social Psychology, 1,* 262–266.

Gerbner, G., Gross, L., Eleey, M. F., Jackson-Beeck, M. Jeffries-Fox, S., & Signorelli, N. (1977). TV violence profile No. 8: The highlights. *Journal of Communication, 27,* 171–180.

Gerbner, G., Gross, L., Morgan, M., & Signorielli, N. (1982). Charting the mainstream: Television's contributions to political orientation, *Journal of Communication, 32,* 100–126.

Goffman, E. (1979). *Gender Advertisements.* Cambridge, MA: Harvard University Press.

Goldstein, M. J., Kant, H. S., Judd, L. L., Rice, C. J., & Geen, R. (1971). Exposure to pornography and sexual behavior in deviant and normal groups. *Technical reports of the Commission on Obscenity and Pornography* (Vol. 7). Washington, DC: Government Printing Office.

Groth, A. N., & Burgess, A. W. (1977). Rape: A sexual deviation. *American Journal of Orthopsychiatry, 47,* 400–406.

Hayes, S. C., Brownell, K. D., & Barlow, D. H. (1978). The use of self-administered covert sensitization in the treatment of exhibitionism and sadism. *Behavior Therapy, 9,* 283–289.

Henley, N. M. (1977). *Body politics: Power, sex and nonverbal communication.* Englewood Cliffs, NJ: Prentice-Hall.

Higgins, E. T., Rholes, W. S., & Jones, C. R. (1977). Category accessibility and impression formation. *Journal of Experimental Social Psychology, 13,* 141–154.

Huesmann, L. R., & Eron, L. D. (1983). Factors influencing the effect of television violence on children. In M. J. A. Howe (Ed.), *Learning from television: Psychological and educational research.* London: Academic Press.

Johnson, P., & Goodchilds, J. (1973). Pornography, sexuality, and social psychology. *Journal of Social Issues, 29,* 231–238.

Joreskog, K. G., & Sorbom, D. G. (1978). *LISREL IV: Estimation of linear structural equation systems by maximum likelihoods methods.* Chicago: National Educational Resources.

Kaplan, R. (in press). The measurement of human aggression. In R. Kaplan, V. Koencni, & R.

Novaco (Eds.), *Aggression in children and youth*. Rijn, Netherlands: Sijthoff & Noordhuff International Publishers.

Katz, E., Blumler, J. G., & Gurevitch, M. (1973). Uses and gratifications research. *Public Opinion Quarterly, 37*, 509–523.

Koss, M., & Oros, C. (1982). Hidden rape: A survey of the incidence of sexual aggression and victimization on a university campus. *Journal of Consulting and Clinical Psychology, 50*, 445–457.

Lord, C. G., Ross, L., & Lepper, M. R. (1979). Biased assimilation and attitude polarization: The effects of prior theories on subsequently considered evidence. *Journal of Personality and Social Psychology, 37*, 2098–2109.

Lowry, D. T., Love, G., & Kirby, M. (1981). Sex on the soap operas: Patterns of intimacy. *Journal of Communication, 31*, 90–96.

Malamuth, N. M. (September 1978). *Erotica, aggression & perceived appropriateness*. Paper presented at the 86th annual convention of the American Psychological Association, Toronto, Canada.

Malamuth, N. M. (1981a). Rape fantasies as a function of exposure to violent sexual stimuli. *Archives of Sexual Behavior, 10*, 33–47.

Malamuth, N. M. (1981b). Rape proclivity among males. *Journal of Social Issues, 37*, 138–157.

Malamuth, N. M. (1982). *Predictors of aggression against female as compared to male targets of aggression*. Paper presented at the 90th annual meeting of the American Psychological Association, Washington, DC.

Malamuth, N. M. (1983). Factors associated with rape as predictors of laboratory aggression against women. *Journal of Personality and Social Psychology, 45*, 432–442.

Malamuth, N. M. (1984). The mass media and aggression against women: Research findings and prevention. In A. Burgess (Ed.), *Handbook of research on pornography and sexual assault*. New York: Garland Publishers.

Malamuth, N. M., & Check, J. V. P. (1980a). Penile tumescence and perceptual responses to rape as a function of victim's perceived reactions. *Journal of Applied Social Psychology, 10*(6), 528–547.

Malamuth, N. M., & Check, J. V. P. (1980b). Sexual arousal to rape and consenting depictions: The importance of the woman's arousal. *Journal of Abnormal Psychology, 89*, 763–766.

Malamuth, N. M., & Check, J. V. P. (1981a). The effects of mass media exposure on acceptance of violence against women: A field experiment. *Journal of Research in Personality, 15*, 436–446.

Malamuth, N. M., & Check, J. V. P. (1981b). The effects of exposure to aggressive-pornography: Rape proclivity, sexual arousal and beliefs in rape myths. Paper presented at the 89th annual meeting of the American Psychological Association, Los Angeles, CA.

Malamuth, N. M., & Check, J. V. P. (1982). *Factors related to aggression against women*. Paper presented at the annual meeting of the Canadian Psychological Association, Montreal.

Malamuth, N. M., & Check, J. V. P. (1983). Sexual arousal to rape depictions: Individual differences. *Journal of Abnormal Psychology, 92*, 55–67.

Malamuth, N. M., & Check, J. V. P. (in press). Debriefing effectiveness following exposure to pornographic rape depictions. *The Journal of Sex Research*.

Malamuth, N. M., Haber, S., & Feshbach, S. (1980). Testing hypotheses regarding rape: Exposure to sexual violence, sex differences, and the "normality" of rapists. *Journal of Research in Personality, 14*, 121–137.

Malamuth, N. M., Heim, M., & Feshbach, S. (1980). Sexual responsiveness of college students to rape depictions: Inhibitory and disinhibitory effects. *Journal of Personality and Social Psychology, 38*, 399–408.

Malamuth, N. M., Reisin, I., & Spinner, B. (1979). *Exposure to pornography and reactions to rape*.

Paper presented at the 86th annual convention of the American Psychological Association, New York.

Malamuth, N. M., & Spinner, B. (1980). A longitudinal content analysis of sexual violence in the best-selling erotic magazines. *The Journal of Sex Research, 16*(3), 226–237.

Morgan, R. (1980). Theory and practice: Pornography and rape. In L. Lederer (Ed.), *Take back the night: Women on pornography*. New York: William Morrow and Co.

New Zealand Herald, March 24, 1982.

Orne, M. (1962). On the social psychology of the psychological experiment: With particular reference to demand characteristics and their implications. *American Psychologist, 17*, 776–783.

Parke, R. D., Berkowitz, L., Leyens, J. P., West, S. G., & Sebastian, R. J. (1977). Some effects of violent and non-violent movies on the behavior of juvenile delinquents. In L. Berkowitz (Ed.), *Advances in experimental social psychology* (Vol. 10). New York: Academic Press.

Perdue, W. C., & Lester, D. (1972). Personality characteristics of rapists. *Perceptual and Motor Skills, 35*, 514.

Quinsey, V. L., & Chaplin, T. C. (in press). Stimulus control of rapists and non-sex offenders sexual arousal. *Behavioral Assessment*.

Quinsey, V. L., Chaplin, T. C., & Carrigan, W. F. (1980). Biofeedback and signaled punishment in the modification of inappropriate sexual age preferences. *Behavior Therapy, 11*, 567–576.

Rada, R. T. (1978). *Clinical aspects of the rapist*. New York: Grune & Stratton.

Rada, R. T., Laws, D. R., & Kellner, R. (1976). Plasma testosterone levels in the rapist. *Psychosomatic Medicine, 38*, 257–268.

Russell, D. (1975). *The politics of rape*. New York: Stein & Day.

Russell, D. (1980). Pornography and the women's liberation movement. In L. Lederer (Ed.), *Take back the night: Women on pornography*. New York: William Morrow and Co.

Siegel, A. E. (1980). Research findings and social policy. In E. L. Palmer and A. Dorr (Eds.), *Children and the faces of television*. New York: Academic Press.

Singer, D. G., Singer, J. L., & Zuckerman, D. M. (1980). *Teaching television: How to use TV to your child's advantage*. New York: Dial Press.

Smith, D. G. (1976a). *Sexual aggression in American pornography: The stereotype of rape*. Presented at the annual meetings of the American Sociological Association, New York.

Smith, D. G. (1976b). The social content of pornography. *Journal of Communication, 26*, 16–33.

Smithyman, S. D. (1978). *The undetected rapist*. Unpublished doctoral dissertation, Claremont Graduate School, Claremont, CA.

Steinem, G. (1980). Erotica and pornography: A clear and present difference. In L. Lederer (Ed.), *Take back the night: Women on pornography*. New York: William Morrow and Co.

Srull, T. K., & Wyer, R. S. (1979). The role of category accessibility in the interpretation of information about persons: Some determinants and implications. *Journal of Personality and Social Psychology, 37*, 1660–1672.

Thomas, M. H., Horton, R. W., Lippencott, E. C., & Drabman, R. S. (1977). Desensitization to portrayals of real-life aggression as a function of exposure to television violence. *Journal of Personality and Social Psychology, 35*, 450–458.

Thistle, F. (1980). Hollywood goes ape over rape. *Game, 7*, 23–25, 84.

Tieger, T. (1981). Self-reported likelihood of raping and the social perception of rape. *Journal of Research in Personality, 15*, 147–158.

Time (1976, April 5). *The Porno Plague*, 58–63.

Tversky, A., & Kahneman, D. (1973). Availability: A heuristic for judging frequency and probability. *Cognitive Psychology, 5*, 207–232.

Village Voice. (1977, May 9) *Pretty Poison: The selling of sexual warfare*. 18–23.

Wyer, R. S., & Carlston, D. E. (1979). *Social Cognition, inference and attribution*. Hillsdale, NJ: Lawrence Erlbaum Associates.

Wyer, R. S., & Hartwick, J. (1980). The role of information retrieval and conditional inference processes in belief formation and change. In L. Berkowitz (Ed.), *Advances in experimental social psychology* (Vol. 12). New York: Academic Press.

Wyer, R. S., & Srull, T. K. (1980). The processing of social stimulus information: A conceptual integration. In R. Hastie, T. M. Ostrom, E. B. Ebbesen, R. S. Wyer, D. L. Hamilton, & D. E. Carlston (Eds.), *Person memory: The cognitive basis of social perception*. Hillsdale, NJ: Lawrence Erlbaum Associates, pp. 225–300.

Wyer, R. S., & Srull, T. K. (1981). Category accessibility: Some theoretical and empirical issues concerning the processing of social stimulus information. In E. T. Higgins, C. P. Herman, & Mark P. Zanna (Eds.), *Social cognition: The Ontario symposium*. Hillsdale, NJ: Lawrence Erlbaum Associates.

2

Pornography: Its Effect on Violence against Women*

Edward Donnerstein

INTRODUCTION

A major focus of this book is the effect of pornography on sexual violence against women. One interesting aspect, however, is that much of the *experimental* research on pornography and subsequent aggression has concerned itself with primarily male-to-male aggression. For example, in the two chapters to follow (Chapter 3 by Sapolsky and Chapter 4 by Zillmann and Bryant), the major theoretical issues and the actual experimental manipulations revolve around primarily same-sex aggression. There is no question that the vast majority of research on the pornography–aggression link is more related to theoretical issues of human aggression (e.g., arousal) than it is to a discussion of potential sexual assault. One cannot, for obvious reasons, experimentally examine the relationship between pornography and *actual* sexual aggression. One can, however, examine various aspects of this relationship through attitudes, arousal patterns, and aggressive behavior in the laboratory.

It is interesting to note that for many years the issue of pornography and violence against women has been of concern both to writers in the popular media

*The research by the present author which is presented in this chapter was supported in part by grants MH 07788-02 from NIMH, and BNS 8216772 from the National Science Foundation.

and the scientific community. The summary statement of these writings has been a taking for granted that pornography and aggression against women are very much related:

> We are somewhat educated now as to the effects of rape on women, but we know less about the effects of pornography . . . . we can admit that pornography is sexist propaganda, no more and no less. Pornography is the theory, and rape is the practice. (Morgan, 1978)

> Pornography is the undiluted essence of anti-female propaganda . . . . does one need scientific methodology in order to conclude that the anti-female propaganda that permeates our nation's cultural output promotes a climate in which acts of sexual hostility directed against women are not only tolerated but ideologically encouraged. (Brownmiller, 1975)

> Even when they do not overtly depict scenes of violence and degradation of women at the hands of men, such as rape, beatings, and subordination, the tone is consistently anti-feminist. . . . The intention would seem to be simply to degrade women, and it is noteworthy that in many cases of rape the men involved either act in the same manner. . . (Eysenck & Nias, 1978)

What, however, do the data say? In Chapter 1 by Malamuth we saw that certain forms of pornography (specifically, aggressive) can affect aggressive attitudes toward women and can desensitize an individual's perception of rape. These attitudes and perceptions are furthermore directly related to actual aggressive behavior against women (Malamuth, 1983). While this might suggest that exposure to pornography will influence aggression against women, one should keep in mind that *only* violent forms of pornography had an influence on these attitudes. Is there a strong relationship between exposure to such materials and subsequent aggression against females? Is the effect, if it does exist, a function of the pornographic content or is it the images of aggression against women that are important? These issues are the basis of the third section of this chapter. The reader should keep in mind that the review of aggressive pornography and aggression presents studies conducted in the late 1970s and early 1980s.

First, however, we shall explore the effects of nonviolent forms of pornography on subsequent aggression against women. In a number of reviews of the research on pornography and aggression (e.g., Donnerstein, 1980b, 1983a, 1983b; Donnerstein & Malamuth, 1983; Malamuth & Donnerstein, 1982), the general conclusion has been that nonaggressive forms of pornography do not, under most situations, increase violence against women. There are, however, a number of situations in which they do have a direct influence.

The use of the term *nonaggressive* refers to the fact that no overt depictions of physical force are displayed. While this definition is consistent with others that have been used in reviews of the literature (e.g., Malamuth & Donnerstein, 1982), it is quite possible that more subtle forms of aggression (e.g., unequal power relationships) may also influence aggression. This issue is addressed at a later point in the following section of this chapter.

NONAGGRESSIVE PORNOGRAPHY AND
AGGRESSION AGAINST WOMEN

In order to examine the relationship between nonaggressive pornography and subsequent aggression against women, we shall first examine early research conducted for the Commission on Obscenity and Pornography (1971) or soon thereafter. The reader should keep in mind that the materials considered nonaggressive in all studies in this section vary greatly in terms of their content. They also differ in terms of their media mode (e.g., film, magazine pictures). We shall take a brief look at this issue in the summary part of this section.

Early Research

One of the first studies of nonaggressive pornography was by Mosher and Katz (1971) conducted for the U.S. pornography commission. Male college students were asked to aggress verbally against a female assistant for 2 minutes. Subjects were then exposed to either a 10-minute neutral or erotic film. While exposure to the erotic film did not increase later verbal aggression against the female, being told that an increase in aggression would allow subjects to view a more exciting erotic film did heighten the level of verbal insult directed at the female. While some have taken this as evidence that pornography increases aggression against women (e.g., Cline, 1974), others have viewed these data in a different light. For instance, Howitt (1982) in his review of this study notes the following:

> However, it conceals the fact that ''aggression against women'' is a shorthand for saying the subject was required as a part of the experimental procedures to verbally aggress against a female experimenter. Seeing pornography as such definitely did not increase aggression. Telling subjects that they could take part in a further piece of research if their aggression levels against the female experimenter were high enough did. The subjects were perhaps merely keen to take part further in the research. General conclusions about the effects of pornography on aggression against women are meaningless when the truth is revealed. (p. 113)

Furthermore, additional research by Mosher (1971) indicated that exposure to erotica did not increase sex-calloused attitudes or exploitive sexual behavior toward women. Given that attitudes of these types are somewhat related to aggressive behavior, one might conclude that exposure to pornography has no impact on aggression that is directed against females. The reader should note, however, that Chapter 4 in this book by Zillmann and Bryant reveals a different finding with regard to calloused attitudes toward women and exposure to pornography. More will be said about this later.

Two other studies in the literature have also investigated the role of pornography on aggression against women. Jaffe, Malamuth, Feingold, and Feshbach (1974) found that subjects who were sexually aroused by exposure to erotic passages increased their level of aggression equally against both male and female targets. There was no evidence that females were a more likely target of aggression. The general increase in aggression against both male and females following exposure to sexually arousing passages is perhaps best explained in terms of an increase in general arousal (e.g., Donnerstein, 1983a). Baron and Bell (1973) also allowed male subjects an opportunity to aggress against a male or female victim after exposure to sexually arousing stimuli. Not only was there no increase in aggression against a female after exposure, but there was a tendency for aggression to be reduced toward both targets after viewing the sexually arousing pictures. The issue of when and how certain forms of pornography increase or decrease aggression in general is discussed in other chapters (Chapter 3 by Sapolsky and Chapter 4 by Zillmann and Bryant).

This short review points out that, at least until recently, there has been little research on the effects of pornography and aggression toward women. Second, early research indicated that there was no basis for concern regarding the potential for pornography to facilitate aggression against women as a specific population.

Problems with Early Research

There were a number of problems with early research on the relationship between pornography and aggression against women, as suggested by Donnerstein and Barrett (1978), which made a definitive statement about this relationship tenuous. First, other research on pornography and aggression indicated that anger arousal, either prior or subsequent to exposure, was needed in order to obtain a facilitative effect in most situations (e.g., Baron, 1977; Donnerstein, Donnerstein, & Evans, 1975; Zillmann, 1971). In none of the early studies were subjects "instigated" to aggress. Given the general tendency for males to be inhibited about aggressing against a female in a laboratory situation, one might expect that exposure to pornography would not increase aggression unless subjects were disinhibited, perhaps via anger arousal toward a female victim. Second, research seems to indicate that primarily highly arousing pornographic material facilitates subsequent aggression (e.g., Baron, 1977; Donnerstein, 1983a, 1983b). Except, perhaps, for the Jaffe et al. (1974) study, all the early research has employed more mildly arousing materials. Given these basic concerns, which were of course not an issue when these earlier studies were conducted, my colleagues and I began a series of studies that were designed to examine those variables (e.g., anger, arousing stimuli, disinhibitors) that were considered to be important in the pornography–aggression link. By examining how these variables influence aggression against women, one would be able, perhaps, to construct a "fairer" test of the influence on aggression toward females as a function of exposure to nonaggressive pornography.

Again the reader should bear in mind that we are dealing with pornographic materials that are not overtly aggressive in nature. The distinction between aggressive and nonaggressive stimuli is quite important, since many of the limitations on the influence of nonaggressive pornography and violence against women discussed below do not affect more aggressive forms of material. In the following section I examine what this new research on pornography and aggression against women has found.

Experimental Studies on Pornography and Aggression against Women

My colleagues and I conducted three major studies that are examined in the following section. Each is discussed separately, and then I summarize and evaluate the current state on the relationship between pornography and violence against women.

DONNERSTEIN AND BARRETT (1978): THE ROLE OF ANGER AND AROUSAL

In the study by Donnerstein and Barrett (1978) male subjects were first angered or treated in a neutral manner by a male or female accomplice. Following this treatment, all subjects either viewed a 4-minute highly explicit stag film depicting various forms of sexual behavior or viewed a neutral film. Following exposure, subjects were ostensibly given an opportunity to aggress against the male or female accomplice who had previously interacted with them via the administration of shock. Measures of arousal (e.g., blood pressure) were monitored at various points in the experiment. The major results are shown in Tables 2.1 and 2.2.

As Table 2.1 shows the aggression measure reveals two significant interactions. The first, Anger × Sex of Target, indicates that angered subjects were more aggressive than nonangered subjects and that subjects angered by a male were more aggressive than those angered by a female. The second interaction,

TABLE 2.1

Mean Intensity × Duration of Aggression as a
Function of Experimental Conditions[a]

Condition	Anger	No anger
Sex of target		
Male	1.86_a	0.95_c
Female	1.55_b	1.13_c
Films		
Erotic	1.90_a	0.93_c
Neutral	1.45_b	1.15_c

[a]Means with a different subscript differ from each other at the .05 level by Duncan's procedure.

TABLE 2.2

Mean Change in Blood Pressure as a Function of
Experimental Conditions after Film Exposure[a]

	Film	
Condition	Erotic	Neutral
Mean blood pressure		
Anger		
Males	1.8_b	-0.2_b
Females	9.4_a	-3.1_c
No anger		
Males	8.2_a	-3.9_c
Females	7.2_a	-3.9_c
Systolic blood pressure		
Anger		
Males	2.8_b	-1.4_b
Females	11.3_a	-4.8_c
No anger		
Males	11.2_a	-5.6_c
Females	8.6_a	-6.2_c

[a]Means with different subscripts differ from each
other at the .05 level by Duncan's procedure.

Anger × Films, indicates that under no-anger conditions there were no effects
for the films shown, but, when subjects were angry, pornography increased
aggression. Thus, when subjects were exposed to highly sexually arousing stimuli, there was a greater possibility for aggression. More importantly, no differential aggression was observed against females as a function of film exposure. In
fact, as has been the case in past studies (e.g., Taylor & Epstein, 1967), less
aggression was administered to the female targets. Does this imply, therefore,
that such films do not influence aggression against females, as suggested by the
U.S. pornography commission? The physiological data shown in Table 2.2
suggests that perhaps another process was operating with angered subjects. The
blood pressure data indicates higher levels of arousal toward a female target than
a male target after pornography exposure and that this arousal was still present
after aggressing. It might have been expected, therefore, that aggression would
have been greater against females than males. As the data in Table 2.1 reveal,
however, results tend to indicate just the opposite. A study by Taylor and Epstein
(1967) also found increased physiological arousal but nonaggressive behavior in
male subjects who were provoked by a female.

Dengerink (1976) has suggested that in laboratory situations, aggression
against females is generally inhibited due to a fear of disapproval. This might

account for the findings in the Donnerstein and Barrett (1978) study. Although it was expected that anger instigation would act as a facilitator of aggression, it is quite possible that additional disinhibitors are required in order for pornography to influence aggression against a female, if it in fact does. Such disinhibitors are more common in real-world situations (e.g., drugs, alcohol, aggressive cues, environmental stimuli) than in the laboratory. Nevertheless, one can create experimental situations in which aggressive inhibitions are further reduced, thus allowing for the effects of pornography to be more closely examined. The next two studies in this series were designed for this purpose.

DONNERSTEIN, MUELLER, AND HALLAM (SUBMITTED
FOR PUBLICATION): DISINHIBITION VIA MODELING

Data suggest that others who act aggressively can serve as models for an individual's subsequent aggression (e.g., Bandura, 1973). Furthermore, such models can effect aggression even in situations in which such behavior is under normal inhibitions (e.g., Baron, 1977). In the study by Donnerstein, Mueller, and Hallam (1983), therefore, we were interested in further disinhibiting aggression so we could examine the effects of pornography on violence against women.

Male subjects were assigned to a $2 \times 2 \times 2$ design with Sex of Target (male or female), Film Condition (neutral or pornographic), and Model Observation (observation of aggressive model or no observation) treated as factors. At the start of the experiment, half the subjects viewed a live male aggressive model administer high level shocks in the Buss procedure (Buss, 1961) to a male or female target. Subjects in the no-model condition did not observe the actions of the model. Following the modeling manipulation, all subjects were angered by the same target. Subjects then viewed a 5-minute filmclip of an explicit pornographic film or viewed a neutral film. They were then given an opportunity to administer shocks to the target for errors ostensibly made on learning task. Blood pressure readings were taken at various points in this study.

As in the previous study, it was found that male subjects who were angered and exposed to a sexually arousing film were more aroused when the anger was instigated by a female rather than a male. Once again we might have expected that aggression would be greater against the females after exposure to the pornographic film. This was not the case, however. The highest level of aggression was found for subjects exposed to both the model and pornographic film, but paired with a male target. While the model did increase aggression against the female, there were no differential effects across the two film conditions. Once again, then, there was no evidence that exposure to nonaggressive pornography increases aggression against women. In light of studies on aggressive pornography to be discussed later, it is interesting to note that exposure to a male model confederate aggressing against a female did increase subjects' aggressive behavior toward a female target. As we shall see later, symbolic portrayals of women being aggressed against, even without sexual content, can increase subsequent aggressive behavior.

DONNERSTEIN AND HALLAM (1978): MULTIPLE AGGRESSION OPPORTUNITIES

As in the previous two studies, the experiment by Donnerstein and Hallam (1978) was designed to reduce aggressive inhibitions. In this study we adopted a situation similar to that employed by Geen, Stonner, and Shope (1975). These researchers found that multiple opportunities to aggress not only increase aggressive behavior, but act to reduce feelings restraints on aggression. Research that has employed this procedure suggested that many inhibitions toward aggression would be reduced, thus allowing for a judicial test of the effects of pornography on aggression against women. Support for this position comes from Quanty (1976) who notes,

> Laboratory studies that deliberately lower restraints against aggression (e.g., Geen et al. 1975) may be seen as representing a reversal of the normal socialization process. After a subject has been angered, he is allowed (actually told) to attack his adversary. The victim emits no pain cues . . . and the subject not only feels better but learns that, in this laboratory situation, aggression is permissible and socially approved (i.e., condoned by the experimenter). When given a second opportunity to aggress, this subject is more aggressive. (p. 126)

Male subjects in this study were assigned to a $2 \times 3 \times 2$ design with Sex of Target (male or female), Film condition (pornographic, aggressive, no film), and Aggression Opportunity (after film exposure and 10 minutes later) treated as factors. Prior to observing one of the films, all subjects were angered by the male or female target (confederate). Subjects then viewed one of the films. The aggressive film contained no sexual content, and the aggression was primarily male–male. A final group of subjects did not observe a film, but rather waited an appropriate amount of time. All subjects were then given a first opportunity to aggress against their anger-instigator for errors ostensibly made on a learning task. Subjects were then informed that there would be a 10-minute delay in the experiment and were allowed to sit quietly during this time. After this 10-minute wait all subjects were given a second opportunity to aggress. As in previous studies in this series, blood pressure readings were taken at various points during the experiment.

The arousal data indicates that subjects were more aroused by exposure to the pornographic film than the aggressive or no-film condition, and that this increased arousal was maintained even after the first aggression opportunity. The results with regard to aggression are presented in Figure 2.1. As can be seen, when male subjects were given an opportunity to aggress immediately, it was found that the pornographic film increased aggression beyond that of the no-film control. This finding corroborates those of other investigators (e.g., Meyer,

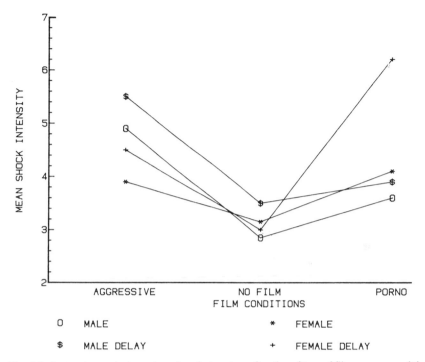

Fig. 2.1 Aggression against a male or female target as a function of type of film exposure and time of aggression opportunity. Subjects aggressed against the male or female target immediately after film exposure and then after a 10-minute delay.

1972; Zillmann, 1971) who have found that highly arousing sexual films can act to facilitate aggression in previously angered individuals. In addition, it was found that during this aggression opportunity there was no differential aggression against male or female targets. However, as can be seen in Figure 2.1, when male subjects were given a second opportunity to aggress against the female target, aggressive responses were increased in the pornographic film condition. This was not the case with regard to the male target.

It is interesting to note in this study that aggression tended to be greater against male targets after exposure to the aggressive film. As noted above, the content of this film was primarily male–male aggression. One possible explanation for this effect is that the male target had acquired aggression-eliciting stimulus properties due to his association with the observed violence in the film (e.g., Berkowitz, 1974), in that the film's victims were primarily males. The obvious implication is that films that depict women as victims of aggression should likewise act to facilitate aggression against women. In addition, given the nature of many pornographic films in which women are depicted in a submissive, passive role, any subtle aggressive content could act to increase aggression because of the women's association with observed violence. This issue of aggressive content is examined in the third section of this chapter. For the moment, however, we should step back and try to summarize the research on the effects of nonaggressive pornography and violence against women.

Summary

The question of whether or not nonaggressive pornography has an influence on aggression against women is not simple to answer. For one thing, there is not that much experimental research on the topic. Also, studies investigating this issue have differed in many ways. The series of studies just discussed were intended to deal with some of these inconsistencies. These studies indicate that under certain conditions exposure to pornography *can* increase subsequent aggression against women. What seems to be required, however, is a lowering of aggressive inhibitions. This change in aggressive predisposition can come about in a number of ways. First, a higher level of anger, or frustration, than that exhibited in a laboratory setting could influence the effects of pornography on aggression against women. There is no question that such levels are present in the real world. Second, as mentioned earlier, drugs, alcohol, and other aggression disinhibitors very likely increase the aggressive response to pornography. The main mediating factor, however appears to be the type of material viewed prior to an aggressive opportunity.

As we know from previous reviews on the relationship of pornography to aggression (e.g., Donnerstein, 1983a; Sapolsky, Chapter 3 in this volume), certain types of sexually explicit materials do not increase subsequent aggressive behavior. In many respects, this material is either mildly arousing or it leads to a positive affective reaction. This type of material does not depict aggression or unequal power relationships with women. This type of material falls more under the heading of "erotica" than pornography.

More pornographic material, in contrast, tends to portray women as sexual objects and to depict coercion. It is quite possible that such representations act to reduce aggression inhibitions. This is, in many ways, the effect of aggressive pornography that is discussed shortly. But even nonaggressive material may promote the same reaction. Chapter 4 by Zillmann and Bryant on long-term, massive exposure to pornography may be seen in this light. Although the material presented to subjects was nonaggressive, it was standard pornographic film material, material tending to feature women in submissive and objectified roles. It would not be considered erotica by common definition (i.e., Malamuth & Donnerstein, 1982). This study found that long-term exposure increased sex-calloused attitudes on the part of males as well as a trivialization of rape. There is now good evidence to suggest that attitudes like these can directly influence aggressive behavior against women (e.g., Malamuth, 1983; Malamuth & Donnerstein, 1982).

The influence of pornography on aggression against women requires much more investigation. The effect of viewing pornography on aggression may not occur with a single exposure (as is the case with aggressive material) or in the presence of inhibitions. However, the possibility does exist that, under certain conditions or with heavy usage, aggression against women may well be activated. We need to examine more closely the types of materials being defined as pornography, individual reactions to such material, already-established attitudes regarding violence and women, results of more massive and long-term exposure to such materials, and perhaps more real-world analogues of aggression-provoking situations.

AGGRESSIVE PORNOGRAPHY: A MORE DIRECT RELATIONSHIP

In Malamuth's discussion on the U.S. Commission on Obscenity and Pornography in Chapter 1, he notes the increase in the availability of aggressive pornography (see also Court, Chapter 5). The focus of Malamuth's chapter is that exposure to such material can influence a number of attitudinal and behavioral responses. Other research has shown that a single exposure to aggressive pornography can result in (1) self-generated rape fantasies (Malamuth, 1981a), (2) an increase in sexual arousal in both normal and rapist populations (Malamuth, 1981b), (3) a less sensitive attitude toward rape (Malamuth & Check, 1980), and (4) an increased acceptance of rape myths and violence against women (Malamuth & Check, 1981). The most important aspect of this research, however, in regard to this chapter is the finding that these changes in attitudes and arousal are directly related to aggression against women (Malamuth, 1983). The interesting observation in this research is that these effects have occurred after only one exposure of a relatively short duration. What can we say, then, about the direct effects of this type of stimuli on aggression against women? Would such studies be comparable to the research on nonaggressive pornography? My colleagues and I have been investigating this question for a number of years. In the sections that follow I describe this research. First, I look at research that has compared aggressive and nonaggressive pornography in its effect on violence against women. Next I examine how the aggressive and sexually explicit components of the material operate to influence this potential aggression.

Experimental Studies on Aggressive Pornography and Aggression against Women

There are a number of theoretical reasons to expect that aggressive pornography influences aggression against women. First, exposure to aggressive pornography could act to reduce aggressive inhibitions. This expectation is based upon the research showing a reduction in inhibitions after exposure to aggressive media (e.g., Geen, 1976). Given the nature of aggressive pornography in which the female victim repeatedly displays signs of pleasure, or arousal, one would expect a general disinhibition of aggressive behavior toward women. Second, as the work of Berkowitz and his colleagues (e.g., Berkowitz, 1974) suggests, aggressive pornography may provide aggressive cues, one important determinant of aggression. Observed aggression may very possibly provide an individual with aggressive cues. Exposure to aggressive pornography could influence aggression against women because repeated association of women with the victims of observed violence increases the aggression-eliciting stimulus properties of a female (see following discussion of study by Donnerstein, 1980a).

This issue of the association of women with violence in aggressive pornography and media violence in general is quite important. We shall look further at this relationship when we examine those studies that deal with exposure to aggression without sexual content. First, however, let us review three studies dealing directly with aggressive pornography and violence against women.

DONNERSTEIN (1980A): AGGRESSIVE AND NONAGGRESSIVE PORNOGRAPHY

In the study by Donnerstein (1980a) male subjects were first angered or treated in a neutral manner by a male or female accomplice. Following this treatment all subjects were exposed to one of three films. The aggressive-pornographic film depicted the rape of a woman by a man who breaks into her house and forces her into sexual activity at gunpoint. The second film depicted a couple in various stages of sexual intercourse, but did not contain aggressive content. In terms of physiological arousal it was equal to the first film. The third film was neutral with regard to aggression and sexual content. Following exposure, subjects were given an opportunity to aggress against the male or female with whom they were paired. The results of this study, which are presented in Figure 2.2., show that exposure to an aggressive-pornographic film increased aggressive behavior to a level higher than was found for a nonaggressive film. These findings were most noticeable in subjects who had previously been angered. With respect to the sex of the aggressive target, when angered subjects were paired with a male, the aggressive film produced no more aggression than the nonaggressive version. Those subjects paired with a female, however, *only* displayed an increase in aggression after viewing the aggressive film. In fact, this increase occurred even if subjects were not angered. Given that both films were equally arousing, why would aggression be increased against the female only after exposure to the aggressive pornography film? One explanation is that the male associated the female confederate with the victim in the film and an aggressive response was thereby elicited (e.g., Berkowitz, 1974). The combination of anger arousal and

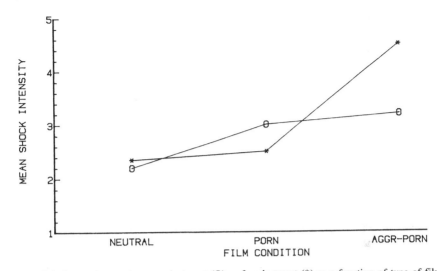

Fig. 2.2 Aggression against a male target (O) or female target (*) as a function of type of film exposure.

film arousal heightened this response and led to the highest level of aggression against the female. But, even under nonanger conditions aggression was increased. This was not the case for subjects paired with a male. It seems, then, that the male's association of the female confederate with the victim in the film was an important factor in the aggression that directed against her.

DONNERSTEIN AND BERKOWITZ (1981): FIRST PART OF STUDY ON VICTIM REACTIONS

A very common theme in pornography is that women derive pleasure from sexual aggression (e.g., Brownmiller, 1975; Gager & Schurr, 1976). We have seen from the work of Malamuth presented in Chapter 1 what effects this type of victim reaction has upon sexual arousal and rape-related attitudes. It seems quite reasonable to assume that viewing an act of aggression in which the *victim* responds in a positive manner should reduce aggressive inhibitions on the part of the viewer. Furthermore, viewing aggression should reinforce any aggressive tendencies stimulated from the film as well as reinforcing any prior anger instigation. We can predict, therefore, that a male subject who is predisposed to aggress against a female would show an increase in aggression following exposure to aggressive pornography in which the female victim in the film shows a positive reaction to aggression.

What about the effects of a film in which the victim does not react in a positive manner? From the work of Malamuth (see Chapter 1) we know that aggressive-pornographic depictions that present a victim who show a *negative* reaction do not generally tend to increase sexual arousal or negative attitudes. For some individuals, however, such stimuli do influence their reactions. For instance, male subjects who have a high likelihood to rape are sexually aroused by exposure to aggressive pornography in which the victim reacts negatively (Malamuth, 1981b). One might consider such individuals predisposed to aggression, and the reactions of the victim act to "reinforce" aggressive tendencies. In the human aggression literature there is ample support for this proposition. Research shows that victim pain cues do increase aggression (e.g., Baron, 1977) and take on a reinforcing value (e.g., Berkowitz, 1974) in angered individuals. Bandura (1973) has also speculated on the effects of observed pain cues. He noted that an increase in arousal increases the conditioning of pain cues as a reinforcer. The highly arousing nature of aggressive pornography in conjunction with an already angered individual should act to facilitate this conditioning. Second, pain cues can acquire reinforcement value if they are repeatedly associated with sexual gratification. No doubt this is the case with aggressive pornography.

The above reasoning suggests that aggressive pornography increases aggression against women in previously angered individuals regardless of the reactions of the victim. The positive reaction film will be effective due to its reducing aggressive inhibitions and justifying aggression. The negative reaction film will have its influence on aggression due to its reinforcing potential.

In this first part of the study by Donnerstein and Berkowitz (1981) male subjects were first angered by a male or female confederate. Following this instigation they were given the opportunity to view one of four films. The first was a neutral film that did not contain aggressive or sexual content. The second presentation was a nonaggressive-pornographic film used in previous studies. The third and fourth films were of an aggressive-pornographic nature. They depicted a young woman who comes to study with two men. Both men have been drinking, and when she sits between them she is shoved around and forced to drink. She is then tied up, stripped, slapped around, and raped. Each of the aggressive-pornographic films had a different ending (30 seconds out of 5 minutes) as well as a different narrative. In the positive–aggressive film the ending shows the woman smiling and in no way resisting the two men. The narrative also indicates that she becomes a willing participant in the events at the end. In the negative–aggressive version the woman's actions are difficult to judge and the narrative indicates that at the end she finds the experience humiliating and disgusting. Pretesting indicated that viewers of the negative–aggressive film perceived the victim as suffering more and not enjoying the experience. After viewing the film, all subjects were given an opportunity to administer electric shocks to the male or female confederate. Physiological reactions were also monitored during the study.

After having viewed the films all subjects were asked to rate them on a number of scales. These ratings are presented in Table 2.3. As can be seen, the negative–

TABLE 2.3

Mean Self-Report and Physiologic Changes under Various Film
Conditions: Experiment I

	Film condition[a]			
	Neutral	Erotic	Positive	Negative
Ratings of film				
Interesting	1.6_a	3.4_b	3.3_b	3.2_b
Sexually arousing	1.1_a	3.7_b	3.7_b	3.9_b
Aggressive	1.4_a	1.4_a	3.5_b	4.8_c
Sexual content	1.4_a	6.0_b	5.9_b	5.6_b
Ratings of victim				
Suffering		1.7_a	2.7_b	4.8_c
Enjoyment		6.3_a	5.1_b	2.6_c
Responsible		5.6_a	4.1_b	2.9_c
Mean blood pressure	-0.9_a	$+6.1_b$	$+8.5_b$	$+5.5_b$

[a]Means with different subscripts differ from each other at the .05 level
by Duncan's procedure. Film ratings are on a 7-point scale.

aggressive film was perceived as more aggressive than the positive version. This
is interesting in light of the fact that the actual aggressive content was the same in
both films. In addition the victim in the negative film was perceived as suffering
more and enjoying herself less than her positive counterpart. Further, the women
in the positive–aggressive sexual film was seen as being more responsible for
what had happened. The physiological data indicates that all pornographic films
were more arousing than the neutral film but did not differ substantially from
each other in arousal effects. The aggression data is presented in Figure 2.3. As
can be seen, none of the films affected aggression against a male target. However, both the positive– and negative–aggressive pornographic films increased
aggression against the female. This level of aggression was higher than the male
target conditions except for the pornographic film.

These results suggest, again, that aggressive pornography does increase aggression against women. While both types of films increased aggression equally,
it appears that the effects were obtained for different reasons. For the positive–
aggressive film, perhaps, in addition to the aggressive cue value in the film, the
positive ending reduced any aggressive inhibitions. In a sense, it suggested that
aggression was acceptable in this situation. Malamuth (1978) has shown that
when male subjects are provoked by a female and exposed to aggressive sexual
pictures, aggression will be increased when subjects are given disinhibitory cues
to aggress (e.g., it is acceptable to behave aggressively). It is highly likely that
this process was operating in this study.

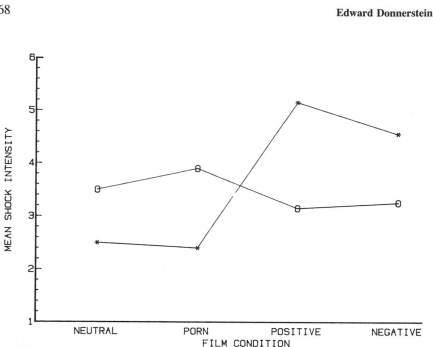

Fig. 2.3 Aggression against a male target (O) or female target (*) as a function of film exposure. Positive and negative refer to the endings of the aggressive-pornographic films.

With regard to those subjects who were exposed to the negative film, we hypothesize that the increase in aggression directed at the female target was a function of the reinforcement of the pain cues in the film. The fact that subjects in this study were angered by the female target, and that the film was highly arousing, supports this position. What, however, if subjects were not angered? Would exposure to an aggressive-pornographic film with a negative victim reaction still increase aggression? There is some suggestion to indicate that it would not. For example, Malamuth (1981b) has found that male subjects who do not have a high likelihood to rape are not sexually aroused by a rape story in which the victim displays a negative reaction. This suggests that these subjects are not predisposed to aggression against women. Baron (1977) also indicated that, for nonangered individuals, pain cues tended to actually reduce rather than increase aggression. In other words, if aggressive pornography that emphasizes the pain and suffering of the victim influences aggression against women because it reinforces already-established aggressive tendencies, then one should see this effect only with previously angered subjects.

Perhaps the more interesting question about aggressive pornography concerns the positive outcome depiction. This type of victim reaction is quite common in these fictional stories (see, e.g., Gager & Schurr, 1976; Malamuth & Check,

1981). While we have seen that this type of aggressive pornography can increase aggression against women in male subjects who are angered, what are the potential effects on individuals who are not predisposed to aggress? Given the findings that show that exposure to such depictions increase sexual arousal and negative attitudes regarding rape and women (see Malamuth, Chapter 1 in this volume; Malamuth & Donnerstein, 1982), we might expect an increase in aggressive behavior following exposure. In many ways this positive reaction on the part of the victim justifies aggression and reduces inhibitions. The aggressive cues present, the highly arousing nature of the film, and the reduced inhibitions should increase aggression. The second study by Donnerstein and Berkowitz (1981) was conducted to examine these considerations.

DONNERSTEIN AND BERKOWITZ (1981): SECOND PART
OF STUDY ON VICTIM REACTIONS

In the second part of the experiment by Donnerstein and Berkowitz (1981), male subjects were paired with a female accomplice. As in previous studies they were angered or treated in a neutral manner by the female. Following this treatment, they were shown one of the four films used in the first part of this study (neutral, nonaggressive pornography, aggressive pornography with a positive outcome, and aggressive pornography with a negative outcome). The rest of the procedure was identical.

Table 2.4 presents the film ratings for subjects from this second part of the study. As can be seen the ratings are identical to those in the first part of the study. The negative version was experienced as more aggressive, and the woman was perceived as suffering more, enjoying less, and being less responsible than her positive-aggression counterpart. Physiological data also indicated that the three pornographic films were more arousing than the neutral presentation, but did not substantially differ from each other in their arousal effect. Figure 2.4 presents the results for the aggression data. As can be seen, for nonangered subjects only the positive–aggressive film *increased* aggression against the female victim. For angered subjects, however, both the negative and positive versions of the film increased aggression. This is similar to the results in the first part of this study.

Results from both parts of this study indicate that aggressive pornography can directly influence aggression against women. While depictions that emphasized the pain and suffering of the victim only affected male subjects who were predisposed toward aggression, the more common story line in aggressive pornography of a willing and positive-reacting victim influenced all subjects. Even with subjects who were not mistreated by the female accomplice, we found an increase in aggressive behavior. If a viewer finds via vicarious means that aggression is in some way beneficial to a victim, this can influence their own aggressive behavior.

TABLE 2.4

Mean Self-Report and Physiological Changes under Various Film
Conditions: Experiment 2

	Film condition[a]			
	Neutral	Erotic	Positive	Negative
Ratings of film				
Interesting	1.6_a	3.8_b	3.8_b	3.2_b
Sexually arousing	1.6_a	4.7_b	3.7_c	3.7_c
Aggressive	1.2_a	1.8_a	4.3_b	6.2_c
Sexual content	1.3_a	6.4_b	5.9_{bc}	5.5_c
Ratings of victim				
Suffering		1.7_a	3.0_b	5.7_c
Enjoyment				
No anger		5.6_{ac}	5.9_{ac}	1.6_b
Anger		6.5_a	4.9_c	3.2_d
Responsible		5.6_a	4.3_b	2.3_c
Mean blood pressure	-0.5_a	$+8.3_b$	$+10.7_b$	$+8.9_b$

[a]Means with a different subscript differ from each other at the .05 level
by Duncan's procedure. Film ratings are on a 7-point scale.

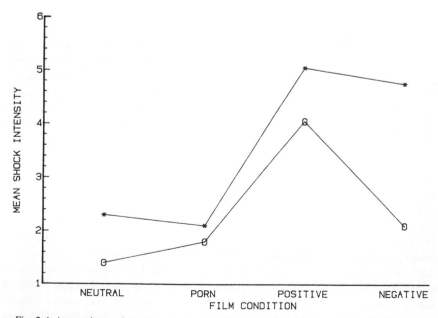

Fig. 2.4 Aggression against a female as a function of anger (*) or no anger (O) and film condition.
Positive and negative refer to the endings of the aggressive-pornographic films.

The Influence of Nonpornographic Images
of Aggression against Women

Images of violence against women in the media have increased over the years both in sexually oriented films and magazines and in mass media materials that would not be considered sexual in nature (e.g., Malamuth & Check, 1981). Scenes of rape and other forms of aggression against women are popular story lines in many commercially released films that are not considered pornographic in nature. In fact, such films are R-rated. Maslin (1982, November 11) explains the nature of this type of material in the following manner:

> Violence in the real world becomes much more acceptable after you've seen infinitely greater violence on the screen. And this kind of horror film, in addition to inuring its audience to genuine violence, has a debasing effect as well. In this respect it harkens back to hard-core sexual pornography, the tactics of which it carries to the most extreme. Years ago, when sexual explicitness on screen seemed to have advanced as far as it possibly could go, it was often remarked that only by actually penetrating the body could the camera go farther. That in a sense, is what the camera does now. The carnage is usually preceded by some sort of erotic prelude: footage of pretty young bodies in the shower, or teens changing into nighties for the slumber party, or anything that otherwise lulls the audience into a mildly sensual mood. When the killing begins, this eroticism is abruptly abandoned, for it has served its purpose, that of lowering the viewer's defenses and heightening the film's physical effectiveness. The speed and ease with which one's feelings can be transformed from sensuality into viciousness may surprise even those quite conversant with the links between sexual and violent urges. (p. 2) Copyright © 1982 by The New York Times Company. Reprinted by permission.

In the study by Malamuth and Check (1981), male subjects viewed full-length films without sexual content that depicted violence against women. The victim's reaction was always positive. It was found that subjects became more accepting of rape myths and violence against women after such exposure.

Studies also show the association of a female target of aggression with an aggressed-against victim in a film (see, e.g., Berkowitz, 1974). As we know from the research on media violence (see, e.g., Geen, 1978), aggression can be facilitated without a sexually arousing film, that is, nonarousing aggressive images may likewise increase aggression. Thus, a film depicting nonsexual aggression against a woman, even if the content is not sexually arousing, may increase subsequent aggression.

It seems reasonable to expect that stimuli that combine sexual arousal and violence would have a stronger impact than films without sexual content. This type of film combines sex and violence in a more soft-core or R-rated format (e.g., the August 1982 issue of *Penthouse* on sex and violence; the genre of horror films alluded to by Maslin). Research by Donnerstein and Linz (1984) indicates that massive exposure to these types of R-rated films can have an influence on rape-related attitudes. In this research, Donnerstein and Linz had subjects view 5 full-length feature films over a one-week period that depicted graphic forms of violence against women. The violence was frequently preceded by some sexually arousing or erotic scene (like those noted by Maslin). It was found that subjects became less bothered by this type of material, felt less anxious and depressed, and began to change their perceptions of the violence in the films by the end of the week period. Subjects saw less overall violence, less violence against women, fewer scenes of rape, and less graphic violence at the end of the week. More important, when subjects were asked to evaluate a rape victim after viewing a reenactment of a rape trial, they saw less injury, more responsibility, and more worthlessness on the part of the victim in comparison to a control group who had not seen the five films. This type of research suggests that exposure to violent images against women can act to desensitize subjects to the plight of a female victim. They also suggest the importance of the violent component in the forms of aggressive pornography that were discussed earlier. In the studies to be discussed next, the emphasis is on trying to determine the important component in aggressive pornography that accounts for the increased aggressive behavior and rape-related attitudes. The following studies were designed to examine the relative importance of the various components of aggressive pornography systematically: (1) aggression, (2) sexual content, and (3) the combination of the two. In this research the sexual explicitness of aggressive pornography was removed (and thereby its arousing aspect) so that images more common in the media and potentially viewed by more individuals could be examined.

Donnerstein (1983b): Nonpornographic Aggression and Subsequent Aggression

In order to examine the relative roles of aggression against women, arousal, and sexual content, male subjects in the study by Donnerstein (1983b) were either angered by a male or female confederate as was done in previous studies of this nature. All subjects were then exposed to one of four different films. The first was nonaggressive pornography. It was identical to that used in the studies already discussed. The second film was aggressive pornography and was also the same as that used in the previous studies. The third film was a nonsexual aggressive presentation in which a woman is taunted by a man at gunpoint. She is tied up, slapped around, and generally aggressed against. There was no nudity or even simulated sexual activity. It was chosen to be as close as possible in content, including aggression, to the aggressive-pornographic film but without portraying sexual behavior. The fourth film was a neutral presentation. Self-report data from subjects indicated that the aggressive film was perceived as being less sexual than the two pornographic films, which did not differ substantially from each other in arousal effect. In addition, the aggressive film and the aggressive-pornographic film were also experienced as equally aggressive. Physiological data also showed that the two pornographic films were equal in arousal effect but higher in that effect than the neutral and aggressive film. This study, then, seems to be a reasonable test of the contributions of arousal, pornographic, and aggressive content on subsequent aggression against women.

The results of this study are presented in Figure 2.5. When subjects were angered by a male, only the nonviolent-pornographic film increased aggression. This finding is quite similar to past research discussed in this chapter. For those subjects who were angered by a female, the aggressive-pornographic film produced the highest level of aggression, higher in fact than any male target condition. The aggressive film, however, also increased the level of subsequent aggression, although the level differed from the aggressive-pornographic presentation.

This study seems to indicate that sexual arousal is not a necessary component in facilitating aggression against women. The more crucial factor seems to be the aggressive cue value of the female target, which is established through the association of the target with observed violence. This does not mean that arousal, or pornographic content, is not important. As we have seen in this and other studies the aggressive responses elicited by the aggressive-pornographic film were heightened by the arousal from previous anger instigation and the arousal from the film itself. The fact that no increase in aggression was observed for male targets after exposure to the aggressive and aggressive-pornographic film further supports the idea that the films need to have some aggressive meaning to the individual.

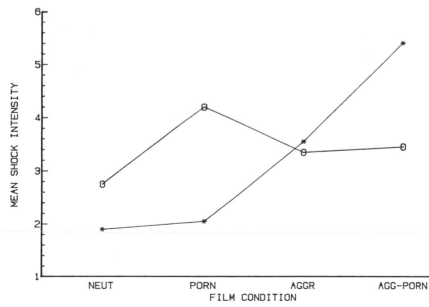

Fig. 2.5 Aggression against a male target (O) or female target (*) as a function of film type.

In this study it is interesting to note the relationship between the self-reported attributes of the films and aggressive behavior. When aggressive behavior was directed against a male, both self-reported sexual arousal and sexual content were correlated with aggression. There was no association with aggressive content. In addition, actual physiological arousal was related to aggression. For subjects aggressing against a female, however, *only* the aggressive content of the films was correlated with actual aggression ($r = .57$). Again, this is strongly suggestive of the importance of aggressive images in pornography and other forms of media as an influential factor in aggression against women. A second study in this series was designed to take this finding a step further.

DONNERSTEIN (SUBMITTED FOR PUBLICATION): AGGRESSIVE IMAGES, VICTIM ASSOCIATION, AND RAPE-RELATED ATTITUDES

I have suggested that one major factor in the influence of aggressive pornography on violence against women is the aggressive cue value of the female victim. This cue value occurs through the association of the victim with the female in the film. This association is also a prime explanation for the increase in aggression observed after exposure to the nonpornographic film of aggression discussed above. In the study by Donnerstein (submitted for publication) it was decided to strengthen the association of the female with the aggression in the film. This was done by establishing a name connection between the female victim in the film and the female confederate in the study. This name-association procedure is well known from the work of Berkowitz on media violence (Berkowitz, 1974). There were, in addition, a number of other aspects of this study that are important.

First, in the Donnerstein (1983) study previously described all subjects were angered. We have seen that aggressive pornography can increase aggression against women even in nonangered male subjects, particularly if the victim's reactions in the film are of a neutral or positive variety. This increase in aggression is attributed to association of females with the victim in the film as well as to the arousal aspect of the film. If subjects are nonangered and exposed to a nonarousing aggressive film would there still be an increase in aggression? Perhaps the simple association of the female with the film's victim is enough. In order to examine this possibility, subjects in this study were either angered or nonangered.

A second purpose of this study was to examine the influence on rape-related attitudes of an aggressive film that does not contain pornographic content. The research of Malamuth and Check (1981) has shown that scenes of nonexplicit sexual violence can increase the acceptance of rape myths. We also know that exposure to aggressive pornography is associated with the willingness to say one would commit a rape (see Malamuth, Chapter 1 of this volume). This study examined how nonpornographic aggression affected the following measures: (1)

the acceptance of rape myths, (2) the willingness to use force to have sex with a woman, and (3) the likelihood that an individual would commit a rape if not caught. A comparison of these previously used measures (see Malamuth, Chapter 1 in this book) was made with respect to exposure to three film types: pornography, aggressive pornography, and aggressive (which portrayed a female victim, but no sexual content).

In this study male subjects were first angered or treated in a neutral manner by a female accomplice. They were then given an opportunity to view one of three films. Each film had a narrative that introduced the woman in the film and mentioned her first name five times during the $4\frac{1}{2}$ minute exposure. This name was either the same or different from that of the female confederate, whose name was also mentioned throughout the study. Following film exposure, subjects completed a number of scales in which they rated various attributes of the film. In addition they completed a questionnaire on rape-related attitudes. Subjects were then given an opportunity to aggress against the female confederate.

Both the film attributes and effects are shown in Table 2.5. As can be seen the aggressive film was considered to have less sexual content and be less sexually arousing, and produced lower levels of physiological arousal (measured by change in blood pressure) than the two pornographic films. The effects regarding

TABLE 2.5

Mean Self-Reported Film Attributes and Film Effects
on Rape-Related Attitudes

	Film		
	Pornography	Aggressive	Aggressive porn
Blood pressure	10.01	2.94	9.83
Sexually arousing	4.00	2.25	3.75
Aggressive content	1.54	4.61	5.45
Sexual content	5.68	3.72	5.88
Rape myth acceptance[a]	14.68	18.82	17.57
Use force[b]	1.13	1.61	1.34
Rape (score)[c]	1.18	1.68	1.34
Rape (%)[d]	11	50	25

[a]Higher score indicates more acceptance of the rape myth on the Rape Myth Acceptance scale.

[b]Willingness to use force to have sex with a woman. Subjects indicated agreement on a 5-point scale. Higher score indicates more likelihood to use force.

[c]Willingness to say you would commit a rape if not caught. A 5-point scale was used in which 5 is very likely to rape.

[d]Percentage of subjects who received a score of 2 or higher on the rape likelihood scale.

rape-related attitudes were, however, not related to sexual content or arousal but rather to aggression. Both the aggressive-pornographic film and the nonpornographic-aggressive film produced higher scores than the nonaggressive pornographic film on the following measures: (1) the Rape Myth Acceptance scale, (2) willingness to use force, and (3) willingness to rape. The finding that nonviolent pornography does not influence rape-related attitudes is similar to research by other investigators (see Malamuth, 1981b; Malamuth, Chapter 1 in this volume). We should keep in mind, however, that this effect occurs with a single and rather short exposure. The research of Zillmann and Bryant (see Chapter 4) suggests that longer exposure to such material could influence attitudes regarding women and rape.

The aggression results are presented in Figures 2.6 and 2.7. In Figure 2.6 we see the effects of anger instigation and film exposure. While there tended to be little aggression from exposure to the pornographic film, both aggressive films increased aggression. This increase in aggression was higher for those subjects who had been angered, as well as for those who had seen the aggressive-pornographic film. As in the first study, the aggressive film did influence aggression more than the purely sexual film. This was observed for both angered and nonangered male subjects. The combination of violence with sexual arousal in the film produced the highest aggression level.

Again we see that aggressive pornography is a strong contributor to violence against women. The main factors in this aggressive facilitation, however, seems to be the aggressive nature of the film. In looking at the correlations of aggres-

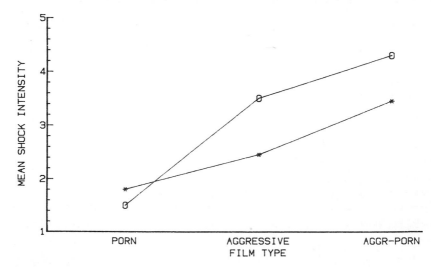

Fig. 2.6 Aggression against a female as a function of anger (O) or no anger (*) and film type.

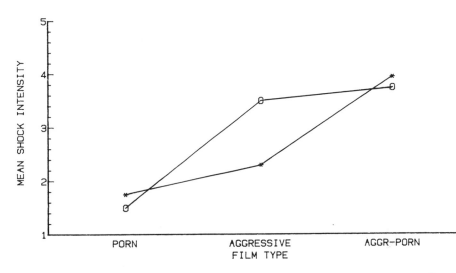

Fig. 2.7 Aggression against a female with the same name as film character (O) and with a different name from the film character (*) as a function of film type and name.

sion with the film ratings, we find that only aggressive content ($r = .44$) was related to aggression. Self-reported arousal, sexual content, and actual arousal did not have a significant association with aggression. It is also of interest to note that both attitudes about rape and the willingness to say one would commit a rape were also correlated with aggression against women.

I have stated that one key factor in the influence of these types of aggressive media on violence against women is the association of a potential aggressive target with the victim in the films. Evidence from this study suggests that an increase in this association can influence aggression against women. As seen in Figure 2.7, when subjects were exposed to the nonsexually explicit aggressive film, there was an increase in aggression beyond that of the pornographic film. When the female target of aggression had the same name as the women who was aggressed against in the film, this increased aggression was similar to that observed for the aggressive-pornographic films. Perhaps the aggressive film did not increase aggression to the same degree as its pornographic counterpart, due to its low level of arousal. However, when subjects were angered or the victim of aggression had a strong association with the observed film, then the nonarousing aggressive film did reveal patterns of aggressive behavior similar to that of aggressive pornography. Such findings again point to the factors of aggressive cues and aggressive imagery as the important contributors in the relationship of even nonpornographic material to violence against women.

Summary

This series of studies point to a number of important factors in the relationship of aggressive pornography and violence against women. First, they point to the importance of the association of the female with observed violence as a critical component in the facilitation of aggression against women. As we have seen, aggression against male targets is not affected by exposure to aggressive pornography in which a female is the victim. Furthermore, while anger instigation does tend to heighten the level of aggression, increased aggression can occur in the absence of prior instigation. The same seems to be true for film arousal. While the highest levels of aggression were obtained with films that juxtaposed aggression with sexual content, films that were nonarousing yet aggressive with regard to women also increased subsequent aggression. Second, the victim's reaction in the film also played a crucial role in terms of how male subjects behaved toward a female. The data from these two studies suggest that positive victim reactions (those that are most common in pornography) can act to justify aggression and also to reduce general inhibitions against aggression (see also Malamuth, 1981b). Negative reactions, on the other hand, seem to reinforce aggression in angered individuals and also to raise the threshold for empathy reactions that should occur when suffering is observed. Finally, these studies support those findings reported by Malamuth in Chapter 1, in that exposure to aggressive pornography seems to affect a general pattern of behavior and attitudes that have the capacity to stimulate various negative reactions against women. As we have seen from the work of Malamuth discussed in Chapter 1, male subjects exposed to various forms of aggressive pornography became sexually aroused, more accepting of rape myths and interpersonal violence against women, and reported a greater likelihood of committing a rape. These attitudinal and behavioral intention changes also correlated with actual aggression and desire to hurt a female. We have now seen that there is a direct causal relationship between exposure to aggressive pornography and violence against women.

CONCLUSION

A straightforward, definitive conclusion on the relationship between pornography and aggression against women is difficult to make. While it seems that certain types of pornography can influence aggression and other asocial attitudes and behaviors toward women, this is not the case for other forms of pornography, especially nonaggressive pornography. As we have seen, nonaggressive materials only affect aggression when inhibitions to aggress are quite low, or with long-term and massive exposure (see Chapter 4). With a single exposure and normal aggressing conditions, there is little evidence that nonviolent pornography has any negative effects. As we have seen in this chapter, it is the aggressive content of pornography that is the main contributor to violence against women. In fact, when we remove the sexual content from such films and just leave the aggressive aspect, we find a similar pattern of aggression and asocial attitudes.

We would be, perhaps, on safe ground therefore to say that aggressive pornography does have a negative effect. But, what about the other type of pornography? The problem here is what we mean by pornography. Are we discussing just sexually explicit material? All the research to date does not suggest any harmful effects from such exposure. In the studies I conducted on the effects of aggressive pornography, all the nonaggressive sexual films were chosen to be void of not only aggressive content but also any male–female power roles. In one sense the films may be considered erotic rather than pornographic. There was no evidence from these studies that the sexual content, arousal, or other aspects of the stimuli were related to aggression against women. Perhaps longer exposure, more massive exposure, or other factors might change this effect. However, in the important study by Zillmann and Bryant (Chapter 4 in this book), in which long-term massive exposure to nonaggressive pornography was examined, I suspect that the types of materials used in that study differed from standard erotica. As I noted earlier in this chapter, more subtle forms of aggression in terms of power roles, objectification, and female submissiveness could all play a role in affecting negative attitudes and behavior toward women. Such depictions of aggression do not depend on sexual explicitness, just as aggressive pornography is not some form of erotica. In other words, the issue of whether or not pornography is related to aggression against women might best be served by doing away with the term *pornography*. There is no question that the term encompasses portrayals from mere sexual explicitness to scenes of rape, torture, and mutilation. Longino (1980) suggested that pornography be defined in terms of its degrading and dehumanizing portrayal of women, not in terms of sexual content. All of the studies reviewed in this chapter that revealed any aggressive outcomes utilized material that was overtly aggressive or of the standard stag film genre. When materials were chosen to reflect consenting, equal power (or nonpower), or truly erotic content, then no negative effects were observed. This is also true for the research of Malamuth presented in Chapter 1. No doubt the long-standing issue of how to define pornography will be with us for some time. Yet an examination of its effects on aggression must begin with a closer look at the term itself. Pornography is not what influences aggression against women, but rather how women are depicted in the media—as victims of aggression or degradation—that is the concern.

Where do we go from here? No doubt more long-term exposure studies are needed. Also material that depicts R-rated sexual violence should be more extensively examined. This type of material, in many ways may have a more negative effect on aggression against women due to its more general availability and acceptability. But, more importantly, we need to be more certain as to what the causal factor is, if there is one, in the relationship between pornography and violence against women. Perhaps the research discussed in this chapter will provoke some thoughts on this issue as well as initiate more systematic work in this area.

REFERENCES

Bandura, A. (1973). *Aggression: A social learning analysis*. New York: Prentice-Hall.

Baron, R. A. (1977). *Human aggression*. New York: Plenum Press.

Baron, R. A., & Bell, P. A. (1973). Effects of heightened sexual arousal on physical aggression. *Proceedings of the 81st Annual Convention of the American Psychological Association, 8*, 171–172.

Berkowitz, L. (1974). Some determinants of impulsive aggression: The role of mediated associations with reinforcements for aggression. *Psychological Review, 81*, 165–176.

Brownmiller, S. (1975). *Against our will: Men, women and rape*. New York: Simon & Schuster.

Buss, A. (1961). *The psychology of aggression:* New York: Wiley.

Cline, V. B. (1974). Another view: Pornography effects, the state of the art. In V. B. Cline (Ed.), *Where do you draw the line?* Provo, UT: Brigham Young University Press.

Committee on Obscenity and Pornography (1971). *Presidential Commission on Obscenity and Pornography*. Washington, DC: Government Printing Office.

Dengerink, H. A. (1976). Personality variables as mediators of attack-instigated aggression. In R. Geen & E. O'Neal (Eds.), *Perspectives on aggression*. New York: Academic Press.

Donnerstein, E. (1980a). Aggressive erotica and violence against women. *Journal of Personality and Social Psychology, 39*, 269–277.

Donnerstein, E. (1980b). Pornography and violence against women. *Annals of the New York Academy of Sciences, 347*, 277–288.

Donnerstein, E. (1983a). Aggressive pornography: Can it influence aggression against women. In G. Albee, S. Gordon, and H. Leitenberg (Eds.), *Promoting sexual responsiblity and preventing sexual problems*. Hanover, NH: University of New England Press.

Donnerstein, E. (1983b). Erotica and human aggression. In R. Geen and E. Donnerstein (Eds.), *Aggression: Theoretical and empirical reviews*. New York: Academic Press.

Donnerstein, E. (submitted for publication). Aggressive pornography: The role of sexual and aggressive content.

Donnerstein, E., & Barrett, G. (1978). The effects of erotic stimuli on male aggression towards females. *Journal of Personality and Social Psychology, 36*, 180–188.

Donnerstein, E., & Berkowitz, L. (1981). Victim reactions in aggressive erotic films as a factor in violence against women. *Journal of Personality and Social Psychology, 41*, 710–724.

Donnerstein, E., Donnerstein, M., & Evans, R. (1975). Erotic stimuli and aggression: Facilitation or inhibition. *Journal of Personality and Social Psychology, 32*, 237–244.

Donnerstein, E., & Hallam, J. (1978). The facilitating effects of erotica on aggression toward females. *Journal of Personality and Social Psychology, 36*, 1270–1277.

Donnerstein, E., & Linz, D. (1984). Sexual violence in the media: A warning. *Psychology Today*. January, 14–15.

Donnerstein, E., & Malamuth, N. (1983). Pornography: Its consequences on the observer. In L. B. Schlesinger (Ed.), *Sexual dynamics of antisocial behavior*. Springfield, IL: Charles C. Thomas.

Donnerstein, E., Mueller, C., & Hallam, J. (submitted for publication). Erotica and aggression toward women: The role of aggressive models.

Eysenck, H. J., & Nias, H. (1978). *Sex, violence, and the media*. London: Spector.

Gager, H., & Schurr, C. (1976). *Sexual assault: Confronting rape in America*. New York: Grosset & Dunlap.

Geen, R. G. (1976). Observing violence in the mass media: Implications of basic research. In R. Geen and E. O'Neal (Eds.), *Perspectives on aggression*. New York: Academic Press.

Geen, R. G. (1978). Some effects of observing violence upon the behavior of the observer. In B. Maher (Ed.), *Progress in experimental personality research* (Vol. 8). New York: Academic Press.

Geen, R. G., Stonner, D., & Shope, G. L. (1975). The facilitation of aggression by aggression: Evidence against the catharsis hypothesis. *Journal of Personality and Social Psychology, 31*, 721–726.

Howitt, D. (1982). *Mass media and social problems*. New York: Pergamon Press.

Jaffe, Y., Malamuth, N., Feingold, J., & Feshbach, S. (1974). Sexual arousal and behavioral aggression. *Journal of Personality and Social Psychology, 30*, 759–764.

Longino, H. E. (1980). Pornography, oppression, and freedom: A closer look. In L. Lederer (Ed.), *Take back the night: Women on pornography*. New York: Morrow.

Malamuth, N. (1978). Erotica, aggression and perceived appropriateness. Paper presented at the 86th annual convention of the American Psychological Association.

Malamuth, N. (1981a). Rape fantasies as a function of exposure to violent-sexual stimuli. Archives of Sexual Behavior, *10*, 33–47.

Malamuth, N. (1981b). Rape proclivity among males. *Journal of Social Issues, 37*, 138–157.

Malamuth, N. (1983). Factors associated with rape as predictors of laboratory aggression women. *Journal of Personality and Social Psychology, 45*, 432–442.

Malamuth, N., & Check, J. (1980). Penile tumescence and perceptual responses to rape as a function of victim's perceived reactions. *Journal of Applied Social Psychology, 10*, 528–547.

Malamuth, N., & Check, J. (1981). The effects of mass media exposure on acceptance of violence against women: A field experiment. *Journal of Research in Personality, 15*, 436–446.

Malamuth, N., & Donnerstein, E. (1982). The effects of aggressive erotic stimuli. In L. Berkowitz (Ed.), *Advances in experimental social psychology*, (Vol. 15). New York: Academic Press.

Maslin, J. (November 11, 1982). Bloodbaths debase movies and audiences. *New York Times*.

Morgan, R. (1978). *Going to Far*. New York: Vintage Press.

Meyer, T. P. (1972). The effects of sexually arousing and violent films on aggressive behavior. *Journal of Sex Research, 8*, 324–33.

Mosher, D. L. (1971). Psychological reactions to pornographic films. In *Technical Report of the Commission on Obscenity and Pornography* (Vol. 8). Washington, DC: Government Printing Office.

Mosher, D. L., & Katz, H. (1971). Pornographic films, male verbal aggression against women and guilt. In *Technical Report of the Commission on Obscenity and Pornography* (Vol. 8). Washington, DC: Government Printing Office.

Quanty, M. B. (1976). Aggression catharsis: Experimental investigations and implications. In R. Geen & E. O'Neal (Eds.), *Perspectives on aggression*. New York: Academic Press.

Taylor, S. P., & Epstein, S. (1967). Aggression as a function of the interaction of the sex of the aggressor and the sex of the victim. *Journal of Personality, 35*, 474–486.

Zillmann, D. (1971). Excitation transfer in communication-mediated aggressive behavior. *Journal of Experimental Social Psychology, 7*, 419–434.

PART II

Experimental Studies on Pornography and Aggression

In the preceding two chapters we examined how certain forms of pornography can influence asocial attitudes and aggressive behavior. The prime emphasis of these two chapters was on aggression against women and rape-related attitudes. In addition, we looked primarily at aggressive forms of pornography. Although those chapters touched upon the role of nonaggressive pornography, they did not give us a complete overview of these types of materials. Are the effects for pornography different when aggressive content is eliminated? Does exposure to pornography influence aggression against males in the same manner as it does against females? What about the influence of prolonged exposure? Do we become bored or satiated, and/or are there some long-term effects on our behavior and attitudes? These are the types of questions that the next two chapters address. Both of these chapters present data of an experimental nature in contrast to the next section of the book which examines similar issues from a more correlational perspective. In addition, both chapters provide data relevant to the arousal–affect theoretical model that has been proposed to account for the effects of pornography on aggressive responses.

In the first chapter of Part II, ''Affect, Individual Differences, and the Aggression-Moderating Effect of Erotica,'' Sapolsky examines some recent theoretical issues that address the impact of pornography on aggressive behavior. What accounts for the fact that under some conditions, and for some types of indi-

PORNOGRAPHY AND
SEXUAL AGGRESSION

viduals, pornography can either increase or decrease subsequent aggression? Sapolsky considers the ability of a model based on arousal and affective reactions to account for such effects. He also discusses various factors that may determine an individual's reactions to pornography. The author suggests a number of individual characteristics in interaction with certain content themes in pornography to account for differences in affective responses. Additionally, Sapolsky considers how this two-factor model of arousal and affect can address the relationship of aggressive pornography and violence against women (as discussed in the first two chapters of the book).

Much of the research on the effects of pornography and aggression has examined somewhat short-term influences in addition to short-term exposure. In their chapter, "Effects of Massive Exposure to Pornography," Zillmann and Bryant address the issue of long-term exposure to pornography. Will prolonged exposure influence arousal? The authors demonstrate in their ambitious study that the answer is "yes," with arousal decreasing, thereby leading to a reduction in subsequent aggression. While this might suggest that large dosages of pornography are harmless, there is in some way a "Catch-22" to this *habituation* to pornography. For while aggressive behavior may be reduced from long-term exposure to pornography, there is a definite change in attitudes—toward the asocial side—with regard to attitudes toward women. Zillmann and Bryant's findings on attitudinal changes are very different from those observed by the U.S. Commission on Obscenity and Pornography over a decade ago, with the commission's research failing to assess the impact of prolonged exposure to pornography on attitudes adequately. As the authors suggest in their chapter, further research is needed on the long-term impact of constant exposure to pornographic images.

3

Arousal, Affect, and the Aggression-Moderating Effect of Erotica

BARRY S. SAPOLSKY

INTRODUCTION

A watershed in research on the effects of erotica occurred with the work of the Commission on Obscenity and Pornography. Its controversial conclusion that exposure to explicit sexual materials is not a cause of social or individual harms has received strong criticism (Cline, 1974; Eysenck & Nias, 1978). Inspired in part by the controversy and shortcomings of the commission report, the emphasis of research on erotica effects has shifted to a greater use of the experimental method and an increased focus on the development and testing of theoretical rationales to account for the varied human response to sexual stimuli. In particular, a substantial number of investigations in the past decade have focused on the effects of exposure to erotica on aggressive behavior. Recent studies of the aggression-moderating impact of erotica have included violent and exploitative stimuli largely overlooked in the commission report.

This chapter reviews the body of research on the consequences for human aggression of exposure to both nonaggressive and aggressive sexual stimuli. Particular attention is given to the appraisal of a model, incorporating the relevant factors of arousal and affect, that may most parsimoniously explain the bulk of the research evidence on intermale aggression. The affective component of response to erotica is regarded as the pivotal determinant of a stimulus's aggression-moderating effects. Subsequent sections of the chapter provide an overview of the primary influences on an individual's affective responsiveness to sexual stimuli. Various strategies for exploring individual differences in affective orientation are detailed, and, finally, investigations conducted in the late 1970s and early 1980s that examine affective reactions to both nonaggressive and sexually violent pornography are reported.

NONAGGRESSIVE EROTICA AND AGGRESSIVE BEHAVIOR

Aggression Facilitation or Inhibition

Despite the "no harm" conclusion on the effects of viewing pornography found by the Commission on Obscenity and Pornography, the report contains findings that suggest a positive association between exposure to erotica and aggression-related attitudes and moods (Byrne & Lamberth, 1971; Mosher, 1971; Schmidt & Sigusch, 1970) as well as verbal and physical aggressive behavior (Mosher & Katz, 1971; Tannenbaum, 1971). In the decade following release of the commission report, researchers have systematically explored the erotica–aggression connection. Initial investigations of the relationship between exposure to erotica and intermale aggression generally utilized stimuli depicting nonaggressive, nondeviant sexual postures and activity (e.g., nudes and coitus). Nearly all of the studies employed a provocation manipulation leading to anger arousal in the subject. These investigations yielded contrasting results: One group of studies found an aggression-enhancing effect for erotica (Fisher & Harris, 1976; Jaffe, 1974; Jaffe, Malamuth, Feingold, & Feshbach, 1974; Meyer, 1972; Rosene, 1971; Sapolsky, 1977; Zillmann, 1971; Zillmann, Hoyt, & Day, 1974) whereas another group established an aggression- or annoyance-reducing effect (Baron, 1974a, 1974b; Baron & Bell, 1973, 1977; Donnerstein, Donnerstein, & Evans, 1975; White, 1979; Zillmann & Sapolsky, 1977). In studies of interfemale aggression, both a facilitory (Cantor, Zillmann, & Einsiedel, 1978; Jaffe et al., 1974; Sapolsky & Zillmann, 1981) and an inhibitory (Baron, 1979) effect for erotica were again observed.

Theoretical Perspectives

AROUSAL

Researchers are faced with the dilemma of accounting for the discrepant findings between aggression facilitation or inhibition. One explanation appears to lie in the choice of the experimental stimuli. Whereas an increase in aggression occurred following exposure to highly arousing, explicit films, a decrease in aggression was found subsequent to viewing mildly arousing, less explicit still photographs. In light of the evidence that motion pictures induce greater sexual arousal than still photographs (Adamson, Romano, Burdick, Corman, & Chebib, 1972; McConaghy, 1974; Sandford, 1974), it would seem, then, that an explanation for the divergent findings resides in the differential arousal capacities of the erotica.

According to the arousal perspective, the aggression-moderating effect of a communication is a function of its excitatory potential (Zillmann *et al.,* 1974). Specifically, following exposure to highly arousing erotica, residues of excitation intensify feelings of anger and aggressive behavior. In contrast, after exposure to less arousing, mild erotica, minimal residues of excitation are available to intensify subsequent aggression. An important element in aggression facilitation is the emotional state of the aroused individual: An aggressive disposition is first established (through provocation) and then later reinstated. Aggression enhancement would not be expected (and, generally, has not been observed) for individuals not predisposed to behave in an aggressive fashion. More simply, the "excitation-transfer" paradigm suggests that individuals would be expected to behave more aggressively when (1) they are angered, (2) they are then exposed to arousing erotica, and (3) residues of arousal are available to "energize" the motivated aggression when they are again confronted with an annoyer (cf. Tannenbaum & Zillmann, 1975).

The arousal mechanism does not, however, provide a satisfactory explanation for erotica's effects on aggressive behavior. First, it does not account for those studies in which mild erotica have been shown to *reduce* aggression (e.g., Baron, 1974a). Second, research has shown some erotic films, but not others, to facilitate aggression, even though all the films were empirically demonstrated to elevate arousal equally (e.g., Sapolsky & Zillmann, 1981). Apparently, when evaluating a stimulus's capacity to alter aggressive behavior, we must consider more than the role of excitation.

EMOTIONAL INCOMPATIBILITY

An explanation for the aggression-reducing effect of mild erotica is derived from the notion of emotional incompatibility (Bandura, 1973). According to this explanation, exposure to mild erotica, which is generally experienced as pleasurable, creates positive affective reactions that are incompatible with anger emotions (Baron, 1974b; Baron, 1983; Zillmann & Sapolsky, 1977). Once an annoyed person is immersed in pleasant erotica his anger dissipates, thus making it difficult to return to the prior state of anger. The emotional incompatibility argument fails to explain the aggression-enhancing effects of strong erotica. Strong erotic stimuli should be even more capable of inducing emotional incompatibility, thereby lowering aggressive behavior. The emotional incompatibility rationale, like that of arousal, appears to fall short of explaining the bulk of research findings.

It has also been suggested that a biological incompatibility of aggressive and sexual arousal responses (Fromm, 1973) may account for the lowering of hostile aggressive behavior (Malamuth, Feshbach, & Jaffe, 1977). Aggression-reducing effects dependent upon a sex–aggression linkage are challenged by findings that show erotica and nonerotica matched for pleasantness and arousal capacity to have identical effects on aggressive behavior (Zillmann, Bryant, Comisky, & Medoff, 1981).

AROUSAL-AFFECT MODEL

As a means of reconciling the apparent contradictory findings, a model has been proposed that integrates the (1) arousal capacity and (2) affect-eliciting qualities ascribed to erotica (Baron, 1983; Sapolsky & Zillmann, 1981; Zillmann, Bryant, Comisky, & Medoff, 1981). Specifically, the excitation-transfer paradigm (Zillmann, 1971) has been modified through the recognition that affective response to an erotic communication may interfere with the aggression-facilitating effect of residual excitation. Likewise, the emotional incompatibility rationale (Baron, 1974b) has been modified through the consideration of affective responses to erotica emotionally *compatible* with annoyance and anger (e.g., disgust and disturbance). Taken together, the components of excitation and affective response are viewed as contributing *additively* to the level of motivated aggressive behavior. The arousal-affect model provides the following predictions for the aggression-moderating effects of erotica based upon a consideration of the combined impact of the stimulus's excitatory potential and its ability to create a positive or negative affective state:

1. Highly arousing erotica inducing negative affective reactions would lead to the highest level of aggression through the summation of the aggression-facilitating effects of residual excitation and of compatible unpleasant emotions.
2. Highly arousing erotica inducing positive affective reactions would facilitate aggression but to a level below that of condition 1 due to the aggression-reducing effect of pleasant emotions counteracting the aggression-enhancing effect of high arousal.
3. Moderately arousing erotica inducing negative affective reactions would lead to an increment in aggression below that of condition 1 due to a reduced level of residual excitation combining with compatible unpleasant emotions.
4. Moderately arousing erotica inducing positive affective reactions would maintain the level of aggression (relative to a control condition) due to the

aggression-reducing effect of pleasant emotions canceling out the aggression-enhancing effect of moderate arousal.

5. Nonarousing erotica inducing negative affective reactions would create an increment in aggression solely on the basis of the aggression-enhancing effect of negative emotions.

6. Nonarousing erotica inducing positive affective reactions would, in the absence of residues of excitation, lead to a reduction in aggression due to the incompatibility of pleasant emotions with anger and aggression.

The comparative strength of the aggression-facilitating effect of conditions 2, 3, and 5 would depend upon the level of residual arousal and/or affect generated by particular erotic contents.

Research Findings

Evidence supporting the arousal–affect model can be found in a study by Zillmann and Sapolsky (1977). Direct measures of excitation and affective response were obtained. Mildly erotic (pictures of nudes) and highly erotic (pictures of intercourse, fellatio, and cunnilingus) stimuli were found to be no more arousing than nonerotica, and the erotica were judged to be equally pleasing and nondisturbing. The erotic stimuli thus possessed qualities that, according to the two-component model, would lead to a lowering of aggressive inclinations. Exposure to the mildly and highly erotic stimuli reduced males' expressions of annoyance (see Table 3.1). The erotica did not, however, affect retaliatory behavior, suggesting a lack of strength of the behavior-modifying impact of exposure to mild erotica. Previous research demonstrating an aggression-inhibiting effect for erotica employed similarly nonarousing erotica[1] and pleasing mild erotica (e.g., semi-nudes, nudes, and sexual acts) and can be considered further evidence in support of the model (Baron, 1974a, 1974b; Baron & Bell, 1977; Donnerstein et al., 1975). In contrast to Zillmann and Sapolsky, these studies found a reduction in *retaliatory* behavior following exposure to mild erotica (refer to Table 3.1). One exception to this pattern should be noted, however. Following exposure to pictures of sexual acts (intercourse and oral sex), Donnerstein et al. (1975) did not observe a reduction in aggressive behavior. This discrepancy may have resulted from Donnerstein et al. using stimuli that evoked a less positive affective state (cf. Baron & Bell, 1977). More recently, White (1979) demonstrated that exposure to affectively positive and presumably trivially arousing erotica reduces aggressive behavior. In addition, affectively negative, minimally arousing erotica were found to enhance aggression slightly (Table 3.1).

[1]No direct measures of excitation were obtained in these studies. Based on the findings of Zillmann and Sapolsky (1977), it is presumed that these stimuli induce only a trivial degree of arousal.

TABLE 3.1

Summary of Investigations Pertinent to the Arousal-Affect Model

Study	Subjects	Stimuli		Dependent measures			
				Arousal	Affect	Hostility–aggression	Support for model
Sapolsky & Zillman (1981)	Males	Films:[a,b]	Nudity	Nonarousing	Calming, pleasing, boring	No effect[c]	Nonsupportive
			Precoitus	Arousing	Disturbing, pleasing, exciting	Increase	Supportive
			R-coitus[d]	Arousing	Calming, pleasing, exciting	No effect	Supportive[e]
			X-coitus[f]	Arousing	Calming, pleasing, exciting	No effect	Supportive[e]
Sapolsky & Zillmann (1981)	Females	Films:[a]	Precoitus	Arousing	Disturbing, displeasing, boring	No effect	Nonsupportive
			X-coitus[f]	Arousing	Disturbing, displeasing, boring	Increase	Supportive
Zillmann, Bryant, & Carveth (1981)	Males	Slides:[a]	Nudes	Nonarousing	Pleasing	No effect	Nonsupportive
		Films:	Bestiality	Arousing	Displeasing	Increase	Supportive
			Sadomasochism	Arousing	Displeasing	Increase	Supportive
Zillmann, Bryant, Comisky, & Medoff, (1981)	Males	Slides:[b]	Nudes	Nonarousing	Pleasing	No effect	Nonsupportive
			Masturbation, bondage	Nonarousing	Displeasing	No effect	Nonsupportive
		Films:	Precoitus, coitus	Arousing	Pleasing	No effect	Supportive[e]
			Sadomasochism, bestiality	Arousing	Displeasing	Increase	Supportive
Baron (1979)	Females	Pictures:[b]	Semi-nudes	Nonarousing[g]	Entertaining, pleasing	Reduce	Supportive
			Nudes	Nonarousing[g]	Disgusting, annoying	No effect	Nonsupportive
			Intercourse, oral sex	Arousing[g]	Disgusting, annoying	Increase	Supportive

(continued)

			Dependent measures			
Study	Subjects	Stimuli	Arousal	Affect	Hostility–aggression	Support for model
White (1979)	Males	Slides:[a,b] Petting, intercourse, oral sex	Arousing[g]	Exciting, entertaining	Reduce	Supportive
Baron & Bell (1977)	Males	Mutual oral sex	Arousing[g]	Exciting, entertaining, disgusting	No effect	Supportive[h]
		Same-sex masturbation	Nonarousing[g]	Disgusting, angering, nauseating	No effect	Nonsupportive
		Pictures:[b] Semi-nudes	Arousing[g]	Attractive	Reduce	Supportive
		Nudes	Arousing[g]	Attractive	Reduce	Supportive
		Intercourse, oral sex	Arousing[g]	Less attractive	Reduce	Nonsupportive
		Passages: Sexual activity	Arousing[g]	Attractive	No effect	Nonsupportive
Zillmann & Sapolsky (1977)	Males	Slides:[b] Nudes	Nonarousing	Nondisturbing, exciting, pleasing	Reduce[i]	Supportive
		Intercourse, oral sex	Nonarousing	Nondisturbing, exciting, pleasing	Reduce[i]	Supportive
Baron (1974a)	Males	Pictures:[b] Nudes	Arousing[g]	Attractive	Reduce	Supportive
Baron (1974b)	Males	Slides:[b] Semi-nudes	Arousing[g]	Positive	Reduce	Supportive
		Nudes	Arousing[g]	Positive	Reduce	Supportive

[a] The study included a no-exposure control condition.

[b] The study included a neutral stimuli control condition.

[c] A finding of "no effect," denotes a particular stimulus condition is not statistically different from the control condition(s).

[d] Coitus without genitalia shown.

[e] As noted in the text, the effects of moderate arousal and positive affect counteract, leading to no effect on hostility/aggression.

[f] Coitus with genitalia shown and oral sex.

[g] No physiological measures of arousal were taken. Self-report ratings of arousal were taken. In terms of assessing support for the Arousal–Affect Model, these stimuli are nonarousing. Physiological evidence (Zillmann & Sapolsky, 1977) suggests these stimuli are nonarousing.

[h] Counteraction of positive and negative affect leads to the expectation of no effect on aggression.

[i] Reduction found for measure of annoyance but not for measure of retaliation.

Sapolsky and Zillmann (1981) exposed males to erotic motion pictures that ranged from suggestive to explicitly sexual (nudity, precoitus, R-coitus [without gentalia shown], and X-coitus [explicit intercourse and oral sex]). As shown in Table 3.1, the precoitus and coitus films were found to be arousing. Males reported positive affective reactions to the nudity and coitus films but not to the film depicting precoital behavior. Nonarousing erotica eliciting positive affective response (nudity) did not reduce retaliatory behavior nor did arousing erotica associated with positive affective response (R- and X-coitus) facilitate such behavior. Rather, the retaliatory actions of provoked males were enhanced by arousing and disturbing erotica: a film of precoital behavior. While the latter finding is projected by the arousal–affect model, the level of retaliatory behavior subsequent to exposure to the remaining erotic films fails to conform to expectations.

One explanation for the coitus films' failure to produce an increase in hostile behavior may derive from the male's habituation to strong erotica. Sapolsky and Zillmann observed increases in systolic blood pressure of 13.6 and 13.9 mm Hg after exposure to the R- and X-coitus films, respectively. In contrast, males in an earlier study (Zillmann, 1971) showed an increase of 19.6 mm Hg after exposure to a milder film of precoital behavior. The male's apparent habituation to some types of explicit erotica suggests that the precoitus and coitus films employed by Sapolsky and Zillmann might be better classified as *moderately* arousing. It would follow from the arousal–affect model that moderately arousing, positively valenced depictions of coitus would not be expected to enhance aggressive behavior. The moderately arousing precoitus film led to a higher level of retaliatory behavior through a boosting effect of negative affective reactions. It can also be speculated that the nonarousing nudity film failed to reduce retaliatory behavior because its positive evaluation (calming, pleasing) was mixed with a judgment that the stimulus was boring. These explanations for the inconsistencies in the Sapolsky and Zillmann findings must remain tentative; according to the data, the arousal–affect model stands only partially confirmed.

Zillmann, Bryant, Comisky, and Medoff (1981) also demonstrated an aggression-enhancing effect for arousing, negatively valenced stimuli (see Table 3.1). This facilitory effect was in evidence regardless of whether the stimulus was erotic or nonerotic. Zillmann *et al.* did not find an increase in males' retaliatory behavior following exposure to arousing erotica eliciting positive affective reactions, nor following nonarousing, negatively valenced erotica. Also, contrary to expectations, nonarousing–pleasing erotica were not shown to reduce the level of retaliatory behavior. The authors point out, though, that in the nonarousing–pleasing erotica condition they were forced to employ stimuli that were not extremely pleasing in an effort to match equivalent nonerotic stimuli. The studies by Sapolsky and Zillmann (1981) and by Zillmann, Bryant, Comisky, and Medoff (1981) are consistent in finding (1) an increase in aggression after exposure to arousing–negative erotica but not after arousing–positive erotica (coital behavior) and (2) no decrease in aggression following the viewing of nonarousing–positive stimuli (nudity). Again, an examination of the physiological data suggests that the arousing–positive erotica used by Zillmann *et al.* were only moderately arousing: The pleasant emotions such stimuli evoke cancel the modest facilitative effect of arousal.

Studies of interfemale aggression have also been generally supportive of the arousal–affect model. In one investigation Baron (1979) exposed females to several types of erotic photographs. Pictures of semi-nude males were assessed as nonarousing and pleasing, and they were found to reduce the females' motivated aggression. Pictures of explicit sexual acts were found to be arousing and disgusting and, as expected, they led to an increase in aggressive responses (see Table 3.1). Sapolsky and Zillmann (1981) exposed females to arousing erotic films (the precoitus and X-coitus films described earlier). Both films were judged to be disturbing and displeasing. However, while both films meet the criteria for aggression-facilitation as set forth in the two-component model, only the explicit X-coitus film enhanced retaliatory behavior in females (see Table 3.1).

In a related line of inquiry, researchers have examined the capacity of erotica to stimulate male aggression against females. Several studies found exposure to nonaggressive erotic stimuli did not differentially affect male–female and male–male aggressive behavior (Baron & Bell, 1973; Donnerstein & Barrett, 1978; Jaffe *et al.,* 1974). Interestingly, Donnerstein and Barrett (1978) observed, irrespective of film exposure, less aggression directed at female targets. It was speculated that, since aggression against a female is generally disapproved of, males were inhibited from retaliating against a female. When the restraints for aggressing against a female were lowered (e.g., by giving males two opportunities for retaliation), male aggression against a female target exceeded that for a male target following exposure to arousing, nonaggressive erotica (Donnerstein & Hallam, 1978). This finding may derive from the female target taking on aggressive cue value (Berkowitz, 1974) through her association with the female recipient of *implied* aggression in the erotic films. A subtle form of aggression is said to result from the female's protrayal in a submissive and passive role in most nonaggressive erotic films (Donnerstein & Hallam, 1978). Obviously, the arousal-affect model does not provide a predictive rationale for differential effects of erotica on male and female targets. Apparently, the contribution of disinhibitory influences and aggressive cues must be considered in the circumstance of male aggression directed at females. This issue will be examined further in the third section of this chapter.

Alternative Explanations

Zillmann and Sapolsky (1977) have suggested the possibility that the aggression-reducing effect of relatively nonarousing mild erotica (e.g., nudes) may be in actuality an annoyance-enhancing effect of the control stimuli. Earlier studies (Baron, 1974a, 1974b, 1979; Baron & Bell, 1973, 1977) have employed nonerotica that have proven to be boring (Zillmann & Sapolsky, 1977). To the extent that being bored can be viewed as an aversive reaction, nonerotica can be considered to have induced a negative affective state. The observed differential effect of exposure to selected stimuli on aggressiveness may at least partly be due to the behavior-modifying impact of less pleasant, boring nonerotica. This explanation, it should be noted, remains compatible with the arousal-affect model. It also points to the need for hedonically neutral or no communication controls for more accurate assessment of the aggression-moderating effect of erotica.

Sapolsky and Zillmann (1981) have proposed that their findings regarding both males and females could alternatively be explained as the result of *annoyance summation*. Subjects who had been annoyed by the provocation procedure were further annoyed by being exposed to disturbing erotic films. Insult was added to injury, so to speak, and retaliation was made more intense. This argument fails to explain why provoked females exposed to a disturbing precoitus film did not retaliate more than their counterparts who had seen a nondisturbing control film.

An additional explanation for the differential effects of exposure to erotica on aggressive behavior is that of *cognitive labeling* (Baron, 1979; White, 1979). According to this notion, the label applied to experienced arousal is derived from the affective reaction to a specific stimulus. The cognitive labeling process in turn determines whether the source of arousal will foster or impede aggression. If the affective response is positive, arousal will be labeled in a positive manner, leading to a decrement in later aggression. If the affective response is negative, arousal will more likely be labeled as anger, and the resulting aggressive behavior will be intensified. This argument helps to explain sex differences in retaliatory behavior following exposure to similar erotic contents. Baron (1979) noted that males reported positive affective reactions to photographs of nudes and sexual acts and exhibited a reduced level of aggression. By comparison, females reported negative reactions to these images with an attending increase in aggressiveness. The males labeled their reactions as positive, while females labeled their reactions as negative. The contrasting affective reactions and labels applied by males and females would explain their differential levels of aggressive behavior following exposure to sexual stimuli.

Conclusions

It is apparent that the erotic stimuli found to mediate motivated aggressive behavior differ along a number of dimensions including content (e.g., the specific type of sexual display), potential to arouse, capacity to elicit positive or negative affect, mode of presentation, and degree of explicitness. It has been unclear which of these qualities must be considered in developing a predictive model to explain the impact of erotica on aggressive behavior. Various rationales have been proposed to account for the contrasting effects of erotica, but the question has remained whether a more parsimonious explanation exists that spans the diverse features of sexual stimuli. The arousal–affect model seems to offer a comprehensive means of assessing the aggression-moderating impact of a wide array of stimuli. With this model both arousing and *non*arousing erotica are considered. The model also extends the emotional incompatibility approach by considering the consequences of negatively valenced erotica. In addition, the two-component model accounts for nonerotica as well as erotica. When considering the potential effect of a particular source of sexual stimulation, predictions for an enhancement or reduction of aggression would be based on a prior determination of the excitatory potential and the hedonic valence of the stimulus.

The arousal–affect model provides an adequate explanation for the effect of nonaggressive erotica on same-sex aggression. Does *aggressive* pornography, especially the portrayal of rape, lead to particular aggression-modifying effects not found for nonaggressive erotica? Are there unique effects for *inter*sex aggression? The following section considers these issues in reviewing investigations employing aggressive pornography, particularly in the context of male–female aggressive behavior.

AGGRESSIVE AND DEVIANT PORNOGRAPHY AND AGGRESSIVE BEHAVIOR

Effects of Sexually Violent Stimuli

The report of the Commission on Obscenity and Pornography has been criticized for its failure to consider the consequences of exposure to violent pornography (Cline, 1974; Donnerstein, 1980; Eysenck & Nias, 1978). Yet this oversight is, in part, understandable in light of the changing contents of sexual stimuli. In the years since the commission report research was conducted, there has been an increase in sexually violent themes in the mass media, in particular, portrayals of sadomasochism and rape (Malamuth & Donnerstein, 1982; *Time,* 1976, April 5). Erotica commonly available in the 1960s contained less sexual violence and, not surprisingly, research on the harmful effects of pornography excluded the kinds of aggressive activity found in many of today's X-rated movies.

Since the release of the commission report, there has been increased attention to the issue of aggressive pornography. Many studies have been concerned with measuring outcomes other than aggressive behavior. For instance, Schmidt (1975) reported both males and females rated themselves as feeling more aggressive after seeing films of sadomasochism and group rape than after seeing a film of nonaggressive sex. Malamuth and his colleagues have examined responsivity to sexual violence and its association with rape-related attitudes and behaviors. These researchers have shown that, for males, sexual responsiveness to descriptions of sexual violence is associated with the propensity to rape, callous attitudes toward rape and victims of rape, and the stimulation of sexually violent fantasies (Malamuth, 1981; Malamuth & Check, 1981; Malamuth, Haber, Feshbach, 1980; Malamuth, Reisin, & Spinner, 1979, September).

One study in the commission report directly assessed the effect of erotica containing violent overtones on aggressive behavior. Tannenbaum (1971) found greater intermale aggression following exposure to an erotic film accompanied by an aggressive sound track as compared to the same film with an erotic (nonaggressive) sound track. This study lacked specific measures of arousal and, therefore, it is not possible to determine whether the heightened aggression is the result of the contribution of added arousal or of the aggressive content per se.

More recently, aggressive pornography has been employed in an extension of research on male aggression against females. In initial research, males retaliated against their female provoker to a higher degree after viewing aggressive pornography (a film depicting rape) than after viewing nonaggressive stimuli (a film of sexual intercourse) (Donnerstein, 1980). Furthermore, subsequent to exposure to the sexually violent film the level of male–*female* aggression exceeded that of male–*male* aggression. A later study found angered males' heightened aggression against a female target was in evidence whether aggressive pornography had a positive or negative outcome (Donnerstein & Berkowitz, 1981). By comparison, aggressive pornography (including portrayals of rape, sadomasochism, and bondage) does not facilitate intermale aggression more than nonaggressive materials, but does promote it more than neutral or no-exposure conditions (Donnerstein, 1980; Zillmann, Bryant, & Carveth, 1981; Zillmann, Bryant, Comisky, & Medoff, 1981). Thus, it appears that, for angered males, aggressive pornography (1) is a more potent stimulator of aggression against females than nonaggressive erotica and (2) can facilitate intermale aggression above the level found in control conditions.

Pornography featuring deviant sexual practices (e.g., bestiality) has also been probed for its aggression-altering impact. It has been found that sexual stimuli depicting deviant behavior, regardless of the degree of aggressiveness involved, facilitate intermale aggression relative to a no-exposure control condition (Zillmann, Bryant, & Carveth, 1981; Zillmann, Bryant, Comisky, & Medoff, 1981).

Aggressive Cues Perspective

Donnerstein (Donnerstein, 1980, 1983) has observed that erotic films equated for arousal but varying in aggressive content have been found to lead to differing levels of male–female aggression. The arousal capacity of the stimuli, while contributing to an enhancement of aggressive behavior, is not seen as a necessary component. Rather, an explanation for the differential effects is based on the proposal that an individual can assume aggressive cue value when he or she is associated with film-mediated violence (Berkowitz, 1974). Specifically, when a male views a film depiction of rape and is then given an opportunity to aggress against a female annoyer, he inflicts more harm because of the female target's aggressive cue value—her association with the victim in the film. A nonaggressive erotic film, in contrast, lacks aggressive cues that would lower the male's inhibitions for inflicting harm against women and, therefore, male aggression against the female target is lower. It could be argued that aggressive pornography leads to more male–female aggression because a filmed portrayal of rape may be associated with greater negative affect (cf. Sapolsky & Zillmann, 1981). However, this argument leaves unexplained the nonfacilitation of inter-male aggression subsequent to viewing the rape film (Donnerstein, 1980). The aggressive-cues rationale suggests this discrepancy results from the male target's lack of association with the film's female victim.

The aggressive cues perspective appears to account for heightened male aggression against a female target subsequent to exposure to pornography featuring violence against women, in particular the portrayal of rape. There is also evidence to suggest that *non*erotic stimuli featuring aggression against a female can facilitate male–female aggression (Donnerstein, 1983). The presence of aggressive cues and the sex of the target of aggression are central factors in this rationale. Arousal can facilitate the retaliatory response and is, therefore, seen as interacting with the content of an erotic communication. The contribution of the viewer's affective response to the erotica is not considered.

One study is particularly relevant to the issue of affective response. A film of rape with a positive outcome led to a greater level of retaliatory behavior by nonangered males toward a female target than a rape culminating in a negative outcome (Donnerstein & Berkowitz, 1981). The rape versions were found to be equally arousing, but no measures of affective response were obtained. It is presumed that observing a rape victim's suffering elicits less positive affect than seeing her ultimately express pleasure. Related research has shown this to be the case: The depiction of rape with a pleasurable outcome fosters more positive affect than rape concluding with the victim experiencing disgust (Malamuth, Heim, & Feshbach, 1980). In line with the arousal–affect model, the greater negative affect associated with the suffering outcome should prompt more aggressive behavior. The findings of Donnerstein and Berkowitz (1981), at least for nonangered subjects, are inconsistent with expectations from the two-component model. Donnerstein and Berkowitz alternatively argue that the pleasurable rape outcome stimulates more male–female aggression because it lowers males' restraints against aggression toward women.

The presence of aggressive content in erotic communications has not trans-

lated to an increment in intermale aggression when compared to nonaggressive
erotica. Equally arousing and displeasing nonaggressive and aggressive pornography (sadomasochism) have been shown to elevate male–male aggression to a
similar degree (Zillmann, Bryant, & Carveth, 1981). Donnerstein (1980) has
likewise demonstrated that a film of sexual violence (rape) leads to no greater
intermale aggression than a film of sexual intercourse. These findings suggest
that the aggressive cues perspective identifies an important factor in the relationship between aggressive erotica and violence against *women*. The arousal–
affect model fails to account for this relationship, but it does provide an adequate
explanation for the findings of previous research on intermale aggression subsequent to exposure to sexual stimuli of a nonaggressive, aggressive (i.e.,
sadomasochistic), or deviant nature.

INDIVIDUAL DIFFERENCES IN RESPONSE
TO EROTICA

Researchers investigating the general character of psychosexual stimulation
have recognized the dual capacity of erotica to generate arousal as well as strong
and diverse affective reactions (Griffitt, 1979; Griffitt, May, & Veitch, 1974;
Money, 1973). What is now being acknowledged is the critical role affective
responses play in the relationship between erotica and human aggression (White,
1979; Zillmann & Sapolsky, 1977). Sapolsky and Zillmann (1981) have noted
that only certain arousing, erotic films are capable of engendering a negative
affective state and that different films may do so for males and females. Affective reactions to erotica are complex and unpredictable: They are dependent on
the interaction of many factors, including the contents of the specific stimulus
and individual and sex differences. Research suggests that the effect of erotica on
intermale aggressive behavior hinges on the affective reactions of the observer.
Therefore, it is of even greater importance to examine how various sexual stimuli
evoke specific affective reactions. The remainder of this chapter examines the
nature of several factors thought to mediate affective response to erotica.

Influences on Affective Response

SEXUAL SOCIALIZATION

It is recognized that an individual's cultural background is an important filter
through which erotic stimuli are exposed (Dienstbier, 1977; Malamuth, *et al.*,
1977). Traditionally, childhood and adolescent socialization experiences have
provided only limited opportunities for learning about sex, particularly for
females (Bandura & Walters, 1963; Kinsey, Pomeroy, Martin, & Gebhard,
1953; Simon and Gagnon, 1970). The socialization process often attaches a great

deal of negativity to sexual behavior and to media portrayals of sexual activity. Sex thus becomes associated with guilt, shame, and even disgust (Dienstbier, 1977). The results can be an unusual preoccupation with erotica as an adult (Dienstbier, 1977), the rejection of activities divergent from "approved" sexual practices (Mann, Sidman, & Starr, 1973), or a strong, negative affective reaction to sexual stimuli (Fisher & Byrne, 1978a).

Some observers have suggested that a significant change in the sexual socialization process has occurred. They point to the sexual liberalization of the 1960s with its greater permissiveness and shifting of sexual norms (Christensen, 1966; Johnson & Goodchilds, 1973). As a result, there may be a convergence in the responses of males and females and a lessening of guilt and disgust associated with sex and sexual images (Schmidt & Sigusch, 1970, 1973). Such speculation must be treated cautiously, however. Current research indicates that college-age populations still find more unusual sexual themes disturbing (Zillmann, Bryant, Comisky, & Medoff, 1981), and females remain more displeased than males with depictions of normal sexual practices (Sapolsky, in preparation).

One theoretical approach considers the relationship between sexual socialization and affective and evaluative responses to erotica. According to the reinforcement–affect model, one's learning experiences (either rewarding or punishing) with regard to sexuality have affective consequences that can be classically conditioned to sexual stimuli, thus making the stimuli capable of eliciting positive or negative affective reactions (Byrne, 1977; Fisher & Byrne, 1978a). In other words, affective reactions to erotica are the result of affect-eliciting rewards and punishments linked to sexual experiences during the socialization process (Byrne, Fisher, Lamberth, & Mitchell, 1974). It has recently been demonstrated that individuals with a negative sexual-socialization history rate their affective and evaluative responses to erotica as negative while those with a positive history of sexual experiences express positive affective–evaluative responses to sexual stimulation (Fisher & Byrne, 1978a).

SEXUAL EXPERIENCE

It has been demonstrated that primary experience with emotion-laden behaviors facilitates affective responsiveness (Sapolsky & Zillmann, 1978). In the case of sexual activity, it is generally regarded that individuals with extensive experience will respond to erotica with more positive affect (Athanasiou & Shauer, 1971; Baron, 1979; Brady & Levitt, 1965; Griffitt, 1975). However, some sexual stimuli (e.g., portrayals of flagellantism, bestiality, and sadomasochism) may evoke strong negative reactions from persons in all levels of sexual experience (Mann *et al.*, 1973; Zillmann, Bryant, & Carveth, 1981). Premarital sex differences in arousal from erotica depicting unusual sex practices (e.g., oral sex) disappear when married couples are considered (Griffitt, 1975), presumably because married females have greater experience with such behaviors. When affect is considered, though, sexual experience does not appear to account for sex differences in responding to erotica. While there is an increasing convergence of male and female reports of sexual activity (Curran, 1977; Libby & Strauss, 1980, Schmidt, 1975), the sexes maintain rather distinct affective reactions to sexual materials.

PRIOR EXPOSURE TO EROTICA

Previous experience with erotic stimuli is said to be associated with a reduced belief in its harmful effects (Lipton, 1973; Malamuth *et al.*, 1979, September), a lowering of restrictive attitudes toward its availability (Johnson & Goodchilds, 1973), and the creation of more permissive sexual attitudes (Goldstein, 1973). Having witnessed media portrayals of sexual activity, adults come to believe that such exposure does not create sexual deviancy but, instead, provides fantasy material and even a safety valve for sexual desires (Eysenck & Nias, 1978).

According to Zajonc (1968), repeated exposure to a stimulus results in more positive evaluation of the stimulus. Both this mere-exposure proposal and the mechanism of desensitization (Eysenck & Nias, 1978) suggest that greater experience with erotica (greater frequency of exposure) should lead to less fear, shame, and guilt and increasingly positive affect upon later exposure to sexual stimulation. This notion seems particularly relevant to sex differences in affective response to erotica. It has consistently been found that females have less experience with all manner of erotica (McCauley & Swann, 1978; Nawy, 1971; Sapolsky, in preparation; Sapolsky & Zillmann, 1981; Schmidt & Sigusch, 1973). And the less experienced female, as will be later noted, has often been found to exhibit negative affective reactions when confronted with most erotic stimuli. Sapolsky and Zillmann (1981) have suggested that females are less desensitized to strong erotica, and therefore, interpret their affective reaction as being one of disturbance.

What is the consequence for affective reactivity when there has been an overindulgence in sexual stimulation? Overexposure can lead to habituation or satiation (Howard, Liptzin, & Reifler, 1973; Money, 1973), but its effect may be transitory (Cline, 1974; Eysenck & Nias, 1978). Habitual users of erotica may lose their appetite for specific materials, but a more general satiation with sexual stimuli does not appear to occur in real life (Winick, 1971). Greater familiarization with and habituation to strong erotica may reduce its offensiveness, particularly for males (Sapolsky & Zillmann, 1981). An immunity to the shocking and disturbing qualities of certain erotic content can then lead the user to search for newer, even stronger materials. The pornography industry is well aware of the potential for dulling the consumer's arousal and affective responses and, as a result, provides ever more novel erotic stimuli (Money, 1973). The habituation to tame sex themes may, in part, explain the current increase in aggressive pornography (e.g., rape and sadomasochism).

THEMATIC ELEMENTS

It is believed that affective reactions to erotica and, in turn, their aggression-modifying effects are dependent on the specific contents of the material (Baron, in press; Baron & Bell, 1977). In a study by Sapolsky and Zillmann (1981), for instance, male subjects rated themselves disturbed by a film of petting but not by a film of coital behavior; the reverse was true for female subjects. These differences in affective response coincided with differences in the expression of hostile behavior. Other studies have found positive affect associated with exposure to semi-nudes and nudes (Baron, 1974a, 1974b) and forms of heterosexual precoital and coital behavior (Zillmann, Bryant, Comisky, & Medoff, 1981). Negative affect has been shown to be associated with portrayals of masturbation and homosexuality (Mosher & O'Grady, 1979), oral sex (White, 1979), sado-masochism (Malamuth, Haber, & Feshbach, 1980), and bondage and bestiality (Zillmann, Bryant, Comisky, & Medoff, 1981). In general, it would seem that the more the stimulus approaches the extremes of uncommonness and deviancy, the greater the degree of negative affect it will elicit.

Of course, the contents of erotica depicting a class of sexual behavior (e.g., heterosexual intercourse) can differ markedly, and these differences may contribute to the observed inconsistencies in evaluative judgments of experimental stimuli. For instance, the negatively valenced precoitus film employed by Sapolsky and Zillman (1981) featured a fully clothed couple kissing and petting. The positive valenced precoitus film included in the Zillmann, Bryant, Comiskey, and Medoff (1981) study contained nudity. While both films portray the same category of sexual behavior, their unique contents lead to contrasting affective responses.

In a recent investigation of media portrayals of sexual violence, the affect-eliciting qualities of a number of thematic elements were assessed (Malamuth, Heim, & Feshbach, 1980). As might be expected, mutually consenting sex generated more positive affect and less negative affect than rape. Also, rape that depicted the victim as experiencing involuntary orgasm led to more positive affect than an outcome displaying the victim's revolt and disgust. However, neither the degree of victim pain nor the degree to which the sex crime was premeditated was associated with differing levels of positive or negative affect (Malamuth, Heim, & Feshbach, 1980).

Traditionally, erotic passages and images have been oriented to the male consumer and have focused on the female in various poses and acts, exploiting her as a sexual object (Heiman, 1977; Johnson & Goodchilds, 1973; Sigusch, Schmidt, Reinfeld, & Weidemann-Sutor, 1970). The accentuation of the female's sexual anatomy and behavior may partially explain her tendency to respond negatively to such stimuli. Possibly, if erotic contents were more oriented toward stimulating the female, gender differences in response would be reduced.

A content-specific issue considered particularly relevant to sex differences in response to erotica is the "romantic versus hard-core" or "love versus lust" themes (e.g., Fisher & Byrne, 1978b). It has variously been stated that males prefer and are more responsive to explicit, plotless, and impersonal hard-core depictions of sex, whereas females find romantic, sentimental, and aesthetically oriented soft-core treatments more desirable (Fisher & Byrne, 1978b, Heiman, 1977; Jakobovits, 1965; Johnson & Goodchilds, 1973; Kenrick, Stringfield, Wagenhals, Dahl, & Ransdell, 1980; Money, 1973). However, little evidence relative to affective response is available on this point. Fisher and Byrne (1978b) found no gender differences in affect from the themes of love, lust, or casual sex. In studies designed to assess arousal reactions to erotic stimuli, females were no more aroused by themes of romance or affection than by purely sexual themes (Heiman, 1977; Schmidt, 1975). The popular belief that females respond more favorably to or are more stimulated by erotica containing love themes, and the more general notion that gender differences are dependent on the specific erotic contents (Griffitt & Kaiser, 1978; Herrell, 1975), must be treated cautiously at present.

SEX DIFFERENCES

It has been found that females respond to nonaggressive and aggressive sexual stimulation with greater negative affect than males (Byrne & Byrne, 1977; Griffitt, 1973; Izard & Caplan, 1974; Malamuth, Heim, & Feshbach, 1980b, Sapolsky & Zillmann, 1981, Schmidt & Sigusch, 1970, 1973). Sapolsky and Zillmann (1981) found that when males responded positively to erotica, females responded negatively, and when males responded negatively, females did so more strongly. Byrne et al. (1974) suggest that negative affect is the primary indicator of females' evaluations of erotica, whereas a mixture of positive and negative affect determines males' evaluations. What might account for the fact that females, quite unlike males, are often shown to respond to erotica with unfavorable reactions of shock, irritation, and disgust?

As has been discussed, the female's lesser experience with erotica and the tendency for this material to be directed at a male clientele may help to explain sex differences in affective response to sexual stimuli. Byrne and his associates have proposed several explanations for the female's inexperience with and unfavorable reaction to erotica. First, it is argued that the female's negative emotions derive from being taught to avoid sexual excitement as a means of averting exploitation by males. In other words, the female's reaction to erotica is associated with the dangerous advances of the male (Byrne, 1977). Second, females are discouraged from acquiring erotica or using it to generate sexual fantasies, and, in general, females are expected to exhibit disinterest in sexual materials (Byrne et al., 1974; Fisher & Byrne, 1978a). In sum, as a result of negative socialization experiences relative to the use of sexual stimuli, the female demonstrates more negative affect when confronted with such materials, expresses less desire to be exposed to erotica, and indicates more restrictive attitudes concerning the availability of sexual words and images (e.g., Griffitt, 1973).

PERSONALITY DIMENSIONS

A number of personality dimensions have been explored in terms of their mediation of the affect elicited by sexual stimulation. For example, individuals found to rate high on the trait of sex guilt react to erotica with more negative emotions, including disgust, than those rating low on sex guilt (Griffitt & Kaiser, 1978; Mosher, 1971; Schill, Van Tuinen, & Doty, 1980). Likewise, authoritarianism is positively related to negative emotions, higher judgments of the pornographic character of sexual stimuli, and the placing of legal restrictions on their availability (Byrne et al., 1973; Byrne et al., 1974). Eysenck (Eysenck & Nias, 1978) has shown that extroverts are more likely to be turned on by and respond positively to erotica; introverts will be turned off and react with disgust to this material. Other factors shown to be related to negative reactions or judgments include religiosity and conservatism (Byrne, 1977; Byrne et al., 1974).

An approach of Byrne, Griffitt, and their colleagues has been to classify individuals according to the degree to which they respond to erotic stimuli with positive or negative affect. Individual differences in affective orientation are then related to evaluative responses and sex-relevant behaviors (Byrne et al., 1974; Griffitt & Kaiser, 1978; Griffitt et al., 1974). Byrne et al. (1974) exposed subjects to a variety of sexual themes. Subsequently, individuals were classified according to their responses to a feelings scale (Byrne & Sheffield, 1965). Two independent dimensions of positive and negative affect emerged yielding four affective subgroups: pro-sex (high positive, low negative), anti-sex (low positive, high negative), ambivalent (high positive, high negative), and indifferent (low positive, low negative). In line with the reinforcement-affect model (Byrne & Clore, 1970), evaluative judgments were found to be systematically related to affective responses to the stimuli. Both anti-sex and ambivalent females gave more negative evaluations of the stimuli—negative affect, regardless of the level of accompanying positive affect, predicted females' evaluative responses. By comparison, only anti-sex males gave more negative evaluations—for males the interaction of both positive *and* negative affect established evaluative responses.

Griffitt et al. (1974) found that, of the four affect subgroups, only pro-sex individuals responded more positively to and had more eye contact with an opposite-sex person than a same-sex person. In addition, only anti-sex individuals established greater physical distance between themselves and persons of the opposite sex. In a later study (Griffitt & Kaiser, 1978), the opportunity to view erotic slides was found to act as a rewarding mechanism for individuals who react to such stimuli with high positive affect but to function as a punisher for those who respond to erotica with low positive affect.

In an alternative approach to the exploration of individual differences in response to erotica, Fisher and Byrne (1978a) distinguished between persons characterized as *erotophobes* and *erotophiles*. These categorizations were based on responses to three questions probing the individual's reactions to an explicit erotic film: Erotophobes, more so than erotophiles, rated a film depicting genital petting and oral sex as pornographic, shocking, and more explicit than expected. And, in addition, erotophobes were found to have had more negative sexual-socialization experiences, more limited sexual experience, and more conservative sex-related attitudes than erotophiles. Of particular importance, erotophobes (as compared to erotophiles) reacted to the erotic film with more negative affect, and "phobes" expressed less desire to engage in future erotica-related studies. Interestingly, only the erotophobes reported an increase in sexual activity from the pre- to post-exposure periods (it is unclear as to whether the *reporting* or the sexual activity itself was disinhibited).

Dimensions of Affective Response and Aggressive Behavior

Byrne and others have demonstrated the feasibility of characterizing individuals according to the comparative levels of negative and positive affect they experience when confronted with sexual stimulation. These researchers have also shown how the dimensions of affective response to erotica are related to evaluative and interpersonal behaviors. It would seem appropriate to apply their approach to the matter of human aggression. For example, anti-sex persons—those found to respond to erotica with predominantly negative affect—would be expected, according to the two-component or arousal–affect model (Sapolsky & Zillmann, 1981; Zillmann, Bryant, Comisky, & Medoff, 1981), to engage in greater motivated aggressive behavior after exposure to strong erotica than pro-sex persons, or those individuals for whom erotica engenders largely positive affect.

White (1979) has examined how aggressive behavior may be influenced by the capacity of erotic stimuli to generate the patterns of affect delineated by Byrne, Griffitt, and others. Angered (or nonangered) males were exposed to one of four sets of stimuli chosen to elicit the four variations in affective response. Thereafter subjects were given an opportunity to retaliate against their annoyer. White predicted that aggression would be inhibited by erotica creating positive affect (pro-sex), enhanced by erotica fostering ambivalent reactions, and neither enhanced nor reduced by stimuli of negative or neutral character (anti-sex and indifferent). Presuming that the erotic slides employed by White were only minimally arousing (cf. Zillmann & Sapolsky, 1977), the arousal–affect model

(Sapolsky & Zillmann, 1981) would likewise predict a lowering of aggressiveness subsequent to positive stimulation. But, in contrast, the model would predict a slight enhancement of aggressive behavior by negative (anti-sex) stimuli and neither an increase nor reduction resulting from ambivalent stimuli due to a counteracting of positive and negative affect. It was found that the stimuli prejudged to create a positive affective state (pro-sex) inhibited motivated aggressive behavior. No facilitory or inhibitory effects were observed for the negative, ambivalent, or neutral stimuli. There was, however, a tendency for both ambivalent and anti-sex stimuli to enhance aggression. Thus, positive erotic stimulation reduced while disgusting and unpleasant imagery slightly enhanced retaliatory behavior. In general, the study offers support for the notion that knowledge of individual variation in affective response to erotica can contribute to a more accurate assessment of its effect on motivated aggressive behavior.

Fisher and Byrne have demonstrated that, in accord with the reinforcement–affect model, affective response is linked to the individual's evaluation of the erotic stimulus. Those who evaluate erotica negatively (phobes) also respond to this material with negative affect, and those with more positive evaluations (philes) react with positive affect. This relationship is particularly relevant for a model implicating affective response as a key element in the influence of erotica on aggressive behavior. If individuals can be identified for whom erotica is likely to produce either negative or positive affect, then a more accurate prediction of the aggression-modifying effect of erotica can be made. In particular, erotophobes should exhibit more negative affect after exposure to strong erotica and thereby display heightened aggressiveness. By comparison, the positive affect experienced by erotophiles should contribute to a reduction in aggressive behavior.

One study has considered the erotophobe–erotophile factor in examining the effect of exposure to erotica on hostile behavior (Sapolsky, 1977).[2] In this investigation, angered (or nonangered) males viewed one of the several nonaggressive erotic or nonerotic films and were then permitted to express hostility toward their provoker. As a means of exploring the contribution of individual differences in response to erotica, subjects provided retrospective accounts of their experiences with and reactions to explicit erotic (X-rated) films. Questions probed (1) the degree to which subjects considered so-called X-rated films pornographic, shocking, and more explicit than expected (scales identical to those used by Fisher and Byrne, 1978a); (2) the frequency with which they attended erotic films; and (3) how much enjoyment they derived from witnessing these films. Through median splits of their responses, subjects were classified as erotophobes or erotophiles, as well as high versus low experienced and high

[2]Sapolsky (1977) contains additional data on male subjects not reported in Sapolsky and Zillmann (1981).

versus low enjoyers of explicit sexual films. These three factors were subsequently included in analyses of intermale hostility.

Surprisingly, erotophobes displayed no greater level of retaliatory behavior toward their provoker than did erotophiles. Individuals who in the past have had negative affective reactions to erotica did not get back at their annoyer any more intensely than individuals for whom the experience of viewing an explicit film was a positive one. Unlike the phobe–phile distinction, the factors of enjoyment and experience were associated with differences in intermale hostility. Subjects who reported a lower degree of enjoyment from watching explicit films exhibited greater retaliatory behavior. Similarly, those males indicating less experience with such fare expressed more hostility. It is not at all unexpected that findings from the experience and enjoyment factors are highly related due to the obvious circumstance that people who enjoy erotic films are more likely to attend them and people who avoid erotic films do so because they find them unenjoyable. It can be speculated that the characterization of individuals as erotophobes or erotophiles may have failed to reveal differences in hostile behavior because of the provision for a *retrospective* accounting of the subjects' responses to an explicit erotic film. Had respondents been given the opportunity to rate the pornographic, shocking, and explicit qualities of stimuli presented during the experimental session, the differentiation of individuals as phobes or philes may have reflected differences in the level of retaliation. However, this argument fails to explain why the variation in past enjoyment of strong erotica was associated with differences in hostility. Perhaps the measure of enjoyment may better reflect the individual's affective responsiveness to erotica than the measures included in the erotophobe–erotophile factor.

Individual Differences in Response to Aggressive Pornography

With the increasing occurrence and acceptance of sexual violence in the mass media, greater attention is being focused on the effects of aggressive pornography. Initial efforts have been made to gauge the affect-eliciting capacity of this form of sexual stimulation (Malamuth, Haber, & Feshbach, 1980; Malamuth, Heim, & Feshbach, 1980). As previously discussed, a description of rape led to more negative feelings than a passage detailing mutually consenting sex (Malamuth, Heim, & Feshbach, 1980b). Research exploring the aggression-enhancing or -reducing impact of aggressive pornography has generally neglected the issue of affective responsiveness as a contributing influence (Donnerstein, 1983). One study has shown that arousing, negatively valenced aggressive pornography (sadomasochism) can facilitate aggressive behavior (Zillmann, Bryant, Comisky, & Medoff, 1981b).

An investigation by Sapolsky and Potter (in preparation) explored affective responsivity to filmed depictions of rape. Of particular importance, individual differences in affective response to aggressive pornography were evaluated. Males and females were exposed to one of several films: (1) aggressive pornography (rape), (2) nonaggressive erotica (mutually consenting intercourse), or (3) a neutral control film (nature scenes). Two versions of the aggressive-pornographic film were prepared. One version depicted rape accompanied by the *threat of injury* if the victim resisted her assailant; the second version portrayed actual *injury* (beating) as part of the sexual violence. Thus, the rape films contained differing levels of aggressive cues. Subsequent to exposure, subjects responded to a series of scales measuring their affective reactions to the films. Thereafter, subjects completed an array of questions probing their past reactions to explicit erotic films, prior experience with sexual materials and sexual behavior, and attitudes toward erotica.

A consistent pattern of response to the films was in evidence. Subjects responded to the rape films most negatively (e.g., unpleasant, dirty, bad, disturbing). Regardless of whether sexual assault contained verbal or physical aggression, affective reactions were comparable. The consenting intercourse film generated moderate levels of negative affect below that associated with the rape film. And, while all three erotic films elicited negative affective reactions, the neutral film fostered largely positive feelings. Males and females reported equal degrees of negative affect from both versions of the rape film. However, although males responded more positively to nonaggressive erotica, females were as disturbed by this film as by the aggressive-pornographic materials.

Dimensions of individual variation were explored in subsequent analyses of affective responsiveness to the aggressive- and nonaggressive-erotic films. Frequent church attendance, high restrictiveness (the expression of opposition to the showing of sexual films on TV or in theaters), and low experience (exposure) with X-rated films were all associated with greater negative affective response to the experimental erotic films. Also, those who reported experiencing a low degree of sexual arousal from explicit films viewed in the past also expressed stronger feelings of negative affect. In agreement with earlier research (Sapolsky, 1977), inclusion of an erotophobe–erotophile factor did not lead to differences in affective reactivity. The factors of past enjoyment of X-rated films and level of sexual experience (intercourse) were not related to the degree of positive or negative affect elicited by the various experimental films.

The utility of the phobe–phile and enjoyment dimensions to reflect differences in affective response may be limited by the manner in which subjects were asked to characterize their general responsiveness to X-rated stimuli. Individuals are likely to conjure up very different kinds of explicit erotic films when registering the level of their past reactions. As a result, the subjects' retrospective reports are confounded with the specific type of erotica each individual has in mind. To overcome this dilemma, future investigations of individual differences in response to erotica may wish to provide participants with identical erotic materials as a means of more accurately assessing affective and evaluative reactions.

In general, Sapolsky and Potter (in preparation) provide evidence that films of rape, regardless of the level of aggressive cues, are potent generators of negative affect. Therefore, it is expected that exposure to this type of pornography would, as predicted by the arousal–affect model, lead to a heightening of motivated intermale aggressive behavior. It should be remembered that contrary evidence (Donnerstein, 1980) questions the extension of predictions from the two-component model to aggressive pornography. It is apparent that a number of attitudinal and behavioral characteristics of the viewer (e.g., restrictiveness and amount of prior experience with erotica) serve as mediators of affect. It is suggested that a model for predicting the effect of erotica on human aggression may be further refined through the consideration of individual differences in responding to a wide range of sexual stimuli. In the future, probing the degree to which individuals differ on relevant variables such as the belief in rape myths (Barnett & Field, 1977, Burt, 1980) may prove valuable in characterizing affective response to media portrayals of sexual violence.

SUMMARY

It has been proposed that a two-component model implicating both the arousal capacity and affect-eliciting qualities of an erotic stimulus offers a comprehensive means of assessing the effect of nonaggressive sexual stimuli on intermale aggression. It thus becomes an essential matter to determine which experiential factors and thematic elements precipitate an individual's affective response to various erotic materials. Individuals differ along various sex-related dimensions including sexual socialization histories, sexual attitudes and behaviors, and sexual media exposure habits. These factors, in interaction with specific erotic themes, apparently account for the direction of affective response.

When individuals have been classified along various erotica-related evaluative and behavioral dimensions, differences in the positive or negative character of affective response to sexual stimuli have been observed. These dimensions have included the level of previous experience with erotica, restrictiveness, the enjoyment and arousal derived from witnessing sexual activity, and erotophobia versus erotophilia. It has yet to be determined if the inclusion of these and other rape-related dimensions of individual variation can provide further insights into the aggression-modifying effects of pornography.

REFERENCES

Adamson, J. D., Romano, K. R., Burdick, J. A., Corman, C. L., & Chebib, F. S. (1972). Physiological responses to sexual and unpleasant film stimuli. *Journal of Psychosomatic Research, 16*, 153–162.

Athanasiou, R., & Shauer, P. (1971). Correlates of heterosexuals' reactions to pornography. *Journal of Sex Research, 7*, 298–311.

Bandura, A. (1965). Vicarious processes: A case of no-trial learning. In L. Berkowitz (Ed.), *Advances in experimental social psychology* (Vol. 2). New York: Academic Press.

Bandura, A. (1973). *Aggression: A social learning analysis*. Englewood Cliffs, NJ: Prentice-Hall.

Bandura, A., & Walters, R. H. (1963). *Social learning and personality development*. New York: Holt, Rinehart, and Winston.

Barnett, N. J., & Feild, H. S. (1977). Sex differences in university students' attitudes toward rape. *Journal of College Student Personnel, 18*, 93–96.

Baron, R. A. (1974a). The aggression-inhibiting influence of heightened sexual arousal. *Journal of Personality and Social Psychology, 30*, 318–322.

Baron, R. A. (1974b). Sexual arousal and physical aggression: The inhibiting influence of ''cheese-cake'' and nudes. *Bulletin of the Psychonomic Society, 3*, 337–339.

Baron, R. A. (1979). Heightened sexual arousal and physical aggression: An extension to females. *Journal of Research in Personality, 13*, 91–102.

Baron, R. A. (1983). The control of human aggression: A strategy based on incompatible responses. In R. G. Geen & E. Donnerstein (Eds.), *Aggression: Theoretical and empirical reviews*. New York: Academic Press.

Baron, R. A., & Bell, P. A. (1973). Effects of heightened sexual arousal on physical aggression. *Proceedings of the 81st Annual Convention of the American Psychological Association, 8*, 171–172.

Baron, R. A., & Bell, P. A. (1977). Sexual arousal and aggression by males: Effects of type of erotic stimuli and prior provocation. *Journal of Personality and Social Psychology, 35*, 79–87.

Berkowitz, L. (1974). Some determinants of impulsive aggression: The role of mediated associations with reinforcements for aggression. *Psychological Review, 81*, 165–176.

Brady, J. P., & Levitt, E. E. (1965). The relation of sexual preferences to sexual experiences. *Psychological Record, 15*, 377–384.

Burt, M. R. (1980). Cultural myths and supports for rape. *Journal of Personality and Social Psychology, 38*, 217–230.

Byrne, D. (1977). The imagery of sex. In J. Money & H. Musaph (Eds.), *Handbook of sexology*. Amsterdam: Excerpta Medica.

Byrne, D., & Byrne, L. A. (1977). *Exploring human sexuality*. New York: Harper and Row.

Byrne, D., Cherry, F., Lamberth, J., & Mitchell, H. E. (1973). Husband-wife similarity in response to erotic stimuli. *Journal of Personality, 41*, 385–394.

Byrne, D., & Clore, G. L. (1970). A reinforcement model of evaluative responses. *Personality, 1*, 103–128.

Byrne, D., Fisher, J. D., Lamberth, J., & Mitchell, H. E. (1974). Evaluations of erotica: Facts or feelings? *Journal of Personality and Social Psychology, 29*, 111–116.

Byrne, D., & Lamberth, J. (1971). The effect of erotic stimuli on sex arousal, evaluative responses, and subsequent behavior. In *Technical Reports of the Commission on Obscenity and Pornography* (Vol. 8). Washington, DC: Government Printing Office.

Byrne, D., & Sheffield, J. (1965). Response to sexually arousing stimuli as a function of repressing and sensitizing defenses. *Journal of Abnormal Psychology, 70*, 114–118.

Cantor, J. R., Zillmann, D., & Einsiedel, E. F. (1978). Female responses to provocation after exposure to aggressive and erotic films. *Communication Research, 5*, 395–411.

Christensen, H. T. (1966). Scandinavian and American sex norms: Some comparisons with sociological implications. *Journal of Social Issues, 22*, 60–75.

Cline, V. B. (1974). *Where do you draw the line?* Provo, UT: Brigham Young University Press.

Curran, J. P. (1977). Convergence toward a single sexual standard? In D. Byrne & L. A. Byrne (Eds.), *Exploring human sexuality.* New York: Harper and Row.

Davis, K. E., & Braucht, G. N. (1973). Exposure to pornography, character, and sexual deviance: A retrospective survey. *Journal of Social Issues, 29*, 183–196.

Dienstbier, R. A. (1977). Sex and violence: Can research have it both ways? *Journal of Communication, 27*, 176–188.

Donnerstein, E. (1980). Aggressive erotica and violence against women. *Journal of Personality and Social Psychology, 39*, 269–277.

Donnerstein, E. (1983). Erotica and human aggression. In R. Geen & E. Donnerstein (Eds.),*Aggression: Theoretical and empirical reviews,* New York: Academic Press.

Donnerstein, E., & Barrett, G. (1978). Effects of erotic stimuli on male aggression toward females. *Journal of Personality and Social Psychology, 36*, 180–188.

Donnerstein, E., & Berkowitz, L. (1981). Victim reactions in aggressive erotic films as a factor in violence against women. *Journal of Personality and Social Psychology, 41*, 710–724.

Donnerstein, E., Donnerstein, M., & Evans, R. (1975). Erotic stimuli and aggression: Facilitation or inhibition. *Journal of Personality and Social Psychology, 32*, 237–244.

Donnerstein, E., & Hallam, J. (1978). Facilitating effects of erotica on aggression toward women. *Journal of Personality and Social Psychology, 36*, 1270–1277.

Eysenck, H. J., & Nias, D. K. B. (1978). *Sex, violence, and the media.* New York: Harper and Row.

Fisher, W. A., & Byrne, D. (1978a). Individual differences in affective, evaluative, and behavioral responses to an erotic film. *Journal of Applied Social Psychology, 8*, 335–365.

Fisher, W. A., & Byrne, D. (1978b). Sex differences in response to erotica? Love versus lust. *Journal of Personality and Social Psychology, 36*, 117–125.

Fisher, J. L., & Harris, M. B. (1976). Modeling, arousal, and aggression. *The Journal of Social Psychology, 100*, 219–226.

Fromm, E. (1973). *The anatomy of human destruction.* Greenwich: Fawcett Crest.

Goldstein, M. J. (1973). Exposure to erotic stimuli and sexual deviance. *Journal of Social Issues, 29*, 197–219.

Griffitt, W. (1973). Response to erotica and the projection of response to erotica in the opposite sex. *Journal of Experimental Research in Personality, 6*, 330–338.

Griffitt, W. (1975). Sexual experience and sexual responsiveness: Sex differences. *Archives of Sexual Behavior, 4*, 529–540.

Griffitt, W. (1979). Sexual stimulation and sociosexual behaviors. In M. Cook & G. Wilson (Eds.), *Love and attraction.* Oxford: Pergamon Press.

Griffitt, W., & Kaiser, D. L. (1978). Affect, sex guilt, gender, and the rewarding-punishing effects of erotic stimuli. *Journal of Personality and Social Psychology, 36*, 850–858.

Griffitt, W., May, J., & Veitch, R. (1974). Sexual stimulation and interpersonal behavior: Heterosexual evaluative responses, visual behavior, and physical proximity. *Journal of Personality and Social Psychology, 30*, 367–377.

Heiman, J. R. (1977). A psychophysiological exploration of sexual arousal patterns in females and males. *Psychophysiology, 14*, 266–274.

Herrell, J. M. (1975). Sex differences in emotional responses to "erotic literature", *Journal of Consulting and Clinical Psychology, 43*, 921.

Howard, J. L., Liptzin, M. B., & Reifler, C. B. (1973). Is pornography a problem? *Journal of Social Issues 29*, 133–145.

Izard, C. E., & Caplan, S. (1974). Sex differences in emotional responses to erotic literature. *Journal of Consulting and Clinical Psychology, 42,* 468.

Jakobovits, L. A. (1965). Evaluational reactions to erotic literature. *Psychological Reports, 16,* 985–994.

Jaffe, Y. (1974). *Sex and aggression: An intimate relationship.* Unpublished doctoral dissertation. UCLA.

Jaffe, Y., Malamuth, N., Feingold, J., & Feshbach, S. (1974). Sexual arousal and behavioral aggression. *Journal of Personality and Social Psychology, 30,* 759–764.

Johnson, P., & Goodchilds, J. D. (1973). Comment: Pornography, sexuality, and social psychology. *Journal of Social Issues, 29,* 231–238.

Kenrick, D. T., Stringfield, D. O., Wagenhals, W. L., Dahl, R. H., & Ransdell, H. J. (1980). Sex differences, androgyny, and approach responses to erotica: A new variation on the old volunteer problem. *Journal of Personality and Social Psychology, 38,* 517–524.

Kinsey, A. C., Pomeroy, W. B., Martin, C. E., & Gebhard, P. H. (1953). *Sexual behavior in the human female.* Philadelphia: Saunders.

Libby, R. W., & Strauss, M. A. (1980). Make love not war? Sex, sexual meanings, and violence in a sample of university students. *Archives of Sexual Behavior, 9,* 133–148.

Lipton, M. A. (1973). Fact and myth: The work of The Commission on Obscenity and Pornography. In J. Zubin & J. Money (Eds.), *Contemporary sexual behavior: Critical issues in the 1970's.* Baltimore: The Johns Hopkins University Press.

Malamuth, N. M. (1981). Rape fantasies as a function of exposure to violent sexual stimuli. *Archives of Sexual Behavior, 10,* 33–47.

Malamuth, N. M., & Check, J. V. P. (1981). The effects of mass media exposure on acceptance of violence against women: A field experiment. *Journal of Research in Personality, 15,* 436–446.

Malamuth, N. M., & Donnerstein, E. (1982). The effects of aggressive-pornographic mass media stimuli. In L. Berkowitz (Ed.), *Advances in experimental social psychology* (Vol. 15). New York: Academic Press.

Malamuth, N. M., Feshbach, S., & Jaffe, Y. (1977). Sexual arousal and aggression: Recent experiments and theoretical issues. *Journal of Social Issues, 33,* 110–133.

Malamuth, N. M., Haber, S., & Feshbach, S. (1980). Testing hypotheses regarding rape: Exposure to sexual violence, sex differences, and the "normality" of rapists. *Journal of Research in Personality, 14,* 121–137.

Malamuth, N. M., Heim, M., & Feshbach, S. (1980). Sexual responsiveness of college students to rape depictions: Inhibitory and disinhibitory effects. *Journal of Personality and Social Psychology, 38,* 399–408.

Malamuth, N. M., Reisin, I., & Spinner, B. (1979, September). *Exposure to pornography and reactions to rape.* Paper presented at the meeting of the American Psychological Association, New York.

Mann, J., Sidman, J., & Starr, S. (1973). Evaluating social consequences of erotic films: An experimental approach. *Journal of Social Issues, 29,* 113–131.

McCauley, C., & Swann, C. P. (1978). Male-female differences in sexual fantasy. *Journal of Research in Personality, 12,* 76–86.

McConaghy, N. (1974). Penile volume responses to moving and still pictures of male and female nudes. *Archives of Sexual Behavior, 3,* 565–570.

Meyer, T. P. (1972). The effects of sexually arousing and violent films on aggressive behavior. *Journal of Sex Research, 8,* 324–331.

Money, J. (1973). Pornography in the home: A topic in medical education. In J. Zubin & J. Money (Eds.), *Contemporary sexual behavior: Critical issues in the 1970's.* Baltimore: The Johns Hopkins University Press.

Mosher, D. L. (1971). Psychological reactions to pornographic films. In *Technical Report of the*

Commission on Obscenity and Pornography (Vol. 8). Washington, DC: Government Printing Office.

Mosher, D. L., & Katz, H. (1971). Pornographic films, male verbal aggression against women, and guilt. In *Technical Report of the Commission on Obscenity and Pornography* (Vol. 8). Washington, DC: Government Printing Office.

Mosher, D. L., & O'Grady, K. E. (1979). Homosexual threat, negative attitudes toward masturbation, sex guilt, and males' sexual and affective reactions to explicit sexual films. *Journal of Consulting and Clinical Psychology, 47,* 860–873.

Nawy, H. (1971). The San Francisco erotic market place. In *Technical Report of the Commission on Obscenity and Pornography* (Vol. 9). Washington, DC: Government Printing Office.

Rosene, J. M. (1971). *The effects of violent and sexually arousing film content: An experimental study.* Unpublished doctoral dissertation. Ohio University.

Sandford, D. A. (1974). Patterns of sexual arousal in heterosexual males. *Journal of Sex Research, 10,* 150–155.

Sapolsky, B. S. (1977). *The effect of erotica on annoyance and hostile behavior in provoked and unprovoked males.* Unpublished doctoral dissertation. Indiana University.

Sapolsky, B. S. (in preparation). Sex of featured partner and point of view: Sex differences in response to erotic films.

Sapolsky, B. S., & Potter, W. J. (in preparation). Affect, individual differences, and response to rape.

Sapolsky, B. S., & Zillmann, D. (1978). Experience and empathy: Affective reactions to witnessing childbirth. *The Journal of Social Psychology, 105,* 131–144.

Sapolsky, B. S., & Zillmann, D. (1981). The effect of soft-core and hard-core erotica on provoked and unprovoked hostile behavior. *Journal of Sex Research, 17,* 319–343.

Schill, T., Van Tuinen, M., & Doty, D. (1980). Repeated exposure to pornography and arousal levels of subjects varying in guilt. *Psychological Reports, 46,* 467–471.

Schmidt, G. (1975). Male-female differences in sexual arousal and behavior during and after exposure to sexually explicit stimuli. In E. A. Rubinstein, R. Green, & E. Brecher (Eds.), *New directions in sex research.* New York: Plenum Press.

Schmidt, G., & Sigusch, V. (1970). Sex differences in response to psychosexual stimulation by films and slides. *Journal of Sex Research, 6,* 268–283.

Schmidt, G., & Sigusch, V. (1973). Women's sexual arousal. In J. Zubin & J. Money (Eds.), *Contemporary sexual behavior: Critical issues in the 1970's.* Baltimore: The Johns Hopkins University Press.

Sigusch, V., Schmidt, G., Reinfeld, A., & Wiedemann-Sutor, I. (1970). Psychosexual stimulation: Sex differences. *Journal of Sex Research, 6,* 10–24.

Simon, W., & Gagnon, J. M. (1970). *The sexual scene.* New York: Transaction, Inc.

Tannenbaum, P. H. (1971). Emotional arousal as a mediator of erotic communication effects. In *Technical Report of the Commission on Obscenity and Pornography.* (Vol. 8). Washington, DC: Government Printing Office.

Tannenbaum, P. H., & Zillmann, D. (1975). Emotional arousal in the facilitation of aggression through communication. In L. Berkowitz (Ed.), *Advances in experimental social psychology* (Vol. 8). New York: Academic Press.

Time. (1976, April 5). *The porno plague,* 58–63.

White, L. A. (1979). Erotica and aggression: The influence of sexual arousal, positive affect, and negative affect on aggressive behavior. *Journal of Personality and Social Psychology, 37,* 591–601.

Winick, C. (1971). Some observations on characteristics of patrons of adult theatres and bookstores. In *Technical Report of the Commission on Obscenity and Pornography* (Vol. 9). Washington, DC: Government Printing Office.

Zajonc, R. B. (1968). Attitudinal effect of mere exposure. *Journal of Personality and Social Psychology Monograph Supplement, 9,* 1–27.

Zillmann, D. (1971). Excitation transfer in communication-mediated aggressive behavior. *Journal of Experimental Social Psychology, 7,* 419–434.

Zillmann, D., Bryant, J., & Carveth, R. A. (1981). The effect of erotica featuring sadomasochism and bestiality on motivated intermale aggression. *Personality and Social Psychology Bulletin. 7,* 153–159.

Zillmann, D., Bryant, J., Comisky, P. W., & Medoff, N. J. (1981). Excitation and hedonic valence in the effect of erotica on motivated intermale aggression. *European Journal of Social Psychology, 1981, 11,* 233–252.

Zillmann, D., Hoyt, J. L., & Day, K. D. (1974). Strength and duration of the effect of aggressive, violent, and erotic communications on subsequent aggressive behavior. *Communication Research, 1,* 286–306.

Zillmann, D., & Sapolsky, B. S. (1977). What mediates the effect of mild erotica on annoyance and hostile behavior in males? *Journal of Personality and Social Psychology, 35,* 587–596.

4

Effects of Massive Exposure to Pornography

Dolf Zillmann
Jennings Bryant

The findings of research on the effects of massive exposure to sexually explicit films are discussed in this chapter. First, a two-component model of erotica effects on motivated aggressive behavior is presented and applied to available research data. Second, the model is expanded to incorporate changes in the response to erotica that result from repeated exposure. In particular, excitatory habituation and changes in the hedonic reaction are traced. Third, the methodology employed in the massive-exposure work is summarized, and the research findings are reported. Effects on habituation and valence are detailed. The modification of aggressive behavior that is mediated by these effects is explored and related to the two-component model. Finally, numerous nontransitory effects of massive exposure to pornography on the perception of sexuality and on sex-related dispositions are reported. Among them are those concerning uncommon sexual practices, sexual callousness toward women, and the punitive treatment of rape.

A TWO-COMPONENT MODEL OF EFFECTS ON AGGRESSION

A large body of research on the immediate consequences of exposure to erotica on aggressive behavior (cf. Donnerstein, 1982) has consistently produced

PORNOGRAPHY AND
SEXUAL AGGRESSION

type-specific effects. Exposure of provoked individuals to strongly arousing, explicitly sexual materials (such as graphic depictions of coition and related activities in films) was found to increase retaliatory behavior (e.g., Baron, 1979; Cantor, Zillmann, & Einsiedel, 1978; Donnerstein & Hallam, 1978; Meyer, 1972; Zillmann, 1971). Exposure of these individuals to sexually suggestive but comparatively nonarousing fare (such as photographs of nudes in sexually enticing poses), in contrast, was found to decrease hostile and aggressive activities (e.g., Baron, 1974a, 1974b; Baron & Bell, 1973; Donnerstein, Donnerstein, & Evans, 1975; White, 1979).

Zillmann (1978, 1979, 1982) has explained the aggression-enhancing effect of arousing erotica as excitation transfer. He argued, in short, that exposure to erotica fosters increased sympathetic activity as an accompaniment to more specific genital responses (such as vasocongestion and myotonia) and that, after sexual stimulation, residues of the slowly dissipating nonspecific sympathetic activity enter into unrelated affective states and potentially intensify them. If the subsequent state is one of annoyance and anger, residual sympathetic excitation from sexual arousal thus is likely to intensify these experiences and to energize the hostile and aggressive actions incited by them. On the other hand, researchers (Baron, 1974a, 1977; Zillmann & Sapolsky, 1977) have suggested that the aggression-reducing effect of nonarousing but usually pleasant erotic fare results from incompatible affective stimulation. They have argued that the elicitation of hedonically opposite responses interferes with the maintenance of a particular state. More specifically, they have suggested that pleasant erotic stimulation diminishes annoyance, disrupts anger, and thereby reduces hostile and aggressive activities.

The transfer of excitation from exposure to erotica and the hedonic valence of the response to such exposure have been shown to act in concert in their effect on aggressive behavior. In an investigation by Zillmann, Bryant, Comisky, and Medoff (1981), the effects of the following erotica on motivated intermale aggression were determined: nonarousing and pleasing erotica (such as photographs of attractive nude females in sexually enticing poses); nonarousing and displeasing erotica (such as photographs of masturbating, highly pregnant women and unattractive women smeared with menstrual blood); arousing and pleasing erotica (such as films depicting fellatio, cunnilingus, and coition); and arousing and displeasing erotica (such as films depicting women fellating and masturbating various animals, heterosexual flagellation, and the painful deformation of genitals in sadomasochistic activities). Residual excitation and hedonic valence were found to have noninteractive, additive effects (i.e., the independent aggression-facilitating effects of residual excitation and of negative hedonic valence simply added up to the joint facilitatory effect of these variables on aggression). Motivated aggressive behavior, then, increases with the magnitude of transferable residual excitation from erotica and jointly with the negativeness of the affective response to erotica.

The findings lead to a model that makes the following predictions: (1) Pleasing, nonarousing erotica reduce aggressiveness because of hedonic incompatibility in the absence of residual arousal that would counteract this effect; (2) Displeasing, nonarousing erotica increase aggressiveness because of the summation of negative affect or annoyance (i.e., the reaction to provocation and the reaction to erotica) in the absence of further facilitation through transfer; (3) Displeasing, arousing erotica increase aggressiveness most strongly because the aggression-enhancing effect of negative affect combines with that of excitation transfer; and (4) Pleasing, arousing erotica, however, constitute a condition in which the effects of transfer and valence tend to cancel each other. Aggression enhancement results only if the aggression-modifying effect of transfer dominates that of valence, and aggression reduction occurs only to the extent that the modifying effect of valence dominates that of transfer.

The discussed excitation-and-valence model of the effects of erotica on motivated aggression is presented in graphic form in Figure 4.1. The broken line projects the aggression facilitation from transfer as a linear function of residual excitation. The solid lines define the summative effect of transfer and hedonic valence. The arrow pointing upward indicates the contribution of negative affect to aggression. The arrow pointing downward indicates the aggression-reducing effect of positive affect. As can be seen, the model projects the most powerful effects on aggression as the results of exposure to erotica that are both highly arousing and displeasing, if not disturbing and disgusting.

FREQUENT EXPOSURE, EXCITATORY HABITUATION, AND VALENCE CHANGES

Although arousing erotica (such as films of coition) have repeatedly been found to enhance postexposure aggression (cf. Donnerstein, 1982), the findings are not entirely consistent. For instance, Sapolsky and Zillmann (1981) and Donnerstein and Berkowitz (1981) failed to obtain an enhancement of aggressive behavior after exposure to sexually explicit, purely erotic films. Why these failures to replicate previously replicated findings? Inspection of subjects' responses to erotica in early and recent investigations—both in excitatory and in hedonic terms—suggests that changes have taken place that call for adjustments in the projection of effects. Compared to excitatory reactions to pornography that were recorded more than a decade ago (e.g., Zillmann, 1971), recent assessments of responses to potentially stronger stimuli yielded about half of the magnitude of the earlier reactions (e.g., Donnerstein & Berkowitz, 1981; Sapolsky & Zillmann, 1981). Additionally, much of the initial disturbance that exposure to pornography produced seems to have dissipated and faded away (e.g., Sapolsky & Zillmann, 1981). Why? A rather obvious answer lies in the fact that explicit erotica have become more readily available and socially accept-

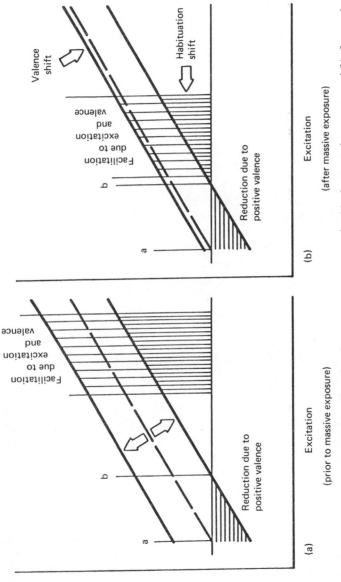

Fig. 4.1 A two-component model of the effect of erotica on postexposure aggression (a) prior to massive exposure and (b) after massive exposure. The broken line projects aggression facilitation as a linear function of excitation. The upper solid line defines the added effect of negative hedonic valence. The lower solid line defines the counterfacilitative effect of positive hedonic valence. The horizontally shaded area specifies the effect of pleasing but nonarousing erotica (point a) and of pleasing and somewhat arousing erotica. At point b, the aggression-facilitating effect of excitation is nullified by the aggression-reducing effect of positive valence. The vertically shaded areas specify the effect of arousing erotica of negative valence (light plus dark) and of positive valence (dark only) prior to and after excitatory habituation and valence changes from massive exposure. See text for further explanation.

ed over the past 10 years or so, and that, as a result, subjects are likely to have had frequent exposure to these stimuli.

Can, as has been implied, frequent exposure to pornography diminish excitatory responsiveness and alter appraisals from shock to acceptance, even liking? The evidence on this point is rather inconclusive. Due to the difficulties in conducting research that requires the subjects' repeated return to the laboratory for extended periods of time, experimental research on the effects of repeated exposure is scarce; and the little that does exist has pursued objectives other than the specific determination of the possibly diminishing sympathetic responsiveness—not to mention its consequences for aggressive behavior. There are, in fact, only two investigations that pertain to diminishing responsiveness as the result of repeated exposure to erotica.

Mann, Sidman, and Starr (1971; see also Mann, Berkowitz, Sidman, Starr, & West, 1974) exposed married couples in four consecutive weekly sessions to sexually explicit films or, in a control condition, to nonerotic films. During the treatment period, subjects recorded their sexual activities in diaries. Attitudes about pornography were assessed initially and after the treatment. Exposure to erotica was found to stimulate sexual behavior only shortly. Sexual activities were more frequent on exposure days than on the days thereafter. More important to this discussion is the finding that the transitory, sex-stimulating effect grew weaker over the weeks and became negligible in the fourth week. Mann *et al.* emphasized that the stimulating effect was rather nonspecific, manifesting itself in a variety of sexual activities with which the couples were familiar. This is to say, the couples did not readily adopt depicted sexual practices that were not already a part of their behavioral repertoire. Many dormant practices were revived, however. This finding, together with the fact that all couples were married for at least 10 years, would seem to suggest that exposure to erotica failed to exhibit sexual novelties for the subjects of this particular investigation and that the lack of specific emulation might not generalize to more sexually naive persons. The sexual maturity of the subjects might also explain the finding of no appreciable attitudinal changes. The only significant effect was obtained in the control group. Women who had been repeatedly subjected to nonerotic films became more strongly opposed to the legalization of pornography. Only if it is assumed that this change reflects extralaboratory influences that also affected the views of the experimental group, could it be argued that, in the absence of these influences, the experimental group might have shifted toward a greater acceptance of pornography.

An investigation conducted by Howard, Reifler, and Liptzin (1971; see also Reifler, Howard, Lipton, Liptzin, & Widmann, 1971) addressed the dissipation of sexual arousal more directly. On 15 days distributed over a 3-week period, male college students were given access to pornographic films, photographs, and readings or were not given such access in a control condition. The experimental subjects were free to choose from among these materials and from among non-erotic ones in the first 10 sessions. In the following 3 sessions, the original pornographic materials were replaced by new ones; and in the last 2 sessions, the nonerotic materials were removed. Each session lasted 90 minutes, and during this time the subjects recorded their activities in regular intervals. Both experimental and control subjects were shown an explicitly sexual film prior to and following the extended exposure treatment. Eight weeks after the treatment, the experimental subjects were once more shown an explicitly erotic film. Numerous measures of sexual arousal were taken during and after exposure to these films, and a battery of self-perception and attitudinal measures was recorded following exposure.

The findings show, first of all, that the young men initially had a strong interest in erotic films. This interest, however, faded rapidly with repeated exposure. Erotic photographs and readings received continued attention, but such attention was at comparatively low levels. After unrestricted exposure to pornography, even the introduction of novel materials failed to revive initial levels of interest. In fact, such unrestricted exposure to pornography led subjects to appraise their reaction to explicit erotica as boredom. Although interest in erotica was maintained to some degree, the findings give no indication that frequent exposure fosters favorable reactions such as enjoyment.

Analysis of the physiological data yielded results that are consistent with decreased interest or increased boredom. It reveals, generally speaking, a loss of responsiveness as the result of frequent exposure. Compared with responses to the pretreatment film, exposure to an explicitly sexual film immediately after the conclusion of the longitudinal treatment produced diminished reactions of sexual excitedness. On the most direct measure of sexual arousal, penile circumference, diminished responsiveness was obtrusively evident: Erections were less pronounced and more poorly maintained than prior to frequent exposure to pornography. Release of acid phosphatase, a prostatic secretion, exhibited redundant changes. As a concomitant of erectile responses, sympathetic activity underwent parallel changes as well. Heart rate, respiration rate, and skin temperature (measured from the earlobe) indicated reduced responsiveness. The loss of specifically sexual responsiveness, however, appeared to be more consistent and more pronounced than that of its sympathetic accompaniment. Finally, the remeasurement of reactions to explicit erotica after a period of 8 weeks during which subjects were not treated in any particular way (i.e., during which they presumably had little exposure to erotica) revealed some recovery from the loss in responsiveness. Although sexual and sympathetic reactions, when compared to initial responses, were still subdued, the differentiation generally failed to be statistically reliable.

The findings reported by Howard *et al.* (1971) and Reifler *et al.* (1971) are highly suggestive of habituation of sexual and autonomic arousal to erotica as the result of massive and continued exposure. However, since in their investigation the longitudinal treatment was both an independent and a dependent variable (i.e., exposure was both a measured effect and a potential cause for later effects), amount of exposure varied across individuals and was by no means massive throughout. Had exposure been more massive, stronger habituation effects might have occurred and have been maintained over longer periods of time. On the other hand, effects might have been weaker, had the subjects been provided with a sufficient, less readily exhaustible supply of erotic materials, especially films, so that exposure could always have been to novel stimuli. The severely limited supply of materials during the first 10 sessions might also account for the development of boredom with erotica. Notwithstanding these ambiguities, the research shows that exposure to erotic films within a relatively short period of time (about 30 minutes on the average per session, amounting to an average of $7\frac{1}{2}$ hours in all) is capable of habituating sexual and excitatory reactions, potentially for extended periods of time.

Regarding habituation, the discussed findings accord well with the fate of excitatory responsiveness in emotional behaviors generally. Repeated exposure to emotion-inducing stimuli characteristically leads to rapid habituation of the excitatory component of the reaction, especially under conditions that do not require overt reactions to the stimulus (cf. Grings & Dawson, 1978). Habituation of this type, though not permanent, usually extends over long periods of time. It is so secure an effect that many behavior-modification programs have been based on it (cf. Bandura, 1969). The finding of growing boredom with erotica, in contrast, seems in conflict not only with the growing commercial success of pornography but with common sense and theoretical considerations as well. Surely, if someone were more or less continually exposed to erotica, boredom must set in sooner or later. The standard situation, however, is occasional exposure, and such exposure may never reach the point at which boredom becomes likely. In fact, there are reasons to expect that increased occasional exposure will foster increased liking of erotica rather than boredom.

Byrne (1977; see also Byrne & Byrne, 1977), for instance, projected increased enjoyment of and preoccupation with erotica as the result of repeated exposure. He assumed that, initially, exposure to pornographic materials may offend and disturb some and produce apprehensions in others. Based on Zajonc's (1968) empirical generalization that repeated exposure to any stimulus results in more favorable evaluations of that stimulus, he then proposed that frequent exposure to erotica, in part because of excitatory habituation, diminishes negative reactions and negative appraisals of these reactions. Once individuals have thus grown more tolerant of pornography, Byrne continued to argue, the stimuli are more likely to entice them to engage uninhibitedly in pleasurable sexual fantasy—a response that should foster reports of enjoyment. In fact, he suggested that repeated exposure not only leads to increased enjoyment of erotica, but that

persons who are introduced to sexual practices of which they are initially ap-
prehensive or disapproving will eventually be inspired to perform the behaviors
in question because of the promise of pleasure from erotica-induced imaginative
rehearsals.

Concerning the modification of aggressive behavior, Byrne's proposal leads to
expectations opposite to those derivable from reports of increased boredom.
Acute boredom may be construed as a negative affective reaction, and this
reaction, as a form of annoyance, may be expected to add to the annoyance in
responses to provocation and thereby facilitate hostile and aggressive behavior
after exposure. Increased appreciation of erotica, in contrast, may be expected to
reduce annoyance and aggressiveness because of hedonic incompatibility. This
possibility is expressed in Figure 4.1b. The arrow pointing downward indicates
the change. The solid line it points at projects only a small contribution to
aggression, due to the expected loss of negative valence of erotica as a result of
frequent exposure.

Figure 4.1b also shows the expected consequence of habituation. The arrow
pointing to the left indicates a shift toward decreased excitatory reactions. The
vertically shaded areas in both graphs refer to hard-core materials that were
initially highly arousing. The shift toward decreased responsiveness exhibits the
hypothesized decrease in the facilitation of aggression. A comparison of the
light-plus-dark vertically shaded areas in Figure 4.1b, and Figure 4.1a exhibits
the corresponding hypothesized effect of decreased negative affect.

RECENT RESEARCH ON THE EFFECTS OF MASSIVE
EXPOSURE

We conducted a series of interrelated investigations to determine the validity
of the preceding projections. This research first examined the habituation phenomenon. Specifically, it examined excitatory habituation to sexually explicit
films as a function of controlled, massive exposure. It examined, moreover, the
extent to which habituation to such erotica generalizes to less explicit depictions
of sexual behavior and to portrayals of less common forms of sexual practices to
which respondents are relatively unaccustomed. Changes in the hedonic reactions were ascertained in conjunction with habituation. The nontransitory nature
of habituation and valence changes was ascertained as well. After this assessment of the hypothesized effects of massive exposure on excitation and hedonic
valence, the implications for postexposure aggression were examined. Finally,
the effects of massive exposure to pornography on sex-related beliefs and dispositions were recorded. The latter effort was inspired mainly by the assertion
that exposure to pornography fosters distorted beliefs about sexuality, especially
female sexuality, and that it leads to sexual callousness toward women, possibly

even to sexual aggression against women (e.g., Brownmiller, 1975; Barry, 1979; Clark, 1980; Lederer, 1980).

The findings of this research are summarized below. After a brief description of the research methodology, we present the findings on excitatory habituation and on corresponding affective changes, then those on the implications of these changes for postexposure aggression, and finally those on beliefs and dispositions concerning sexual behaviors and sexual aggression.

Design and Procedures

Eighty male and 80 female undergraduates from a large eastern university were randomly assigned to four experimental groups. Three of the groups participated in weekly experimental sessions over a period of about 9 weeks. The remaining group served as a no-treatment control, and the subjects participated in a session in the final week of the experiment only. Table 4.1 gives an overview of design and procedures.

EXPOSURE TREATMENTS

Subjects in the three experimental groups met in six consecutive weekly sessions. They watched six films of about 8 minutes duration and evaluated aesthetic aspects concerning the production of these films, this evaluation being the ostensible purpose of the research in which they were assisting. In the *massive-exposure* condition, subjects saw six explicitly sexual films per session (about 48 minutes of exposure per session). Over the 6-week treatment period, they watched 36 erotic films, a total of about 4 hours and 48 minutes of exposure. In the *intermediate-exposure* condition, subjects saw three erotic films and three nonerotic ones. They consequently saw 18 erotic films in all, an exposure time of about 2 hours and 24 minutes. In the *no-exposure* condition, all 36 films were nonerotic. All exposure treatments were identical in all respects other than the described variation in erotic stimulation.

All erotic films depicted heterosexual activities, mainly fellatio, cunnilingus, coition, and anal intercourse. None of these activities entailed coercion or the deliberate infliction or reception of pain. The nonerotic films were educational and entertaining materials that had been judged to be interesting. None of these films depicted or made reference to sex-related behaviors. None of the erotic or nonerotic films was repeatedly presented.

ASSESSMENT OF EXCITATORY HABITUATION
AND VALENCE CHANGES

Subjects of all three treatment groups returned to the laboratory 1 week after their final session. At that time, all subjects were exposed to three films in the following order: (1) a sexually suggestive film depicting heterosexual petting and precoital behavior, (2) a sexually explicit film depicting fellatio, cunnilingus,

TABLE 4.1

Overview of Design and Procedures

Time of event	Exposure to explicit erotica featuring fellatio, cunnilingus, coition, and anal intercourse			No exposure
	Massive	Intermediate	None	
Initial treatment in six consecutive weekly sessions	6 erotic films per session; 36 erotic films in all	3 erotic and 3 nonerotic films per session; 18 erotic films in all	6 nonerotic films per session; 0 erotic films in all	No exposure, no assessments
1 week after initial treatment	Exposure to (1) suggestive erotica (petting, precoital), (2) explicit erotica (coition, fellatio, cunnilingus), and (3) unusual erotica (sadomasochism, bestiality) Assessment of (1) heart rate, (2) systolic and diastolic blood pressure, (3) enjoyment, and (4) repulsion			No exposure, no assessments
2 weeks after initial treatment	Provocation by same-gender peer of all subjects who received exposure treatment; subdivision of each treatment group into four conditions Exposure to (1) explicit erotica, (2) sadomasochism, (3) bestiality, or (4) no exposure Assessment of (1) retaliatory aggression, (2) heart rate (during provocation, during erotica exposure), (3) enjoyment of erotica, and (4) repulsion by erotica			No treatment, no exposure, no assessments
3 weeks after initial treatment	Survey of all subjects, including those without prior exposure or treatment Assessment of (1) perception of usage of common and uncommon sexual practices in society, (2) recommendation of punishment for rape, (3) support for women's liberation movement, (4) dispositions regarding the harmfulness (or innocuousness, respectively) of pornography, and (4) men's sexual callousness toward women			

and heterosexual intercourse, and (3) a film depicting both bestiality and sadomasochistic activities (such as a woman fellating and having intercourse with a dog and a man being whipped by a woman during cunnilingus). All films were of about 8 minutes duration. Recovery periods of equal duration (i.e., 8 minutes) were allowed between exposures. Excitatory responses (i.e., heart rate, systolic and diastolic blood pressure) were assessed prior to and immediately after exposure. Additionally, subjects reported their affective reaction immediately after exposure (i.e., the degree to which they were displeased or disgusted by the film and the degree to which they enjoyed it). Ratings were made on 100-point scales.

ASSESSMENT OF EFFECTS ON AGGRESSION

Within initial exposure treatments, subjects were now randomly assigned to one of four conditions: (1) exposure to a sexually explicit film depicting fellatio, cunnilingus, and heterosexual intercourse; (2) exposure to a film depicting sadomasochistic activities (such as flagellation during coition and the apparently painful deformation of genitals); (3) exposure to a film featuring bestiality (such as men and women having intercourse with various animals of the opposite sex); and (4) a no-exposure control. All films were of about 8 minute's duration. Subjects in the no-exposure condition waited during this period of time.

Subjects returned to the laboratory 2 weeks after their final session of the prior-exposure treatment. All subjects were provoked by a same-gender confederate, exposed or not exposed to erotica, and then provided with an opportunity to retaliate against their annoyer. The provocation procedure and the measurement of retaliation are detailed in a report by Zillmann, Bryant, and Carveth (1981). In brief, a confederate treated the subjects rudely and seemingly deliberately caused them pain when, in violation of instructions, he or she overinflated a blood-pressure cuff and did not deflate it promptly. Subjects later assessed the confederate's blood pressure—at least, they believed they were. This gave them an opportunity to reciprocate the infliction of pain by overinflating the cuff, again in violation of instructions. Excessive pressure-time (i.e., pressure above an allowed maximum multiplied by its duration) served as the measure of retaliation. In addition to the assessment of aggressive behavior, subjects' excitatory reactions were monitored (i.e., heart rate was recorded prior to and after provocation as well as prior to, midway through, and after exposure to erotica—or the waiting period in the control condition) and affective reactions were recorded in ratings (repulsion, enjoyment).

ASSESSMENT OF PERCEPTUAL AND DISPOSITIONAL CHANGES

During the third week following the completion of the initial exposure treatment, the subjects who had received one of the three treatments and the subjects who had not received any prior treatment participated in a final session. They first estimated, as a percentage, the portion of American adults performing particular sexual acts, common ones as well as uncommon ones. Among other things, they estimated the portion of sexually active adults, of adults employing oral-genital stimulation techniques, and of adults practicing anal intercourse, group sex, sadomasochism, and bestiality.

Subjects were then introduced to a rape case. They read the newspaper coverage of a hitchhiking that resulted in the sexual offense. The rapist's jury conviction was reported, but a sentence was not stated. Subjects were asked to recommend a prison term for the particular offense. The length of the term was considered to indicate disapproval or condemnation of rape. Sexual callousness toward women was expected to find expression in minimal prison sentences. Subjects also indicated their support for the female liberation movement on a scale ranging from 0 (no support) to 100 (maximal support). This assessment was included to learn whether callousness, should it be created, generalizes from sex to gender (i.e., from specifically sexual issues to gender-associated issues generally).

Subjects were then exposed to a sexually explicit film and asked to (1) report their affective reactions (e.g., it offends me, it is pornographic) and (2) register the degree to which they deemed it desirable to curtail the distribution of pornography (e.g., restrictions for minors or for broadcasting). All ratings were made on 100-point scales. The second set of measures was employed to assess the general acceptance of pornography.

Finally, the male subjects filled in a questionnaire designed to measure men's sexual callousness toward women (Mosher, 1971). Prior to the subjects' dismissal, all were debriefed about the purpose of the investigation. The experimenter explored whether anybody felt disturbed about the extensive exposure to pornography, in particular. Counseling was offered. However, none of the subjects reported any kind of disturbance or felt the need for counseling.

Excitatory Habituation

As can be seen from the upper portion of Table 4.2, massive exposure to sexually explicit erotica produced strong habituation effects on heart rate and

TABLE 4.2

Excitatory Habituation and Judgmental Adjustment to Various Erotic Stimuli 1 Week after Massive Exposure to Explicit Erotica[1]

Measure	Initial exposure[2]	Erotic stimulus			Stimuli combined
		Suggestive[3]	Explicit[4]	Unusual[5]	
Δ Heart rate	None	9.4[c]	20.6[d]	11.3[c]	13.8[C]
	Intermediate	5.3[b]	10.0[c]	11.1[c]	8.8[B]
	Massive	4.4[b]	0.4[a]	11.2[c]	5.4[A]
Δ Systolic blood pressure	None	12.4[bc]	24.8[d]	15.1[bc]	17.4[C]
	Intermediate	10.5[bc]	11.2[bc]	14.3[bc]	12.0[B]
	Massive	8.0[b]	0.8[a]	16.3[c]	8.3[A]
Repulsion	None	21.3[a]	54.1[c]	92.8[e]	56.1[C]
	Intermediate	20.7[a]	31.9[b]	84.6[d]	45.7[B]
	Massive	20.4[a]	19.2[a]	79.1[d]	39.6[A]
Enjoyment	None	61.8[d]	27.9[b]	14.8[a]	34.9[A]
	Intermediate	67.6[d]	54.7[c]	29.2[b]	50.5[B]
	Massive	51.2[c]	51.8[c]	36.8[b]	46.6[B]

[1]Means having no letter in their superscripts in common differ at $p < .05$ by Newman-Keuls' test.
[2]Exposure was in weekly sessions over a 6-week period. Per session, subjects saw 6 erotic films (massive), 3 erotic films, and 3 nonerotic films (intermediate), or 6 nonerotic films (none).
[3]Heterosexual petting and precoital behavior.
[4]Heterosexual intercourse, including fellatio and cunnilingus.
[5]Sadomasochistic activities and bestiality.

TABLE 4.3

Excitatory Habituation and Judgmental Adjustment to
Various Erotic Stimuli and Mediated Effects on
Motivated Aggressive Behavior 2 Weeks after Massive
Exposure to Explicit Erotica

Measure	Initial exposure[1,2]		
	None	Intermediate	Massive
Heart rate	81.1[b]	78.7[ab]	77.4[a]
Repulsion	75.4[c]	65.0[b]	54.8[a]
Enjoyment	22.8[a]	40.2[b]	45.0[b]
Aggression[3]	63.8[b]	53.2[ab]	48.8[a]

[1]Exposure was in weekly sessions over a 6-week period.
Per session, subjects saw 6 erotic films (massive), 3 erotic
films, and 3 nonerotic films (intermediate), or 6 nonerotic
films (none).
[2]Means having no letter in their superscripts in common
differ at $p < .05$ by Newman-Keuls' test.
[3]Aggression was measured in the transgressive infliction
of pain (i.e., extent and time of overinflation of a blood-
pressure cuff).

systolic blood pressure. The effect, evident 1 week after the initial exposure treatment, was most pronounced for stimuli of great affinity. This is to say that materials similar to those to which the subjects had been massively exposed had lost most of their excitatory capacity. There is some indication that habituation generalizes to similar sexual themes despite a less explicit portrayal. Both massive and moderate exposure to explicit erotica prompted a decrease in the heart-rate response to suggestive erotica. There is no indication, however, that habituation generalizes to erotica that feature substantially different sexual activities, especially those with which respondents are not accustomed. These habituation effects were observed for males and females alike. There were no gender differences or interactions with gender. Diastolic blood pressure did not yield any reliable effects.

Two weeks after the initial exposure treatment, heart rate—the only index of excitation employed at this time—was still strongly differentiated. The overall differentiation is reported in Table 4.3. The more informative interaction with time of measurement is displayed in Figure 4.2. As in the earlier assessment, there were no effects involving gender. The previously observed interaction of initial treatment and immediate exposure was lost, however. Heart-rate responses to the three films employed were not critically affected by initial exposure. This finding 3 weeks after the prior treatment seems inconsistent with

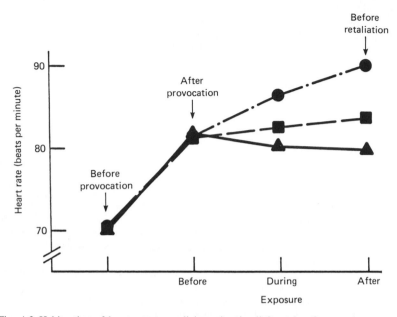

Fig. 4.2 Habituation of heart rate to explicit erotic stimuli 2 weeks after massive exposure to sexually explicit erotica for no-exposure (●), intermediate exposure (■), and massive exposure (▲) conditions. The graph also shows the equally strong excitatory reactions to provocation in the three experimental conditions.

that obtained 1 week earlier. The lack of generalization from standard erotic fare to erotica featuring less commonly practiced sexual behaviors that was observed earlier apparently no longer applied. Does this mean that habituation generalizes more as time goes by? Although the data are consistent with such an interpretation, they in no way demand it. In fact, this interpretation is untenable. Not only did the erotic stimuli that produced or did not produce the interaction differ, but the statistical test of this interaction was more powerful when it yielded significance than when it failed to do so. In the initial test of habituation, all subjects were exposed to all types of erotica (i.e., repeated measures were taken). In the treatment 2 weeks after initial exposure, measures could not be repeated but were independent. Within initial exposure treatments, subjects were assigned to four experimental groups (see p. 124), and thus only one-fourth of the original group saw a particular erotic film. This change resulted in a substantial loss of power in the statistical evaluation of the interaction, and it can be argued that the appearance of increased generalization of excitatory habituation as a function of time is the direct result of this loss of power. The findings, then, do not allow definitive statements about changes in generalization. What can be said with confidence, however, is that they indicate strong, nontransitory habituation effects to erotica, and that these effects do not necessarily generalize to erotica that are substantially different from those that produced habituation.

Valence Changes

The lower portion of Table 4.2 shows the expected effects of massive exposure to sexually explicit erotica on repulsion and enjoyment. As can be seen, massive and moderate exposure diminished negative affective reactions to materials of the kind that produced habituation. This effect generalized to materials depicting less common sexual practices. It did not generalize, however, to non-explicit, suggestive materials. Enjoyment mirrored these effects, but not precisely. Massive and moderate exposure facilitated reactions of enjoyment to materials similar to those that produced habituation. This response tendency also generalized to materials featuring unusual sexual practices. Responses to suggestive fare are inconsistent with expectations, however. Subjects who had been massively exposed to explicit erotica enjoyed suggestive materials less than did other subjects. Massively exposed subjects, accustomed to the explicit portrayal of sexual behaviors, may have been disappointed, if not frustrated, with seeing suggestive materials only.

A significant aspect of these findings on repulsion and enjoyment is the absence of gender effects. Although the differences in means pointed toward greater repulsion and lesser enjoyment in females than in males, the differences were trivial statistically. All interactions involving gender were equally trivial in magnitude.

The strong effects of massive exposure to explicit erotica on repulsion and enjoyment were still in evidence 2 weeks after the termination of the initial treatment. As can be seen from Table 4.3, in both the massive and intermediate exposure conditions, repulsion was significantly reduced and enjoyment significantly enhanced. These effects again apply to males and females equally, as no gender effects or gender interactions were obtained.

Finally, Table 4.4 reports data that show that valence changes endured a 3-week period after the conclusion of the initial treatment. Compared with unexposed subjects, both massively and moderately exposed subjects at this time reported being less offended by pornography, and in fact, they considered pornography, a concept laden with negative connotations, less pornographic. In these appraisals, significant gender differences did emerge. Females considered the particular film more pornographic than did males, and they reported being more offended by it. Gender interactions were not observed, however.

Taken together, the findings show rather compellingly that massive exposure to pornography promotes acceptance of such material. Reactions of repulsion diminish, and enjoyment tends to increase. Both valence changes are nontransitory and potentially long lasting. The findings on both repulsion and enjoyment

TABLE 4.4

Evaluation of an Explicit Erotic Film and Recommendation Concerning
Accessibility 3 Weeks after Massive Exposure to Explicit Erotica[1]

Measure	Initial exposure[2]			No prior treatment
	None	Intermediate	Massive	
Is offensive	75.2[c]	42.9[b]	26.3[a]	68.8[c]
Is pornographic	70.1[c]	47.3[b]	28.9[a]	68.2[c]
Need for restrictions for minors	83.5[c]	53.6[b]	36.8[a]	76.4[c]
Need for restrictions for broadcasting	80.8[c]	61.2[b]	43.6[a]	80.5[c]

[1]Means having no letter in their superscripts in common differ at
$p < .05$ by Newman-Keuls' test.

[2]Exposure was in weekly sessions over a 6-week period. Per session,
subjects saw 6 erotic films (massive), 3 erotic films, and 3 nonerotic films
(intermediate), or 6 nonerotic films (none).

accord with the earlier discussed proposals of Byrne (1977), but those on increasing enjoyment are inconsistent with projections of growing boredom with erotica as a function of massive exposure (Howard *et al.*, 1971).

Effects on Aggression

Table 4.3 shows the predicted aggression-modifying effect of excitatory habituation and valence changes. Initial massive and moderate exposure to explicit erotica produced a significant trend toward decreased motivated aggression following exposure to equally explicit erotic materials. In particular, massive prior exposure reduced aggressiveness sharply. A close correspondence is evident between decreased excitatory reactions to erotica, decreased repulsion (or increased enjoyment, respectively), and reduced aggressiveness. All these changes are consistent with the excitation-and-valence model. More specifically, they are consistent with the projection that a reduction of excitatory responsiveness to erotica due to habituation and a corresponding reduction in negative affect jointly mediate a reduction in aggressiveness.

The joint operation in these response components is also evident from Table 4.5, which reports the immediate effects of exposure to stimuli across conditions of initial exposure. As can be seen, exposure to standard erotic fare produced aggressive behavior at a level above that observed in the no-exposure control condition. Exposure to erotic films featuring less common sexual activities (i.e., sadomasochism and bestiality) produced aggressiveness at levels that exceeded that of exposure to standard erotic fare. Although the aggression-facilitating

TABLE 4.5

Excitatory and Judgmental Response to Various Erotic Stimuli and
Mediated Effects on Motivated Aggressive Behavior 2 Weeks after
Massive Exposure to Explicit Erotica

Measure	Erotic stimulus[1]			
	None	Coitus	Sadomasochism	Bestiality
Heart rate	76.5[a]	79.4[b]	80.4[b]	80.0[b]
Repulsion	—	32.4[a]	80.2[b]	82.7[b]
Enjoyment	—	48.8[b]	29.7[a]	29.5[a]
Aggression[2]	33.2[a]	49.7[b]	68.0[c]	70.2[c]

[1]Means having no letter in their superscripts in common differ at
$p < .05$ by Newman-Keuls' test.
[2]Aggression was measured in the transgressive infliction of pain (i.e.,
extent and time of overinflation of a blood-pressure cuff).

effect of the erotic stimuli—compared with the control—is predictable from the
observed excitatory changes, the differences between the erotic stimuli are not—
as excitatory reactions to the various erotic films were virtually identical. A look
at affective responses shows, however, that repulsion and enjoyment differed
substantially among these films. The consideration of these affective reactions,
as required by the excitation-and-valence model, explains the greater degree of
aggression facilitation in the unusual-erotica conditions. The model thus predicts
all reported findings accurately.

There were no gender effects or interactions with gender in the mediation of
aggression. Additionally, there was no interaction between the initial exposure
treatment and the immediately preceding exposure to stimuli.

The findings on aggression, then, accomplish four things. First, they corroborate earlier findings (e.g., Baron, 1979; Cantor et al., 1978; Jaffe, Malamuth,
Feingold, & Feshbach, 1974) by showing that in same-gender interactions, exposure to erotica affects aggressiveness in females much the same way it affects
aggressiveness in males. Second, they show that both the immediate effect of
exposure to erotic stimuli and the effect of the initial exposure treatment accord
with the excitation-and-valence model (see Figure 4.1) and thus lend further
support to its accuracy and usefulness. Third, the findings demonstrate that the
effect of excitatory habituation and valence changes on aggression is nontransitory and potentially long lasting. Fourth, and perhaps most significantly, the findings suggest that the frequent and massive exposure to pornography—mainly
through the mechanics of excitatory habituation, but also because of growing
hedonic response incompatibilities—will diminish the likelihood of aggression
facilitation after erotic stimulation.

Perceptual and Dispositional Changes

Numerous perceptual and dispositional changes concerning sexuality, especially female sexuality, were recorded during the third week after the conclusion of the initial exposure treatment. These changes are obviously nontransitory and potentially long lasting.

As can be seen from Table 4.6, massive and moderate exposure to pornography significantly affected the perception of the popularity of specific sexual practices in society. Related estimates, such as the proportion of sexually active persons, were analogously affected. In general, massive exposure to explicit erotica produced visions of more of anything pertaining to sex, and it did so for males and females alike—as no gender effects or interactions involving gender were observed. Visions of more of anything sexual are, of course, relative to the two control conditions employed (i.e., relative to the estimates of persons without massive or moderate exposure to erotica). Massive exposure to pornography did not necessarily distort the perception of prevalent sexual practices. Estimates of the use of oral-genital stimulation, for instance, approximate estimates based on survey data (e.g., Hunt, 1974) more closely the more subjects were exposed to sexually explicit materials. Massive exposure to pornography thus could be said to correct distorted views of sexuality. However, estimates of less widespread sexual behaviors—such as intercourse with more than one partner at a time, sadomasochistic actions, and animal contacts—approximate survey projections less closely the more subjects were exposed to erotica. The popularity of unusual sexual behaviors was grossly overestimated. Massive exposure, then,

TABLE 4.6

Projections of Common and Uncommon Sexual Behaviors 3 Weeks
after Massive Exposure to Explicit Erotica[1]

Measure[3]	Initial exposure[2]			No prior treatment
	None	Intermediate	Massive	
Fellatio–cunnilingus	34.0[a]	49.6[b]	67.2[c]	36.2[a]
Anal intercourse	12.1[a]	19.6[b]	28.5[c]	12.4[a]
Group sex	10.9[a]	18.2[b]	30.2[c]	11.8[a]
Sadomasochism	7.4[a]	8.4[a]	14.8[b]	8.6[a]
Bestiality	6.6[a]	7.9[a]	12.0[b]	8.0[a]

[1]Means having no letter in their superscripts in common differ at $p < .05$ by Newman-Keuls' test.

[2]Exposure was in weekly sessions over a 6-week period. Per session, subjects saw 6 erotic films (massive), 3 erotic films, and 3 nonerotic films (intermediate), or 6 nonerotic films (none).

[3]All projections are estimates of the percentage of adults practicing the sexual behaviors in question.

TABLE 4.7

Incarceration Recommended for Rape 3 Weeks after Massive Exposure
to Explicit Erotica[1,2]

Gender of respondent	Initial exposure[3]			No prior treatment	Combined
	None	Intermediate	Massive		
Male	94.6	78.0	49.8	93.7	79.0[y]
Female	143.6	101.4	77.0	119.7	110.4[z]
Combined	119.1[b]	89.7[ab]	63.4[a]	106.7[b]	

[1]Recommendations are in months, but were made in years and months in response to a specific case.

[2]Means having no letter in their superscripts in common differ at $p < .05$ by Newman-Keuls' test.

[3]Exposure was in weekly sessions over a 6-week period. Per session, subjects saw 6 erotic films (massive), 3 erotic films, and 3 nonerotic films (intermediate), or 6 nonerotic films (none).

can be said to distort the perception of many aspects of sexuality by producing the lasting impression that relatively uncommon sexual practices are more common than they actually are. It should be noticed that this perceptual shift from the uncommon to the common resulted from massive exposure to erotica that featured common, not uncommon sexual practices.

The lower half of Table 4.4 exhibits general dispositional consequences of massive and moderate exposure to pornography. As can be seen, the more extensive the exposure, the more accepting of pornography subjects became. This effect was observed for females as well as for males. Females, however, expressed significantly less acceptance than males. That is to say that although massive exposure to pornography created some degree of acceptance among females, they continued to object more strongly to the unlimited distribution of such material.

Perhaps the most astonishing of the findings on perceptual and dispositional consequences of massive exposure to pornography are those concerning rape. As can be seen from Table 4.7, massive exposure resulted in recommendations of significantly shorter terms of imprisonment. After massive exposure to pornography, rape is apparently considered a lesser offense. Inspection of the frequency of recommendations of minor sentences (incarceration up to a maximum of 1 year) agrees with such an interpretation. The number of subjects recommending minimal sentences was markedly higher under conditions of massive exposure than in the other conditions. Unexpectedly, these effects of massive exposure applied to males and females equally. The females' dispositions toward rape and its punishment were apparently just as much influenced as those of males.

However, whereas there was no evidence of an interaction between gender and initial exposure, females recommended longer prison terms overall.

According to these findings, massive exposure to pornography fosters a general trivialization of rape. It can only be speculated that this effect results from the characteristic portrayal of women in pornography as socially nondiscriminating, as hysterically euphoric in response to just about any sexual or pseudosexual stimulation, and as eager to accommodate seemingly any and every sexual request. Such portrayal, it seems, convinces even females of the hyper-promiscuous, accepting nature of women. What appears to be trivialized, then, is the impact of rape. The credibility of the victim's suffering during rape is being undermined. Since the massive-exposure treatment did not entail depictions of sexual access through coercion, it is difficult to see how the trivialization of rape could have been mediated by changing views concerning the use of power and/or violent means in a sexual context.

The suggestion that massive exposure to pornography trivializes rape through the portrayal of women as hyperpromiscuous and socially irresponsible is supported by further findings. Table 4.8 presents data that exhibit a loss of faith in women—by females and males alike. Massive and moderate exposure to pornography led to sharp declines in the support of the female liberation movement. Furthermore, the assessment of men's sexual callousness toward women, presented in Table 4.9, exhibits the same loss of respect. Massive exposure increased sex callousness considerably.

The present findings relate to recent observations concerning the trivialization of men's violence against women, including rape (Malamuth & Check, 1980, 1981). For example, Malamuth and Check (1981) reported that exposure to films that portray women as craving sexual violence tend to foster in men an accep-

TABLE 4.8

Support for the Female Liberation Movement 3 Weeks after Massive Exposure to Explicit Erotica[1]

Gender of respondent	Initial exposure[2]			No prior treatment	Combined
	None	Intermediate	Massive		
Male	71.0	48.7	25.0	66.8	52.8[y]
Female	82.0	59.2	52.2	76.2	67.4[z]
Combined	76.5[c]	54.0[b]	38.6[a]	71.5[c]	

[1]Means having no letter in their superscripts in common differ at $p < .05$ by Newman-Keuls' test.

[2]Exposure was in weekly sessions over a 6-week period. Per session, subjects saw 6 erotic films (massive), 3 erotic films, and 3 nonerotic films (intermediate), or 6 nonerotic films (none).

TABLE 4.9

Men's Sexual Callousness toward Women 3 Weeks after
Massive Exposure to Explicit Erotica[1,2]

Initial exposure[3]			No prior treatment
None	Intermediate	Massive	
10.5[a]	15.6[a]	23.8[b]	10.5[a]

[1]Callousness was assessed on Mosher's scale.
[2]Means having no letter in their superscripts in common differ at
$p < .05$ by Newman-Keuls' test.
[3]Exposure was in weekly sessions over a 6-week period. Per
session, subjects saw 6 erotic films (massive), 3 erotic films, and 3
nonerotic films (intermediate), or 6 nonerotic films (none).

tance of the use of force against women. Presumably, such attitudinal changes
are again mediated by a disrespect for women that these films are capable of
producing.

This research focused on callousness toward women. It is conceivable, of
course, that massive exposure to pornography promotes women's sexual callousness toward men as well. Men, after all, are also portrayed as socially
nondiscriminating in their relentless pursuit of sexual gratifications. Perceptual
changes might be less dramatic, however, as men never seem to have been
believed to be particularly responsible in their sexual ventures. Be this as it may,
massive exposure to pornography appears to contribute to beliefs about sexual
desire and sexual conduct that are not conducive to respect for the opposite (or
the same) sex. Whether the creation of seemingly cynical beliefs and attitudes
undermines social relationships by instilling distrust or, in fact, corrects erroneous, romantic, and idealistic views of human sexuality is a different matter,
however; and the issue cannot be decided one way or another by the data at hand.

A CALL FOR LONGITUDINAL RESEARCH

The reported findings concerning the consequences of massive exposure to
pornography urge the use of specific approaches in the study of these consequences. Almost all past experimentation has concentrated on the effects on
aggression immediately after exposure to erotic stimuli. These effects are in part
mediated by residual excitation (e.g., Zillmann, 1971), and they are known to be
short-lived (e.g., Zillmann, Hoyt, & Day, 1974). Excitatory habituation further
diminishes this type of effect. Effects not mediated by residual arousal are likely
to be similarly short-lived. The disinhibition of aggression against specific tar-

gets (e.g., Donnerstein & Berkowitz, 1981), for instance, is likely to dissipate as unrelated environmental stimuli intervene and make particular target-associations less accessible (Wyer & Srull, 1980). Additionally, the one-exposure procedure that has been commonly employed in the convenient one-session experiments may be considered a poor simulation of exposure to pornography under standard conditions, and to expect lasting effects from it may be considered unrealistic. It would seem imperative, then, to conduct investigations in which exposure is repeated and in which effects are ascertained at different times after exposure. This seems especially important now that numerous nontransitory effects have been recorded. What are the consequences of these effects that transcend immediate excitatory and valuative reactions to erotic stimuli? Do they mediate interpersonal distrust, conflict, hostility, or sexual aggression? Do they promote alienation? Or do they merely reflect the adoption of a more realistic view of human sexuality and human nature? We cannot tell the consequences at present. And we cannot hope to gain much understanding by conducting one-exposure, one-session studies. We shall have to conduct longitudinal investigations. There is no alternative.

REFERENCES

Bandura, A. (1969). *Principles of behavior modification.* New York: Holt, Rinehart & Winston.

Baron, R. A. (1974a). The aggression-inhibiting influence of heightened sexual arousal. *Journal of Personality and Social Psychology, 30,* 318–322.

Baron, R. A. (1974b). Sexual arousal and physical aggression: The inhibiting influence of "cheesecake" and nudes. *Bulletin of the Psychonomic Society, 3,* 337–339.

Baron, R. A. (1977). *Human aggression.* New York: Plenum Press.

Baron, R. A. (1979). Heightened sexual arousal and physical aggression: An extension to females. *Journal of Research in Personality, 13,* 91–102.

Baron, R. A., & Bell, P. A. (1973). Effects of heightened sexual arousal on physical aggression. *Proceedings of the 81st Annual Convention of the American Psychological Association, 8,* 171–172.

Barry, K. (1979). *Female sexual slavery.* Englewood Cliffs, NJ: Prentice-Hall.

Brownmiller, S. (1975). *Against our will: Men, women and rape.* New York: Simon & Schuster.

Byrne, D. (1977). The imagery of sex. In J. Money & H. Musaph (Eds.), *Handbook of sexology.* Amsterdam: Elsevier/North-Holland Biomedical Press.

Byrne, D., & Byrne, L. A. (Eds.). (1977). *Exploring human sexuality.* New York: Crowell.

Cantor, J. R., Zillmann, D., & Einsiedel, E. F. (1978). Female responses to provocation after exposure to aggressive and erotic films. *Communication Research, 5,* 395–411.

Clark, L. (1980). Pornography's challenge to liberal ideology. *Canadian Forum, 3,* 9–12.

Donnerstein, E. (1982). Erotica and human aggression. In R. Geen & E. Donnerstein (Eds.), *Aggression: Theoretical and empirical reviews.* New York: Academic Press.

Donnerstein, E., & Berkowitz, L. (1981). Victim reactions in aggressive erotic films as a factor in violence against women. *Journal of Personality and Social Psychology, 41,* 710–724.

Donnerstein, E., Donnerstein, M., & Evans, R. (1975). Erotic stimuli and aggression: Facilitation or inhibition. *Journal of Personality and Social Psychology, 32,* 237–244.

Donnerstein, E., & Hallam, J. (1978). Facilitating effects of erotica on aggression against women. *Journal of Personality and Social Psychology, 36,* 1270–1277.

Grings, W. W., & Dawson, M. E. (1978). *Emotions and bodily responses: A psychophysiological approach.* New York: Academic Press.

Howard, J. L., Reifler, C. B., & Liptzin, M. B. (1971). Effects of exposure to pornography. In *Technical report of The Commission on Obscenity and Pornography* (Vol. 8). Washington, DC: Government Printing Office.

Hunt, M. (1974). *Sexual behavior in the 1970s.* New York: Dell Books.

Jaffe, Y., Malamuth, N., Feingold, J., & Feshbach, S. (1974). Sexual arousal and behavioral aggression. *Journal of Personality and Social Psychology, 30,* 759–764.

Lederer, L. (Ed.). (1980). *Take back the night: Women on pornography.* New York: Morrow.

Malamuth, N. M., & Check, J. V. P. (1980). Penile tumescence and perceptual responses to rape as a function of victim's perceived reactions. *Journal of Applied Social Psychology, 10,* 528–547.

Malamuth, N. M., & Check, J. V. P. (1981). The effects of mass media exposure on acceptance of violence against women: A field experiment. *Journal of Research in Personality, 15,* 436–446.

Mann, J., Berkowitz, L., Sidman, J., Starr, S., & West, S. (1974). Satiation of the transient stimulating effect of erotic films. *Journal of Personality and Social Psychology, 30,* 729–735.

Mann, J., Sidman, J., & Starr, S. (1971). Effects of erotic films on sexual behavior of married couples. In *Technical report of The Commission on Obscenity and Pornography* (Vol. 8). Washington, DC: Government Printing Office.

Meyer, T. P. (1972). The effects of sexually arousing and violent films on aggressive behavior. *Journal of Sex Research, 8,* 324–333.

Mosher, D. L. (1971). Sex callousness toward women. In *Technical report of The Commission on Obscenity and Pornography* (Vol. 8). Washington, DC: Government Printing Office.

Reifler, C. B., Howard, J., Lipton, M. A., Liptzin, M. B., & Widmann, D. E. (1971). Pornography: An experimental study of effects. *American Journal of Psychiatry, 128,* 575–582.

Sapolsky, B. S., & Zillmann, D. (1981). The effect of soft-core and hard-core erotica on provoked and unprovoked hostile behavior. *Journal of Sex Research, 17,* 319–343.

White, L. A. (1979). Erotica and aggression: The influence of sexual arousal, positive affect, and negative affect on aggressive behavior. *Journal of Personality and Social Psychology, 37,* 591–601.

Wyer, R. S., & Srull, T. K. (1980). Category accessibility: Some theoretical and empirical issues concerning the processing of social stimulus information. In E. T. Higgins, C. P. Herman, & M. P. Zanna (Eds.), *Social cognition: The Ontario Symposium on Personality and Social Psychology.* Hillsdale, NJ: Erlbaum.

Zajonc, R. B. (1968). Attitudinal effects of mere exposure. *Journal of Personality and Social Psychology Monograph Supplement, 9,* 1–27.

Zillmann, D. (1971). Excitation transfer in communication-mediated aggressive behavior. *Journal of Experimental Social Psychology, 7,* 419–434.

Zillmann, D. (1978). Attribution and misattribution of excitatory reactions. In J. H. Harvey, W. J. Ickes, & R. F. Kidd (Eds.), *New directions in attribution research* (Vol. 2). Hillsdale, NJ: Erlbaum.

Zillmann, D. (1979). *Hostility and aggression.* Hillsdale, NJ: Erlbaum.

Zillmann, D. (1982). Transfer of excitation in emotional behavior. In J. T. Cacioppo & R. E. Petty (Eds.), *Social psychophysiology.* New York: Guilford Press.

Zillmann, D., Bryant, J., & Carveth, R. A. (1981). The effect of erotica featuring sadomasochism and bestiality on motivated intermale aggression. *Personality and Social Psychology Bulletin, 7,* 153–159.

Zillmann, D., Bryant, J., Comisky, P. W., & Medoff, N. J. (1981). Excitation and hedonic valence in the effect of erotica on motivated intermale aggression. *European Journal of Social Psychology, 11,* 233–252.

Zillmann, D., Hoyt, J. L., & Day, K. D. (1974). Strength and duration of the effect of aggressive, violent, and erotic communications on subsequent aggression. *Communication Research, 1,* 286–306.

Zillmann, D., & Sapolsky, B. S. (1977). What mediates the effect of mild erotica on annoyance and hostile behavior in males? *Journal of Personality and Social Psychology, 35,* 587–596.

PART III

Correlational and Cross-Cultural Studies on Pornography and Aggression

For the most part, the research on the effects of pornography that has been presented heretofore has concerned itself primarily with studies conducted in the United States or Canada, as well as research of an experimental nature. Pornography is obviously not confined to these countries. In fact, some of the more interesting studies on the long-term impact of pornography have been undertaken in Denmark and were quoted extensively by the U.S. Commission on Obscenity and Pornography in support of the ''non-effects'' conclusion of this commission. What can differences within the U.S. and among other countries tell us about the effects of pornography? Using correlational data, regarding pornography consumption and the frequency of rape, the three chapters of this section are intended to shed new light on the possible effects of pornography.

In the first chapter, ''Sex and Violence: A Ripple Effect,'' John Court takes great exception to the early findings of the 1970s that indicated no antisocial effects of exposure to pornography. He believes that the laboratory research of recent years has demonstrated negative effects of exposure to violent pornography, and his cross-cultural examination of sexual violence shows similar indications. He examines first the well-known Denmark data on the reduction of sexually related crimes and the lifting of legal restrictions on pornography. The

PORNOGRAPHY AND
SEXUAL AGGRESSION

Denmark studies are extremely important for they have been seen as the "prototypical" social experiment on the influence of pornography. Court goes on to suggest that changes in legalization of pornography have influenced the incidence of sexual crimes in numerous countries (e.g., the United States, England, Australia, and New Zealand). He also makes reference to Japan, a country with little incidence of rape, yet with a trend toward increases in violent forms of pornography. He suggests that in future years there may be a rise in sexual crimes in Japan. The reader should compare this prediction, however, to the comments of Abramson and Hayashi in the second chapter of this section. In general, Court feels there is a "ripple effect" occurring as a result of increased exposure to pornography. It may be years, however, before the full impact of this effect is seen.

In their chapter "Pornography in Japan: Cross-Cultural and Theoretical Considerations," Paul Abramson and Haruo Hayashi give us a historical and contemporary examination of the pornography industry in Japan in the context of discussing the incidence of sexual crimes in that nation. Their conclusions appear to stand in contrast to the earlier research presented in this book, which demonstrate an effect on attitudes and on laboratory aggression after exposure to violent forms of pornography. The authors reveal that Japanese pornography is often violent in nature. However, they indicate that despite this, Japan's rape rate is one of the lowest in the world. Why? The authors address this question and at the same time offer a number of policy implications for the United States.

In the chapter by Baron and Straus entitled, "Sexual Stratification in American States" the authors test three hypotheses derived from feminist theories of rape. In comparing the rape rates in the differing states of the U.S., they find support for two of these hypotheses: 1) Higher circulation of sex magazines is significantly related to higher rape rates, and 2) the higher the incidence of nonsexual violent crime, the higher the rape rate. Contrary to the third hypothesis, it was found that the higher the status of women, the higher the rape rate. The authors suggest that this relationship may reflect a backlash against the women's movement.

While the chapters in this section primarily focus on crime statistics, it should be noted that such rates constitute but one possible measure of the potential undesirable effects of violent pornography or similar media stimuli. The views and data cited in previous chapters suggest that certain forms of pornography may reflect, perpetuate, and cause a sexist ideology, greater acceptance of violence against women, and increased aggression under certain conditions. Such effects may indeed occur without any direct influences on crime statistics, particularly when, as Abramson and Hayashi note, powerful cultural and situational forces inhibit the expression of aggression within Japanese culture. In examining the research of these investigators (which focuses on crime in Japan in the context of media violence), the reader may wish to consider whether other aspects of Japanese society (e.g., degree of equality between the genders, history of violence against other societies, etc.) may be additional indexes by which to evaluate the potential role of violent pornography and other media in that and other societies. Furthermore, as the research presented in this volume shows, there may be considerable variations among individuals within a culture in susceptibility to media influences. Similarly, cultural factors may create major individual differences in the role and impact of media stimuli on members of differing societies.

5

Sex and Violence: A Ripple Effect

JOHN H. COURT

SHORTCOMINGS OF PREVIOUS PORNOGRAPHY STUDIES

In 1970 the possibility that widespread availability of sexually explicit materials might have harmful consequences was rejected by the U.S. Commission on Obscenity and Pornography, but this conclusion was not universally accepted as valid, given the evidence available to that commission. It was challenged at the time in a Minority Report, notably incorporating an extensive critique by Cline (1970) of the research studies that served as the basis for this conclusion. Among the many objections raised by Cline at that time, and on several subsequent occasions (1974, 1976), was the observation that no studies of "porno-violence" (i.e., explicit sexual themes presented within a context of aggression) were conducted by the commission, hence the possibility of harm arising from access to such materials could not be excluded. The possibility of harmful effects from exposure to porno-violence deserves serious attention today since, if harm does arise, this is likely to become apparent in indirect ways in those places where it has since become widespread.

In 1979 the British report of the Committee on Obscenity and Film Censorship, chaired by Professor Bernard Williams, came to conclusions about the evidence very similar to those reached by the U.S. commission in 1970. Specifically it concluded that "it is still possible to say, as Mr. Yaffe points out in his updated review, that there does not appear to be any strong evidence that ex-

PORNOGRAPHY AND
SEXUAL AGGRESSION

posure to sexually explicit material triggers off anti-social behavior'' (Williams, 1979, p. 66).

The committee recommended removal of all censorship of the written word ''since its nature makes it neither immediately offensive nor capable of involving the harms we identify, and because of its importance in conveying ideas'' (Williams, 1979, p. 160).

In coming to such conclusions the committee was relying on evidence based on a literature research review conducted by Yaffe and commissioned for the committee. However, as with the 1970 report, the Williams committee report has also been the subject of criticism. For example, Court (1980) points out that

> one would have to conclude that whatever else it is, Yaffe's review has not been ''brought up to date for our benefit'' as indicated in para 1.9. Hence the conclusion reached in para 6.16 that ''there does not appear to be any strong evidence that exposure to sexually explicit material triggers off anti-social behavior'' must be limited by the fact that *significant research remains unconsidered.* (p. 59)

Such a situation might not be serious if a balanced review of the literature were to permit an assessment of the general state of knowledge within an area of research. This cannot be said of a review that substantially ignores those research studies during the past decade by Baron (1974a,b, 1978; Baron & Bell, 1977), Donnerstein (Donnerstein & Barrett, 1978; Donnerstein, Donnerstein, & Evans, 1975), Malamuth (Feshbach & Malamuth, 1978; Malamuth & Check, 1981; Malamuth, Feshbach, & Jaffe, 1977), and Zillmann (Cantor, Zillmann, & Eisiedel, 1978; Zillmann, Hoyt, & Day, 1974; Zillmann & Sapolsky, 1977). Such experimental studies have been extended more recently to include further work in more naturalistic settings (e.g., Malamuth, Heim, & Feshbach, 1980) and complement the clinical work on sexual arousal of rapists in response to specific sexual stimuli (Abel, Barlow, Blanchard, & Guild, 1977, Barbaree, Marshall, & Lanthier, 1979).

Such studies have led to a variety of theoretical models to explain the linkage between exposure to sexual and violent themes and an increased probability of sexually aggressive behavior. These models are examined elsewhere in this volume. What emerges is that, whatever the mechanisms involved, there is now a strong case for postulating a positive enhancement of sexually aggressive behavior after exposure to porno-violence without adequate evidence for a decline in such behavior. The possibility of a negative correlation was widely held during the 1970s but now lacks experimental support.

STUDYING PORNO-VIOLENCE AND SOCIETY

Pursuit of the evidence for a coherent description of the effects of porno-violence must be undertaken in various ways. One approach is anecdotal evidence of cases in which exposure to such materials is linked to subsequent behaviors. Evidence is accumulating from therapists and sex offenders that offenses often relate closely to the use of pornographic materials, and this is repeatedly confirmed in legal evidence coming to the courts (Court, 1980). Additionally, the powerful effect of porno-violence on behavior is demonstrated through carefully conducted single-case studies such as those reported by Abel, Blanchard, Barlow, and Mavissakalian (1975).

Laboratory studies can provide the context for examining paradigms, with the opportunity to discriminate between competing hypotheses relating to psychological mechanisms and subject groups. Such studies have permitted the identification of disinhibition as an important mechanism (Malamuth, Heim, & Feshbach, 1980). Research has also shown that studies of normal populations cannot be readily generalized to account for the responses of clinically deviant populations (Barbaree *et al.*, 1979), although there is some overlap (Malamuth, Haber, & Feshbach, 1980). There is also increasing attention to the importance of sex differences in responsiveness since the majority of porno-violence is created for men and directed against women (Griffitt, 1973, 1975; Griffitt & Kaiser, 1978; Hartfield, Sprecher, & Traupmann, 1978; Kenrick, Stringfield, Wagenhals, Dahl, & Ransdell, 1980; Schmidt, Sigusch, & Schafer, 1973).

The more problematic question remains of whether those effects observed in laboratory and clinical studies have implications for society. One possible source of evidence could be obtained from the observation of trends in behavioral indexes of some kind, together with changes related to social reforms (Campbell, 1969, 1979), if one is to observe the effects of exposure to porno-violence in the wider context. Such effects are unlikely to be directly linked to specific stimuli as in controlled experiments. Instead the effects of exposure to porno-violence represent a ripple effect on behavior. That is, while laboratory studies can identify direct linkages between exposure and behavior–attitudes, studies of social trends identify more general influences on those same people and on others with whom they come in contact. The whole question of effects would be much easier to explore if a simple and direct impact of a particular experience of pornography led immediately to a measurable behavior change. In reality, just as a stone thrown in a pool creates ripples far away and interacts with other influences, so pornography has widespread, subtle, long-term, and interacting influences on the users of pornography, together with indirect influences on the values and attitudes of others. The conventional wisdom of the 1970s was that the major ripple effect would be a reduction in the incidence of sexual offenses with increased availability of pornography. This view, which derived its major impetus from the Commission on Obscenity and Pornography (1970), can be taken as a starting point for examining societal effects, leading to a refinement of some hypotheses and a reformulation of others.

EVIDENCE FOR REDUCTION IN SEX CRIMES:
LIMITATIONS OF THE DATA

The relationship between access to sexually explicit materials and sexual offenses committed was investigated by the U.S. Commission on Obscenity and Pornography and the primary data reported in its Technical Reports, especially volumes 7–9 (Commission on Obscenity and Pornography, 1971). A number of retrospective studies relying heavily on self-report led to ambiguous results, given reassuring treatment by the main commission (pp. 169–308) but interpreted very differently in the Minority Reports (pp. 463–490). In addition to studies of individual responses, volume 7 included studies of the Danish experience (Ben-Veniste, 1971; Kutchinsky, 1971).

Since the commission's findings have been widely quoted, though typically relying on secondary or tertiary sources, their conclusions should serve as a starting point for considering the relationship between pornography and sex crimes.

Ben-Veniste (1971) describes the context of his study in Denmark as one in which written and then pictorial pornography became increasingly available throughout the 1960s. He examined sex crime rates in Copenhagen (based on reports recorded by police), and, after commenting cautiously about changing reporting attitudes and police practice, concluded that "pornography of the type disseminated in Denmark apparently has caused no increase in the rate of sex crime. Not to be ruled out at this stage, however, is the possibility that pornography portraying some forms of deviant sexual behavior, especially sadism, may adversely affect potential offenders" (Ben-Veniste, 1971, p. 252).

Difficulty in predicting the outcome of exposure to porno-violence arises in part because it was only just becoming available in Denmark. Hence a footnote to Ben-Veniste's paper states that "a surprising feature of Danish magazine pornography is the infrequency of sadomasochism, bondage and transvestism as a theme" (1971, p. 261).

Kutchinsky (1971) reports a survey of Copenhagen residents intended to cast light on the apparent drop in sexual offenses throughout the 1960s. The U.S. commission interpreted his work as showing that "neither public attitudes about sex crimes nor willingness to report such crimes had changed sufficiently to account for the substantial decrease in sex offences between 1959 and 1969" (Commission on Obscenity and Pornography, 1970, p. 274).

Kutchinsky's own interpretation, based on detailed analysis of four offenses, was actually much less simplistic and more careful as well as being very cautious:

> We have completed an analysis in which we have tried to combine information from
> several different sources, including the tentative findings in the present survey, in order
> to explain the recent decrease in the numbers of four different types of sex crimes

registered by the police in Copenhagen. Concerning three of these types of crimes—exhibitionism, peeping and (physical) indecency towards girls—it was possible, without restraint or ad hoc construction tentatively to explain this registered decrease as being due to the influence on either the victims or the potential offenders of one single factor, namely the development in the availability of pornography. While the general change in the sexual behavior and attitudes of the Danes may, in different ways, have had a contributory influence on the decrease of the above three types of sex crimes, the analysis tentatively indicated that the influence of such a change on the *victims* was the major reason for the registered decrease in (physical) indecency towards women.

For two types of sex-crimes—peeping and (physical) indecency towards girls—the analysis led to the tentative conclusion that the abundant availability of hard-core pornography in Denmark may have been the direct cause of a veritable decrease in the actual amount of crime committed. . . . We should like to stress once more that the conclusions are tentative and will have to be re-examined on the basis of a more complete analysis of this survey and the crime statistics. (Kutchinsky, 1971, pp. 296–297)

These tentative conclusions have indeed been subjected to further analysis. Limitations in the actual sex crime trends have been identified by Bachy (1976), Court (1977), and Bart and Jozsa (1980).

Types of Sex Crimes Considered

The Minority Commission Report also noted the importance of considering the more serious sexual offenses (rape, rape with robbery, attempted rape and intercourse on threat of violence), which did not show evidence of decline over the period in question.

In the survey conducted by Kutchinsky to study whether people's definition of sex crimes or their readiness to report sex crimes had changed, the most serious offense considered was that of physical indecency with a young girl, characterized in the following survey question: "Imagine that a five-year-old girl comes home and says that a strange gentleman has made her touch his penis. Apart from that nothing has happened and the girl is not frightened. What would you do if that was your child?"

It should therefore be acknowledged that the evidence from Denmark that was tentative and incomplete originally has since been shown to have serious flaws. It provides no evidence that serious sex offenses, like rape, decreased or could be expected to decrease. It contributes little to our understanding either of the impact of porno-violence on behavior or to understanding of trends in serious sex offenses.

Similar caution has to be exercised in relation to the attempt of the U.S. commission to pursue pornography and sex crime relationships in the United States by Kupperstein and Wilson (1971). They found great complexity in their data and found the rise in adult sex crimes (using report and arrest data) was not greater than the rise for other offenses during the period 1960–1969). They concluded that "for the moment, the question of the relationship between avail-

ability of erotic materials and sex crimes must remain open to further question''
(p. 32).

In the interval since that time it has been possible to clarify various aspects of
that open question. It has become evident that the use of sex crimes as an index
of effects is open to confusion and conflicting interpretations (Court, 1977;
Biles, 1979a; Williams, 1979). A very minimal requirement is that one distinguishes between *major* and *minor* sexual offenses since the trends for these do
not correlate well at all (Court 1980). Reports of minor sex offenses (e.g., carnal
knowledge, voyeurism) have typically declined over the past decade: this trend
probably says more about changed attitudes to reporting and actual changes in
the law than about any real reduction in incidence. By contrast, reports of the
more serious offenses such as rape have typically increased over the same period
(Geis & Geis, 1979; Court, 1980). Since the minor offenses are cumulatively
greater in number than the major offenses, it follows that a reduction in the
former will result in the aggregated total giving false reassurance about trends by
masking an increase in serious offenses.

A further consideration is that the evidence advanced in 1970 was at most
tentative and based on information of dubious quality. Both Ben-Veniste (1971)
and Kutchinsky (1971) gave considerable attention to the preliminary and uncer-
tain nature of their own findings, and little is published to substantiate those
impressions. Ben-Veniste's suspicion that hard-core pornography could produce
adverse effects in some offenders had already received some support from the
U.S. commission—in sponsored studies of Davis and Braucht (1973), Mosher
and Katz (1971), Propper (1971), and Walker (1971). There was also a commis-
sion-sponsored study by Goldstein, Kant, Judd, Rice, and Green (1971) that
came to a ''no harm'' conclusion, but a detailed critique of this study by Cline
(1974) indicates that it has a number of serious limitations and even concludes
that it contains ''considerable evidence suggesting possible cause–effect harm
for some viewers of pornography—if we can accept retrospective self-report data
as valid'' (Cline, 1974, p. 218). Pursuing the evidence through the examination
of rape reports to the police on Stockholm, Geis and Geis (1979) found, rather to
their surprise, a steep increase in such reports throughout the 1970s. Using the
same measure in Copenhagen, the trend is closely similar (Court, 1980) although
this observation has not been substantiated by Kutchinsky as he has preferred to
introduce certain (unpublished) procedural variations to his data (see Williams,
1979, p. 83).

The earlier studies also make it necessary to clarify the kinds of data that are to
be used for determining sex crime trends. Some authors have in the past relied on
arrest data rather than police report data, while another line of argument can be
derived from victimization studies. One is always seeking to get as near as
possible to real incidence in order to minimize the dark figure of unreported

crime, and police reports, while subject to limitations, remain for this purpose the most satisfactory (Fox, 1976).

Availability of Porno-Violence in the 1960s

It is important, furthermore, to note that studies of sex crimes up to 1970 were conducted in settings where porno-violence was relatively unusual. Hence it was too soon for evidence from sex crime rates to be attributable to porno-violence. Kupperstein and Wilson (1971) make the point that any rise observed is no greater than the rise for other types of crime and hence has no special significance. It is only in the more recent past that porno-violence has become generally accessible and found its way into the more widely distributed magazines such as *Playboy* and *Penthouse* (Malamuth and Spinner, 1980), as well as pervading general release films. Hence, evidence relating to pornography from the 1970s is much more pertinent than that derived from the 1960s.

If one is to pursue the implications of research on porno-violence (e.g., Donnerstein, 1980) (which shows rather different effects on behavior from that observed with less extreme material, which may actually decrease aggressive behavior) (Baron, 1974a; Donnerstein, Donnerstein, & Evans, 1975), then it is necessary to look closely at those sex crimes that involve a degree of violence, distinguishing them from sexual offenses involving no violence. Hence evidence regarding a rise or fall in sex crime data is too crude to relate to the availability of porno-violence. It is necessary to consider offenses such as rape and attempted rape as appropriate dependent variables, while exhibitionism and peeping reports would be irrelevant to the case.

Obsolete Data

The dangers of relying on outmoded data are nowhere more evident than in the 1980 account of work published in the *British Journal of Sexual Medicine* reported by Schmidt and Sigusch. They reject the Kinsey findings of 1953 as out of date and note the changes that have occurred since that time. There then follows an apparently up-to-date report of experiments on sexual responsiveness to pornography, with the conclusion

> this short survey of our findings shows clearly that the nature and intensity of male and female reactions to pornography are basically the same. Contrary to widespread public fears, our experiments give no indication of any kind of an increase in uncontrolled sexual activity or of reduced effectiveness of controlling mechanisms. . . . There is therefore no question of a sexual "disinhibition." (Schmidt and Sigusch, 1980, p. 6)

The report fails to alert the reader to the fact that these findings were drawn from experiments that were completed in the 1960s and reported in 1970 in the *Journal of Sex Research*. Such obsolete data based on material quite different

from today's pornography and involving only student volunteers are highly misleading without reference to the more recent findings that so thoroughly negate
that work (Court, 1981).

Volume of Pornography Now Available

The same is true in relation to the sheer *volume* of material now in circulation.
While the U.S. commission of 1970 commented on the massive traffic in sexually oriented materials, estimating a total of $537 to 574 million for the United
States in 1968 (p. 85), there is little doubt that there has been a great increase
beyond that throughout the 1970s as many countries have subsequently relaxed
their laws against the distribution of pornography. McCarthy (1980) reports that
the combined circulation of the porn magazines is increasing, while a 1980
estimate for the United States is of a $4 billion business (Lederer, 1980). In
Britain, while Williams (1979) remarks that exact information on the amount of
materials available is unattainable, he nonetheless provides results of a survey of
some of the better-known sexually explicit magazines with clear indications of
increase over the period 1970–1978 (Williams, 1979, p. 257).

There has been both an increase in the volume of pornography available in
many Western countries, as well as a change in the types of material available.
When it has been shown that even generally released films are capable of inducing attitude changes to sexual violence against women among student populations (Malamuth & Check, 1981), it is clear that the great increase in exposure to
films incorporating powerful presentations of sex with violence must also be
taken into account. What was previously a restricted taste, widely disregarded by
most people, has now created a ripple that affects many young adults viewing
popular films. The representation of porno-violence has become part of the
culture. Over the same period, serious sexual offenses have increased significantly in many places. A significant association between these two observations
can at least be advanced as a plausible hypothesis. Before looking at ways of
testing it, it is necessary to consider a number of alternative hypotheses contributing more or less to the total picture.

ALTERNATIVE INTERPRETATIONS OF TRENDS

In seeking to establish an association between porno-violence and serious
sexual offenses, one has difficulty in accepting numerical indices for either as
reliable. It would be meaningless to attempt correlation coefficients using indices
of circulation (or sales or availability) and numbers of serious sex crime reports.
Even if precise data were available, it would still be inadequate to rely on
correlation coefficients as a means of showing a causal relationship since correla-

tional data cannot sustain this interpretation. At best one can identify broad trends for both the independent and the dependent variables and then rely on logical and methodological procedures to test alternative hypotheses.

For the present purposes it will be taken as axiomatic that pornography has become increasingly available in the United States, in England and Wales, in Australia, in Denmark, and in Sweden. Support for these assumptions comes from legislative changes, the establishment of commissions in response to public concern, and evidence reported both in the reports of such commissions (Commission on Obscenity and Pornography, 1970; Longford, 1972; Williams, 1979) and other published sources (Court, 1977; Holbrook, 1972; Kraus, 1979; Lederer, 1980).

It has occasionally been argued that in Denmark, a decline in the market followed liberalization. This argument, advanced by Kutchinsky (1973, 1978) does not enjoy strong factual support. Even following the simplistic approach of counting the number of retail outlets, one may compare Ben-Veniste's observation that "by the summer of 1968 there were at least 25 shops in Copenhagen dealing exclusively in erotic publications, pictures and films" (1971, p. 259), with an up-to-date count showing that

> A district in Copenhagen, Vesterbro, has been completely changed into a district with porno-shops, massage clinics and prostitution. . . . In a street in this district, Istedgade, there are 30 porno-shops with "cinemas" showing non-stop films, in a distance of 400 metres. In the Copenhagen main street, the Strøget, and in most provincial towns there are similar shops and "cinemas." (Krogh, 1980)

It is clear that over the past 10 years especially, the genre of porno-violence has figured more than in the previous decade (Ben-Veniste, 1971; McCarthy, 1980; Malamuth & Spinner, 1980). The increase, however, has not been uniformly distributed. Within countries the size of the United States and Australia, it is possible for regional differences to arise in response to state legislation, as well as general sociocultural differences. At the same time, other countries have adopted different national policies regarding availability. These provide the basis for some useful comparisons.

Before doing so, however, it is important to consider some of the factors that could influence changes in the dependent variable that is, reported sex-crimes. A rise or fall in the frequency of reports of an offense like rape can be the result of a variety of factors, so it is necessary to determine whether they are sufficient to explain observed trends or merely responsible for noise in the system.

Change in Reporting Rates

It is commonly argued that observed changes in reported crime levels are a function of reporting rates. This possibility is especially important with crimes in which the reporting level is known from victimization data to be low. It is also important for offenses that themselves are relatively infrequent since a small change in reporting patterns can lead to a larger percentage change than would occur with changes in reporting of high-frequency offenses.

Rape is a low-frequency offense that victimization data indicates has a large dark figure of unreported offenses. Hence a rise or a fall in police reports could arise from changes in reporting practice.

Kutchinsky (1971) specifically addressed himself to these issues in relation to sex crimes in Copenhagen. He conducted an interview with 398 persons to determine readiness to report certain offenses and sought victimization data at the same time. Among the conclusions (drawn cautiously for methodological reasons) was the confirmation that "the dark figures for minor sex crimes are indeed very high" (p. 274). Furthermore, he provided an estimate of reporting readiness for several offenses, seeking to determine whether a relative change in reporting readiness had occurred over a 10-year period (1959–1969). Without exception the trends were toward a reduced probability of reporting, ranging as high as 40% for exhibitionism.

He concludes that this change in readiness to report is not sufficient in itself to account for the steep decrease in all sex crime reports over the period. It is however clearly an important factor in some offenses and may even be a sufficient explanation in relation to exhibitionism (Kutchinsky, 1971, p. 285). Whatever the extent of this contribution may be, the point to note is that people were consistently less likely to report sex crimes as pornography became increasingly available. When we move to a situation in which report rates are *increasing,* it is not immediately apparent why such an increase should be attributed to changed reporting rates.

Whether the dark figure in crime reports is increasing or decreasing was fully discussed by Radzinowicz and King (1977) and they concluded

> Nor can I see any justification for claiming, or hoping, that the gap between crimes hidden and crimes recognised, has been narrowing. . . . On the contrary, there is much to suggest that, taking crime as a whole, it is becoming wider. . . . The dark figure tends to increase as society becomes more urbanised and anonymous, and also as it becomes more mobile. (p. 49)

Radzinowicz and King's data are similar to Kutchinsky's, and lead to the conclusion that increases in reports are real, though increasingly muted by the growing dark figure.

Chappell (1976), addressing himself specifically to the question of rising rape rates and the possibility that changed reporting rates might be responsible, concluded that

> quite apart from the influence of the debates about women's rights, race and the death penalty upon the contemporary response of the criminal justice system to forcible rape, concern about this crime has been further stimulated by the apparent startling increase in the incidence of this type of sexual assault (rape). During the last decade, rates of

forcible rape have more than doubled. The pace of increasing rates has become more rapid since 1976 and in the early 1970s reached a speed outstripping all other major categories of violent crime. (p. 10)

It is growth in public concern about such offenses that has brought about a number of changes, including visibility of the offenses in the media, changes in police and legal procedures, and the development of rape crisis centers. These changes are largely a response to an ongoing real rise in offenses rather than the cause of an apparent increase due only to reportage. Evidence for this interpretation includes the fact that these changes have typically appeared no earlier than 1975 whereas increased rape reports had been evident for several years before that. Moreover, the changes have produced neutralizing effects on the data. The introduction of well-trained policewomen in rape squads and changes in legal procedure to give victims greater protection encourage increased reporting rates. In some places changes in definition of rape have also resulted in slight increases in reportage, again later than 1975.

Contrary influences on reporting rates stem from the growth of the rape crisis centers. While the centers have encouraged victims coming forward to report, these reports are commonly not turned over to the police because victims have preferred emotional support without medical and legal investigations.

Estimates of the gap between the two rates (commission and reports) vary: the National Victimization Study conducted in 1967 for the President's Crime Commission suggested a ratio of between three and four actual rapes for each one reported. A more recent Law Enforcement Assistance Administration pilot survey in two American cities suggested a two to one ratio, possibly indicating a change in victim reporting behaviour since 1967. (Wilson, P.R. 1978, p. 17)

On this basis, it strains credulity to explain increases in reports of more than 100% as merely attributable to increased willingness to report. There is no evidence that *all* attacks are now being reported. On the contrary Wilson gives evidence of the larger proportion of victims who reported at a women's center but did not go on to the police: "between October 1974 and January 1976, of 221 victims seen by persons connected with the (Sydney) centre only about eighty-eight were reported to the police" (Wilson, P.R., 1978, p. 19). Thus, even among the selected sample of those willing to come forward in this way, only 40% appear in police figures.

Two further factors lead one to suspect no increase in reporting rates and possibly a decrease. One is that when the level of offenses becomes very high, the probability of effective action against offenders is reduced to the point that it appears useless to report. This point is exemplified in evidence from Los Angeles where in 1960, the reports rate was 43.4/100,000 and the arrest rate was 12.4. The comparable figures for 1972 were 78.4 and 10.55. That is, in 1960, there was a 29% chance that a report would lead to an arrest, but this had dropped to a 13.5% chance by 1972" (Court, 1980, p. 197).

Second, in two ways, the disposition of offenders makes a difference to the number of offenses and reports received. There has been a trend toward rapists receiving little or no sentence even after an arrest has been made (Soothill & Jack, 1975). This outcome reduces the willingness of victims to report. At the same time, it means a greater number of offenders remain free within society to reoffend, thereby increasing actual offenses (Wilson, P.R., 1978).

It is impossible to provide weightings for these conflicting influences. What does appear is that changes in reporting patterns are identifiable in relation to the period since about 1975, and such changes give as much credibility to reduced rates of police reports as to increased rates.

Changed Definitions

Changing definitions of sex crimes arise within the context of changed attitudes to those crimes. Kutchinsky (1971) wrote within a context in which a number of formal legal changes were introduced, including the removal of a number of offenses from legal sanctions. Such changes tend to produce a change of threshold of acceptance of behavior within that society such that even those offenses that do have legal sanctions are viewed less seriously. These combined influences reduce police offense statistics even if the behavior is itself unchanged.

For this reason, it is difficult to attach significance to undifferentiated sex crime figures in a period of such social change. There has been less change in the definition of rape, although extensions to include oral and anal rape, as well as rape in marriage have in recent years provided the basis for some increase by definition. The social acceptance of this offense that would lead to reduced reporting does not appear to have developed. Hence, specifying rape as the dependent variable in studies of the impact of pornography makes more sense than the diffuse and changing category of "sex crime."

The Influence of Race and City Size on Rape Statistics

That rape is not simply a sex crime is apparent from some of its related variables. It is widely recognized that in the United States, rape has been more common among blacks than among whites (Amir, 1971). The rate is also much greater in urban than in rural communities. One possible interpretation is therefore in terms of powerlessness of subcultures who express their rage against society. Svastolga (1962) proposed that rape is a feature of communities in which males substantially outnumber females.

The high association of rape with blacks has certainly been evident in the American culture, as has the rate found in large cities. Such evidence provides only a partial explanation and may be proportionately less and less significant as the rape rate rises. Lester (1974) found only a low positive correlation of .22

($p < .01$) of blacks and rape across the whole of the United States. Even such a low correlation must itself be taken cautiously since the percentage of blacks is confounded as a variable with city size.

Partial correlations for black population and city size enable one to identify variables more clearly. Taking the 15 cities used in FBI statistics as representative of U.S. cities (Kelley, 1972), size of population and percentage of blacks were correlated with the rate of reports of rape. The same variables were related to reports of crimes of violence. High correlations were found for violent crime. The partial correlation between violent crime and city size, holding black percentage constant, was .84 and .88 for violent crime and black population, holding city size constant. The corresponding figures for rape, however, were .23 and .39. This different relationship suggests that at least some factors are discordant and that the influence of race and city size should not be overemphasized.

Such a conclusion is at first counterintuitive. It must be noted however that these figures relate to data from 1973. (A date later than 1973 cannot be safely used for the present purpose without confounding the data with changes in reporting patterns discussed above). Generalizations about the relevant variables based on the early 1960s are inadequate for the 1970s. The rates of rape reports in the United States for the years 1961–1965 were 8.8, 9, 8.7. 10.7, and 11.9 per 100,000 population, respectively. By contrast the figures for 1971–1973 were 20.5, 22.5, and 24.5 per 100,000 population, respectively. In other words, a larger percentage of the population were offenders during the latter period. Discussions about the meaning of rape and the characteristics of rapists commonly draw on information based on rape as it was in the 1960s. There are now indications that the offense is changing in certain respects. By 1973, there were 51,400 cases reported in the United States and this had risen to 82,090 by 1980 (a rate of 36.4 per 100,000 population).

The Influence of Changing Age Groupings on Rape Statistics

It is appropriate to consider whether such rises in sexually violent crime have arisen because of a greater proportion of the population falling within the young adult group, following the baby boom of the 1950s. Certainly demographic studies indicate an increased proportion of young adults in the 1970s, but it is too slight to account for the very large increase in reports of sexual violence. Whereas Chappell (1976) referred to a doubling of rape reports in the decade prior to 1976, the U.S. population change for those in the age group 15–29 rose from 8.8 to 9.8% of the total population (Demographic Year Books, 1965, 1974).

Without rejecting these four factors entirely, they remain insufficient explanations for the steep increase in rape reports being widely encountered. This increase is sometimes in close parallel with a general increase in crimes of violence, but not in all cases, nor is the timing of these increases well matched (Court, 1980).

Hence the possibility remains that freely available porno-violence is making a contribution. In a comment on the ripple effect of pornography on attitudes and behavior,McCarthy (1980) says:

> Increasingly, a primary source of sex education for teenager boys is pornography. . . . Much of pornography and indeed our objections to it, hinges on violence and degradation rather than sexuality. . . . There is a principle highly thought of in the sciences called the Principle of Parsimony. It states that one should never employ a more complex explanation for an event when a less complex one will suffice. In a culture that promotes the cult of macho, rape should have been expected. (pp. 15, 18).

The probability of a link between pornography and porno-violence is increasingly frequently claimed as rape reports increase and porno-violence pushes to and beyond the limits of obscenity legislation (Brownmiller, 1975; Metzger, 1976; Russell, 1977, Lederer, 1980).

ARGUMENTS FOR AN ASSOCIATION BETWEEN RAPE AND PORNO-VIOLENCE

1. As noted previously it was argued in the U.S. 1970 commission report that increased availability of pornography had been associated with a reduction in sex crimes. Here it is argued that, allowing for a refinement to restrict observation to the incidence of rape reports, the impact of porno-violence can be detected in changing rates.

2. If the association is more than arbitrary, it should also be found that where porno-violence is not made more readily available, there will correspondingly be no significant increase in rape reports.

3. Furthermore, if an increasingly restrictive attitude to porno-violence is adopted, this should be reflected in a decrease in rape reports.

4. If a policy change occurs such that porno-violence is made available or restricted on some intermittent basis, then one has the elements (i.e., the alternating presence and absence of the independent variable) of an ABAB design experiment to test hypotheses more exactly.

5. In all these cases, the argument for a positive association will be strengthened if the time of increased rape reports follows fairly closely that of changes in the availability of porno-violence. One need not postulate an immediate impact since exposure to pornography does not necessarily produce an immediate change in either attitude or behavior. Indeed, it is clear from Goldstein's work that "most of the reported imitation occurred some time after the exposure to erotica, suggesting that a type of latent learning took place which was not

expressed until a later time when an appropriate partner was available'' (1977, p. 11). Hence one is looking for increased rape reports typically over the years following liberalization of laws, with a cumulative effect occurring.

6. The link would be more convincing if the nature of rape offenses were shown to be somehow changing and related to the images contained within porno-violence. Such an association is particularly difficult to determine scientifically since behavior is rarely triggered by a simple stimulus, but general patterns may emerge and become apparent to those working in the area of sexual violence.

7. If the link between porno-violence and rape were a simple causal one, there should be no negative instances contrary to the above expectations. It would of course be naive in the extreme to postulate a simple cause–effect relationship, since rape has existed long before porno-violence became available, and many (probably most) of those exposed to porno-violence neither attempt rape nor have any urge to do so. Both phenomena clearly exist within a social context, with many other variables affecting behavior and attitudes. If significant increases in rape are found in places where there is no evidence for increased availability of porno-violence, the general proposition needs reexamination but not necessarily rejection. Certain specific factors may apply in a local context that create a special case.

8. Finally, if the impact of porno-violence is having its own special contribution to sexual violence, it is possible that the rise in rape reports will occur at a different rate from other types of offense, including violent crime generally. Sexual arousal to porno-violence can lead both to increased sexual activity and increased aggression (e.g., Donnerstein, 1980; Malamuth *et al.*, 1977; Meyer, 1972). Hence porno-violence may play some part in trends toward increased nonsexual violence, but it is more likely that modeling of sexual violence will occur. Hence one would look for a trend of rising rape reports rather more serious than the general level of increasing violence (where that is occurring). Conversely, where porno-violence is *not* available, one might expect a relatively lower level of both rape reports and other forms of violent crime. The next section discusses evidence bearing upon each of the seven arguments I have just summarized.

PROPOSITIONS FOR AN ASSOCIATION BETWEEN RAPE AND PORNO-VIOLENCE

Proposition 1   Rape reports have increased where pornography laws have been liberalized. While some will challenge the reasons why, few will reject the fact that rape reports have steeply increased over the past decade in some places.

TABLE 5.1

Rape Reports to Police 1964–1974 per 100,000
Population

	1964	1974	% Change
United States	11.00	26.30	139
England and Wales	1.10	2.13	94
Copenhagen	8.88	16.32	84
Stockholm	10.64	15.05	41
Australia	2.35	6.10	160
New Zealand	4.40	9.12	107

Data for the period 1964–1974 (both before and after the 1970 U.S. commission report) shows evident trends that cannot be ascribed to complicating factors like changed laws or changed reporting rates.

The availability of pornography has undoubtedly increased, as has porno-violence, in the United States, in Scandinavia, in Britain, and in Australia following legislative and administrative liberalizations. To a lesser extent availability of pornography has increased in New Zealand. In all these places there has been a notable increase in rape reports over the decade 1964–1974, as shown in Table 5.1.

Because of varying methods of defining rape and police practice in recording rapes, these previous figures cannot be used legitimately to compare absolute levels, thereby assuming one place has a higher or lower rate of rape than another (Chappell, Geis, Schafer, & Siegel, 1977), but they do represent large enough raw data over a long enough period for the percentage changes to be meaningful. All the places noted have an upward trend consistent with the observation that liberalization of pornography laws corresponds to an increase in rape reports.

An important exception to this proposition has been advanced by Kraus (1979) who examined trends in violent crime in New South Wales. He relates rape rates specifically to the availability of pornography to argue that an increase in pornography has *not* been associated with increased rape reports. Reporting on the years 1967–1976, he remarks, "the period covered by the present study witnessed in New South Wales an unprecedented in Australia relaxation of censorship, and an exponential growth of "soft" and "hard-core" pornography, which according to numerous crusading groups should have resulted in a dramatic increase of rapes" (1979, p. 184). He presents evidence to show that there has been no such increase. Using crime reports to the police in New South Wales (1967–1976) with the figures for rape and attempted rape (reported as a rate per 100,000 males 18–39 years of age), the data appeared to show no increase in reports (see Table 5.2). The data are, however, strikingly discrepant with the data provided by

TABLE 5.2

Comparison of Rape Report Data for New South Wales

	Kraus (1979)			Biles (1979b)	
	Reports	Rate		Reports	Rate
1967		9.7	1966–1967	69	1.6
1968		11.7	1967–1968	91	2.1
1969		12.0	1968–1969	105	2.4
1970		11.0	1969–1970	116	2.6
1971	203	10.8	1970–1971	173	3.8
1972	174	9.1	1971–1972	184	4.0
1973	187	9.7	1972–1973	206	4.4
1974	219	11.2	1973–1974	308	6.5
1975	204	10.3	1974–1975	364	7.6
1976	186	9.3	1975–1976	342	7.1

Derived from Kraus (1979) and Biles (1979b). Rates are offenses per 100,000 males age 18–39.

Biles (1979b) from the Australian Institute of Criminology. While Kraus has relied on state figures that are not comparable with figures from other states, Biles has reported data collected according to standardized criteria for the Australian Bureau of Statistics.

Correspondence with these authors reveals two different sets of data, with Kraus relying on "accepted reports," which are typically fewer than the standardized data collated for federal statistics (Court, 1982). The source for his data has been reported as unreliable (Swanton, 1976).

Hence, evidence presented as a direct refutation of a corresponding increase in rates with liberalization of pornography must at best be treated with great caution. The uniform crime data for Australia actually support the case for an increase quite convincingly.

Proposition 2   Areas where porno-violence is not liberalized do not show a steep rise in rape reports. This proposition must be exemplified in several ways in order to eliminate competing hypotheses. First, one way is to compare the situation in Singapore with those places noted in Table 5.1. In Singapore, the government has taken a firm stand against permissiveness, and pornography is controlled (Court, 1977). Over the same period (1964–1974) rape reports increased from 2.01 to 3.40 per 100,000 population (69%). This figure is less than for any place listed in Table 5.1 except Stockholm, and is in contrast to the upward trend for the places with liberal pornography laws. The Singapore figure for 1974 is actually unrepresentatively high, with those for every year from 1975 to 1980 lower, resulting in a horizontal linear trend for the period 1964–1980 (personal communication, Statistics Department, Singapore, April 1982). One might object that cultural differences invalidate a comparison of Singapore with Western nations. This point deserves attention, even though the careful statistical approach of a small nation with only one police force does make for reliability of the data.

A second example that reduces the cultural gap is South Africa, if one considers only the white population. (This restriction is necessary if one is to minimize the problems of cross-cultural comparison. It is further justified since the use of pornography is very much greater among whites than among blacks in South Africa. Moreover, the provisions of the Immorality Act making sexual activity across races illegal mean that sex offense data can only be meaningfully related to one race at a time). The corresponding rape rates for 1964 and 1974 are 10.80 and 13.87 per 100,000 population, respectively, that is, a 28% increase (Court, 1979). It cannot be denied, however, that a factor capable of further affecting both these countries and distinguishing them from those in Table 5.1 is the manner in which offenders are treated. Tough penalties for rapists are characteristic for both Singapore and South Africa, so the absence of a major rise in rape may be partly attributable to this.

A third comparison sheds further light by examining two states within Australia. While federal practice has liberalized pornography since 1970, it is possible for individual states to adopt local criteria. Queensland has been characterized by a conservative policy while South Australia has been the most liberal (Biles, 1979a; Overduin and Fleming, 1980.) In neither place are stiff penalties of the kind seen in Singapore and South Africa imposed.

Figure 5.1 gives rape report data for the two states. Acceptable figures are available only from 1964 to 1965 for Queensland, at which time the incidence was closely similar to that in South Australia. The trend for Queensland shows no upturn throughout the period, whereas in South Australia, an upward trend departing from a previous horizontal line started from 1970 (Court, 1980). The data in Figure 5.1 based on Australian Bureau of Statistics information indicate an upturn for Queensland from the period 1964–1965 to 1974–1975 of only 23%, but for South Australia of 284%, and the separation has continued.

It should be acknowledged that when these data were first published they were challenged by Cochrane (1978) who claimed that the South Australian data could be best explained by a curvilinear trend originating well before 1970. If this were so, then the hypothesized relationship of increased incidence of rape with pornography would be open to question. However, analysis of his data reveals that he failed to test the curve statistically, and relied for his interpretation on visual inspection, facilitated by the deletion of 7 of 13 data points. The data in Figure 5.1 go beyond the original figures, so that more recent information permits more rigorous analysis of the entire series to 1977 to 1978. Regression analyses were carried out, showing Cochrane's solution to be less adequate than a solution

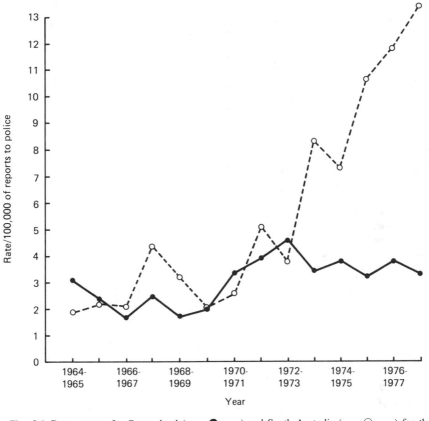

Fig. 5.1 Rape reports for Queensland (———●———) and South Australia (———○———) for the period 1964–1965 to 1977–1978.

involving two straight lines. A linear trend not rising significantly occurs until 1970, but thereafter rises steeply. The best-fitting break-point in 1970 corresponds closely to the legislative change liberalizing censorship laws in Australia. Taking the period 1959–1970, a fitted quadratic has an error mean square of 1.151, whereas the solution with two straight lines involves the more satisfactory error mean square of 0.607 (Court, 1980).

Together these comparisons provide support for the proposition that places that exercise control over pornography also experience a lower rate of rape reports, while other factors can be identified as contributory. The most parsimonious explanation for the data is that the public policy adopted in relation to pornography has had a disinhibitory influence on the disposition to sexual aggression.

Proposition 3   Where restrictions have been adopted, rape reports have de-creased. Evidence to support this proposition is sparse indeed, since in most Western countries liberalizing policies have prevailed since the 1970s. One possible example is presented by Japan, which has traditionally accepted porno-violence as part of its cultural expression (Roth, 1977). However, changed policies in the 1970s relating to the import of Western publications have meant that confiscation and airbrushing of pictorial magazines was introduced (*Time,* 1976). It should be noted, as discussed in the next chapter in this book, that the specific focus of the restrictions on pornography imposed by the Japanese au-thorities (e.g., not showing pubic hair) may not correspond to the content that may indeed be most objectionable (e.g., violence).

Reports available from the police in Japan show a decline in rape reports over the period 1965–1974 from 11.5 to 6.28 per 100,000 population (Court, 1980). This downturn has coincided with a downturn in violent crime generally, and an additional factor to be acknowledged is a highly efficient and respected police force. The downturn is remarkable at a time when so many places are troubled by an upsurge of violent and sexual crime and when Japan is increasingly identified with Western culture.

Evidence, as yet unsubstantiated, suggests that pornography is becoming more available once again. If this proves to be so, the trend in rape statistics could provide a further test of the proposed linkages by serving as a reversal experi-ment as is shown in the following case.

Proposition 4   Intermittent policy changes are reflected in rape report data.
It would be particularly satisfying to experiment using an ABAB design with a complete country, changing laws affecting the availability of pornography every few years and observing the consequences. Campbell (1979) advocates this approach where possible, but it is unusual for social policy to be decided on scientific rather than a political basis.

The only available evidence that approximates such a design comes from Hawaii. Hawaii is a particularly favorable place for study since traffic across borders is minimized by its geographical isolation. Since Hawaii is also a tourist area, disinhibiting influences such as anonymity in combination with alcohol are operating. Figure 5.2 illustrates the steep increase in rape reports troubling that state from 1965. It was from about that time that pornography became in-creasingly available throughout the United States. In the late 1960s, Hawaii also experienced an influx of U.S. troops on stopover from Vietnam.

For the present purpose, the most important observation is not the steep increase in rape reports to 1974 but the change that occurred when restraints were temporarily applied from 1974 to 1976. A significant downturn occurred in rape reports. The very close time relationship is surprising unless one considers that the potential offender population producing the increase consists predominantly

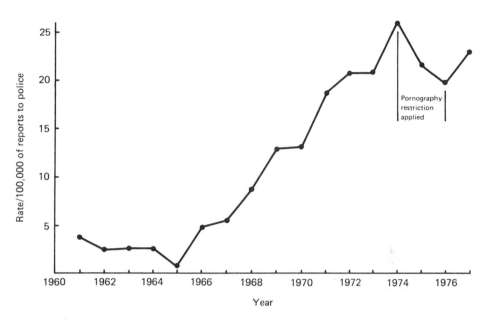

Fig. 5.2 Rape reports for Hawaii during the period 1960–1978. During the period 1964–1974, rape reports rose by 900%.

of visitors under unusually facilitating circumstances (i.e., alcoholic disinhibition, anonymity, opportunity). Scientifically, it would have been desirable for the restriction period to have been extended longer. When the laws were relaxed again in 1977, an upward turn in rape reports occurred. The relationship since that time has become more complex as the proportion of native Hawaiians committing offenses has greatly increased (Hawaii Criminal Justice Centers, 1981).

Proposition 5   Changed laws on pornography are temporally related to changed rates of rape. For a simple causal association, a precise and close temporal relationship would be essential. If one postulates that porno-violence erodes society's taboos, generates disinhibition, and gradually extends its influence to affect attitudes and behavior, then a less precise time relationship would be more likely. Among the examples cited, the temporal relationships for changes in rape reports are unusually close for South Australia (1970) (see Figure 5.1) and for Hawaii (1974, 1976) (see Figure 5.2). The time when porno-violence became widely available in the United States and in Scandinavia is not clearly identifiable, being gradual rather than sudden, so no clear disjunctions are detectable.

In England and Wales, a major change in the law (the Obscene Publications

Act) occurred in 1959, allowing greater freedom for obscenity to circulate. This change antedated the availability of more than a tiny amount of porno-violence. An amendment in 1964 encouraged the distribution of magazines such as *Penthouse* (Williams, 1979), and then the publication of the U.S. commission report in 1970 undoubtedly strengthened the view that pornography could circulate without causing harm. The type of material changed, so that by 1976 it was reported that "sex shops . . . are proliferating with the help of 30 importers who are said to be marking up their wares by 2000%. Especially unsettling to the British public is the marked increase in violent, sado-masochistic pornography, which, although still illegal, is reaching a growing underground market" (*Time*, 1976, p. 46). Over the same period, the ripples spread wider with increasing numbers of X-rated movies being screened, with sex and violence predominating.

The period 1964–1974 in England and Wales was characterized by an increase in rape reports from 1.10 to 2.13 per 100,000 population (94%) and has continued to rise since that time, whereas over the period 1945–1958 no significant increase occurred. Williams (1979) comments that "this period of ten years (1964–74) was clearly a bad one for offences of rape" (p. 76). That other types of violent crime were also increasing over the same period does not invalidate the time relationship noted here, though that may again lead one to speculate about a more general disinhibition, with porno-violence having a contributory role. It has been postulated that "the elicitation of sexual arousal within a violent context may result in a conditioning process whereby violent acts become associated with sexual pleasure, a highly powerful unconditioned stimulus and reinforcer" (Malamuth, Heim, & Feshbach, 1980, p. 407).

The situation in New Zealand may also be related to certain specific events (see Figure 5.3). The upward trend in rape reports from 1964 to 1974 has been very steep (40%). Among the factors one may implicate was the introduction of the Indecent Publications Act, taking effect in 1964, which liberalized laws on obscenity. The increased stable level of 1965 to 1969 then moved steeply upward after it was so widely claimed by the U.S. commission report in 1970 that no harm was associated with pornography. After several years of steep increase the trend was reversed in 1974. It is possible that the decline arose due to the introduction of the Auckland Task Force, established to take a tough line with crime and led by Gideon Tait. Following his retirement, Tait in his autobiography gave his opinion that

> It is a matter of police record rather than opinion that a great many offenders convicted of sex crimes possessed libraries of pornograpic books. . . . I am certain that competent sociological research would establish a link between the flood of pornographic material to which young people are subjected and the increase in sex crimes. (Tait, 1978, p. 159)

Proposition 6   The nature of the rape attack is changing. This proposition is not open to clear scientific investigation. Official records are inadequate for

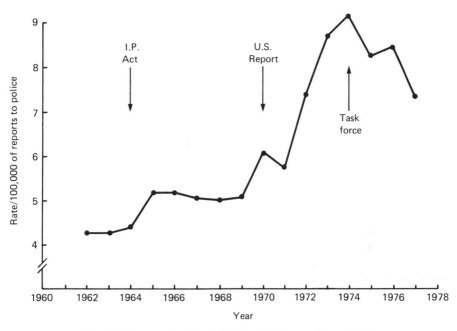

Fig. 5.3 Rape reports for New Zealand for the period 1960–1978.

showing that the actual nature of serious offenses against women has changed in line with the kinds of images presented in books and films. If the kind of modeling postulated by Bandura (1973), Berkowitz (1971), and others does occur in this context, one would expect the proposition to find support in some way. A good many press reports of rape attacks give anecdotal support for such an association. Changes in the law to include oral and anal rape in the definition of rape (Mitchell, 1976) seem to point to a concern over the increased incidence of this form of activity, while Superintendent McAulay of the South Australian Police was reported as saying that "teenagers are making an increasingly high proportion of the attacks. . . . Furthermore, rapes are becoming more violent. The offenders are using more force. And we have noticed rapists are subjecting women to indecent acts far more than before" (de Luca, 1977). There appears, therefore, to be some support for this proposition, but it deserves further investigation.

Proposition 7   Discrepant cases should not occur without adequate explanation. In citing examples of an association between an increase in porno-violence and rape, it would be misleading to ignore instances where a positive correlation does not exist. Much of the debate over the social consequences of making pornography available has arisen because of the widely cited claims for reduced sexual offenses in Copenhagen (Kutchinsky, 1971) and Denmark (Ben-Veniste, 1971). Nowhere, however, have any claims been made that rape reports have declined where pornography has been liberalized. Hence that side of the argument does not appear to need further defense. At issue is the question of the mechanisms whereby the observed positive correlations are mediated. Factors other than pornography per se can be implicated.

There are examples of steeply increased rape rates where factors other than the availability of porno-violence may even play a major role. Two such places are Alaska and the Northern Territory in Australia. Both have experienced very high and increasing per capita rates of rape reports. Alaska showed a rate increase in rape reports over the period 1964–1974 from 22.4 to 49.3 per 100,000 population (and to 71.9 by 1979, which is more than twice the national average). Northern Territory rates are typically high also (Biles, 1979b) but unreliable as they are based on small absolute frequencies. Both places are frontier states with social characteristics different from the rest of the country. Alaska has a disproportionate male–female ratio and an unusually high accessibility to alcohol— one bar for every 550 persons, compared with one for every 1470 generally in the United States. (*Los Angeles Times,* 1977). The Northern Territory is also known to be characterized by a very high rate of alcohol intake and an atypical population with a high proportion of males to females.

Svastolga (1962) postulated that the male–female ratio is a significant factor in the rate of rape reports in communities where males substantially outnumber females. Lester (1974), however, has not found this to be the case in surveys across the whole of the United States.

Proposition 8   The increase in rape reports does not parallel the increase in serious nonsexual offenses. If changes in rape reports coincide closely with changes in other types of offenses, then nothing specific can be advanced to explain such changes. Fluctuations in crime levels are undoubtedly multifactorial, thus, to advance the influence of a particular factor such as porno-violence, the trends for rape must be in some way discriminable. In the light of theory advanced by Baron and Bell (1977) and by Donnerstein (1980) to show that both aggressive and sexual impulses can be stimulated by exposure to porno-violence, the distinction between sexual and aggressive crimes is not entirely justified. It is possible that factors other then porno-violence can contribute to increased rape reports (e.g., changing sex roles [Kenyon, 1975] and availability of alcohol) while concurrently porno-violence may facilitate a growth in nonsexual violence.

Depending on the time frame adopted and the mode of comparisons selected, it is in some cases possible to show an increase in rape that is greater than that for nonsexual violent crime (Court, 1977). However, there are many instances where no differences can be detected, or where little association exists at all

(Court, 1980). Some of the ambiguity that arises from this state of affairs can be related to changing definitions and police practice, but whatever the explanation, the evidence is at this stage insufficient to support or deny the proposition. Since changes in the availability of pornography have occurred concurrently with a growth in violence in the media, it may be that the only way to test this proposition will be through laboratory studies.

DISCUSSION

While one might approach the question of a relationship between pornography and sexual offenses by adopting a null hypothesis, this chapter has started from the presumption, based on Danish evidence, of a negative correlation between the availability of pornography and the incidence of sexual offenses.

After showing that there are serious difficulties with this interpretation of the effects of the availability of pornography, the case is made for an association between the availability of pornography and the increased incidence of serious sexual offenses, specifically, rape. This association also needs further refinement since related experimental work suggests that not all types of pornography are equally implicated. Porno-violence proves to be particularly powerful in its potential for generating antisocial sexual behavior and attitudes.

If an association between availability of porno-violence and incidence of rape exists, one must ask whether the link is causal or of some other type. The answer to this depends as much on one's definition of causality as it does on the criteria deemed sufficient to demonstrate causality.

A series of eight propositions is advanced which provide support for positive and negative relationships and for reversals. In a tight experimental design context such arguments would be sufficient to conclude that a causal relationship exists. However, the data reported here are naturalistic and based on information with many uncertainties. That rape reports are increasing in places where pornography is also increasing is not a matter for serious doubt, but attention has been drawn to factors that make precise measurement and interpretation impossible.

Hence, while one cannot exclude a causal relationship (Roth, 1977), it is safer to assume a multifactorial situation in which pornography is playing a significant part. Porno-violence appears from experimental work to have a fairly direct effect on specific types of response and attitude change (Donnerstein, 1980; Malamuth & Check, 1981). Beyond that immediate effect, a ripple effect is occurring.

The existence of porno-violence both validates and further facilitates a hostile, exploitative view of women (Lederer, 1980; McCarthy, 1980). The wide availability of pornography of a softer kind appears to support the market and extend the demand for porno-violence as consumers move from one type of material to another. It is clear that without a period of widely available soft pornography, the present genre of porno-violence would never have gained the acceptance it has (Clunies-Ross, 1970; Williams, 1971). A period of desensitization and adaptation has occurred over the past 15 years.

Those studies showing contrary results for soft and hard-core materials (Baron, 1974a) also raise questions about a ripple effect for nonviolent pornography. Mildly erotic stimulation leads to a reduced likelihood of the expression of aggression with more sexually arousing materials facilitating aggression. It would appear that erotica can therefore claim to be successful in generating a higher level of sexual arousal and activity. Indeed, if it were not so, it is difficult to know how its enormous sales would be maintained. This facilitation is commonly argued to be a social benefit, especially when specifically applied in therapy to those with sexual difficulties. That there could be negative consequences from such sexual facilitation involves a moral rather than a scientific evaluation.

One further sense in which a ripple effect applies relates to actual exposure to pornography, including porno-violence. In this area, statistical estimates are particularly hazardous. However, if one combines the observations of increased sales of publications, reduced police activity in relation to public access to such materials, liberalized censorship laws, and extensions into new media such as video-cassettes, one may reasonably conclude that more people are being exposed to more pornography than ever before. This could be even more pronounced in the teenage age group because of increased access of young people to such materials, due to increased mobility and money. Postulating that media effects operate according to principles of modeling, and that the psychosexual stages of teenage development make for high receptivity, the outcomes of this kind of ripple effect on sexual behavior are likely to appear over the next decade. They will be difficult to distinguish from other sociological changes concurrent with exposure to pornography (Schmidt & Sigusch, 1973), yet deserving attention as the balance of benefit and harm is determined.

The question of how society should respond to the increasing availability of pornography is not easily answered. The dangers of advocating censorship are widely recognized since the principle of restraining harmful material can easily be too widely applied for political and other purposes. Yet the indications of harm from certain types of material have accumulated now to the point that the demand for freedom of one kind (of expression) is threatened by the loss of freedom experienced by the victims of sexual assault, and hence by extension, the whole society suffers.

For this reason, this chapter has highlighted the term *porno-violence* as a subcategory of pornography in order to identify a circumscribed class of materials that is more readily identifiable than pornography and that for both theoretical and experimental reasons can be linked with indisputable harm. One may argue for the containment of porno-violence while having a quite different view in relation to other forms of pornography.

The evidence that countries allowing porno-violence also experience an escalation in rape rates needs to be treated as seriously as the observation that countries that restrain porno-violence have not experienced steep increases in rape rates. Taken without a context these relationships might be merely associations without significance. When interpreted in relation to what is now known about modeling, about the responsiveness of various normal and pathological groups to erotica and porno-violence, and the closely similar lines of evidence derived from studies of media violence, a strong case can be made for the restraint of porno-violence in contemporary society.

REFERENCES

Abel, G. G., Blanchard, E. B., Barlow, D. H., & Mavissakalian, M. (1975). Identifying specific cues in sexual deviations by audio-taped descriptions. *Journal of Applied Behavioral Analysis, 8,* 274–260.

Abel, G. G., Barlow, D. H., Blanchard, E. B., & Guild, D. (1977). The components of rapists' sexual arousal. *Archives of General Psychiatry, 34,* 895–903.

Amir, M. (1971). *Patterns of forcible rape.* Chicago: University of Chicago Press.

Bachy, V. (1976). Danish "permissiveness" revisited. *Journal of Communication, 26*(1), 40–43.

Bandura, A. (1973). *Aggression: A social learning analysis.* Englewood Cliffs, NJ: Prentice-Hall.

Baron, R. A. (1974a). The aggression-inhibiting influence of heightened sexual arousal. *Journal of Personality and Social Psychology, 30,* 318–322.

Baron, R. A. (1974b). Sexual arousal and physical aggression: The inhibiting influence of "cheesecake" and nudes. *Bulletin of the Psychonomic Society, 3,* 337–339.

Baron, R. A. (1978). Aggression inhibiting influence on sexual humor. *Journal of Personality and Social Psychology, 36,* 189–198.

Baron, R. A., & Bell, P. A. (1977). Sexual arousal and aggression by males: Effects of erotic stimuli and prior provocation. *Journal of Personality and Social Psychology, 35*(2), 79–87.

Barbaree, H. E., Marshall, W. L., & Lanthier, R. D. (1979). Deviant sexual arousal in rapists. *Behavior Research and Therapy, 17,* 215–222.

Bart, P. B., & Jozsa, M. (1980). Dirty books, dirty films and dirty data. In L. Lederer (Ed.), *Take back the night: Women on pornography.* New York: William Morrow and Co.

Ben-Veniste, R. (1971). Pornography and sex-crime: The Danish experience. *Technical Reports of the Commission on Obscenity and Pornography,* Vol. 8. Washington, DC: U.S. Government Printing Office.

Berkowitz, L. (1971, December). Sex and violence: we can't have it both ways. *Psychology Today,* pp. 14, 18, 20, 22, 23.

Biles, D. (1979a). Minor sexual offences in Australia: A research note. *Australian and New Zealand Journal of Criminology, 12,* 33–40.

Biles, D. (1979b). *The size of the crime problem in Australia.* Canberra: Australian Institute of Criminology.

Brownmiller, S. (1975). *Against our will: Men, women and rape.* New York: Simon and Schuster.

Campbell, D. T. (1969). Reforms as experiments. *American Psychologist, 24,* 409–429.

Campbell, D. T. (1979). Assessing the impact of planned social change. *Evaluation and Program Planning, 2,* 67–90.

Cantor, J. R., Zillmann, D., & Einsiedel, E. F. (1975). Female responses to provocation after exposure to aggressive and erotic films. *Communication Research, 5*(4), 395–411.

Chappell, D. (1976). Forcible rape and the Criminal Justice System: Surveying present practices and projecting future trends. In M. J. Walker and S. L. Brodsky (Eds.), *Sexual Assault*. Lexington, MA: Lexington Books.

Chappell, D., Geis, G., Schafer, S., & Siegel, L. (1977). A comparative study of forcible rape offences known to the police in Boston and Los Angeles. In D. Chappell *et al.* (Eds.), *Forcible rape: The crime, the victim and the offender.* New York: Columbia University Press.

Cline, V. B. (1970). *Minority report of the U.S. Commission on Obscenity and Pornography.* New York: Bantam Books.

Cline, V. B. (1974). *Where do you draw the line? An exploration into media violence, pornography and censorship.* Provo, UT: Brigham Young University Press.

Cline, V. B. (1976, February). The scientists vs. pornography: An untold story. *Intellect,* pp. 574–576.

Clunies-Ross, B. (1970). How to change censorship in Australia. *The Bulletin, 92,* 43–44.

Cochrane, P. (1978). Sex crimes and pornography revisited. *International Journal of Criminology and Penology, 16,* 307–317.

Commission on Obscenity and Pornography. (1971). *Technical Reports of the U.S. Commission on Obscenity and Pornography* (Vols. 1–9). Washington, DC: U.S. Government Printing Office.

Commission on Obscenity and Pornography. (1970). *U.S. Presidential Commission on Obscenity and Pornography.* New York: Bantam Books.

Court, J. H. (1977). Pornography and sex crimes: A re-evaluation in the light of recent trends around the world. *International Journal of Criminology and Penology, 5,* 129–157.

Court, J. H. (1979). Rape and pornography in white South Africa. *De Jure, 12*(2) 236–241.

Court, J. H. (1980). *Pornography and the harm condition.* Adelaide: Flinders University.

Court, J. H. (1981, May). Pornography update. *British Journal of Sexual Medicine,* pp. 28–30.

Court, J. H. (1982) Rape trends in New South Wales: A discussion of conflicting evidence. *Australian Journal of Social Issues, 17,* 3, 202–206.

Davis, K. E., & Braucht, G. N. (1973). Exposure to pornography, character and sexual deviance: A retrospective study. *Journal of Social Issues, 29*(3) 183–196.

de Luca, G. (1977, July). Rape cases at record level in S.A. *The News,* p. 8.

Demographic Year Book (1965, 1974). New York: United Nations.

Donnerstein, E. and Barrett, G. (1978) Effects of erotic stimuli on male aggression toward females. *Journal of Personality and Social Psychology, 36,* 2, 180–188.

Donnerstein, E. (1980). Aggressive erotica and violence against women. *Journal of Personality and Social Psychology, 39*(2), 269–277.

Donnerstein, E., Donnerstein, M., & Evans, R. (1975). Erotic stimuli and aggression: Facilitation or inhibition. *Journal of Personality and Social Psychology, 32,* 237–244.

Donnerstein, E., & Hallam, J. (1978). The facilitating effects of erotica on aggression against women. *Journal of Personality and Social Psychology, 36,* 1270–1277.

Feshbach, S., & Malamuth, N. (1978). Sex and aggression: Proving the link. *Psychology Today, 12*(6) 111–122.

Fox, J. A. (1976). *Forecasting crime data: An econometric analysis.* Lexington: Lexington Books.

Geis, G., & Geis, R. (1979). Rape in Stockholm: Its permissiveness relevant? *Criminology, 17*(3) 311–322.

Goldstein, M. J. (1977). A behavioral scientist looks at obscenity. In B. D. Sales (Ed.), *The crimincal justice system* (pp. 1–21). New York: Plenum.

Goldstein, M. J., Kant, H. S., Judd, L. L., Rice, C. J., & Green, R. (1971). Exposure to pornography and sexual behavior in deviant and normal groups. *Technical Report of the Commission on Obscenity and Pornography,* (Vol. 7). Washington, DC: U.S. Government Printing Office.

Griffitt, W. (1973). Response to erotica and the projection of response to erotica in the opposite sex. *Journal of Experimental Research in Personality, 6,* 330–338.

Griffitt, W. (1975). Sexual experiences and sexual responsiveness: Sex differences. *Archives of Sexual Behavior, 4,* 5, 529–540.

Griffitt, W., & Kaiser, D. L. (1978). Affect, sex-guilt, gender and the reward-punishing effects of erotic stimuli. *Journal of Personality and Social Psychology, 36,* 850–858.

Hatfield, E., Sprecher, S., & Traupmann, J. (1978). Men's and women's reactions to sexually explicit films: A serendipitous finding. *Archives of Sexual Behavior, 7,* 583–592.

Hawaii Criminal Justice Statistical Analysis Center (1981). *Comparative crime trends: State of Hawaii, 1970–79.*

Holbrook, D. (1972). *The pseudo-revolution.* London: Tom Stacey.

Kelley, C. M. (1972). *Crime in the United States: Uniform crime reports.* Washington, DC: FBI Department of Justice.

Kenrick, D. T., Stringfield, D. O., Wagenhals, W. L., Dahl, R. M., & Ransdell, H. J. (1980). Sex differences, androgyny and approach responses to erotica: A new variation of the old volunteer problem. *Journal of Personality and Social Psychology, 38*(3), 517–524.

Kenyon, F. E. (1975). Pornography, the law and mental health. *British Journal of Psychiatry, 126,* 225–233.

Kraus, J. (1979). Trends in violent crime and public concern. *Australian Journal of Social Issues, 14*(3), 175–191.

Krogh, I. (1980, November). British Report proven wrong on impact of pornography in Denmark. *Newsweekly* (Melbourne) pp. 8–9.

Kupperstein, L. R., & Wilson, W. C. (1971). Erotica and antisocial behavior: An analysis of selected social indicator statistics. *Technical Report of the Commission on Obscenity and Pornography* (Vol. 7). Washington, DC: U.S. Government Printing Office.

Kutchinsky, B. (1971). Towards an exploration of the decrease in registered sex crimes in Copenhagen. *Technical Report of the Commission on Obscenity and Pornography* (Vol. 7). Washington, DC: U.S. Government Printing Office.

Kutchinsky, B. (1973). Eroticism without censorship. *International Journal of Criminology and Penology, 1,* 217–225.

Kutchinsky, B. (1978). Pornography in Denmark - A general survey. In R. Dhavan and C. Davies (Eds.), *Censorship and obscenity.* London: Martin Robertson.

Los Angeles Times. (1977). Alaskans heaviest drinkers in U.S. March 6.

Lederer, L. (1980). *Take back the night: Women on Pornography,* New York: William Morrow & Co.

Lester, D. (1974). Rape and social structure. *Psychological Reports, 35,* 146.

Longford, Lord (1972). *Pornography: The Longford Report.* London: Coronet Books.

McCarthy, S. J. (1980, September/October). Pornography, rape and the cult of macho. *The Humanist,* pp. 11–20, 56.

Malamuth, N. & Check, J. V. P. (1981). The effects of mass media exposure on acceptance of violence against women: A field experiment. *Journal of Research in Personality, 15,* 436–446.

Malamuth, N., Feshbach, S., & Jaffe, Y. (1977). Sexual arousal and aggression: Recent experiments and theoretical issues. *Journal of Social Issues, 33*(2), 110–133.

Malamuth, N., Haber, S., & Feshbach, S. (1980). Testing hypotheses regarding rape: Exposure to sexual violence, sex differences and the 'normality' or rapists. *Journal of Research in Personality, 14*(1), 121–137.

Malamuth, N., Heim, M., & Feshbach, S. (1980). Sexual responsiveness of college students to rape depictions: Inhibitory and disinhibitory effects. *Journal of Personality and Social Psychology, 38,* 399–408.

Malamuth, N., & Spinner, B. (1980). A longitudinal content analysis of sexual violence in the best selling erotica magazines. *Journal of Sex Research. 16,* 226–237.

Metzger, D. (1976). It is always the woman who is raped. *American Journal of Psychiatry, 133,* 405–407.

Meyer, T. P. (1972). The effects of sexually arousing and violent films as aggressive behaviour. *The Journal of Sex Research, 8,* 324–331.

Mitchell, R. (1976). Criminal Law and Penal Methods Reform Committee of South Australia. *Rape and other sexual offences: Special report.* Adelaide.

Mosher, D. L., & Katz, H. (1971). Pornographic films, male verbal aggression against women, and guilt. *Technical Report of the Commission on Obscenity and Pornography* (Vol. 8). Washington, DC: U.S. Government Printing Office.

Overduin, D. Ch., & Fleming, J. (1980). *Wake up, lucky country.* Adelaide: Lutheran Publishing House.

Propper, M. M. (1971). Exposure to sexually oriented materials among young male prisoners. *Technical Report of the Commission on Obscenity and Pornography* (Vol. 9). Washington DC: U.S. Government Printing Office.

Radzinowicz, H., & King, J. (1977). *The growth of crime.* London: Hamish Hamilton.

Roth, M. (1977). Sexual pornography in society, a psychiatric perspective. Fifth Goodman Lecture, Society of Opticians, London.

Russell, D. E. H. (1977). Pornography: A feminist perspective. Symposium paper, *Women against Violence and Pornography in the Media.* San Francisco.

Schmidt, G., Sigusch, V., & Schafer, S. (1973). Responses to reading erotic stories: Male–female differences. *Archives of Sexual Behavior, 2,* 181–199.

Schmidt, G., & Sigusch, V. (1973). Women's sexual arousal. In J. Zubin and J. Money (Eds.), *Contemporary sexual behavior: Critical issues in the 1970s.* Baltimore: John Hopkins University Press.

Schmidt, G., & Sigusch, V. (1980, September 3). Comment: The effects of pornography. *British Journal of Sexual Medicine, 7,* pp. 3,6.

Soothill, K., and Jack, A. (1975). How rape is reported *New Society, 32,* 702–703.

Svastolga, K. (1962). Rape and social structure. *Pacific Sociological Review, 5,* 48–53.

Swanton, B. (1976). Police in Australia. In D. Chappell and P. Wilson (Eds.), *The Australian criminal justice system.* Sydney: Butterworths.

Tait, G. (1978). *Never back down.* Christchurch: Whitcoulls.

Time (1976). The porno plague. 5 April, pp. 40–47.

Walker, C. E. (1971). Erotic stimuli and the aggressive sexual offender. *Technical Report of the Commission on Obscenity and Pornography* (Vol. 7). Washington DC: U.S. Government Printing Office.

Williams, B. (1979). *Report of the Committee on Obscenity and Film Censorship.* London: Her Majesty's Stationery Office. Command 7772.

Williams, D. (1971). *Trousered apes.* London: Churchill press.

Wilson, P. R. (1978). *The other side of rape.* Sr. Lucia. University of Queensland Press.

Wilson, W. C. (1978). Can pornography contribute to the prevention of sexual problems? In C. B. Qualls, J. P. Wincze, and D. H. Barlow (Eds.), *The prevention of sexual disorders.* New York: Plenum Press.

Zillmann, D., Hoyt, J. L., & Day, K. D. (1974). Strength and duration of the effect of aggression, violent and erotic communications on subsequent aggressive behavior. *Communication Research, 1,* 286–306.

Zillmann, D., & Sapolsky, B. (1977). What mediates the effect of mild erotica on hostile behavior in males? *Journal of Personality and Social Psychology, 35,* 587–596.

6

Pornography in Japan:
Cross-Cultural and Theoretical
Considerations

PAUL R. ABRAMSON
HARUO HAYASHI

This chapter examines the historical precedence of contemporary pornography in Japan in terms of explicitness and manifest themes. Despite the economic prominence of Japanese society today, there is a near void of psychological literature about this culture, especially in the area of sexuality. And more importantly, even though pornography historically has been an integral part of Japanese culture, there are no psychological writings on this subject. Consequently, this chapter provides both a review of Japanese pornography and a discussion of the cross-cultural variations between Japanese and American pornography, particularly the concepts of compartmentalization, consistency, and internal versus external constraints.

HISTORICAL PERSPECTIVE

Prior to the enthronement of Emperor Meiji in 1868 (often called the Meiji Restoration), sexually explicit stimuli served one of three purposes: (1) to symbolize fertility, (2) to illustrate a sex manual, and (3) to create sensual feelings.

PORNOGRAPHY AND
SEXUAL AGGRESSION

173

Copyright © 1984 by Academic Press, Inc.
All rights of reproduction in any form reserved.
ISBN 0-12-466280-3

Early Agricultural Society

Because agriculture played a predominant role in Japan, religious ceremonies incorporated symbols that were believed to ensure a bountiful harvest. Since the penis and the vagina are explicitly related to fruition, religious objects (called *do so shin*) and festivals (*matsuri*) often featured a model or symbol of the penis and the vagina. Today, remnants of this practice are still evident in rural communities, as well as in the nearly 2000 extant shrines housing the *do so shin*.

In addition to the parades and shrines, the early Japanese agricultural communities also utilized sexuality in their festivals. Although it was assumed to be tangentially connected to bountiful harvests, these festivals encouraged open sexual relations. Characterized by the following folk poem, "I will make love with someone else's wife, so why doesn't someone make love with my wife," these festivals permitted unlimited sexual expression, usually initiated by a black-out at midnight. Children conceived from these relations were referred to as products of god's love, with the analogy extended to a successful harvest.

The Edo Period of the Tokugawa Shogunate (1603–1867)

Sexually explicit themes were also evident in Japanese art, especially in the form of wood block prints known as *ukiyo-e* (literally "floating world paintings"). *Ukiyo-e* was a hydrid school of print design and painting that used popular everyday images as its predominant theme (Lane, 1978). *Ukiyo-e* was one of the last movements of Japanese classical art, and it coincided with the Edo period (1603–1868) of the Tokugawa Shogunate.

Some of the earliest *ukiyo-e* featured scenes from the Kabuki theater. Developed around 1600 by a young Shinto priestess named O-Kuni, Kabuki featured impromptu performances by women, often in a sexually enticing manner. To limit the seductive nature of Kabuki theater, the government in 1629 banned all female performers. However, the young boys who replaced the women merely continued the seductive style, thereby creating a theater of "pederasty." Consequently, in 1652 it was proclaimed that only grown men could act in Kabuki—a tradition that exists today.

Although there are isolated examples of erotic scrolls as early as the twelfth century, *ukiyo-e* established erotica as a legitimate genre of Japanese art. Sensualism and the techniques of sexual relations were evident in *ukiyo-e* throughout the course of its popularity. These erotic prints, called *shunga* ("spring pictures"), were often commissioned by ruling lords as wedding gifts to the mothers of prospective brides in order to instruct the daughter in sex education. The money made from this commissioned erotic art is often credited with establishing *ukiyo-e* as a prevalent art form. Eventually, the *shunga* were collected and bound into sex manuals. These sex manuals had two purposes: to depict the variety of sexual positions (the Japanese believed that there were 48) and to rate the local courtesans (*oyiran*). The rating system often included pictures and poetic verses, plus information on the courtesan's beauty, faults, address, and price. An example of the type of verse included with each picture is as follows: "Indeed, indeed / with all their hearts' sharing love's pillow: / stroking her Jeweled Gateway and taking / the girl's hand, causing her to grab his / Jade Stalk: what girl's face will not / change color, her breath come faster?" (Lane, 1978).

Although *ukiyo-e* often focused upon erotic themes, it was also incorporated in the most prominent literature of its time. *Tales of Genji,* which is *the* classic Japanese novel, was published in an illustrated edition, using *shunga* as vivid description. Consequently, *ukiyo-e* served the dual purpose of providing sexually relevant information to the viewer (the genitals were often prominently displayed) and creating a sensual ambiance to any theme or material it accompanied. Although not a predominant theme, rape is periodically represented in *ukiyo-e*. Scenes of forced entry and resistance are subtly portrayed in a variety of ways (hand gestures, facial expressions, looks of surprise, doors ajar, and so on), as well as in more explicit depictions.

The Meiji Restoration and Post-World War II Japan

In 1868, Japan restructured its govenment, caste system, and ethics. This period was known as the Meiji Restoration (named after Emperor Meiji). In contrast to the Edo period of the Tokugawa Shogunate, which stressed an isolationist policy among its reigning feudal lords, the Meiji Restoration reinstated power for the emperor and embarked on a policy of industrialization and expansion. The caste system was abolished in 1896, which provided considerable social mobility, with education and wealth being the primary agents of change. Finally, considerable efforts were also made to adhere to a Confucian ethos. Although these ethics were often part of the samurai creed, the Meiji Restoration had the effect of generalizing this belief system throughout the populace. The Japanese viewed this conservative moral code as being more consistent with its policy of industrialization. At a time when England was thoroughly Victorian, Japan sought to establish standards of propriety that reinforced its new industrial status.

The Confucian ideology had a specific set of moral precepts. Often called noble moral customs, these precepts stressed filial piety, decorum based on rank, loyalty, fearlessness, trust, truthfulness, and so on—all of which were ultimately integrated into the preservation of the family. Dore (1958) suggests that this ideology was translated into four separate policies. First, the government sought to establish a clear distinction between masculine and feminine roles. Purity was emphasized for women, whereas men were given tacit approval of sexual freedom, as long as it was limited to prostitution or concubines. These prostitution

176 Paul R. Abramson and Haruo Hayashi

districts (or *yū ka ku*) were justified as "an essential means of preserving the purity of the home" (Dore, 1958, p. 159). On the other hand, restrictions were invoked for rural phallicism and ritual promiscuity, plus pornography. However, by 1930 the pornography restrictions were relaxed in order to "reduce labor unrest and to take the students' minds off politics" (Kawashima, 1954, p. 221).

The second policy focused upon changing customs that might draw criticism from foreign nations. Included among the edicts were bylaws forbidding nakedness in the streets and mixed-sex bathing in public bathhouses. The populace was warned that "although this is the general custom and is not so despised among ourselves, in foreign countries this is looked on with great contempt. You should therefore consider it a great shame" (Dore, 1958, pp. 159–160).

In the third policy, the circumstances of married life were also addressed. Concubines, who were regarded as second-degree relatives in the early Meiji period. lost this status in a Supreme Court judgment in 1897 that became law in the Civil Code of 1898. Consequently, monogamy became an increasingly accepted ideal, despite the availability of prostitution. Also, a law was passed that stated that a husband must gain the wife's permission before the family would recognize a child by another woman and adopt it into the household. In the same vein, legislation was introduced that made adultery by the husband grounds for divorce (the inverse was true), but the proposal was deemed "impractical given the prevailing state of society."

The fourth policy reflected the finding that Western literature had a profound effect on the characteristics of Japanese male–female relations. Although the samurai scorned love as a detraction from masculine dignity, Japanese men now read of love as a regal emotion with many spiritual and personal commitments. Hence, Japanese civil codes started to incorporate references to "emotional bonding" between men and women. The impact of these changes on male–female relationships has continued throughout the twentieth century.

It is interesting to note that although restrictions were imposed, the Japanese did not equate sexuality with sin. Sexuality was still a natural human feeling that was capable of evoking considerable pleasure. However, sexual indulgence was largely curtailed by the relative importance of one's family, social, and governmental obligations. Consequently, an indirect form of sexual regulation occurred, and as such, the Japanese never institutionalized a specific set of morals about sex (Benedict, 1946).

Following World War II, Japan underwent a number of additional changes. First, the expansionistic policy and the militaristic hegemony were abolished. Second, the confusion and famine surrounding defeat forced a breakdown in social policy. Crime and prostitution increased, sexual segregation was relaxed, sexual relations were more open, and pornography became more prevalent. It is interesting to note that the pornographic literature that grew out of this period (known as *Nikutai-Bungaku* or "Literature of the Flesh") is unique in its combination of sexual and sadistic elements. Bondage, rape, and sadomasochistic themes became more prevalent, and the numbers of consumers increased proportionally. Kuro (1954) indicates that this literature was heralded as the "liberation of instinctual forces from the artificial restraints of feudal morality."

Besides the governmental and social changes, post-World War II Japan also sought to establish amiable relations with the Western powers and to revitalize the Japanese economy. To achieve this objective, Japan turned to the United States. Although this course of action is obviously related to the United States occupation, Japan also took considerable initiative in developing a comparable technology. However, besides incorporating the technological advances, Japan also emulated the social restrictions of the United States as a means of gaining further approval.

Presently, the laws governing pornography in Japan can be traced directly to this circumstance. As one of many gestures aimed at gaining acceptance and approval from the United States, Japan decided to avoid creating further offense to the American people. Consequently, what America deemed pornographic, Japan deemed likewise. However, as the reader will note in the following section, despite the similarities in post-World War II policy, the psychology of contemporary Japanese pornography is uniquely Japanese.

PORNOGRAPHY IN JAPAN IN 1984

It is still illegal in Japan to show pubic hair and adult genitals in sexually explicit stimuli. This is true for Japanese and imported pornography. Although magazines such as *Playboy* and *Penthouse* are available in Japan, the genitals are scratched off or blacked out with a large circle, and pubic hair (where marginally visible) is air-brushed away.

Despite the restrictions, uncensored film and pictorial pornography is available through underground sources or from Japanese travellers abroad. In this context it is interesting to note that the most prevalent form of contraband seized by custom agents in Japan is American and European film and pictorial pornography. Pornographic literature, however, is not banned since written pornography obviously does not violate the prohibition of pubic hair in visual display. Listed under English titles such as *Hungry Pussy,* cheap English-language erotica is as accessible as the more classic forms of erotic novels. Actually, prior to the availability of translated pornography, the Japanese would joke that one of the benefits of learning English was being able to read better pornography.

The Japanese restriction of pubic hair and adult genitals in visual depiction is a direct consequence of emulating an American policy. Following World War II, there were strict limitations on both visual and written pornography in America. Consequently, the Japanese sought to establish standards that approximated (and thus did not offend) American customs. Since the Japanese-language novels were unlikely to offend many Americans, the major initiative in Japan was to have the visual stimuli consistent with American norms. Consequently, visual stimuli would depict only the breasts and buttocks of adult men and women.

Although nearly 40 years have passed since World War II, and America has drastically changed its obscenity laws, Japan still maintains its ban against the visual display of pubic hair and adult genitals. This ban continues despite the accumulating evidence (contraband, public opinion, etc.) that the Japanese have considerable interest in more explicitly sexual material (Komatsu, 1974). Since prostitution is still illegal (though certainly available) pornography represents one of the more popular forms of sexual diversion. Strip shows, massage parlors, and atriums (a kind of stylized peep show that includes "artists" [male customers] and "female models") are also popular with Japanese men.

Of particular note in Japanese pornography (film and novel) is the recurring theme of bondage and rape. Although movies are much less explicit than their American and European counterparts, the plot often involves the rape of a high school girl. This theme is also evident in the cheap erotic novels (with titles like *Gang-Raped Daughter*) and sexual cartoons. In fact, one of the best ways to ensure the success of a Japanese adult film is to include the bondage and rape of a young woman. This juxtaposition of sexuality and aggression is evident in almost all forms of Japanese sexual material, including cartoons, films, and sexological museums. Consequently, it should come as no surprise to learn that such stimuli is designed solely for a male audience. Although sexual information is readily available for Japanese women, visual pornography is not created for that aduience.

CROSS-CULTURAL AND THEORETICAL CONSIDERATIONS

One of the most obvious differences between Japanese and American pornography is that American pornography is substantially more explicit. Genitals, pubic hair, sexual intercourse, oral-genital sex, and many variations thereof are readily apparent in American pornography.

Although American pornography is more explicit than Japanese pornography, it is compartmentalized within American society. For instance, *Playboy* and *Penthouse* are legal magazines, but are sold only in selected stores. Moreover, in many stores, although such magazines are purchasable, they are not accessible to the customer. Whereas this latter procedure is often utilized to control theft and loitering, it is clear that such stimuli, though legal and widespread, are only selectively available. Second, although it is legal to publish photographs of nude men and women, such photographs are limited to sexually identified books and magazines. Exceptions include anthropological magazines (such as *National Geographic*) when nonwhite races are the focus of study and photography books and magazines. General circulation magazines such as *Time, Newsweek, TV Guide,* and *Business Week* do not contain sexually explicit photographs. Consequently, it is evident that there are clearly delineated vehicles for the display of sexually and nonsexually explicit stimuli. Finally, even though it is legal to include explicit sexual material in a film, all films are categorized (i.e., rated) according to the amount of sexual content. Moreover, despite the prevalence of nudity in a predominant number of American films, American public television is void of nudity. Once again, although it is legal and available, sexuality on film is compartmentalized according to transmission (public TV vs. private TV and movies) and outlet (X-rated theater vs. general access theater).

In contrast, the Japanese are more consistent in their presentation of sexuality in the media. Nudity is evident in both sexually identified and general circulation magazines. For instance, the weekly general-interest magazines will often include several photographs of nude women (plus ratings of local massage parlors). Although such magazines are oriented predominantly for businessmen, the inclusion of sexual photographs is also assumed to interest the business audience. In this regard, it is apparent that rigid boundaries do not exist for the publication of sexual material. In fact, nudity or sexual themes appear in Japanese teen magazines, sports magazines, fashion magazines, and so on. Consequently, the magazines are different in theme and emphasis; differences do not result from self-imposed barriers to the publication of sexual material.

Japanese public television is also different from its American counterpart. Overtly sexual material and nudity are permissible. For example, a Japanese television program known as the *11 P.M. Show* can feature a strip tease, bare breasts and buttocks, reportage on massage parlors, expert authorities on sex, and so on. Similarly, the Japanese public-access movie channels can feature R-rated movies such as *Emanuelle* (with some air-brushing). Finally, even Japanese commercials and advertisements have more flexibility in sexual content. Thus, as long as certain prohibitions (like the ban on pubic hair and adult genitals) are maintained, there is considerable freedom in the publication of sexual material. In fact, prepubescent girls are occasionally featured in the nude (in books with such titles as *Nymphs*). Since these girls are void of pubic hair, the publication of such photographs is not identified as a violation of Japanese obscenity laws (as long as intercourse is not portrayed or implied).

Although the Japanese have considerable flexibility in the display of sexual material, their publications, movies, and television shows are far from being inundated with such stimuli. In fact, in most regards, they approximate American standards, except for the lack of rigid boundaries. Consequently, while Americans will publish informative (and clearly labeled) sexuality texts, the Japanese will include this information in popular magazines. One such Japanese teen magazine, call *Hot Dog Press,* recently presented an exhaustive review of sexuality. The issue was called "Thinking About Adam and Eve," and it included a thorough and informative discussion of sexual anatomy, contraception, sexual myths, sexual intercourse, oral-genital sex, masturbation, orgasm, and so on. Selected coverage was also provided for homosexuality, bisexuality, sado-masochism, swinging, vibrators, sex toys, Masters and Johnson's research, and the Hite Reports.

The consistency in Japanese sexual behavior is evident in other domains. The initiation of sex in adolescence is a good example. The initiation of petting (mean age for males is 16.38, for females, 16.82) and the initiation of sexual inter-course (mean age for males is 16.90, for females, 16.67) occur at approximately the same time (Mamiya, 1981). Another example of this consistency is evident in contemporary Japanese novels. As early as the 1930s, critically acclaimed novel-ists could include sexually explicit passages without violating obscenity laws or diminishing the widespread appeal of their work. Consequently many of the classic twentieth-century novels, by authors such as Yasunari Kawabata (a Nobel Prize winner), Kobo Abe, Junichiro Tanizaki, or Yukio Mishima, contain sexu-ally explicit material within the context of their highly regarded stories.

One other area of major difference between Japanese and American pornogra-phy is the prevalence of bondage and rape in Japanese adult movies. Although when compared to American standards, these Japanese movies are only mildly sexually explicit, they contain vivid rape and bondage themes, which are usually curtailed or isolated in America cinema. The remainder of this chapter discusses the theoretical and cultural implications of this curious finding.

Rape and Aggressive Pornography

Rape is a tragic and increasing crime in the United States. Legislators, en-forcement officials, feminist organizations, and parents are desperately trying to curtail the incidence of rape. By law, it is a felony, with the possibility of life imprisonment. In practice, it is a crime that is often difficult to prove. Moreover, women are reluctant to report a rape; the trial proceedings are usually humiliat-ing; plea bargaining for aggravated assault, or assault and battery, is often involved; and so on (Federal Bureau of Investigation, 1977). Consequently, concerned citizens and organizations are trying to minimize some of the pre-cipitating factors in rape. Women are cautioned about traveling alone, security procedures are stressed, self-defense is taught, and stimuli that might elicit rape are severely restricted. In the latter case, such stimuli might include a movie that depicts rape, especially if the outcome is positive or void of negative conse-quences. The underlying assumption (which is discussed in more detail in many of the other chapters in this book) is that such stimuli might facilitate rape through either modeling or minimizing the tragic abuse of this behavior.

In comparison to Western nations, Japan has a substantially lower incidence of rape: in the United States there are 34.5 reported rapes per 100,000 population;

in England, 10.1; in West Germany, 10.7; in France, 3.2; and in Japan, 2.4. (In fact, all crimes are substantially lower in Japan). The discrepancy in the incidence between the United States and Japan cannot be attributed to variance in the laws because the laws are basically the same (although prosecution rates may vary). Moreover, Japanese women are just as reluctant to report a rape and similarly view the trial proceedings as humiliating. Consequently, it is of considerable value to isolate those factors that contribute to the diminished incidence of rape in Japan. The remainder of this discussion focuses upon internal contraints (i.e., within the person) versus external (i.e., societal) constraints.

If there is a direct connection between the prevalence of rape imagery and rape behavior, Japan should have an overwelming occurrence of rape. As indicated in the preceding paragraph's rape statistics, it does not. Consequently, it is our suggestion that mediating circumstances are involved, especially in the form of internal constraints to maladaptive behavior.

In Benedict's (1946) discussion of the Japanese people, she cites "a strong sense of obligation" as a salient factor in Japanese psychology. In this context, obligation implies responsibility, respect, and commitment in primary relationships (parents, children, husband–wife, employer–employee, and so on). Benedict suggested that the Japanese are conscientious in their obligatory responsibilities because those responsibilities are relevant to their self-respect. If they are derelict in their obligations, the Japanese experience shame (*haji*) in regard to self and family. This shame is a critical factor in Japanese psychology, especially in terms of sensitivity to evaluation by others. Benedict indicates that shame is also a fundamental part of Japan's system of morality. Thus, failure to adhere to explicit signposts of good behavior, failure to balance obligations, and so on, induces *haji*. The Japanese also view shame as being aligned with virtue, since a person who is sensitive to shame will abide by the rules of good behavior. Consequently, a man who knows shame is sometimes translated as either a "virtuous man" or a "man of honor" (Benedict, 1946).

It is not surprising that a culture that emphasizes order, obligation, and virtue should have a low crime rate. Prosecution and penalty are only one aspect of the punitive consequences of criminal behavior. Intense shame drawn to self and family is an equally viable constraint. Where rape is concerned, the Japanese also provide extensive media coverage of the rapist's name, thereby ensuring that public shame will result. It is interesting to note that cultures that utilize guilt as a major sanction (such as the United States) also utilize confession and atonement as a means of relieving guilt. Cultures, such as the Japanese, that emphasize shame, do not provide a system of relief. Shameful behavior is shameful behavior whether it is confessed or not. This later circumstance is related to the Japanese perception of self. Again, it is less compartmentalized than American standards. To the Japanese, every overt action is representative of the entire person. If any shameful behavior is exhibited, the entire person is assumed to be shameful. Similarly, the Japanese do not have a word for self-identity. A Japanese person is identified (by self and others) by virtue of overt behavior.

There are several other factors that contribute to the low incidence of rape in Japan. Since the tenth century, the Japanese have integrated commercial sexuality into their social system. In the past, prostitution has been widely accessible and publicly endorsed. In present-day Japan, massage parlors satisfy a similar objective. In each instance the Japanese government and people have recognized the necessity of sexual availability. The Japanese have been direct and forthright with this objective because they do not connect sexuality with sin. When sexual prohibitions are instituted, they are usually in response to critical evaluation by foreign countries (i.e., a shame response). It is our opinion that sexual availability, void of public condemnation, has contributed to the low incidence of rape.

Finally, a number of Japanese authors (e.g., Komatsu, 1974) have also suggested that Asian populations are less sexualized than Caucasian or black populations. They cite secondary sex characteristics (less pubic hair, smaller breasts, etc.) as evidence. Unfortunately, the data on sexual frequencies (intercourse, etc.) are not particularly reliable, and it is not clear whether competing responses (such as nurturance) are mediating sexual expression.

The relatively low frequency of rape behavior, in the presence of abundant rape stimuli, is also interesting from a theoretical perspective. The Japanese view the availability of such stimuli (which has existed since the *ukiyo-e*) as a cathartic valve. It is presumed to provide vicarious satisfaction of a socially unacceptable behavior. In a culture that endorses strict codes of behavior and highly defined roles, the depiction of rape also provides a context in which Japanese men can vicariously abandon all of the explicit signposts of good behavior. This assumption is in contrast to the prevailing American perspective that suggests that sexual stimuli associated with rape will provoke rape (Liebert, Neale, & Davison, 1973). Obviously, when examined within a cross-cultural framework, the relationship between such stimuli and rape behavior is more complex. Perhaps, as Abramson (1982, 1984) has suggested, sexual expression is ultimately an existential phenomenon whereby a variety of determinants are cognitively evaluated for the acceptability of response. In Japan, the internal constraints are usually sufficient to exert cognitive control. In the United States, the internal constraints are not as stringent, which may account for the greater incidence of rape. Moreover, in addition to the absence of internal constraints, the American rapist will often minimize the external constraints—given the difficulty in proving rape, the victim's humiliation in the trial proceedings, the lack of convictions and penalties, and so on.

In conclusion, we offer some policy suggestions. If the United States is truly committed to lowering the incidence of rape, a macrocosmic intervention is necessary. First, it is not clear that rape stimuli are directly related to rape behavior. Although a number of experimental studies have provided tangential evidence, the cross-cultural data suggest that this relationship is far from being a direct causal relationship. Rape stimuli may be prohibited for a variety of reasons (demeaning to women, etc.), but such restrictions may have little relevance for the frequency of rape. Also, given the cumbersome U.S. legal system, it is unlikely that drastic changes will result from alterations in this domain. That is, the trials will always be humiliating, plea bargaining will always be involved, convictions will always be difficult, and so on. Therefore, we suggest five interrelated alternatives: (1) recognition and support for harmonious family relations, including readily accessible and affordable therapeutic centers that provide family therapy, parent training, mutual support systems, and so on; (2) educational programs within the school and religious systems specifically designed to malign rape; (3) governmentally sanctioned prostitution; (4) an aggressive advertising campaign designed to ridicule and humiliate the act of rape; and (5) public humiliation, within the media, of all convicted rapists. Although these procedures are certainly short of internal constraints, over time they could be integrated into American social consciences.

What do we think is the likelihood that the United States will adopt these (or comparable) procedures? Frankly, we are not optimistic. Yet, if we truly care about this tragic crime, we are going to need more than symbolic gestures (such as limiting rape stimuli in movies) to effectuate substantial change.

REFERENCES

Abramson, P. R. (1982). Implications of the sexual system for the contraceptive process. In D. Byrne and W. Fisher (Eds.) *Adolescents, sex, and contraception* (pp. 49–61) Hillsdale, NJ: Erlbaum.

Abramson, P. R. (1984) *Sarah: A sexual biography*. Albany, New York: State University of New York Press.

Benedict, R. (1946). *The chrysanthemum and the sword*. New York: Houghton, Mifflin.

Dore, R. P. (1958). *City life in Japan*. Los Angeles: University of California Press.

Federal Bureau of Investigation (i977). *Uniform crime reports*.

Kawashima, Takeyoshi (1954). *Kekkon*.

Komatsu, S. (Ed.) (1974). *Seibunka o kangaeru*. Miya Shobō..

Kuro, Hyoosuke (1954). Nikutai bungaku no seiri. *Shisoo no Kagaku, 4*(3)

Lane, R. (1978). *Images from the floating world: The Japanese print*. New York: Putnam.

Liebert, R. M., Neale, J. M., and Davison, E. S. (1973). *The early window*. New York: Pergamon Press.

Mamiya, T. (1981). Seisa o meguru shomondai—Seisa shinrigaku kara mite *psychology*, (Saikorogi) *19*, 30–37.

7

Sexual Stratification, Pornography, and Rape in the United States*

LARRY BARON
MURRAY A. STRAUS

Current public concern with the crime of rape has its roots in the threefold increase in officially reported rapes since 1960 and in the activities of the women's movement (Brownmiller, 1975; Largen, 1976; Rose, 1977a, 1977b). Feminists, although not of one mind in theoretical discussions of the causes of rape, do seem to agree that analysis of rape must consider the constellation of political, economic, and ideological institutions that together constitute the macrosociological background for sexual violence against women (Clark & Lewis, 1977).

Despite the theoretical importance attributed to macrostructural factors in the feminist explanation of rape, there appears to be a paucity of research using social system level data in both feminist and nonfeminist research of rape (for

*Paper presented at the American Society of Criminology annual meeting, Denver, November 11, 1983. The research reported in this paper is part of the Family Violence Research Program (FVRP), and the State And Regional Indicators Archive (SRIA). A bibliography listing papers and books of the FVRP and SRIA is available from the Family Research Laboratory, University of New Hampshire.

We are pleased to express our appreciation to participants in the FVRP seminar and Kersti Yllo for many helpful suggestions and criticism of an earlier draft, and to the Graduate School of the University of New Hampshire and NIMH grant T32 MH15161 for financial support.

PORNOGRAPHY AND
SEXUAL AGGRESSION

185

three exceptions see Blau & Blau, 1982; Ellis & Beattie, 1983; Stack & Kanavy, 1983). Our intention in this paper is to test three hypotheses derived from feminist discussions of rape, using the 50 states and the District of Columbia as the units for analysis.

THE FEMINIST VIEW OF RAPE

Fundamental to the feminist view of rape is that violence against women, both sexual and nonsexual violence, is an expression of a patriarchical (male dominant) social system. The subjugation of women by men is seen as built into the organization of society—in the opportunity and reward structure—so that women are systematically disadvantaged in respect to attaining valued socioeconomic resources on which the perpetuation of male power depends. Thus, rape is construed as integral to the historic powerlessness of women in male-dominated societies.

Cross-cultural evidence for this view has been offered by Sanday (1981). Sanday hypothesized that the incidence of rape would vary according to the degree of power and status attributed to women in tribal societies. She found that, in societies where women are excluded from positions of power and their contributions to the functioning of society are assigned little significance, there is a high incidence of rape. By contrast, in societies based on the equal distribution of power, mutual respect, and appreciation for the contribution that women make to society, rape is infrequent or almost nonexistent.

Others have suggested that rape is a manifestation of the asymmetrical pattern of male–female sex-role socialization in which males are taught to be aggressive and dominant, while females are taught to be passive and submissive (Greer, 1973; Griffin, 1971, September; Russell, 1975; Weis & Borges, 1977). The suggestion is that normal sex-role socialization is responsible for shaping men into assailants and women into victims. According to Weis and Borges, (1977), "Rooted in a social structure which is characterized by male domination, the socialization processes of the male and female act to mold women into victims and provide the procedure for legitimizing them in this role" (p. 44).

Research indicates that the belief in traditional sex roles is correlated with attitudes endorsing violence against women as well as aggression against women. In one study, McConahay and McConahay (1977) examined 17 primitive cultures from the Human Relations Area Files and found a higher degree of violence in cultures marked by an inflexible sex-role system. In another study, Burt (1980) interviewed a representative sample of 598 Minnesota adults and found that the belief in sex-role stereotypes was positively correlated with the endorsement of rape myths, violence against women, and the belief that sexual relationships are necessarily deceptive, manipulative, and exploitative. Burt's findings have recently been corroborated by Check and Malamuth (1983). In the same study, Check and Malamuth also found that college students who scored high on Burt's Sex Role Stereotype scale were more likely to become sexually aroused by rape depictions and to report a greater likelihood of raping than were those who did not hold stereotypical beliefs.

Early feminist writing on rape emphasized that rape functions as an instrument of social control whereby "all men keep all women in a state of fear" (Brownmiller, 1975, p. 15; see Griffin, 1971, September, for several parallel statements). While Brownmiller has been amply criticized for her hyperbolic indictment of all men (Curtis, 1976; Elshtain, 1976–1977; Geis, 1977; Schwendinger & Schwendinger, 1983), there is evidence that rape and the fear of rape act to restrict the behavioral options of women and to prevent their full participation in society (Riger & Gordon, 1981).

The feminist literature suggests, then, that rape and the fear of rape are a reflection of a sexual stratification system in which women are subordinate members. This suggests the following hypothesis:

Hypothesis
1 The lower the status of women in a state,
     the higher the incidence of rape.

Although feminist writers agree that rape is an effort to keep women subordinate, there might be disagreement about whether rape will be positively or negatively related to the status of women. Russell (1975) argues that the desire of feminist women to break out of traditional sex roles may anger men and increase the number of rapes. In Russell's (1975) words: "Rape is the way some men express their hostility to women. More threatened male egos may mean more rapes" (p. 14).

Pornography and Rape

A fundamental issue in discussions of pornography is the effect of various types of erotica on the incidence of sex crimes. Much of the current concern over this issue has been generated by feminist organizations such as Women Against Pornography, Women Against Violence Against Women, and Women Against Violence in Pornography and Media. Feminists are far from agreement in their assessment of the definition, meaning, and effects of pornography (see Elshtain, 1982; English, 1980; Orlando, 1982, December; and Willis, 1982, December). However, most feminists would probably agree with Laura Lederer (1980), who holds that "pornography is the ideology of a culture which promotes and condones rape, woman-battering, and other crimes against women" (pp. 19–20).

The feminist contention that the proliferation of pornography is linked to rape and other violent crimes against women is at odds with the report of the Commission on Obscenity and Pornography published in 1970. The findings of the various researchers (who used a variety of methodologies. research designs, and samples in their studies) are startling in their similarity. The commission felt that the weight of evidence indicated that there was no relationship between exposure to pornography and the incidence of sex crimes.

Since the report on pornography was published, there have been a number of criticisms leveled at the commission's findings and a series of new studies by experimental social psychologists (see Donnerstein, 1983; Malamuth & Donnerstein, 1983; and Nelson, 1982, for three excellent reviews of this literature). These studies show that exposing male subjects to pornography with violent content (e.g., rape depictions) results in significant increases in self-reported likelihood of raping, endorsement of rape myths and attitudes supporting violence against women, and aggression against women using the Buss shock apparatus (see Malamuth and Donnerstein, 1983, for a review). These data suggest a modification rather than a contradiction of the pornography commission conclusions because those conclusions were not based on experiments using pornography with *violent* content. Therefore the commission's conclusion of no relationship between pornography and antisocial behavior is limited to pornography that contains nonviolent depictions of nudity and sexual acts.

The issue, however, is far from settled. Almost all the new research on pornography and rape is laboratory experimental studies. As excellent as these studies are, the external validity of the findings is unknown.[1] Moreover, none of these studies addresses the structural conditions that are at the heart of the feminist theory of rape. Since this research uses societal level data, it can throw

---

[1]One of the few macrosociological investigations of the relationship between pornography and rape is Kutchinsky's (1973) study of sex crimes in Denmark. In the 1960s Denmark provided the context for a unique natural experiment by gradually legalizing pornography. This was done by decriminalizing the sale of pornographic fiction in 1967 and then in 1969 decriminalizing pornographic photographs. Kutchinsky demonstrated that as pornography became more accessible there was a parallel drop in the number of reported sex crimes. More specifically, there were considerable reductions in reports of exhibitionism, peeping, statutory rape, verbal indecency, child molesting, and physical indecency against women. In attempting to explain these changes, Kutchinsky argued that the widespread availability of pornography was the direct cause of the drop in sexual offenses. Kutchinsky went on to suggest that the pronographic novels served as a safety valve for the more intelligent sex offenders while the pornographic photographs provided the same function for the less imaginative and less intelligent sex deviates.

Kutchinsky's data are usually taken as evidence that the availability of pornography siphons off potentially dangerous sexual impulses (the catharsis hypothesis). However, almost no empirical evidence supports the idea of catharsis (Berkowitz, 1971, December; Straus, 1974). In addition, a close look at his data shows that, although the total number of sexual offenses decreased, the number of *rapes* reported either stabilized or increased (Kutchinsky, 1973, p. 166). The change in the composite number of sex offenses hides increases in the number of rapes. The fact that rape, one of the most serious sex crimes, did not decrease after the legalization of pornography, led Court (1976, p. 144) to contend that this outcome represents a "pyrrhic victory."

light on the question of the extent to which the laboratory findings are generally applicable. The specific hypothesis we tested for this purpose is:

Hypothesis
2   The higher the readership of pornography
    in a state, the higher the rape rate.

Rape as a Crime of Violence

For several years now, the conceptualization of rape as either a sex crime or a violent crime has been an issue of debate. Those who see rape as a crime of violence claim that, when rape is defined as sexual, attention is shifted away from the assailant to the victim's role in precipitating the attack and often results in victim blaming. As a result, feminists have relentlessly argued that rape is not a sexual act, but an act of violence in which men exert their power, dominance, and control over women (Brownmiller, 1975; Griffin, 1971, September; Russell, 1975; Sanday, 1981; see Groth, 1979, for clinical evidence of this view).

If there is validity to the argument that rape is a crime of violence, we would expect rape to be positively correlated with other violent crimes such as murder, assault, and robbery. Thus, rape may be seen as part of a general pattern of violence in society and subject to many of the same determinants as other violent crimes. This leads us to the following hypothesis:

Hypothesis
3   The higher the rate of nonsexual violent
    crime, the higher the rape rate.

DATA AND METHODS

The variables used in this study are discussed in two groups. The first group consists of the dependent variable (the incidence of rape) and control variables (state characteristics such as the percentage of urban dwellers and the percentage of blacks). These variables are described in this section because they figure in all subsequent sections of the chapter. The second group of variables consists of the independent variables needed to examine the theoretical issues of this chapter. Since some of these are composite indexes that require considerable explanation, they will be described at the beginning of the sections in which the results are presented, thus avoiding the need for readers to remember or look up the details when considering the findings.

Rape Statistics

The data on rape used in this chapter are for rapes known to and recorded by the police, as given in the annual FBI Uniform Crime Reports (UCR) publication

TABLE 7.1

Rank Order of States with Respect to Rape, Status of Women, and Sex Magazine Circulation

Rank	Rapes known to the police per 100,000 population, 1979		SWX, 1970–1979		Rate per 100,000 adults, 1979 Hustler		Playboy		SMCX, 1979	
	State	cke29[a]	State	z57[a]	State	ma151r[a]	State	ma239r[a]	State	xma32[a]
1	ALAS	71.9	ALAS	70	ALAS	3247	ALAS	10208	ALAS	4.58
2	NEV	59.5	CONN	62	NEV	2594	NEV	9641	NEV	2.94
3	CAL	53.9	MD	61	HAWA	1924	WYO	8072	HAWA	1.89
4	COLO	53.1	VT	61	N.H.	1683	COLO	6588	D.C.	1.28
5	FLA	51.6	COLO	61	DEL	1653	OREG	5785	OREG	1.07
6	N.M.	46.9	N.J.	60	ARIZ	1627	IDA	5700	WYO	1.01
7	WASH	46.4	N.H.	60	KANS	1517	D.C.	5587	ARIZ	0.88
8	ARIZ	45.7	WASH	59	NEBR	1479	ARIZ	5572	KANS	0.78
9	D.C.	45.3	WIS	57	ILL	1479	WASH	5570	N.H.	0.42
10	TEX	45.1	NEBR	57	OREG	1419	HAWA	5496	CAL	0.32
11	MICH	44.5	HAWA	55	VT	1411	MONT	5425	GA	0.21
12	OREG	44.4	OREG	55	TEX	1407	CAL	5234	MD	0.11
13	GA	43.3	ARIZ	55	CAL	1388	MINN	4920	WASH	0.08
14	MD	39.4	MASS	55	MICH	1359	OKLA	4891	VT	0.07
15	LA	38.6	N.Y.	55	S.D.	1294	KANS	4852	ILL	0.04
16	TENN	34.5	D.C.	55	FLA	1289	N.M.	4728	IDA	0.03
17	S.C.	34.3	CAL	54	W.VA	1281	IOWA	4542	FLA	0.03
18	MO	33.6	S.D.	54	N.J.	1249	TEX	4318	COLO	0.02
19	OKLA	33.0	IOWA	53	WYO	1215	NEBR	4253	TEX	0.01
20	HAWA	32.3	MINN	53	N.D.	1214	VT	4243	MICH	0.00
21	OHIO	31.8	KANS	53	WASH	1195	N.H.	4216	OKLA	-0.01

190

	A		B		C		D		E	
22	INDI	31.1	FLA	53	N.C.	1183	S.D.	4180	DEL	−0.01
23	N.Y.	30.6	MICH	52	N.M.	1182	FLA	4062	N.M.	−0.03
24	ILL	29.4	WYO	51	MD	1173	ILL	3961	VA	−0.06
25	UTAH	27.9	DEL	50	OHIO	1159	VA	3898	OHIO	−0.14
26	N.J.	27.8	ME	50	PA	1139	MICH	3846	N.J.	−0.16
27	DEL	27.8	TENN	49	ME	1137	MD	3845	NEBR	−0.16
28	WYO	27.6	R.I.	49	KY	1125	GA	3834	MONT	−0.18
29	ALA	27.5	ARK	49	MASS	1117	WIS	3814	MINN	−0.38
30	ARK	27.3	INDI	49	VA	1095	DEL	3810	N.D.	−0.38
31	VA	27.1	PA	48	INDI	1078	UTAH	3745	INDI	−0.41
32	KANS	26.4	N.D.	48	D.C.	1074	N.D.	3723	MASS	−0.42
33	MASS	24.8	N.C.	47	N.Y.	1059	INDI	3658	S.D.	−0.42
34	CONN	24.1	MONT	46	TENN	1058	CONN	3547	N.Y.	−0.45
35	VT	22.9	KY	45	MONT	1051	N.J.	3495	IOWA	−0.47
36	MISS	21.7	GA	45	ALA	1028	MASS	3395	ME	−0.51
37	PA	21.6	MO	44	LA	1015	OHIO	3356	LA	−0.52
38	MINN	21.5	NEV	44	WIS	1014	LA	3345	WIS	−0.54
39	NEBR	21.5	TEX	44	CONN	988	ME	3339	N.C.	−0.57
40	IDA	20.6	OHIO	43	COLO	972	R.I.	3109	ALA	−0.61
41	MONT	20.6	IDA	43	S.C.	898	PA	3070	PA	−0.63
42	KY	20.4	MISS	42	IOWA	888	MO	2942	S.C.	−0.65
43	N.C.	20.3	VA	41	MINN	882	N.Y.	2839	TENN	−0.66
44	N.H.	17.1	N.M.	41	GA	860	N.C.	2693	CONN	−0.67
45	S.D.	16.4	ILL	39	MISS	852	ALA	2629	KY	−0.69
46	WIS	16.1	S.C.	36	ARK	758	KY	2613	W.VA	−0.82
47	W.VA	15.5	OKLA	34	R.I.	670	TENN	2594	R.I.	−0.84
48	R.I.	15.2	W.VA	34	MO	632	S.C.	2501	ARK	−0.98
49	ME	11.9	UTAH	28	OKLA	606	ARK	2244	MO	−1.12
50	IOWA	11.0	ALA	28	IDA	488	W.VA	2195	MISS	−1.15
51	N.D.	8.2	LA		UTAH	299	MISS	2179	UTAH	−1.17

[a]Variable identification code names, as used in the State and Regional Indicators Archive, University of New Hampshire.

"Crime In The United States." The underreporting of rape in the UCR, as well as many other problems with the UCR data, is well known (see Hindelang, 1974, for a summary and analysis). We used the UCR data despite these problems for two reasons. First, other presumably more complete data [such as the National Crime Survey (NCS)] are not available by state. For example, the NCS data are available for a few large cities. Even if there were a sufficient number of cities, city data would not be satisfactory because data on some of the theoretically crucial independent variables (such as the legal status of women) are only available for states. The second reason for using the UCR data despite problems such as underreporting, is that the deficiencies of the UCR may not be as serious as is widely believed, especially when the research focus is to estimate the degree of association between variables rather than to estimate the number of rapes (see Hindelang, 1974).

SIZE AND CONSISTENCY OF STATE DIFFERENCES IN RAPE

Two important preliminary questions are whether there is sufficient state-to-state variation in the UCR rape rate to be worth analysis and whether such differences are consistent from year to year. To begin answering these questions, we ranked the states from highest to lowest incidence of rape in 1960, 1970, 1979, and 1980 (the rank for 1979 is shown in Table 7.1).[2] These rankings showed large differences between top and bottom states, and these differences tended to persist over the 20-year period examined. In 1960, for example, the top-ranking state (Alaska) had a rate of 20.3 rapes per 100,000 population. This was 9.5 times the rate for North Dakota, the state with the lowest incidence of rape. In 1980, rape rates in general had tripled, but Alaska was still almost at the top (second) and North Dakota still had the lowest incidence of rape.

The fact that the same states have tended to remain at the top and bottom of the ranking since 1960 is shown by the correlations in Table 7.2. In addition to the correlations shown in Table 7.2, we also computed the correlations for each year since 1975 (i.e., 1975 with 1976, 1976 with 1977, etc.). The mean of these five correlations is .97. Nevertheless, over longer time spans there have been some important shifts. The correlation of the rate for 1980 with the rate for 1960 is only .62.

The fact that the year-to-year correlations for each successive year from 1975 to 1980 are almost perfect suggests that, whatever the processes underlying the production of these rates, they are consistent. At the same time, the gradual decrease in the correlations as the time interval between measurements increases suggests that the rates can and do reflect changes over time—either in the true incidence rate or the recording methods.

---

[2]We began with 1960 because this was the first census year for which UCR data on rape became available by state. We ended with 1980 because it was the most current available data at the time this project began.

TABLE 7.2

Temporal Consistency of UCR Rape Rates,
1960–1980

Year	Between-state correlation[a]		
	1960	1970	1980
1960	—	.81	.62
1970		—	.74
1980			—

[a]All correlations are statistically significant at the .001 level.

Control Variables

Analyses such as those in this chapter could produce misleading or spurious results if the independent and dependent variables are correlated with a common third variable. Suppose the Status of Women index (SWX) is found to be correlated with the rape rate. If both the status of women and the incidence of rape are greater in the more urban states, the correlation between the status of women and rape might simply reflect the degree to which the states are urbanized rather than an intrinsic association between the status of women and rape. The same possibility of spurious correlation could occur because of confounding with certain other variables. To deal with this problem we introduced statistical controls for the following five variables which are known to be related to the incidence of rape at the individual level: (1) percentage living in Standard Metropolitan Statistical Areas (SMSAs), (2) percentage black, (3) percentage with incomes below federal poverty level, (4) percentage age 18–24, and (5) sex ratio for 15–24 year olds.

Method of Analysis

The procedure followed to test each hypothesis started with computing zero order correlations and the inspection of scatterplots for outliers and possible nonlinear relationships. Next we computed the correlations of all the independent and control variables with each other to determine if any were high enough to produce a problem with multicolinearity. Since the highest correlation among the nine independent variables (four theoretically based independent variables and five control variables) was .74, and since most of the correlations were well below that, we did not consider multicolinearity to be a serious threat.

The main findings of the study are those resulting from multiple regression analyses. These were computed to determine whether each of the theoretically posited independent variables are significantly related to the incidence of rape after partialing out the effects of the other hypothesized and control variables. Finally, certain regressions were replicated to deal with methodological threats to the validity of the results, such as outliers that might be unduly influencing the results and artifacts from the use of ratio variables.

THE STATUS OF WOMEN AND RAPE

The Status of Women Index

In a study entitled "The Demographic Aspects of the Changing Status of Women in Europe," Hommes (1978) defined the status of women as "the position women have as a group, compared with men as a group, in different fields of society" (p. 27). For example, if women were to earn the same as men, they would have equal status in this aspect of the economic–occupational structure. To the extent that they do not, there is sexual inequality.

The term *patriarchy* has been used by several feminist writers to refer to societies in which such sexual inequalities are typical of all social institutions, including the family, church, political, educational, and legal institutions. Thus, to measure sexual inequality adequately requires a multifaceted index covering many spheres of life. The Status Of Women Index (SWX) used in this research was developed by Yllo and Straus (Yllo, 1983; Yllo & Straus, 1981, April). Although lack of data prevented inclusion of several key institutional spheres, such as the church, the SWX is a step in the direction of creating a comprehensive index. It uses 22 indicators of sexual equality, covering four key aspects of society: economic, educational, political, and legal.[3]

The procedure for constructing the index was first to z score each of the indicators and then sum them to obtain a score for each of the four dimensions. The overall SWX used in this chapter was obtained by z scoring and then

---

[3]The indicators making up this index (grouped by dimension) are (1) *ecnonomic dimension:* percentage of women in the labor force; percentage of females in professional and technical occupations; percentage of females in managerial, administrative occupations; male unemployment rate as percentage of female rate, female median income as percentage of male, for full-time workers; (2) *educational dimension:* percentage of females graduating from high school as a percentage of male rate; percentage of females enrolled in post-secondary schools; percentage of female high school interscholastic athletes; percentage of female high school administrators; (3) *political dimension:* percentage of female members in U.S. Congress; percentage of female members of state senate; percentage of female members of state house; percentage of female judges on major appellate and trial courts; (4) *legal dimension:* no occupations barred to women; equal pay laws; fair employment practices act; no maximum hour restrictions for females; proof of resistance not required for rape conviction; corroboration of testimony not required for rape conviction; husband and wife jointly responsible for family support; husband and wife have equal right to sue for personal injury; husband and wife have equal right to sue for loss of consortium; wife's property rights unrestricted; wife's right to use maiden name unrestricted; wife's right to maintain separate domicile unrestricted; ratified federal Equal Rights Amendment; passed a state Equal Rights Amendment.

summing each of the four dimensions. Thus the overall SWX is based on the combining of four conposite items. The alpha coefficient of reliability is .54. Given the diversity of the four dimensions, even this moderately sized alpha coefficient is noteworthy. The second column of Table 7.1 gives the SWX scores for each state.

Previous research using this index revealed a nonlinear relationship between the status of women and the rate of wife-beating (Yllo & Straus, 1981, April). Wife beating was highest in states in the lowest quintile on the SWX. As the SWX score increased, the rate of wife-beating declined—up to a point. In the quintile of states where the status of women is highest, the rate of wife-beating went up sharply. The tendency for wife-beating to decrease as the status of women increases in the first four quintiles was interpreted as reflecting the principle that the greater the degree of social inequality, the more coercion is needed to keep subordinates in their place. On the other hand, the increase in wife-beating in states where women have the highest status may reflect increased marital conflict growing out of rapid social change in the sex roles and in the balance of power between husband and wife. In the light of these findings, there may be a similar nonlinear relationship between the status of women and the incidence of rape.

Correlation Analysis

The simple correlation between the SWX and the 1979 UCR rape rate is .17, which is not statistically significant. Nevertheless, the fact that there should be any tendency for the rape rate to go up as the status of women increases is directly contrary to the hypothesis. Inspection of the scatterplot, however, revealed that what little correlation there is was due to one extreme outlier case— Alaska. Alaska has both a very high SWX score and a very high rape rate. The correlation without Alaska is essentially zero (.03).

We also investigated the possibility of a nonlinear relationship. The SWX was grouped into deciles, and the mean rape rate was plotted for each decile. No meaningful nonlinear relationship could be observed. The test for nonlinearity produced by the SCSS program Breakdown was also not significant. Our findings, like those of Ellis and Beattie (1983), therefore provide no support for the hypothesis that the higher the status of women, the lower the rape rate.

PORNOGRAPHY AND RAPE

The Sex Magazine Circulation Index

There is virtually no agreement on either the conceptual or operational definition of *pornography* (Baron & Straus, 1983). This situation leads some social scientists to follow the example of the Commission on Obscenity and Pornography (1970), which decided not to use the term pornography at all. Some authors, for example, use the term *erotica*.

Given the strong disagreements over the term pornography we debated using erotica as an alternative. However, that is not a real solution since those who use the term erotica fail to state what distinguishes erotica from pornography. Moreover, those who regard *Playboy, Hustler, Penthouse,* and other such mass circulation magazines as pornography would object to labeling them erotica; just as those who regard them as erotica will undoubtedly object to applying the term pornography to these magazines. As a result of the disagreement over these concepts, each reader will have to decide if the conceptual focus of the research is pornography, erotica, sexually explicit materials, or some other concept. However, in respect to operationalization, we think it is best to identify the measure as simply Sex Magazine Circulation Index.

The raw data for this measure are the number of copies sold in 1979 (both subscription and newsstand sales) for each of eight sexually explicit magazines (*Chic, Club, Forum, Gallery, Genesis, Hustler, Oui,* and *Playboy*). The data were obtained from the Audit Bureau of Circulation (an independent nonprofit organization that audits and certifies magazine sales figures). These magazines are "soft-core" rather than "hard-core" sex literature, in the sense that they do not show the penis errect or show acts of copulation. However, just a few years ago they would have been considered hard-core because all show details of female genitals. With the exception of *Penthouse* (which is not included in our index because it does not provide circulation data to the Audit Bureau of Circulation), these are by far the most widely read, sexually oriented material in the United States. Several sell millions of copies every month. They reach a much wider audience than other sex literature and are therefore important for both theoretical and policy issues.

We began by converting the number of copies sold to a rate per 100,000 population for each state. The next step was a factor analysis using the SCSS principal components method with varimax rotation. The factor analysis revealed a single factor that explained 76% of the variance. We therefore computed a single index using all eight magazines, weighted according to their factor scores. This index will be referred to as the Sex Magazine Circulation Index (SMCX).

As with almost all the variables so far examined in the various State and Regional Indicators research projects, large differences between states were revealed in the readership of sex magazines. The right-hand columns of Table 7.1 show the circulation rates for each state of *Hustler* and *Playboy*[4] and the score of

---

[4]These two magazines were chosen to illustrate specific magazines because they are two of the largest circulation newsstand sex magazines, and because of the contrast in the image that each presents. *Playboy* seeks to portray itself as a highbrow magazine and *Hustler* as a macho magazine. Given this difference between the two magazines, it was surprising to us that they have a correlation of .68 between their circulation rates. This high correlation is typical of the correlations between the eight magazines and is the reason for their high loading on the factor.

TABLE 7.3

Basic Correlation Matrix

Variable	1	2	3	4	5	6	7	8	9	10	11
1 Rape, 1979		.17	.63***	.64***	.56***	.66***	.43***	.21	.01	.15	.23
2 SWX, 1970–1979			.40**	−.40**	.11	−.10	.13	−.24*	−.50***	−.01	−.15
3 SMCX, 1979				.24*	.24*	.16	.06	−.05	−.31*	.33**	.50***
4 Murder, 1979					.53***	.60***	.24*	.50***	.45***	.01	.16
5 Robbery, 1979						.51***	.74***	.43***	−.01	−.16	−.23
6 Aggravated assault, 1979							.36**	.34***	.17	−.08	−.04
7 % Residing in SMSAs, 1980								.29*	−.26*	−.09	−.22
8 % Black, 1980									.60***	.14	−.37**
9 % Poor, 1979										.01	−.18
10 % Age 18–24, 1980											.33**
11 % Male of population 15–24, 1980											
Mean	31.2	49.5	0.0	8.1	147.3	245.4	62.1	10.3	12.6	13.5	50.4
Standard deviation	13.5	8.7	1.0	4.4	107.8	113.2	23.3	12.5	3.5	0.8	1.2

*p < .05, **p < .01, ***p < .001.

each state on the SMCX (in z-score form). For both magazines there are large differences between the top- and bottom-ranking states. For example, the readership per 100,000 population for Hustler is 10.8 times greater in Alaska (the highest state) than in Utah (the state with the lowest readership rate).

Correlation of the SMCX with Rape and Nonsexual Violent Crimes

We found an unusually high correlation between the SMCX and the UCR rape rate (Table 7.3, second correlation in row 1). The importance of this correlation is further emphasized by the comparison with the low correlations between the SMCX and nonsexual violent crimes (first three coefficients in the third row of Table 7.3) for 1979 (the year of the SMCX data). In addition to the correlations in Table 7.3, we also computed the correlation of the SMCX with 1980 crime data. Although these correlations (.58, .08, .23, .26) differ somewhat from the corresponding four correlations in Table 7.3 (.63, .24, .24, .16), the pattern is consistent. Both sets of correlations indicate that readership of this particular type of sex literature is highly correlated with rape but has relatively low correlations with nonsexual violent crimes.

The fact that the SMCX is strongly and consistently correlated with rape supports the theory that pornography endorses attitudes that increase the likelihood of rape. However, there are also a number of other plausible explanations for this correlation. One of the strongest of the alternatives is that the state-to-state variations in both sex magazine readership and rape is spurious in the sense that it might reflect the correlation of both sex magazine readership and rape with some common third factor. For example, NCS data show that rapists and rape victims tend to be young. If sex magazines are also more widely read in states with a youthful population, the correlation between sex magazine readership and rape could be due to the fact that both are related to age, rather than to any causal link between this material per se and rape. There are many other state characteristics that could produce a spurious correlation. Consequently, later in this chapter we use multiple regression to control for this possibility statistically.

NONSEXUAL VIOLENCE AND RAPE

The theory that rape is primarily an act of violence, rather than primarily an act to secure sexual gratification, must be approached more indirectly than was the case with the links between rape and the status of women and sex magazine readership. This is because the measure of violence currently available to us on a statewide basis is the UCR data on violent crimes. At best this measures general proclivity to violence, rather than violence intended to injure women physically

TABLE 7.4

Correlation of Nonsexual Violent Crime with Rape,
1960, 1970, and 1980

Year	Correlation with rape[a]		
	Murder	Robbery	Assault
1960	.44	.62	.51
1970	.56	.53	.71
1980	.75	.62	.73

[a]All r's are significant at $p < .001$.

and psychologically. Consequently, the use of UCR data stacks the cards against finding a relationship that is consistent with the theory.

Despite the qualifications just listed, Table 7.3 shows that there are substantial correlations between each of the three nonsexual violent crimes and the incidence of rapes reported to the police (row 1, columns 4, 5, and 6). Moreover, Table 7.4, which shows these same correlations for three additional years, indicates that this link has been present for at least 20 years. We interpret these correlations as showing that rapes tend to occur in social systems characterized by violence, even when that violence is not sexual.

MULTIPLE REGRESSION ANALYSIS

The findings presented up to this point suggest that the large differences between states in rape rates are associated with the incidence of other crimes and with the readership of mass circulation pornography. However, as noted in the discussion of the pornography–rape correlations, all the correlations presented so far could be spurious. To investigate this possibility, variables that might be correlated with both the independent and dependent variables need to be controlled before one can talk with much confidence about the association between pornography and rape or between other crimes and rape. This section therefore presents the results of multiple regression analyses which provide estimates of the net association of the SWX, SMCX, and three nonsexual violent crimes with the incidence of rape.

In addition to the five variables of theoretical interest just listed, the regression equations included five other variables from the 1980 census (listed in the lower half of Table 7.5). As explained previously, these variables were introduced to control for possible spurious associations (such as might occur due to confounding with urbanization of the states), or to control for limitations of the UCR (for e.g., UCR rates are not age standardized or age specific).

TABLE 7.5

Multiple Regression Analysis of Rape Rate, 1979

Independent variable	Regression coefficient	Beta	t	p<
SMCX	6.99	.52	5.55	.001
Murder and manslaughter rate	1.70	.55	4.09	.001
Aggravated assault rate	0.04	.32	4.21	.001
SWX	0.43	.27	3.06	.014
Robbery	−0.03	−.25	2.00	.052
% Resident in SMSAs	0.26	.45	4.26	.001
% Black	−0.41	−.38	3.63	.001
% Below poverty income level	1.11	.29	2.67	.011
% Male of population age 18–24	−2.60	−.23	2.45	.019
Sex ratio for 15–24-year-olds	2.12	.12	1.73	.09

Original Regression Analysis

The multiple regression analysis was done using the SCSS regression program, with backward elimination. Of the 10 independent variables, 9 proved to be significantly related to the incidence of rape. After adjusting for degrees of freedom, these nine variables accounted for 83% of the state-to-state variation in rape ($F = 27.79$, $p< .001$).

The regression statistics are listed in Table 7.5 in three groups: first, the theoretically chosen independent variables (SMCX, UCR crime rates, and SWX), then the statistically significant control variables, and finally a nonsignificant control variable. Within each group, the list begins with the variable with the largest t (most statistically significant).

Heading the list is the SMCX. It has a regression coefficient of 6.99. This means that each change of 1 standard deviation in the circulation of sex magazines is associated with an average increase of about seven rapes per 100,000 population. Moreover, this is the net association of sex magazine readership with rape after controlling for all the other variables listed in Table 7.5.

Table 7.5 also shows that the three nonsexual violent crime variables (murder, aggravated assault, and robbery) are each significantly related to rape after controlling for all other variables in the equation. The relationship with murder is especially strong. Moreover, the correlations presented earlier (Table 7.4) indicate that this relationship has existed at least since 1960 and is therefore a relatively stable aspect of American society.

The significant regression coefficients for the SWX are surprising because the simple correlation analysis did not show a significant relationship with rape. This suggests that the true relationship between the status of women and rape was obscured by confounding with the variables partialed out in the multiple regression analysis. It is important to note that the regression analysis shows that the higher the status of women, the *higher* the incidence or rape. This is opposite to Hypothesis 1 but consistent with the male "backlash" theory suggested by Russell (1975).

Table 7.5 also shows that four of the control variables are significantly related to rape: two positively and two negatively. Since these variables were entered in the equation as controls for possibly spurious associations, rather than for purposes of testing a hypothesis, we shall not comment on them because of space limitations.

Supplementary Methodological Analyses

We carried out a series of additional analyses to investigate various threats to validity (Cook & Campbell, 1979) of the results just presented.

RELIABILITY OF RESULTS

The basic regression analysis shown in Table 7.5 was replicated using 1980 data for rape and nonsexual violent crime as a partial test of the replicability of the findings shown in Table 5. The use of 1980 crime data resulted in lower regression and beta coefficients. None of the control variables except the percentage living in metropolitan areas were significantly related to rape. Of the theoretically specified variables, the beta for robbery was $-.24$, which is almost identical to the coefficient using 1979 data, but not significant ($p = .17$). The beta coefficient for the SWX dropped from .27 to .17 ($p = .10$). The other three variables specified in the hypotheses remained statistically significant at the .01 level: SMCX was $= .40$; assault, .29; and murder, .37. These results using 1980 data question the support for Hypothesis 1 shown in Table 7.5, but strengthen the case for accepting Hypotheses 2 and 3.

RATIO VARIABLE ARTIFACTS

Both the independent variables and the dependent variable in this study use rates to control for the size of the state. However, this means that the population of the state appears in all variables as the denominator. In principle this could produce an artifactual correlation. In practice the results of methodological studies have been inconclusive, leading to the recommendation that the issue should be studied empirically in each research (Bolen & Ward, 1980). We did this in two ways. First, we replicated the regression, but with the addition of the population of the state as a control variable. Second, we replicated the analysis using only raw data for all variables and including the population size as a control variable. The regression coefficients produced by these analyses of course differed from those in Table 7.5, but all that are significant in Table 7.5 were also found to be statistically significant in these two replications.

OUTLIERS

Washington, D.C., was included in the analyses presented up to this point. However, inspection of the regression diagnostics showed a high value for Cook's D (1.112), indicating that the inclusion of the District of Columbia as though it were a state might be unduly influencing the results. We therefore replicated the analysis without the District of Columbia. The regression coefficients for the SWX, SMCX, and nonsexual violent crime all remained statistically significant, and similar in size to the coefficients in Table 7.5.

The section on the status of women with rape showed that what little correlation there was reflected the influence on one extreme state—Alaska. We therefore replicated the multiple regression analysis without Alaska to see if the regression results for the status of women changed as did the simple correlations without Alaska. The results are very similar to those shown in Table 7.5. The regression coefficients for SWX remained highly significant ($p < .007$), and the regression coefficient (.43) and the beta (.27) are almost identical to the original values.

WESTERN STATES

The key theoretical variables in this study (status of women, sex magazine readership, and rape) tend to be highest in the western part of the United States. This raises the possibility that the associations are spurious in the sense of reflecting a regional concentration of the variables, rather than a real relationship between them. We therefore replicated the analysis omitting the 13 states in the region designated as the West by the census.

The explanatory power of the model is almost identical for the 38 nonwestern states, as indicated by the adjusted R square of .82 ($F = 29.11$, $p < .001$). The results for the individual predictor variables do not differ importantly from the results given in Table 7.5, except that the significance levels are lower because the smaller N.

REPORTING EFFECTS ANALYSIS USING NATIONAL
CRIME SURVEY DATA

Perhaps the most serious threat to validity comes from the possibility that the large state-to-state differences in rape reflect differences in willingness to report rape, or in police policies in respect to recording rape, rather than differences in the true incidence of rape. If such differences are the results of random error, then the effect is likely to be one of underestimating the true regression coefficients. On the other hand, if differences in willingness to report are correlated with the independent variable, such "correlated error" can inflate the coefficients.

The NCS data on rape victimization can provide information on whether the results reported in this chapter are a function of error in the UCR crime rates, provided one assumes that the NCS does not have the same errors as the UCR. The NCS data is known to be far more complete than the UCR, since the incidence rates are several times greater. On the other hand, there are numerous problems with the NCS data (see the discussion and references in O'Brian, 1982). ''Record check'' studies, for example, reveal many crimes reported to the police that are *not* reported to the NCS interviewer—about one-third in the case of rape. Consequently, one cannot take state-to-state differences in NCS rates as necessarily more valid than state-to-state differences in UCR rates. Specifically, one cannot interpret a correlation of less than 1.0 as a measure of error in the UCR. It could be error in the UCR, or error in the NCS, or more likely an error in both. Nevertheless, since both are intended to be measures of roughly the same phenomenon, the validity of the findings presented in this chapter would be questioned if there is not at least a moderate correspondence between the two.

The NCS data are available only for the 10 largest states. This is too small a number for a multiple regression. However, the simple correlations are informative. They show a correlation of .49 between the NCS rape rate and the UCR rape rate for all rape victimizations. Moreover, the variables critical for the hypotheses of this study were found to have a similar pattern of correlation with the NCS rape rate to that found when using the UCR rape rate as the dependent variable. Specifically, we found the following correlations with the NCS rape victimization rate: $-.07$ with the SWX, .32 with the SMCX, .59 with the NCS aggravated Assault rate, and .46 with the UCR murder rate.

CONTROL FOR PROPENSITY TO REPORT RAPE

The NCS analysis is limited not only by the small N but also because there is no real measure of state-to-state differences in the willingness of respondents to report rape. Consequently we searched for measures that could be considered as proxies for this phenomenon. We investigated five such measures, but only two revealed even moderate correlations with the UCR rape rate.

The first of these is the availability of rape crisis services. We reasoned that, if there are many such services per 100,000 women in a state, it may give women greater hope of securing justice (or at least of being treated humanely) and hence a greater willingness to report.[5] The simple correlation of .33 is consistent with this idea since it shows that the more such services are available, the higher the

---

[5]The data on the number of rape crisis services in each state was obtained by counting the number of services listed for each state in the National Directory of Rape Prevention and Treatment Resources, published by the National Center For the Prevention and Control of Rape, NIMH (Department of Health And Human Services Publication ADM 81-1008, 1981). The number of services in each state was converted to a rate per 100,000 population. There are large differences between states on this measure. It ranged from a low of 1.5 per 100,000 population to a high of 46.9, with a mean of 8.6 and a standard deviation of 7.8. There is therefore more than enough state-to-state variance to use in correlation and regression analysis.

rape rate. Of course, many other processes than reporting effects could produce this correlation. For example, state-to-state differences in the availability of rape crisis services could be a *response* to real differences in the incidence of rape.

The second possible indirect indicator of willingness to report rape to the police is the membership in the National Organization for Women (NOW) per 100,000 women. Since rape has been an issue that NOW has focused on for several years, including emphasis on women's legal rights, it is possible that states with a larger membership in NOW will appear to have a higher incidence of rape because more of the rapes are reported than in other states. Although the correlation of NOW membership is barely statistically significant (.23), it is in the predicted direction.

Despite the ambiguity inherent in these correlations, the issue is important enough to make further exploration worthwhile. We therefore replicated the regression reported in Table 7.5, but with the addition of the rape crisis service rate and the NOW membership rate to the model. We used both variables because they are essentially uncorrelated with each other ($r = -.08$). The results do not suggest any alternative interpretations of the findings of the original regression analysis since it produced regression coefficients that are very similar to those shown in Table 7.5.

Uniform Crime Reports Coverage

It is possible that the state-to-state differences in rape rates reflect (at least partly) the assiduousness of reporting effort by police departments. We therefore used the percentage of each state's population that was covered by the UCR system in 1970 and 1979 as proxies for reporting effort by the police. Even with the growth in coverage by 1980, some states still had a much lower coverage than other states. For example, in 1980 in Indiana, 12% of the population living in standard metropolitan statistical areas (SMSAs) was not covered, 14% of the population living in other cities in Alabama was not covered, and 30% of the population living in rural areas was not covered by the UCR system.

Separate correlations were computed for metropolitan areas, other cities, and rural areas of the states. The correlations between the percentage of the population covered in 1970 and rape are .13 for metropolitan areas, .12 for other cities, and −.14 for rural areas. Using coverage in 1980 as the independent variable, the correlations are −.15, .05, and .09.

If percentage covered is a proxy for police reporting effort, and if differences in such reporting effort accounts for part of the state-to-state variation in rape rates, these correlations should all be positive. Instead, there is a mix of nonsignificant positive and negative correlations that is typical of random fluctuations around a true correlation of zero. In view of these findings, we did not think it worth replicating the regression analysis to control for state-to-state differences in the completeness of UCR coverage.

INTERACTION EFFECTS

Laboratory experimental studies of pornography and violence cited earlier in this chapter found that exposing men to pornography resulted in an increase in the level of aggression against women, but only if the pornography depicted acts of physical violence. Perhaps a similar process also operates at the societal level. We therefore investigated the possibility that the link between sex magazine circulation rates and the incidence of rape might be found only in social systems that have a high rate of violence.

This hypothesis was tested by including an interaction effect term in the regression equation. The interaction term was obtained by converting the non-sexual violent crime rate to a dummy variable (by dichotomizing at the median) and multiplying this by the SMCX. The test of this model showed no significant interaction effect. Consequently, the linear additive model summarized in Table 7.5 remains the best estimate.

SUMMARY AND CONCLUSIONS

There are extremely large state-to-state differences in the reported incidence of rape, and these differences have been relatively consistent from 1960 to 1980. Such large and consistent state-to-state differences in rape need to be understood. As a step in that direction, we investigated three hypotheses that according to many feminist writers, account for the high incidence of rape in American society: (1) the use of rape as a means of keeping women in a subordinate status, (2) the idea that pornography provides cultural ideation that endorses and legitimizes rape, and (3) the idea that rape is a a crime of violence rather than a crime motivated by a desire for sexual gratification.

Since these ideas refer to characteristics of societies, our research used a macrosociological approach by investigating differences between the 50 states. Each of the three factors hypothesized as accounting for state-to-state variation in the incidence of rape were studied using multiple regression. The regression equations included controls for five variables that could produce a spurious association between the independent variables and rape. The results can be summarized as follows.

Status of Women and Rape

The SWX was used to measure the extent to which women have achieved equality with men in respect to four spheres of life: educational, economic, occupational, and political. Despite large state-to-state differences in this measure, the simple correlation analysis did not show a statistically significant relationship. However, the multiple regression analysis showed that, when various other factors are controlled, there is a significant tendency for rape to increase as the status of women increases. This finding is opposite to our hypothesis but is consistent with the "backlash" theory put forward by authors such as Russell (1975). It is also possible that the apparent tendency for the incidence of rape to increase as the status of women increases indicates a "reporting effect," rather than a true relationship. This could occur because there are many more rapes than are reported to the police. If women in states where there is more nearly equality with men have a greater tendency to report being raped, this could produce a higher officially reported rate, even though the true incidence of rape is no different from that of other states.

Pornography and Rape

The SMCX was constructed to measure the extent to which mass circulation sex magazines are part of the popular culture of each state. This index was found to be highly correlated with the incidence of rape. Moreover, the significance of this finding is enhanced by (1) the contrast with the low correlations of the SMCX with nonsexual violent crimes, (2) the confirmation of the relationship when the analysis was replicated for a second year, and (3) the persistence of the association despite controls for possible confounding variables such as the youthfulness of the population.

Does the finding that rape increases in direct proportion to the readership of sex magazines mean that exposure to this type of pornography induces men to rape? This is a plausible interpretation. However, it must be remembered that, despite the controls for confounding variables, the evidence presented shows only that there is a strong association between sex magazine readership and rape, not that one causes the other. Even more caution is required because there are a number of other plausible interpretations of what underlies the tendency for rape to be highest in states with the highest circulation of sex magazines.

First, the relationship between sex magazine readership and rape may be due to an unspecified third variable that is a common determinant of both. We controlled for five such variables, but there are many others for which no control variable was available. We think it is quite plausible, for example, that the findings could reflect state-to-state differences in a cultural pattern emphasizing "compulsive masculinity" (Toby, 1966). Such a pattern could include norms and values that promote male interest and involvement in sex, male sexual aggressiveness, the perception of women as sex objects, the belief in rape myths, male dominance, and female subordination. The association of violence with this type of cultural and social organization is suggested by a number of studies (Check & Malamuth, 1983; Holmstom & Burgess, 1983; Libby & Straus, 1979; McConahay & McConahay, 1977; Prescott, 1975, March–April). If such a hypermasculine culture pattern independently influences the purchase of sex magazines and the incidence of rape, the original association between sex magazine readership and rape could be an artifact of their relationship to compulsive masculinity. Moreover, if this orientation produces a social climate that is favorable to both pornography and rape, the rape rate would not be altered if sex magazines did not exist.

A second explanation for the relationship between sex magazine readership and rape is that each varies directly with the degree of sexual openness within states. Thus, states that provide a more relaxed and casual atmosphere for sexual relations may also produce conditions that make men more comfortable buying sex magazines. Similarly, an open sexual milieu might make some men feel sexually deprived relative to others and promote the belief that they are entitled to sex even if it means using coercion or force to obtain it. It could also be argued that a sexually open atmosphere might reduce the stigma attached to a rape victim and increase the likelihood of her reporting the incident. This would increase the number of reported rapes in states relative to those states that have a more sexually repressive orientation.

Rape and Nonsexual Violence

The theory that rape is an act of violence was investigated by computing the extent to which nonsexual crimes of violence are correlated with rape. Each of the nonsexual violent crimes reported in the UCR were found to be strongly correlated with rape. These associations persisted despite controls and were essentially similar over a 20-year period. This finding is clearly consistent with the feminist theory that forms the focus of this chapter. However, it is also consistent with other plausible interpretations. For example, the correlation of nonsexual violent crimes with rape may be interpreted as showing that rape is not unique among violent crimes. The high incidence of rape in some states could reflect a climate of violence against both men and women, of which rape is but one manifestation.

Conclusion

From the perspective of feminist theory, the findings suggest that the combination of a society that is characterized by a struggle to secure equal rights for women, by a high readership of sex magazines that depict women in ways that may legitimize violence, and by a context in which there is a high level of nonsexual violence, constitutes a mix of societal characteristics that precipitates rape. To the extent that this interpretation is correct, it suggests social policies directed toward eliminating or mitigating the conditions that make rape more likely to occur. These steps would include reducing the cultural acceptability of violence, of which rape is a part; and restructuring male gender roles (in both sexual and nonsexual relationships) to specify equality, warmth, and supportiveness, rather than dominance, aloofness, toughness, and violence. Such a restructuring of relationships between the sexes, while it will not eliminate rape, could reduce the high-incidence rates that now characterize American society.

REFERENCES

Baron, L., & Straus, M. A. (1983). *Conceptual and ethical problems in research on pornography.* Paper presented at the 1983 annual meeting of the Society for the Study of Social Problems, Detroit, Michigan.

Berkowitz, L. (1971, December). Sex and violence: We can't have it both ways. *Psychology Today,* pp. 14, 18, 20, 22–23.

Blau, J. R., & Blau, P. M. (1982). Metropolitan structure and violent crime. *American Sociological Review, 47,* 114–128.

Bolen, K. A., & Ward, S. (1980). Ratio variables in aggregate data analysis: Their uses, problems and alternatives. In Edgar F. Borgatta and David J. Jackson (Eds.), *Aggregate data: Analysis and Interpretation.* Beverly Hills, CA: Sage.

Brownmiller, S. (1975). *Against our will: Men, women, and rape.* New York: Simon and Schuster.

Burt, M. R. (1980). Cultural myths and supports for rape. *Journal of Personality and Social Psychology, 38,* 217–230.

Check, J., & Malamuth, N. (1983). Sex role stereotyping and reactions to depictions of stranger versus acquaintance rape. *Journal of Personality and Social Psychology, 45,* 344–356.

Clark, L., & Lewis, D. (1977). *Rape: The price of coercive sexuality.* Toronto: Women's Press.

Cook, T. D., & Campbell, D. T. (1979). *Quasi experimentation: Design and analysis issues for field settings.* Chicago: Rand McNally.

Court, J. H. (1976). Pornography and sex-crimes: A re-evaluation in the light of recent trends around the world. *International Journal of Criminology and Penology, 5,* 129–157.

Curtis, L. A. (1976). Sexual combat. *Society, 13* (May–June), 69–72.

Donnerstein, E. (1983). Erotica and human aggression. In R. Geen and E. Donnerstein (Eds.), *Aggression: Theoretical and empirical reviews.* New York: Academic Press.

Donnerstein, E., & Berkowitz, L. (1981). Victim reactions in aggressive-erotic films as a factor in violence against women. *Journal of Personality and Social Psychology, 41,* 710–724.

Ellis, L., & Beattie, C. (1983). The feminist explanation for rape: An empirical test. *Journal of Sex Research, 19* (February), 74–93.

Elshtain, J. B. (1976–1977). Review of Susan Brownmiller's *Against Our Will. Telos,* 30, 237–242.

Elshtain, J. B., (1982). The victim syndrome: A troubling turn in feminism. *The Progressive, 42,* (June), 42–47.

English, D. (1980). The politics of porn: Can feminists walk the line? *Mother Jones, 5*(April), 20, 22–23, 43–44, 48–50.

Geis, G. (1977). Forcible rape: An introduction. In D. Chappell, R. Geis, and G. Geis (Eds.), *Forcible Rape: The crime, the victim and the offender.* New York: Columbia University Press.

Greer, G. (1973). Seduction is a four-letter word. *Playboy, 20*(January), 80–82, 164, 178, 224–228.

Griffin, S. (1971, September). Rape: The all-American crime. *Ramparts,* pp. 26–35.

Groth, N. A. (1979). *Men who rape.* New York: Plenum.

Hindelang, M. J. (1974). The uniform crime reports revisited. *Journal of Criminal Justice, 2,* 1–17.

Holmstrom, L. L. & Burgess, A. W. (1983). Rape and everyday life. *Society, 6,* 33–40.

Hommes, R. (1978). The status of women. In M. Hipheua-Nell (Ed.), *Demographic aspects of the changing status of women in Europe.* Boston: Martin Dyboff.

Kutchinsky, B. (1973). The effect of easy availability of pornography on the incidence of sex crimes: The Danish experience. *The Journal of Social Issues, 29,* 182–183.

Largen, M. A. (1976). History of the women's movement in changing attitudes, laws, and treatment toward rape victims. In Marcia J. Walker and Stanley L. Brodsky (Eds.), *Sexual assault.* Lexington, MA: D. C. Heath.

Lederer, L. (1980). *Take back the night.* New York: Morrow.

Libby, R., & Straus, M. A. (1979). Make love not war? Sex, sexual meanings, and violence in a sample of college students. *Archives of Sexual Behavior, 9*(2), 133–148.

Malamuth, N., & Spinner, B. (1980). A longitudinal content analysis of sexual violence in the best selling erotic magazines. *Journal of Sex Research,* 16, 226–237.

Malamuth, N., & Donnerstein, E. (1983). The effects of aggressive–pornographic mass media stimuli. In L. Berkowitz (Ed.), *Advances in experimental social psychology* (Vol. 15). New York: Academic Press.

McConahay, S. A., & McConahay, J. B. (1977). Sexual permissiveness, sex-role rigidity, and violence across cultures. *Journal of Social Issues, 33*(2), 134–143.

Nelson, E. C. (1982) Pornography and sexual aggression. In Maurice Yaffe and Edward C. Nelson (Eds.), *The influence of pornography on behavior.* New York: Academic Press.

O'Brien, R. M. (1982). Metropolitan structure and violent crime: Which measure of Crime? *American Sociological Review, 48*(June), 434–437.

Orlando, L. (1982, December). Bad Girls and "Good" Politics. *Village Voice Literary Supplement,* 2 pp. 16–19.

Prescott, J. W. (1975, March–April). Body pleasure and the origins of violence. *Futurist,* pp. 64–80.

Report of the Presidential Commission on Obscenity and Pornography. (1970). Washington, DC: U.S. Government Printing Office.

Riger, S., & Gordon, T. (1981). The fear of rape: A study in social control. *Journal of Social Issues, 37*(4), 71–92.

Rose, V. M. (1977a). Rape as a social problem: A by-product of the feminist movement. *Social Problems, 25*(October), 75–89.

Rose, V. M. (1977b). The rise of the rape problem. In Armand Mauss and Julie C. Wolfe (Eds.), *Our land of promises: The rise and fall of social problems in America.* Philadelphia: Lippincott.

Russell, D. E. H. 1975 *The politics of rape: The victim's perspective.* New York: Stein and Day.

Sanday, P. R. (1981). The socio-cultural context of rape: A cross-cultural study. *Journal of Social Issues, 37*(4), 5–27.

Schwendinger, J. R., & Schwendinger, H. (1983). *Rape and inequality.* Beverly Hills: Sage.

Stack, S., & Kanavy, M. J. (1983). The effect of religion on forcible rape: A structural analysis. *Journal for the Scientific Study of Religion, 22*(1), 67–74.

Straus, M. A. (1974). Leveling, civility and violence in the family. *Journal of Marriage and the Family,* 36(February), 13–29, plus addendum August 1974.

Toby, J. (1966). Violence and the masculine ideal: Some quantitative data. In Suzanne K. Steinmetz and Murray, A. Straus (Eds.), *Violence in the family.* New York: Harper & Row.

Weis, K., & Borges, S. S. (1977). Victimology and rape: The case of the legitimate victim. In Deanna R. Nass (Ed.), *The rape victim.* Dubuque, IA: Kendall/Hunt Publishing Company.

Willis, E. (1982, December). Who is a feminist? *Village Voice Literary Supplement,* pp. 17–18.

Yllo, K. (1983). Using a feminist approach in quantitative research: A case study. In D. Finkelhor, R. J. Gelles, G. T. Hotaling, and M. A. Straus (Eds.), *The dark side of families.* Beverly Hills: Sage.

Yllo, K., & Straus, M. (1981, April). *Patriarchy and violence against wives: The impact of structural and normative factors.* Paper presented at the Johns Hopkins Symposium on "Feminism and the Critique of Capitalism," Baltimore, MD.

PART IV

Causes of Sexual Aggression: Psychological and Communicative Factors

The chapters in this section examine possible causes of sexual aggression other than pornography. These chapters focus on aggression in nonlaboratory settings, including aggression in dating interactions. The contributions in this section also analyze the role of individual (e.g., psychological) and cultural (e.g., normative) causes of aggression against women.

In the first chapter, "Sexually Aggressive Men: Empirical Findings and Theoretical Implications," Koss and Leonard describe differing approaches that have been used to identify sexually aggressive men. These include judicial identification, self-reported likelihood of raping, and self-reported sexual aggression. Koss and Leonard consider the strengths and limitations of each of these approaches and emphasize the need to replicate findings across the three procedures. The authors then proceed to analyze empirical findings regarding the psychological characteristics of aggressive men. Are men who are more sexually aggressive different from less aggressive men in terms of emotional maladjustment, attitudes and beliefs, patterns of sexual arousal to pornography and general aggressivity? What role might these factors play in causing sexual aggression? After examining data relevant to these questions, the authors consider the ability of two contrasting theoretical models, the psychopathology model and the social

PORNOGRAPHY AND
SEXUAL AGGRESSION

control model, to account for the research findings. In closing, they point to possible areas for incorporating elements from both of these models.

In the second chapter, "Communication and Sexual Aggression in Adolescent Relationships," Goodchilds and Zellman examine how norms and signals used by young couples may affect sexual aggression. Do males and females share understanding about the interpretations of various signals and to what extent do today's youth differ from earlier generations in terms of signaling systems and interpretations? To address such issues, the authors analyze the results of an ambitious survey of male and female teenagers who were interviewed about their expectations and communication about sex. As part of the interview process, subjects responded to vignettes describing interactions among youth that were systematically varied by the experimenters along differing dimensions. These variations enabled the assessment of the impact of diverse signaling and relationship dimensions. The results reveal important areas of convergence and divergence between the genders. Normative and communicative factors that affect the use of force in sexual relations are identified. The data highlight the extent to which adversarial aggressive interactions characterize much of adolescent sexual relations.

8

Sexually Aggressive Men: Empirical Findings and Theoretical Implications

MARY P. KOSS
KENNETH E. LEONARD

Sexual aggression is a general term that refers to a continuum of sexual activity involving increasing degrees of coercion up to and including rape. Sexual aggression includes the legal categories of sexual contacts, sexual acts, sexual imposition, and sexual intercourse when obtained through coercion or force and without consent. The focus of this chapter is the psychological characteristics of males who have engaged in sexual aggression against females. Since sexual aggression, though not uncommon, is not a behavior exhibited by all males, one may legitimately ask whether sexually aggressive men differ from sexually non-aggressive men. To examine this possibility, the literature concerning psychological disorders, attitudes, and sexual behavior of sexually aggressive men is reviewed, and several theoretical models of sexual aggression are presented and discussed.

IDENTIFYING SEXUALLY AGGRESSIVE MEN

The selection of an appropriate sample of sexually aggressive men is a critical methodological issue. Since extreme forms of sexual aggression constitute crimi-

PORNOGRAPHY AND
SEXUAL AGGRESSION

213

nal acts, one cannot simply ask male subjects if they have ever committed rape or attempted rape. Such a question would likely receive an unanimous negative response; even convicted rapists minimize the severity of their sexually aggressive acts or completely deny them. As Weis and Borges (1973) state, "If the man can call the act seduction, he may call himself a winner; if it is rape, he is a loser" (p. 87). Fortunately, there are several alternative sampling approaches available.

Judicial Identification

The most common method of selecting a sample of sexually aggressive men has been to utilize males who have been identified as rapists through judicial procedures. Convicted rapists have been studied both prior to sentencing and following incarceration or institutionalization.

A primary problem with this sampling procedure is that the subjects may not be representative of the entire population of rapists. It has been estimated that for every rape reported 3–10 rapes are committed but not reported (LEAA, 1975). Only a fraction of those reported rapes will eventually result in a conviction. For example, Clark and Lewis (1977) suggested that after allowances are made for nonreporting, the inability by police to acquire evidence, nonapprehension, and failure to convict, the highest justifiable proportion of actual rapists who are ever found guilty is 7%. Brodsky (1976) concluded, "It is not known if nonapprehended assailants are like those who make it through the justice system's progressive filtration process" (p. 5).

At each stage of the judicial process, a portion of the potential rapist sample is excluded from systematic study. However, factors other than judicial may exclude the person from prosecution for rape or may influence the verdict. For example, it has been argued that a rapist who knows the victim may be at less risk for being reported or convicted of rape than a rapist who is a complete stranger (e.g., Clark & Lewis, 1977). Similarly, certain demographic or psychological characteristics (e.g., social class, race, intelligence, presence or mental disorder) may facilitate prosecution and conviction. As a result, psychological characteristics of convicted rapists may reflect as much about the judicial process as about the dynamics of sexual aggression.

Some investigators have utilized samples of men who have been convicted of other violent crimes (murder, assault) in an attempt to obtain a comparison group of nonrapists who have also been selected via potentially biased judicial processes. However, considering the low reporting and low clearance rates (reported cases that resulted in an arrest) for rape even relative to other violent crimes, it is unlikely that this method of controlling for the judicial process could be entirely successful. A second problem related to formation of nonrapist comparison . samples is potential contamination by undetected offenders (i.e., rapists, at-

tempted rapists, and sexually aggressive men who have not been reported, apprehended, or convicted). To the extent that such men are present in the control
group, actual differences between rapists and sexually nonaggressive men would
be attenuated.

Self-Rated Likelihood of Raping

A second sampling approach has been developed by Malamuth (1981). Rather
than selecting men who have committed rape, Malamuth's approach has been to
attempt to identify men who have the potential to commit rape. This is accomplished in a straightforward fashion. A male subject is asked to rate the likelihood that he would rape a female if he could be assured that he would not be
apprehended and punished. Any male who admits to a likelihood above "not at
all likely" is assumed to "possess a relative propensity to rape" (Malamuth,
1981). Under these conditions, approximately 35% of the male college students
admitted to some likelihood of committing rape. Malamuth (1981) has reported
several studies that provide some construct validity for the likelihood-of-raping
measure. For example, rated rape proclivity is related to physical aggression
against a female in an experimental situation as well as to the admission of the
use of force against females in previous sexual situations and the anticipated use
of force in future sexual situations.

Self-Reported Sexual Aggression

The third method of selecting a sample of sexually aggressive men has been
utilized by Koss (Koss & Oros, 1982; Koss, Leonard, Beezley & Oros, in press).
They adopted a continuum approach to sexual aggression and rape. According to
this approach, rape represents the extreme point on a continuum of sexual aggression. Manipulation, coercion, and attempted rape represent increasing levels
of sexual aggression, while the absence of such behaviors would be the low point
on the continuum. To identify samples of males at different points on the continuum of sexual aggression, a sexual experience survey is employed. This
survey consists of 12 circumstances under which sexual intercourse could occur.
These circumstances vary in the degree to which sexual aggression is present and
are ordered from the absence of sexual aggression to high levels of sexual
aggression. The term *rape* is not used.

Subjects were classified as sexually nonaggressive, sexually coercive, sexually abusive, and sexually assaultive on the basis of their responses to this
survey. Males who admitted to obtaining sexual intercourse, oral intercourse, or
anal intercourse through the threat or use of force constituted the sexually assaultive group. These behaviors are legally rape in most states. The sexually
abusive men did not admit to any of the highly sexually aggressive items, but did
admit to one of the following three moderately aggressive behaviors: "used

some degree of physical force (twisting her arm, holding her down, etc.) to make a woman engage in kissing or petting when she didn't want to,'' ''told a woman who did not want to have intercourse that you would use some degree of physical force if she didn't have sexual intercourse with you, but for various reasons intercourse did not occur,'' or ''used some degree of physical force to try to obtain sexual intercourse with a woman who didn't want it, but for various reasons intercourse did not occur.'' This behavior would be attempted rape in most states. The sexually coercive men did not admit to any of the moderately or highly sexually aggressive items. These subjects agreed that they had obtained intercourse with a woman when she did not want it either ''by telling her you would end the relationship if she didn't agree,'' ''after continual discussions and arguments about it,'' or ''by saying things you didn't really mean (false promises of love, etc.).''

Among a campuswide representative sample ($N = 1846$), 4.3% of the males reported sexually assaultive behavior, 4.9% reported sexually abusive behavior, 22.4% reported sexually coercive behavior, and 59.0% reported no sexually aggressive behavior but did report mutually desired sexual experience. Sexually inexperienced subjects, those who responded ''no'' to all items, comprised 9.4% of the sample. The men who took the survey were also asked to indicate whether they would be willing to be interviewed in more depth about their sexual experiences. Approximately 30% of the males agreed to be interviewed. A similar procedure based on self-report in a standardized interview setting was used by Ageton (1983) to identify a sample of sexually aggressive adolescents.

The self-report procedures described above have two major strengths. They are capable of identifying subjects without reliance on judicial process or social labeling. Also, sexually aggressive men have admitted to actual assaultive behavior rather than only to the possibility that they could behave in such a fashion. However, as with the likelihood-of-raping measure, the question of the veracity of self-reports regarding sexual behavior is raised. It is possible that factors such as social undesirability, deviant response sets, or lowered social anxiety could potentially influence an individual's reporting of his sexually aggressive behavior. Additionally, males selected by self-report may not have been involved in acts of sexual aggression that necessarily correspond to the traditional stereotype of a rape incident. For example, among college males, the sexually aggressive acts reported were often ''date'' rapes where the aggressive male and the victim were in a romantic relationship. In contrast, rapes committed by convicted rapists are more frequently ''stranger'' rapes, in which the victim is violently attacked in a clearly nonsexual context by a man whom she does not know. Finally, the consent rates to participate in sexual research can be problemmatic. Some significant differences have been reported between males who do and do not volunteer to participate (Malamuth & Check, 1983).

In summary, there are three available methods of identifying sexually aggressive men; judicial identification, rated likelihood of raping, and self-report of sexually aggressive behavior. Each method has its own implicit limitations. Furthermore, samples selected by one method may differ considerably from samples selected by another method. In reviewing the literature, it is necessary to bear these methodological issues in mind. Findings that are replicated across the three sample-selection procedures would obviously provide the strongest evidence of psychological differences between sexually aggressive and nonaggressive men. Findings that are not replicated across the three procedures may indicate that the psychological characteristic in question is important in only some forms of sexual aggression.

The psychological characteristics of sexually aggressive men that have been studied include emotional adjustment, attitudes and beliefs relevant to rape, patterns of sexual arousal to pornography and erotica, and general aggressivity. These findings are reviewed below. It must be recognized from the outset that studies that examine the psychological characteristics of existing groups represent a correlational approach, and, as such, cannot conclusively indicate causality. Nevertheless, the results of these studies may have important causal and preventative implications.

EMPIRICAL FINDINGS

Psychological Disorder

One of the most prevalent assumptions concerning the psychological characteristics of sexually aggressive men has been that such men are psychologically disturbed. Groth and Birnbaum (1979), for example, state that "rape is always a symptom of some psychological dysfunction, either temporary and transient or chronic and repetitive" (p. 5). Similarly, Cohen (1976) has argued that "every act of rape is expressive of psychopathology: of a disturbance, moderate or severe, in the developmental history of the offender and his current adaptive efforts." Despite these adamant assertions, data concerning psychological disturbance in sexually aggressive men are inconclusive.

The major source of information concerning psychological disorders in sexually aggressive men has been diagnostic impressions of samples of incarcerated rapists. In general, there is agreement that incarcerated rapists are not psychotic. Gebhard, Gagnon, Pomeroy, and Christenson (1965) reported that fewer than 1% of the rapists in their sample could be diagnosed as psychotic. Henn (1978) surveyed police records and psychiatric histories of 2657 rapists for the period 1961–1973. Only 8 or 0.3% had a psychotic diagnosis. This rate of psychosis (schizophrenia) was actually somewhat less than the estimated rate of psychosis in the general population (1.5%). With respect to neurotic disorders, it can be assumed that these disorders were rare among rapists since neurosis is rarely mentioned by the authors.

In contrast to the low incidence of neurotic and psychotic diagnoses, a high incidence of character disorders, especially antisocial or psychopathic personalities, is reported. McCaldon (1967) reported that 50% of his sample of convicted rapists could be diagnosed as antisocial personalities. Henn (1978) estimated that nearly 70% of his court-referred rapists manifested some form of personality disorder. Groth and Birnbaum's (1979) description of chronic rape offenders strongly suggests that their sample consisted largely of psychopaths. For example, the psychological characteristics of rapists noted by these authors were "the absence of any close, emotionally intimate relationships," "little capacity for warmth, trust, compassion, or empathy" (p. 6), "poor judgment," "does not anticipate the consequences of his behavior" (p. 106), "cannot delay or redirect his impulse, but instead seeks immediate need gratification," and views other people as "obstacles to be overcome or objects to be used or manipulated" (p. 107). Cohen, Garofalo, Boucher, and Seghorn (1971) have described three types of rapists and noted a strong similarity between them and three personality disorders: explosive personality, inadequate personality, and antisocial personality. Thus, there is a prominent view that many, if not most, sexually aggressive men or rapists can be diagnosed as personality disorders.

There are major methodological problems present in most of the diagnostic studies of convicted rapists. Several of the papers are simply impressionistic descriptions of rapists. Often the investigators did not use any standardized psychological measures nor provide any statistical treatment of the variables (e.g., Groth, Burgess, & Holmstrom, 1977). Whenever psychiatric diagnoses are presented in support of theoretical contentions, questions of the reliability and validity of the nosological system must be addressed. It is well known that the rate of agreement is low between two independent diagnoses, especially among the subtypes of personality disorder. Additionally, authors seldom report whether the diagnosis of the individual was determined independent of knowledge of the crime he had committed. Such information could bias formulation of the diagnosis. Thus, the preponderance of antisocial personalities in samples of convicted rapists could partially reflect the expectation that rapists have antisocial personalities.

Several studies have addressed the issue of psychopathology in rape offenders in a more rigorous fashion. These studies have utilized objective measures of psychopathology and at least one comparison group. The results of these studies have been inconsistent with respect to the presence of psychological disorders in rape offenders. For example, Perdue and Lester (1972) found no differences between the Rorschach responses of convicted rapists and nonsexually aggressive offenders. Hammer (1954) found pedophiles to be more deviant than rapists on the House-Tree-Person Test. Fisher and Rivlin (1971) compared the responses of rapists, general criminal offenders, and normal adults on the Edwards Personal Preference Scale. These authors suggested that rapists were less self-assured and independent, less dominant, less aggressive and more self-critical and introspective than the general criminal and normal adult samples.

The most widely used objective psychological test has been the Minnesota Multiphasic Personality Inventory (MMPI). Panton (1958) examined the MMPI profiles of over 1300 male convicted criminals. He found few differences between his aggravated sex offender group (rapists and attempted rapists) and the five other crime classification groups. Although none of the clinical scales of the aggravated sex offender group were in a clinically significant range, many of the scales were higher than the standardized norm. The two highest scales were Scale 4 (psychopathic deviate) and Scale 8 (schizophrenia). Similar findings have been reported by Karacon, Williams, Guerraro, Salis, Thornby, and Hursch (1974). Finally, Rader (1977) examined the MMPI records of exposers, assaulters, and rapists who had been selectively referred by the court for preplea or presentence investigation. It seems likely that this selection procedure would result in a psychologically deviant sample of rapists, as well as exposers and assaulters. Thus, the results must be viewed with caution. The rapist group scored significantly higher than the exposers on six of the clinical scales and differed from the assaulters on three of the clinical scales. The rapist groups' highest scores were on Scales 4 & 8.

While the above studies are methodologically superior to the diagnostic studies cited earlier, several problems remain. A major problem is the failure to control for certain demographic variables that could cause spurious elevation on the MMPI scales, such as age, race, and socioeconomic status. For example, scores on both Scales 4 and 8 must be lowered $\frac{1}{2}-1$ SD among black subjects before standard interpretive statements can be applied (Graham, 1977). Also, it is difficult to determine the causal significance of elevated Scale 4 scores among rapists since Scale 4 tends to be elevated in all criminal groups (Dahlstrom, Welsh, & Dahlstrom, 1972). Thus, these studies cannot provide unqualified support for the belief that rapists differ from other incarcerated criminals with respect to psychopathology.

One study has examined the psychopathology of undetected rapists and sexually aggressive men (Koss et al., in press). Koss et al. administered two scales sensitive to antisocial tendencies—Scale 4 of the MMPI and the social anxiety items of the Activity Preference Questionnaire (APQ) (Lykken, Tellegen, & Katzenmeyer, 1973)—to college males who admitted to behavior congruent with the legal definition of rape, as well as to men who admitted lesser degrees of sexual aggression. Scale 4 was significantly correlated ($r = .28$) with level of sexual aggression. However, it failed to add significantly to the prediction of sexual aggression. The APQ score was unrelated to level of sexual aggression.

In summary, the empirical evidence to support the existence of psychopathology among groups of incarcerated rapists is inconclusive and weak, but
clinical impressions rather consistently emphasize aggressive, antisocial character traits. Studies of self-identified sexually aggressive men have failed to
reveal clinically significant levels of psychopathology.

Rape Myths and Rape-Supportive Attitudes

Several researchers have attempted to examine belief in stereotypes or myths
about rape among diverse groups. Burt (1980) defined a rape myth as a "prejudicial, stereotyped, or false belief about rape, rape victims, and rapists" (p.
217). She has reported strong relationships between the acceptance of rape myths
and other deeply held beliefs such as sex-role stereotypes, sexual conservatism,
adversarial sexual beliefs, and acceptance of interpersonal violence. Other workers have reported that acceptance of rape myths appeared to influence the treatment rape victims received from police (Feild, 1978), judges (Bohmer, 1974),
attorneys (Holmstrom and Burgess, 1975), and juries (Scroggs, 1976). It has
also been theorized that acceptance of rape myths and other prejudicial stereotypes supportive of rape could play a role in the etiology of sexual aggression
(e.g., Weis and Borges, 1973). Studies that have attempted to explore the relationship of attitudes to the commission of rape are reviewed briefly below.

Feild (1978) administered an Attitudes Toward Rape questionnaire to rapists
committed to a state mental hospital, rape crisis counselors, police, and citizens.
On the basis of a factor analysis of the questionnaire, eight factor scores were
computed for the subjects. Of interest is the fact that 26 of the 32 attitude items
are included in the first factor, Woman's Responsibility in Rape Prevention.
Thus, this factor could be interpreted as a general rape myth factor. Examples of
the items on this factor are: "It would do some women some good to be raped,"
"Most women secretly desire to be raped," " 'Nice' women do not get raped,"
"Most charges of rape are unfounded," and "If a woman is going to be raped,
she might as well relax and enjoy it."

The four groups—rape crisis counselors, rapists, police officers, and citizens—were compared on each of the eight factors. As might be expected,
rapists and rape crisis counselors held dramatically different attitudes about rape.
On every factor, rapists were significantly different from the counselors. Furthermore, the rapists differed from police officers on four of the factors and from
citizens on five of the factors. These results support the hypothesis that rapists
maintain certain attitudes and beliefs that are supportive of their actions. They
hold these attitudes more strongly than do the police or general citizens and
considerably more strongly than do rape crisis counselors. However, the fact that
these rapists were hospitalized in a state mental hospital should be considered in
interpreting the results.

A more recent study of incarcerated rapists has been reported by Scully and Marolla (1982, January). The administered 3 attitude scales (among a battery of 12 measures) to a sample of 98 convicted rapists and 75 non-sex-offenders incarcerated in medium security prisons. The instruments used were the Attitudes toward Women Scale (Spence, Helmreich, & Stapp, 1973), The Rape Stereotype Scale (Marolla & Scully 1979) and Rape Vignettes (Williams, 1981). Contrary to their expectation, they found no significant differences in attitudes between rapists and nonrapists. However, rapists were significantly more likely to indicate agreement with common rape myths. The analyses of the rape vignettes indicated that both rapists and nonrapists alike were more likely to define an encounter as rape when a weapon was present and when the assailant was a stranger.

Both of these studies of incarcerated rapists are based on typological assumptions that people can be classified as either rapists or nonrapists and that the rapist category is determined by conviction of rape. But as pointed out previously, due to the underreporting and underconviction of rape, it is very likely that a non-rapist control group defined in terms of conviction is contaminated with undetected offenders who have been sexually aggressive to various degrees. If such individuals are present in the comparison sample, differences between the groups would be attenuated. At present, some attitudinal differences between incarcerated rapists and the general population are indicated. Should possible contamination be removed, the pattern of differences might be even stronger.

Koss et al. (in press) have extended the study of rape-supportive attitudes to undetected sexually aggressive men. They administered an attitude questionnaire to sexually coercive, abusive, and assaultive men and sexually nonaggressive men. This questionnaire consisted of three parts. The first part was the 25-item short form of the Attitudes toward Women Scale (Spence, Helmreich, & Stapp, 1973). This scale measures the degree to which an individual accepts traditional sex-role stereotypes. The second part of the questionnaire consisted of 37 items that reflect rape-supportive beliefs adapted from Burt (1980). These items were factor analyzed with pilot data from another sample. Five factors were identified. These factors were quite consistent with the attitude scales constructed by Burt (1980) on a rational–intuitive basis. The final part of the questionnaire consisted of 20 of the rape myth items that compose the factor of Woman's Responsibility in Rape Prevention reported by Feild (1978). As was noted previously, this factor appears to be a general measure of acceptance of rape myths.

The results indicated that the groups of sexually aggressive men could be significantly discriminated by their scores on the attitudinal measures. Sexually aggressive behavior was associated with the beliefs that sexual aggression was normal and that relationships contained a large element of game playing, with a conservative attitude toward female sexuality, and with an acceptance of rape myths as accurate. Additionally, men who reported high levels of sexual aggression scored higher on the Feild factor of Woman's Responsibility for Rape Prevention and lower on the Spence-Helmreich Attitudes toward Women Scale. Thus, with increasing sexual aggression, attitudes tend to be more rape suppor-tive, more accepting of rape myths, and more traditional with respect to sex roles.

Ageton (1983) reported the results of a study of sexually aggressive adoles-cents who were identified through screening questions on the National Youth Study. This study began in 1976 and is a longitudinal, sequential study of a national probability sample of youth aged 11 to 17. During a standardized inter-view in the context of other crime questions, subjects were asked how many times in the last year they had attempted or had sexual relations with someone against their will. A sample of 68 sexually aggressive adolescents were identified who reported engaging in sexually aggressive acts between 1978 and 1980. Among the data available on these youth were sociodemographic variables, attitude measures, and situational factors surrounding the assault. The major strength of this study is that due to the panel design, the attitudinal measures were collected at measurement points prior to the reported occurrence of the sexual assault. Thus, the ability to determine causality is increased. Ageton (1983) found that four variables correctly classified 77% of the subjects in a descriminant analysis: Involvement with Delinquent Peers, Crimes against Per-sons, Attitudes toward Rape and Sexual Assault, and Family Normlessness. However, in a separate analysis, Involvement with Delinquent Peers alone could correctly classify 76% of the subjects. She concluded that adolescent sexual offenders are basically delinquent youth not well integrated into the traditional social order.

Several studies have reported a relationship between rape-supportive attitudes and the attitudes of men who have indicated a self-rated likelihood of raping (Malamuth, Haber, & Feshbach, 1980; Malamuth, 1981). In the first of these studies, Malamuth et al. (1980) provided subjects with the depiction of a rape incident and then asked them to complete a rape questionnaire that assessed their beliefs concerning the victim, the rapist, and the rape situation with respect to the rape scenario. The results indicated that the self-rated likelihood of raping was associated with positive attitudes toward the rapist's behavior, negative attitudes toward the victim, and the belief that women enjoy vicitimization. Tieger (1981) replicated this study and concluded that self-reported likelihood of raping was related to the "belief in the notion that victims acted seductively, enjoyed being raped and that other males would also be likely to rape." Males with a high likelihood of raping were also "more likely to blame the victim (factor 1) and perceive her as more attractive. . . . [These subjects] scored lower in femininity, viewed the crime as less serious (factor 4) and also held a more sympathetic view of the rapist (factor 7)" (pp. 154–155).

A similar study has been reported by Briere and Malamuth (1983). These authors assessed the subjects' likelihood of raping as well as the likelihood that they would force "a female to do something she really didn't want to do." On the basis of these two questions, subjects were classified as one of four groups: (1) no likelihood of force or rape (F−R−), (2) some likelihood of force but no likelihood of rape (F+R−), (3) no likelihood of force but some likelihood of rape (F−R+), and (4) some likelihood of both force and rape (F+R+). Very few subjects admitted to no likelihood of force but some likelihood of rape. Thus, these subjects were excluded from analysis. A series of attitude and sexual variables were utilized in a discriminant analysis of the three groups (F−R−, F+R−, F+R+). Only one of the sexual variables—sexual experience—could significantly discriminate the three groups. However, many of the attitude variables derived from Burt (1980) were significant discriminative factors.

The studies concerning the relationship between sexual aggression and rape-supportive attitudes are remarkably consistent. Sexually aggressive men, whether convicted rapists, undetected rapists, or males with a self-rated likelihood of raping, maintain attitudes that differ considerably from the attitudes of sexually nonaggressive men. The sexually aggressive men tend to view rape as a crime of lesser seriousness and attempt to justify such behavior by directly or indirectly blaming the victim. The victim is viewed, at best, as not acting responsibly in avoiding a potential rape situation, and at worst, provoking or actually desiring the sexually aggressive actions displayed by the male. Behaviors that are only mildly sexual in nature are viewed as indicating that the female desires intercourse. These sexually aggressive men also believe that relationships between men and women are adversarial or manipulative, with men attempting to convince the reluctant woman to have sexual relations. Finally, these men believe that some amount of force is a legitimate strategy to induce a female to behave according to their desire and that a female will not find this force offensive.

Sexual Arousal

The pattern of sexual arousal of sexually aggressive men is a third area that has attracted considerable study. This research has been conducted amidst debate over the primary motivational forces underlying sexual aggression. It is clear, of course, that rape, on the level of overt behavior, is a violent act. What is controversial is whether this overt aggressive act is primarily motivated by deviant sexual arousal or by deviant hostile needs to dominate and humiliate women. Some authors have attempted to develop classification systems that group rapists according to the relative balance of sexual and aggressive motives apparent in the act (e.g., Cohen *et al.*, 1971; Groth, Burgess, & Holmstrom, 1977). Such classifications are difficult to apply because they require attribution of motivational intent to the offender after the crime has already occurred. Nevertheless, these classification systems do indicate that clinicians working with convicted rapists perceive evidence that both deviant hostility and sexual arousal patterns occur to various degrees. Of most relevance to this chapter, however, are attempts to study these motives empirically.

Early studies of sexual arousal in sexually aggressive men utilized retrospective self-reports of the individual's response to pornography (e.g., Thorne & Haupt, 1966; Gebhard, Gagnon, Pomeroy & Christenson, 1965) or estimated sex drive (Kanin, 1965). The results of these studies tended to indicate little difference between rapists and nonrapists on these measures. However, there is some doubt as to the accuracy of such measures of sexual arousal.

Later studies have utilized more objective measures of sexual arousal and penile erection. Kercher and Walker (1973) allowed rapists and non-sex-offenders to view a series of slides that depicted a variety of sexual activities. Each slide was presented for 20 seconds. Penile enlargement, galvanic skin responses (GSR), and subjective ratings of the slides were obtained. The results indicated no difference between rapists and non-sex-offenders in sexual arousal as measured by penile enlargement. However, rapists tended to manifest higher GSR responsivity and to rate the slides as less appealing relative to the control subjects.

Abel, Barlow, Blanchard, and Guild (1977) argued that the absence of sexual arousal differences in the Kercher and Walker (1973) study could be attributed to two factors: the relatively short exposure of the slide and the absence of rape cues in the slides. These authors chose a group of rapists and a group of nonrapists (composed primarily of bisexuals and pedophiles) and presented an audiotaped scenario of mutually consenting intercourse and one of forcible rape. The penile enlargement measure indicated that nonrapists were less aroused to the rape depiction than to the mutually consenting depiction. Rapists, on the other hand, were equally aroused to these two scenarios. Further, rapists and nonrapists did not differ in their sexual arousal to mutually consenting intercourse.

In a second study, these authors assessed the penile enlargement of the rapists from the above study to an aggressive scenario devoid of any sexual material. The degree of erection to the aggressive scene was considerably less than to the rape or mutually consenting scenes. However, a highly significant correlation ($r = .98$) was noted between a rapist's response to the aggressive cues and his response to the rape cues. Rapists with the largest penile enlargement to the rape scenes manifested the largest enlargement to the aggressive scenes. These findings led the authors to suggest that the observed level of sexual arousal to rape scenes was the result of an individual's response to mutually consenting intercourse and to aggression. They hypothesized that in the nonrapist the presence of aggressive cues inhibited arousal, while in rapists, there was no appreciable inhibition. The authors speculated that sadists may be individuals who are aroused by aggressive cues but are relatively unaffected by mutually consenting cues.

Subsequent studies (Barbaree, Marshal, & Lanther, 1979; Hinton, O'Neill, & Webster, 1980; Quinsey, Chaplin, & Varney, 1981) have provided some support for the findings of Abel *et al.* (1977). For example, Barbaree *et al.* (1979) allowed 10 incarcerated rapists and 10 graduate students to listen to verbal descriptions of mutually consenting intercourse, rape, and nonsexual assault. Rapists and nonrapists did not evidence different levels of penile enlargement to mutually consenting intercourse. Rape scenarios, as compared to mutually consenting scenarios, resulted in a reduction of arousal in the nonrapist group but did not affect the arousal of the rapists. The authors suggest that "sexual arousal in these rapists may have been deviant, not necessarily because force and violence and nonconsent of the female evoked their sexual arousal, but perhaps because force, violence, and nonconsent of the female failed to inhibit their sexual arousal" (p. 221). Hinton *et al.* (1980) showed several groups of sex offenders and a nonoffender control group a movie depicting several forms of sexual behavior. None of the groups differed while observing the mutually consenting segment of the film. However, those offenders convicted for sexual attacks on women or girls evidenced higher levels of arousal than nonoffenders or physically aggressive offenders while observing the film segments devoted to rape of a 12-year-old and the abduction of a clothed female.

Malamuth and Check (1980a, 1980b, 1981, August) have reported similar findings with a group of males with a proclivity toward rape. Males with self-reported low and high likelihood of rape were randomly assigned to listen to one of three tapes: a mutually consenting depiction, a rape depiction in which the rape is responded to very negatively by the victim (rape victim adhorrence), and a rape depiction in which the victim involuntarily became sexually aroused (rape victim arousal). Men with some proclivity to rape were more aroused, according to penile tumescence, by the rape victim abhorrence tape than by the mutually consenting tape. For these men, the tape with the rape victim arousal produced the highest level of sexual arousal. Men with a low proclivity to rape were equally aroused by the tapes of mutually consenting intercourse and rape victim arousal but were less aroused by the tape of rape victim abhorrence. Furthermore, men with high likelihood of raping evidenced somewhat higher levels of sexual arousal than did men with low likelihood of raping when listening to the rape depiction tapes. This situation was reversed when listening to the tape of mutually consenting intercourse.

In general, these results do suggest differential sexual responsivity between sexually aggressive and nonaggressive men. The presence of various cues of rape inhibits the arousal of sexually nonaggressive men but not sexually aggressive men. Rape cues potentially congruent with some male fantasies, such as the eventual arousal of the victim, appear to result in high levels of arousal in both sexually aggressive and nonaggressive males.

Hostility

Less attention has been directed to the study of the hostile motivation as compared to the sexual arousal of sexually aggressive men. Three studies have compared incarcerated rapists on measures of hostility. Fisher and Rivlin (1971) reported that rapists scored lower on the California Psychological Inventory Aggression scale than did other prisoners or normal controls. Scully and Marolla (1982, January) found no significant differences between rapist and nonrapist prisoners on the Hostility toward Women Scale (Marolla & Scully, 1979). In contrast, Rada, Laws, and Kellner (1976) found that rapists scored higher than a normal group or child molesters on the Buss-Durkee Hostility Inventory.

The hostility of men who admitted to sexual aggression has also been studied. Kanin (1965) found that sexually aggressive men scored higher on the Zaks and Walter's (1959) Aggression scale. Koss *et al.* (in press) reported that although the total score on the Buss-Durkee Hostility Inventory (1957) was correlated with level of sexual aggression ($r=.17$), it did not significantly contribute to the prediction of group membership.

The self-reported hostility of males with a high likelihood of raping has also been explored. Malamuth and Check (1983) found that the Psychoticism scale of the Eysenck Personality Inventory was correlated ($r = .17$) with likelihood of raping. Eysenck (1977) has noted that Psychoticism is a dimension that runs through the normal range and is related to hostility to women and aggressive sexual encounters.

These studies all utilized self-report measures of hostility. While it seems reasonable that these measures would be related to overt sexual aggression, the extent of the relationship is not well known. Therefore, studies that examine an actual harming response are important. Malamuth (1981) assessed the reported likelihood of raping of male college students; then several days later a female experimenter insulted them. Subsequently, the subjects were allowed to administer different levels of aversive noise to the female in the context of a teacher–learner paradigm. The results suggested that self-reported likelihood of raping was related to anger toward the woman, a reported desire to hurt her, and greater behavioral aggression.

Hostility has been studied among samples using self-reported sexual aggression, self-reported likelihood of raping, and judicial identification. While hostility has rather consistently been reported when the Buss-Durkee was used, and in samples of nonincarcerated subjects; two of three studies of incarcerated rapists failed to find elevated levels of hostility compared to other prisoners. These results are somewhat hard to interpret due to unresolved conceptual problems. For example, it is not known what the clinical significance of an elevated Buss-Durkee score is. Also, the relationship of physical aggression and sexual aggression has not been considered. These problems will be explored in more detail in the final section of this chapter.

THEORETICAL IMPLICATIONS AND DIRECTIONS
FOR FUTURE RESEARCH

In this section we attempt to evaluate the major theoretical models of rape in terms of the empirical findings reported above.

A primary conclusion that emerged from the literature is that the method of sample selection is a critical methodological issue. Rape is both an underreported and underconvicted crime, so studies based on rapists identified by the judicial process are unlikely to be reflective of the entire population of sexually aggressive men. Yet, alternative sampling procedures have been found to result in samples that differ from incarcerated rapists on prominent features such as acquaintance with the victim and the violence used in the assault. In part, these differences may support the contentions of various writers (e.g., Brownmiller, 1975) that certain offender characteristics (e.g., low SES, minority race) and crime characteristics (e.g., extreme violence, no relationship to the victim) facilitate conviction whereas the opposite characteristics greatly reduce the probability of detection. However, no sampling strategy can be touted as the single road to identification of the true domain of rapists since rapists and rape do not appear to be homogeneous categories.

The psychological variables that have been examined among sexually aggressive men include psychological adjustment, rape myths and rape-supportive beliefs, sexual arousal patterns to erotica and pornography, and general hostility and aggressivity. The implications of these empirical findings for the major theoretical models of rape is now considered.

Psychopathology Model

The psychopathology model suggests that sexual aggression is due to an emotional disorder in the offender (Brodsky, 1976). Rape or sexual aggression is simply one manifestation of the psychological disorder of the individual. A direct implication of this model is that the examination of rapists and sexually aggressive men should reveal more manifestations of disorder than an examination of sexually nonaggressive men.

The empirical evidence does not provide clear support for the psychopathology model of sexual aggression. Studies that have examined the diagnoses of incarcerated rapists typically have had severe methodological problems including the absence of comparison groups and the failure to maintain blind conditions in the individuals doing the diagnoses. Methodologically superior studies have often failed to find differences in psychopathology between rapists and other criminal groups (Karacon, Williams, Guerraro, Salis, Thornby, & Hursch, 1974; Panton, 1958). Finally, the only study that employed nonincarcerated rapists found no relationship between level of sexual aggression and two measures sensitive to psychopathology (Koss *et al.*) Even if psychopathology could be demonstrated conclusively among incarcerated rapists, however, the conclusion that psychopathology was a cause of incarceration rather than a cause of rape could still not be refuted.

It should be noted that the studies that have found evidence of psychopathology have typically involved convicted rapists whose victims were most often strangers or nonromantic acquaintances. The absence of psychopathology has been noted among undetected rapists. Sampling techniques to identify undetected rapists frequently result in samples of sexually aggressive men who have victimized romantic acquaintances (e.g., Koss *et al.* [in press] reported that 85% of their highly sexually aggressive men had victimized women with whom they were romantically involved). These differences highlight the problems inherent in treating rape as a unidimensional construct when rapes are known to differ in violence, context (stranger, acquaintance) and form (individual, group). Deming and Eppy (1981) have suggested that comparative studies have been neglected by rape researchers and "theories specific to stranger rape and acquaintance rape have yet to be developed" (p. 362). "Unsocialized" rape involves the total lack of an appropriate social context where the offender chooses a victim with whom he has no ramantic relationship. It is possible that psychopathology plays a more powerful etiological role in this form of rape than in "socialized" rape that involves inappropriate sexual conduct occurring in a superficially appropriate social context.

Future research on the psychopathology of sexually aggressive men should try to specify the level of violence, form and context in which the rape occurred, attempt to remove undetected rapists from comparison samples, administer standard psychological tests that can be statistically treated, and have diagnostic assessments carried out by two independent clinicians who are not informed of the criminal status of the offender.

Social Control Model

The second theoretical model has been referred to as the social control model (Weis & Borges, 1973). This model suggests that certain attitudes and beliefs concerning male–female relationships and sex roles facilitate sexually aggressive behavior. A major set of these attitudes have been labeled "rape myths" (Weis & Borges, 1973). For the male, these rape myths have been hypothesized to allow the sexually aggressive man to avoid defining force or threat of force in the service of his sexual aims as rape. Instead, such force is seen as a normal way in which to instigate sexual intercourse with a woman. As a result, the mythology of rape "allows the man both to engage in the otherwise forbidden behavior and to rationalize and justify it after the event" (Weis & Borges, 1973, p. 87).

The bulk of empirical findings appears to be consistent with the social control model of sexual aggression. Sexually aggressive boys and men, rapists, and men who admit to some likelihood of raping tend to believe in the accuracy of rape myths more than do sexually nonaggressive men and they tend to maintain constellations of attitudes consistent with their behavior. For example, these men minimize the severity of sexually aggressive behavior and blame the female when such behavior occurs. They are more sure that a female desires sexual intercourse when she engages in certain ambiguous behaviors, tend to believe her refusal is simply an aspect of the traditional adversarial nature of heterosexual relationships, and are more likely to view aggressive force as an appropriate and necessary step to induce a female to behave in accordance with their interpretation of the situation.

Future research is needed to address the precursors of rape myth acceptance. It should be determined whether rape myth acceptance can be related to any socialization differences. Alternately, the possibility should be explored that those individuals who strongly adhere to a rape-supportive belief system may have had similar socialization experiences but possess other psychological characteristics that lead them to absorb rape-supportive beliefs differentially. It would be interesting to study individuals who adhere to a rape-supportive belief system but who have not raped to learn something of the factors or controls that may mitigate sexual aggression.

The data regarding the sexual arousal patterns and the levels of hostility displayed by sexually aggressive men are not directly related to either the psychopathology or the social control model of rape. However, any viable explanation of sexual aggression must incorporate these data and both models could be altered to explain them.

For example, the social control model could explain the sexual arousal results as follows. Certain factors such as force by the male or nonconsent or negativity by the female appear to change the interpretation of a sexual situation for sexually nonaggressive men. The belief system of sexually aggressive men may lead them to misperceive this sexual situation as a normal heterosexual relationship. A belief in the normality of sexually aggressive behavior, for example, might prevent such men from viewing the situation as incompatible with sexual behavior and their behavior is, therefore, not inhibited. Alternatively, the psychopathology model could account for the deviant arousal findings by postulating either a generalized or specific defect in impulse control.

The research on deviant arousal patterns is not yet complete. Deviant arousal patterns have been reported among incarcerated rapists and among males with high self-rated likelihood of raping. There have been some failures to replicate the findings reported in the literature as well. The sexual arousal patterns of undetected rapists who became sexually aggressive in a dating situation have not yet been investigated. This group appears to be important to study. If deviant arousal patterns can be identified in the absence of psychopathology, the case for defective impulse control would be weakened.

The last psychological variable that has been investigated among sexually aggressive men is hostility. Data indicative of higher self-reported hostility among sexually aggressive men have been reported. In addition, one study demonstrated greater physical aggression against women in a laboratory setting by men with a high self-rated likelihood of raping. However, questions regarding construct validity plague interpretation of these results. For example, further work must be done to consider whether the hostility reported by sexually aggressive men is generalized or specific to women. Research should also attempt to determine the extent to which self-reported hostility by sexually aggressive men translates into behavioral aggression. It would also be important to learn whether sexual aggression occurs by itself in a specific subgroup of men, or whether it is a manifestation of general physical aggressiveness.

CONCLUSIONS

Deming and Eppy (1981) note that ''recent research supports most theories of rape (p. 374).'' It is premature and overly simplistic to focus on a single theoretical model. This review of the literature on male sexual aggression leads to the conclusion that while there are many fruitful avenues of exploration, methodological refinements are needed in future rape research. Most importantly, the review has highlighted the complexity of rape and the need for future studies to address the topic with more specificity.

REFERENCES

Abel, G. G., Barlow, D. H., Blanchard, E., & Guild, D. (1977). The components of rapists' sexual arousal. *Archives of General Psychiatry, 34,* 395–403.

Ageton, S. S. (1983) Sexual assault among adolescents. Lexington, Mass.: Lexington Books.

Barbaree, H. E., Marshal, W. L., & Lanther, R. D. (1979). Deviant sexual arousal in rapists. *Behavior Research and Therapy, 17,* 215–222.

Bohmer, C. (1974). Judicial attitudes toward rape victims. *Judicature, 57,* 303–307.

Briere, J., & Malamuth, N. M. (1983) Self-reported likelihood of sexually aggressive behavior: Attitudinal vs. sexual explanations. *Journal of Research in Personality, 17,* 315–323.

Brodsky, S. L. (1976). Sexual assault: Perspectives on prevention and assailants. In M. J. Walker & S. L. Brodsky (Eds.), *Sexual assault.* Lexington, MA: D. C. Heath and Company.

Brownmiller, S. (1975). *Against our will: Men, women, and rape*. New York: Simon & Schuster.

Burt, M. R. (1980) Cultural myths and support for rape. *Journal of Personality and Social Psychology, 38,* 217–230.

Buss, A. H., & Durkee, A. (1957). An inventory for assessing different kinds of hostility. *Journal of Consulting and Clinical Psychology, 21,* 343–349.

Clark, L., & Lewis, D. (1977). *Rape: The price of coercive sexuality*. Toronto: The Women's Press.

Cohen, M. L. (1976). Patterns of conflict in the rapist. Paper presented at Butler Hospital Conference, Providence, RI.

Cohen M. L., Garofalo, R., Boucher, R., & Seghorn, T. (1971). The psychology of rapists. *Seminars in Psychiatry, 3,* 307–327.

Deming, M. P., & Eppy, A. (1981) The sociology of rape. *Sociology and Social Research, 65,* 357–380.

Dahlstrom, W. G., Welsh, G. S., & Dahlstrom, L. E. (1972). *An MMPI handbook. Volume I: Clinical interpretation*. Minneapolis: University of Minnesota Press.

Eysenck, H. J. (1977). *Crime and personality* (3rd ed.) London: Granda Press.

Feild, H. S. (1978). Attitudes toward rape: A comparative analysis of police, rapists, crisis counselors, and citizens. *Journal of Personality and Social Psychology, 36,* 156–179.

Fisher, G., & Rivlin, E. (1971). Psychological needs of rapists. *British Journal of Criminology, 11,* 182–185.

Gebhard, P. H., Gagnon, J. H., Pomeroy, W. B., & Christenson, C. V. (1965). *Sex offenders: An analysis of types*. New York: Harper & Row.

Graham, J. R. (1977). *The MMPI: A Practical Guide*. New York: Oxford University Press.

Groth, A. N., & Birnbaum, H. J. (1979). *Men who rape: The psychology of the offender*. New York: Plenum Press.

Groth, A. N., Burgess, A. W., & Holmstrom, L. L. (1977). Rape, power, anger, and sexuality. *American Journal of Psychiatry, 134,* 1239–1243.

Hammer, E. F. (1954). A comparison of H-T-Ps of rapists and pedophiles. *Journal of Projective Techniques, 18,* 346–354.

Henn, F. A. (1978). The aggressive sexual offender. In I. L. Kutash, S. B. Kutash, & L. B. Schlesinger (Eds.), *Violence: Perspectives on murder and aggression*. San Francisco: Jossey-Bass.

Hinton, J. W., O'Neill, M. T., & Webster, S. (1980). Psychophysiological assessment of sex offenders in a security hospital. *Archives of Sexual Behavior, 9,* 205–216.

Holmstrom, L. L., & Burgess, A. (1975). Rape: The victim goes on trial. In I. Drapkin & E. Viano (Eds.), *Victimology: A new focus*. Lexington, MA: Lexington Books.

Kanin, E. (1965). Male sex aggression and three psychiatric hypotheses. *The Journal of Sex Research, 1,* 221–231.

Karacon, I., Williams, R.L., Guerraro, M. W., Salis, P. J., Thornby, J. I., & Hursch, C. J. (1974). Nocturnal penile tumescence and sleep of convicted rapists and other prisoners. *Archives of Sexual Behavior, 3,* 19–26.

Kercher, G. A., & Walker, C. E. (1973). Reactions of convicted rapists to sexually explicit stimuli. *Journal of Abnormal Psychology, 81,* 46–50.

Koss, M. P., & Oros, C. J. (1982). Sexual experiences survey: A research instrument investigating sexual aggression and victimization. *Journal of Consulting and Clinical Psychology. 50,* 455–457.

Koss, M. P., Leonard, K. E., Beezley, D. A., & Oros, C. J. (in press) Nonstranger sexual aggression: A discriminant analysis of psychological dimensions. *Sex Roles*.

LEAA (Law Enforcement Assistance Administration). (1975). Criminal victimization surveys in 13 American cities. Washington, DC: Government Printing Office.

Lykken, D. T., Tellegen, A., & Katzenmeyer, C. (1973). Manual for the Activity Preference Questionnaire. Unpublished manuscript, University of Minnesota.

Malamuth, N. M. (1981). Rape proclivity among males. *Journal of Social Issues, 37,* 138–157.

Malamuth, N., & Check, J. V. P. (1980a). Penile tumescence and perceptual responses to rape as a function of victim's perceived reactions. *Journal of Applied Social Psychology, 10,* 528–547.

Malamuth, N., & Check, J. V. P. (1980b). Sexual arousal to rape and consenting depictions: The importance of the woman's arousal. *Journal of Abnormal Psychology, 89,* 763–766.

Malamuth, N., & Check, J. V. P. (1981, August). The effects of exposure to aggressive pornography: Rape proclivity, sexual arousal, and beliefs in rape myths. Paper presented at the Annual Meeting of the American Psychological Association, Los Angeles.

Malamuth, N., & Check, J. V. P. Sexual arousal to rape depictions: Individual differences. *Journal of Abnormal Psychology, 92,* 55–67.

Malamuth, N., Haber, S., & Feshbach, S. (1980). Testing hypotheses regarding rape: Exposure to sexual violence, sex differences and the "normality" of rapists. *Journal of Research in Personality, 14,* 121–137.

Marolla, J., & Scully, D. (1979). Rape and psychiatric vocabularies of motive. In Gomberg, E. & Franks, V. (Eds.) *Gender and disordered behavior: Sex differences in psychopathology.* Larchmont, NY: Brunner-Mazel.

McCaldon, R. J. (1967). Rape. *Canadian Journal of Corrections, 9,* 37–43.

Panton, J. H. (1958). MMPI profile configurations among crime classification groups. *Journal of Clinical Psychology, 14,* 305–308.

Perdue, W. C., & Lester, D. (1972). Personality characteristics of rapists. *Perceptual and Motor Skills, 35,* 514.

Quinsey, V. L., Chaplin, T. C., & Varney, G. (1981). A comparison of rapists and non-sex offenders' sexual preferences for mutually consenting sex, rape, and physical abuse of women. *Behavioral Assessment, 3,* 127–135.

Rada, R. T., Laws, D. R., & Kellner, R. (1976). Plasma testosterone levels in the rapist. *Psychosomatic Medicine, 38,* 257–268.

Radar, C. M. (1977). MMPI profile types of exposers, rapists, and assaulters in a court services population. *Journal of Consulting and Clinical Psychology, 45,* 61–69.

Scroggs, J. R. (1976). Penalties for rape as a function of victim provocativeness, damage, and resistance. *Journal of Applied Social Psychology, 6,* 360–368.

Scully, D., & Marolla, J. (1982, January). Convicted rapists attitudes toward women and rape. Paper presented at the First International, Interdisciplinary Congress on Women, University of Haifa, Haifa, Israel.

Spence, J. T., Helmreich, R., & Stapp, J. (1973). A short version of the Attitudes Toward Women Scale. *Bulletin of the Psychonomic Society, 2,* 219–220.

Thorne, E. C., & Haupt, T. D. (1966). Objective measurement of sex attitudes and behavior in adult males, *Journal of Clinical Psychology, 22,* 404–407.

Tieger, T. (1981). Self-rated likelihood of raping and the social perception of rape. *Journal of Research in Personality, 15,* 147–158.

Weis, K., & Borges, S. S. (1973). Victimology and rape: The case of the legitimate victim. *Issues in Criminology, 8,* 71–115.

Williams, J. & Holmes, K. A. (1981). The second assault: Rape and public attitudes Westport, Conn: Greenwood Press.

Zaks, M. S., & Walters, R. H. (1959). First steps in the construction of scale and measurement of aggression, *The Journal of Psychology, 47,* 199–209.

9

Sexual Signaling and Sexual Aggression in Adolescent Relationships*

JACQUELINE D. GOODCHILDS
GAIL L. ZELLMAN

Changes in sexual attitudes and behaviors are occurring among adolescents as well as adults. These changes, including a younger age of initiation into sex, greater acceptance of childbearing and rearing among nonwedded persons, and different expectations of marriage have been extensively documented, viewed with enthusiasm or with alarm, and linked in the common parlance with impressive-sounding rubrics such as liberation, epidemic, egalitarianism, and revolution (see Chilman, 1979; Glenn & Weaver, 1979; Hopkins, 1977; Jessor & Jessor, 1975; Zellman & Goodchilds, 1982; Zelnik, Kantner, & Ford, 1981).

Yet the more subtle aspects of these changes have been largely ignored. Little attention or concern has been devoted to understanding how—or if—these new norms are expressed by interacting individuals. One aspect of behavior that has been overlooked is sexual signaling between today's young couples. Has this important form of communication changed to reflect significant societal-level changes? If so, are these signals shared? Do both genders interpret them the same

*The research described was supported by PHS Grant #R01-MH 30655 from the National Center for the Prevention and Control of Rape. Importantly involved in the study, in addition to the two authors, were Paula B. Johnson and Roseann Giarrusso.

233

way? Do new, apparently more liberated behaviors signal liberation or something else? We explore some of these important communication issues in this chapter.

In addressing these issues we draw on the results of a 1978 survey of Los Angeles teenagers designed to examine expectations for and communication about sex across gender (see Giarrusso, Johnson, Goodchilds, & Zellman, 1979; Goodchilds, Zellman, Johnson, & Giarrusso, 1979; Zellman, Goodchilds, Johnson, & Giarrusso, 1981; and Zellman, Johnson, Giarrusso, & Goodchilds, 1979).

THE SURVEY SAMPLE

Survey respondents were 432 volunteer participants recruited through the summer-work job office of the Youth Employment Service of the California State Department of Employment. Written consent was obtained from both parents of each interviewee (whenever possible), and each respondent was paid $5 at the end of the session. All sessions were conducted in a private setting with a specially trained interviewer experienced in work with adolescents and of the same gender and ethnicity as the person being interviewed. The sample was stratified by gender and ethnicity such that there are six equal subcategories of respondent: male or female self-identified as Anglo, black, or Hispanic.

Although limits of project size and resources precluded inclusion of Asian teenagers in the sample, the obtained sample is otherwise representative for the area ethnically and socioeconomically, with the two dimensions seriously confounded.[1] Almost all of our respondents (98.4%) were still living in their family of orientation, half of those with a lone parent (an incidence figure also fairly typical for the area). With few exceptions (less than 4%) they were high-school attendees; the 14% who had graduated that June were planning further training either in college or in trade–professional schools.

A requirement for participation in the study was that participants not have started post-high-school training and that they be between 14 and 18 years of age inclusive. The sample was about equally split into thirds by age: 35% were ages 14 and 15; 31%, exactly 16; 34%, 17 and 18. Nearly all reported interest in cross-gender sexuality. Many were sexually active: 71.7% of males and 57.2% of females reported that they had "gone all the way [had sexual intercourse] with someone of the opposite sex."[2]

---

[1]To index socioeconomic status of an adolescent group, we utilized parents' education and occupation and respondents' aspirations for both.

[2]This question was asked at the end of the interview and in such a way that the answer did not involve self-presentation uncertainties (the reply was placed by the interviewee in a separate sealed envelope).

Interestingly, none of these background characteristics were associated with different response patterns. Although there were some variations from one ethnic group to another in average level of response, within the three groups in our sample the male–female patterns were strongly similar. Chronological age, reported experience with sex, and any of several other background measures (e.g., dating history, place in family constellation) also did not predict the outcome measures. Evidently the development and extent of acceptance of the normative system for sexual encounters among this group of adolescents occur early and quite equally across the entire range of sampled characteristics.[3]

THE SEXUAL SIGNAL SYSTEM

The sexual signaling system—involving nonverbal as well as verbal behavior—helps partners and potential partners learn about the other and express personal needs and desires. A system that works (i.e., one in which signals are clear and straightforward) allows relationships to proceed (or not) based on accurate readings of the partners' needs and wishes. A dysfunctional system, in which signals are distorted by the sender, the receiver, or both, results in relationships that run the risk of being dishonest, exploitative, stereotypical, and unsatisfying. The sexual signal system works, or dysfunctions, at the very first encounter and continues to be important throughout a relationship.

Preliminary Signaling[4]

Communication may begin well before a partner is viewed as such. This earliest phase, preliminary signaling, is important because such signaling creates an impression that influences the partner's expectations and behavior during and often well after the period of initial acquaintance. A key element of this earliest phase concerns selection of the partner from among any number of potential opposite-gender associates. How does one choose dating and/or sexual partners?

A simple, noninteractive criterion might be reputation: If a young man or woman has a reputation for having had sex with other people, would one expect to have sex on a date with this person? Probably yes, according to our respondents. Both genders differentiate between male and female reputations, however, with the female reputation being a much more salient signal.

A second selection criterion might be apparel, that is, are there certain articles

---

[3]These and some other study findings are reported in greater detail in a series of convention presentations (see References).

[4]In the analysis of these data the statistic of choice was for each question an analysis of variance with item option, gender, ethnicity of respondent, and (where appropriate) gender of referent as factors. All reported differences are significant at least at the $p < .01$ level.

of clothing whose wearing is indicative of sexual interest? This set of questions asked first in open-ended fashion, then in a structured way, similarly established the female as the more salient signaler. Neither gender had a ready set of stereotypes about sexy clothing for young males, but both endorsed such items of female apparel as a see-through blouse, low-cut top, no bra, and tight jeans as possible indicators that the young woman wearing them wanted to have sex. Interestingly, males were more confident than females of this interpretation; they saw these garments as potent sexual signals while females were less certain of their meaning. This reflects a potentially dangerous divergence between the genders. A young man can dress himself with impunity. Male and female adolescents agreed that, on a male, an open shirt, tight pants, or jewelry are not clearly communicating anything about his interests or availability for sex. But a young woman's attire may have considerable signal value—the young men may receive what they interpret as a strong sexual signal, but in the view of the wearer and that of her girlfriends, she may simply be trying to keep up with the latest fashion trends.

As a final preliminary type of signal, a person selected as a dating partner may communicate his or her intentions toward having sex by the choice of or agreement with the setting for the date. For five possible "things a guy and a girl might do together," we asked what participating would indicate about each person. The activities rated ranged, according to our respondents, from very indicative of sexual interest (going home to the man's home when they knew they would be alone there) to relatively uninformative of sexual intentions (attending a party where there would be grass, drugs, and drinking). The ordering of the five options was identical across gender, suggesting that place represents a relatively unambiguous set of signals. However, there are two quite distinct and independent main effects in these data consistent with an emerging general pattern. For the five settings combined, all subjects rated the participating male as more interested than the female in having sex. On the same order of magnitude, male interviewees were more confident than females that the dating pair wanted to have sex.

Acting Out: Dating Behaviors

Signaling continues and focuses when two people become a dating pair. We asked our subjects to interpret the sexual cue value of eight behaviors that might occur on a date. Ratings for these behaviors ranged in suggestiveness from the quite obvious and direct "talking about sex" and about the "sexiness" of the partner, and wrestling with and tickling the partner, through the more indirect approaches of professing one's love for the other, looking deeply into the other's eyes, or commenting on the other's beauty, to such relatively ambiguous actions as playing with the partner's hair or finally, remarking on how "understanding" the partner is. Male and female respondents rank-ordered these items identically, and in the same order regardless of the gender of the actor referent. Again male respondents consistently scored behaviors as more indicative of sexual interest than did female respondents, and behaviors by the male actor were seen by all as slightly more provocative. There is, however, a statistical interaction effect. Combining responses across all eight behaviors, we note that for young men the meaning of a behavior is largely independent of the gender of the communicator, whereas women differentiate by actor-gender in assigning meanings, interpreting male behavior as more suggestive than identical behaviors attributed to females.

The complexity of the signal system for young women as contrasted with that for young men is highlighted when we turn to questions of control over sexual interactions and the accompanying interpersonal affect. This area has always been a difficult one for women. Social norms dictate that the woman is responsible for sexual outcomes (and should say "no" to sex). At the same time, her partner may be persistent and threaten abandonment if she fails to deliver. A third element, generally ignored, is that of her own preferences and concerns in the interaction. To get at the notion of *sexual contract,* we presented subjects with 11 specific things a woman might do in a cross-gender encounter. For each, we asked whether the behavior indicated her agreement to have sex and whether a subsequent refusal on her part would give the man "the right to get mad." There was complete agreement between the genders on the ordering of the 11 situations for agreement to sex. However, male interviewees more often perceived that the female was signaling agreement to sex than did their female counterparts.

Subjects also agreed on the rank order of the items in terms of the male partner's right to get angry if the female partner exhibited the behavior, then refused sex. Two female behaviors stand out as inconsequential—responding to the male's kisses and lying down next to him. These are followed in the subjects' ordering by several relatively noncommittal behaviors—dating a man several times, allowing a man to "touch and feel" her body, kissing the man first, and allowing the man to lie on top of her. A significantly more serious breach of contract is entailed if a woman "touches a man below the waist"; worse yet would be to undress or allow herself to be undressed or to undress the man. The most reprehensible action of the 11 behaviors in the eyes of our young people, male and female, is for the woman to change her mind—"to say yes to sex and then say no." Subjects of both genders shared the view that anger was justifiable when the female partner displayed certain behaviors but refused sex. Across items and subject gender, the mean score on the question of the male right to get mad fell on the "maybe yes" side of the scale. However, male subjects saw more justification for anger by the rebuffed male than did female subjects. Male anger is unfortunately but thus demonstrably a predictable and acceptable accompaniment to breach of contract in the sexual arena.

Jacqueline D. Goodchilds and Gail L. Zellman

These findings suggest that if a woman does not want to have sex but wants to forestall male anger, she must be careful to avoid certain behaviors. But what can she do, or how can she act in a positive way to prevent sex but maintain the relationship and positive affect? We presented subjects with eight possible behaviors a woman might employ to forestall an unwanted sexual advance while keeping the relationship friendly. These included pushing him away, acting distant or annoyed, laughing or giggling, being unresponsive to a "come on," saying she does not want a sexual relationship, saying she is tired, cracking jokes, or suggesting they go to a public place. We asked subjects to indicate for each how likely the male would be to stop coming on and (separately) how likely it was that the relationship would remain friendly. Again. we found close agreement between genders on these items. Male and female subjects agreed that simply saying she did not want sex and acting "distant and annoyed" were the two best ways to control the male's behavior and maintain positive affect. Rated next in order of success was the ploy of suggesting going out some place. The remaining five options (being nonresponsive, claiming fatigue, giggling and joking, pushing the partner away) were uncertainly ordered, but all were seen as relatively inadequate to achieve one or the other goal. The problem of the double message did not go unnoticed by the subjects, who accorded "suggesting going out" the best balance across control and affect goals, rated "expressing annoyance" very high on control and relatively low on affect maintenance, and "giggling and joking" (not surprisingly) the reverse. A striking overall gender difference does emerge here, however: Young men are more able than young women to imagine that a friendly relationship can be maintained in the face of sexual rejection. This difference may reflect very different norms for men and women in this domain. Male adolescents are expected every time and with every potential partner insistently to attempt to have sex, a behavior pattern which inevitably involves the expectation and experience of at least occasional failure. Females, however, are expected to control sexual behavior and affect. The balance is a difficult one, and adolescent females often worry whether successful control and positive affect are mutually exclusive.

Men may step out of role and exercise control in some cases. We asked subjects to rate five behaviors in terms of their likely effectiveness in communicating to one's partner that one did not want "to go further." There was no ambiguity for our subjects in ordering the five suggested behaviors in terms of effectiveness, regardless of gender either of interviewee or actor. Complaining that a partner's sexual advances tickle or simply asking the other to stop are seen as ineffective control devices. In comparison, not responding to the partner's kisses is perceived as significantly more effective than any of the other options. Suggesting "doing something else for a while" and removing the partner's hands from "any place but the arms or the back" were rated moderately effective.

Though men exercise control infrequently, they are considered better at doing it. Both genders expected men to be more successful in stopping the action than women. But our subjects recognized that such control exercised by men is rare; many interviewees spontaneously observed that a male adolescent would *never* try to stop the action.

The findings up to this point indicate that the conflicting norms of earlier eras are still very much a part of sexual behavior today. Males are expected to be aggressive always, while females must control sexual behavior, be responsible for sexual outcomes, and maintain positive affect despite rejecting the advances of the male. The female may also try to meet her own needs, which themselves may be in conflict. Our findings also show that males and females learn and follow a similar sexual code. To a remarkable degree, they agree on rank orderings of the sexiness, aggressiveness, and cue value of a wide range of behaviors. At the same time, the mean ratings of these behaviors are significantly different. Males have a more sexualized view of the world than females, attributing more sexual meaning to a wide range of behaviors—a differentiation that has recently come under examination and been confirmed for a slightly older population (college students) in an experimental laboratory setting (Abbey, 1982).

DIFFICULT ENCOUNTERS

Normative expectations about dating interactions held by the sampled adolescents seem a confusing, contradictory, and in some ways self-defeating swirl of prescriptions and proscriptions for both genders. In normal dating situations these expectations may produce awkwardness, discomfort, or disappointment. But what happens when the situation becomes bluntly aggressive? How do adolescents apply norms and evaluate behavior in the context of nonconsensual sex?

To explore these questions, we presented subjects a series of hypothetical stories involving teenage couples who found themselves alone together and at least initially attracted to one another sexually, such that they had progressed to kissing and a bit of mutually accepted exploration. Prominant among these vignettes (as we called them) was a series in which the female rejected any further sexual advance, the male persisted, and the story ended with the identical line, "Though the girl does not want to, they have sexual intercourse." These prototypical nonstranger rape stories varied in the following details:

1. The setting in which the events took place was described as (a) at work (after-school jobs), (b) at the female's home, or (c) at a party.
2. The existing relationship between the actors was presented as (a) newly acquainted, (b) friends but never dated, or (c) "in a dating relationship."

3. The pressure exerted by the male consisted of (a) threatening verbal harm ("I'll tell lies about you," etc.), (b) threatening physical harm, or (c) actually using force (slapping, hitting, etc.).

The three dimensions, each with three levels, generated a 3^3 factorial frame entailing 27 individual vignettes. Any particular interviewee responded to a subset of 9 in a balanced incomplete block design that provided sufficient statistical information to test all main effects and their interactions.

To avoid problems of self-presentation in terms either of the content of these materials or the subject's language fluency, the vignettes were read to the subject, who recorded his or her answers after each story on a separate standardized answer form. We asked six questions about each vignette: (1) How much was the boy responsible for what happened? (2) How much was the girl responsible for what happened? (3) Do you think you would like the boy in this story? (4) Do you think you would like the girl in this story? (5) Do you think this was rape? (6) Do you think this girl would want to see this boy again? Questions 3–6 were answered on the same 5-point scale (1 being definitely yes) used throughout the survey. The first two questions were answered on a percentage line, from 0 to 100%.

Analyses of these vignette data make it unmistakably clear that setting was of no significance to our young people in this context. We had designed the stories to reflect variation among locales in social appropriateness for sex; we found no evidence that adolescents have developed such a concept. A second and more startling outcome was an almost total absence of any difference in response by gender of the evaluator. With the one exception that young men reported more positive affect toward the boys in the stories than young women did, responses of our male and female subjects were identical.

Overall, most of the responsibility for what happened was attributed to the boy, but a surprising amount, nearly one-third, was assigned to the nonconsenting girl. As expected, the greater the pressure exerted by the man, the more responsibility for the outcome was attributed to him and the less was attributed to the female character. However, even in the case where her partner actually forces sex upon her, she was not seen as blameless. On average, she was assigned 20% of the responsibility in this worst-case vignette. At that high force level, the existence of a relationship also affected responsibility attributions. Subjects felt that the female partner in a dating couple shared more responsibility for forced sex than did females who were newly acquainted with their partner or who were just friends.

Subjects generally disliked the insistent young man and found him most unappealing in the high-force and just-met stories. Subjects' evaluation of the female character was unaffected by her relationship with her partner and was most positive when she was the victim of actual force. Generally, they were favorably disposed toward the young woman, seemingly not inclined to stigmatize her as the victim of nonconsensual sex.

The next to last question asked the respondents to decide whether or not the label "rape" was an appropriate descriptor for the event portrayed. This was the first and only time in the interview that the label "rape" was used. It is most informative to compare the average scores on this question with the comparable scores on the two responsibility questions. The ordering is exactly parallel: To the extent that the situation was seen as relatively more the responsibility of the boy and less that of the girl, it was also more likely to be described as rape. The vignette most so labeled describes an encounter between persons who have just met and the male uses actual force, followed next by the other two cases of the use of actual force. At the second level of the force variable (threat of physical force), the average score shifts significantly toward the "unsure" point on the scale, particularly for the nonstranger situation. Regardless of the relationship, when the aggressor merely threatens verbal harm, the respondents were clear that they did not know whether or not to think of this encounter as rape.

Finally, we wondered what such difficult encounters would imply about future contacts between the pair. Subjects assumed across situations that the girl would "probably not" want to see the boy again. But where nonconsensual sex occurred in the face of only a threat and that only of verbal harm, or if at the time of the incident the couple had already established a dating relationship, the scores shifted significantly down the scale toward uncertainty. Despite a carefully reiterated closing line for each story, "Though the girl does not want to, they have sexual intercourse," many subjects thought a continuing relationship might still be acceptable to the girl.

JUSTIFYING ASSAULT

Toward the very end of the interview session, the core question that had most centrally prompted our research was asked directly of the subjects: "Under what circumstances is it OK for a guy to hold a girl down and force her to have sexual intercourse?" With some righteous huffing and puffing, 72% of the adolescents replied that no circumstances would justify such behavior. However, as we spelled out a nine-item list of "what ifs" for them, the 72% adamantly opposed to force diminished to a bare 21% (two-thirds of whom were female) who held out across the nine options. The specific "what ifs" in order of ranking by the total group from least to most justifying assaultive male behavior were (1) he spends a lot of money on her, (2) he's so turned on he can't stop, (3) she is stoned or drunk, (4) she has had sexual intercourse with other guys, (5) she lets him touch her above the waist, (6) she says she's going to have sex with him and then changes her mind, (7) they have dated a long time, (8) she's led him on, (9) she gets him sexually excited. Whereas for the money option, two-thirds of the respondents reported that force was definitely contraindicated, at the other end of the option order those rejecting the acceptability of assault dropped to fewer than one-third of our sample.

While the extent to which male adolescents accept sexual assault as justified is surprising, the numbers of female adolescents who also condone a male attack is truly astounding. While female acceptance was less, the fact that females could accept such behavior at all is deeply disturbing.

Once again, the ordering of the behaviors was essentially the same for male and female respondents, indicating that the genders shared an understanding of the relative seriousness of behaviors as precursors to sexual assault. Clearly, they also shared a less than total aversion to the idea of assaultive acts by men. The similarity in attitudes and expectations between the two groups is all the more impressive in the light of a reported difference between them in their sources of sexual information. When asked how or where the respondents learned what they knew about sex, followed by a request to identify which of the named sources provided "the most useful information," young women were most apt to report learning from a class in school or from a parent and to cite the parent's information as most useful. Young men, on the other hand, typically reported other young males as their major and most useful resource. Irrespective of whether instruction comes from one's peer group or from the adult world, it evidently adds up to a shared picture of sexual behavior fraught with inequality and potential violence.

CONCLUSION

At most these survey data are descriptive of a particular population in a particular place at a particular point in time. Nevertheless the data seem enormously informative of the magnitude of a serious social problem. They also examine and refute a previously untested assumption—that benign social change (progress?) has been occurring in sexual socialization practices in step with increased knowledge about human sexuality and an increased thrust toward greater egalitarianism between the genders.

Our young male respondents report perceiving a world in which sexuality is a more pervasive and salient fact of life than our young females report—certainly not an unexpected finding. What is unexpected, however, is the extent to which both genders agree that this is so. Most sobering is the finding, repeated in several shades and nuances depending on the exact question to which subjects were responding, that both genders accept as the norm an essentially adversarial cross-gender relationship around sexual issues. Our data indicate that adolescents view sexual aggression by the man against the woman as an ever-present and sometimes acceptable possibility in the context of intimate cross-gender encounters.

It is evident that, in this arena, today's young people are echoing the concerns, the uncertainties, and (more ominously) the aggressive adversarial overtones characteristic of the experiences of previous generations. Efforts to change these patterns must, it seems, be directed toward both genders, must begin earlier in the life span of each, and must be more sweeping in scope than anyone had imagined.

REFERENCES

Abbey, A. (1982). Sex differences in attributions for friendly behavior: Do males misperceive females' friendliness? *Journal of Personality and Social Psychology, 42,* 830–838.

Chilman, C. S. (1979). *Adolescent sexuality in a changing American society: Social and psychological perspectives.* Washington, DC: Government Printing Office.

Giarrusso, R., Johnson, P.. Goodchilds, J. D., & Zellman, G. (1979, April). *Adolescents' cues and signals: Sex and assault.* Symposium presentation at the meeting of the Western Psychological Association, San Diego.

Glenn, N. D., & Weaver, C. N. (1979). Attitudes toward premarital, extramarital, and homosexual relations in the U.S. in the 1970s. *Journal of Sex Research, 15,* 108–118.

Goodchilds, J. D., Zellman, G., Johnson, P. B., & Giarrusso, R. (1979, April). *Adolescent perceptions of responsibility for "dating" outcomes.* Symposium presentation at the meeting of the Eastern Psychological Association, Philadelphia.

Hopkins, J. R. (1977). Sexual behavior in adolescence. *Journal of Social Issues, 33*(2), 67–85.

Jessor, S. L., & Jessor, R. (1975). Transition from virginity to nonvirginity among youth: A social-psychological study over time. *Developmental Psychology, 11,* 473–484.

Zellman, G. L., & Goodchilds, J. D. (1982). Becoming sexual in adolescence. In E. Allgeier & N. McCormick (Eds.), *Changing boundaries: Gender roles and sexual behavior.* Palo Alto, CA: Mayfield.

Zellman, G. L., Goodchilds, J. D., Johnson, P. B., & Giarrusso, R. (1981, August). *Teenagers' application of the label "rape" to nonconsensual sex between acquaintances.* Symposium presentation at the meeting of the American Psychological Association, Los Angeles.

Zellman, G. L., Johnson, P. B., Giarrusso, R., & Goodchilds, J. D. (1979, September). *Adolescent expectations for dating relationships: Consensus and conflict between the sexes.* Symposium presentation at the meeting of the American Psychological Association, New York.

Zelnik, M., Kantner, J. F., & Ford, K. (1981). *Sex and pregnancy in adolescence.* Beverly Hills, CA: Sage.

PART V

Legal Implications of Research on Pornography and Sexual Aggression

In the preceding chapters we have seen a good deal of debate concerning the effects of pornography, in particular aggressive forms of pornography, on social behavior and attitudes. This research might suggest to the reader that under some circumstances exposure to certain forms of pornographic materials can lead to greater acceptance of aggression against women, as well as an increase in aggressive behavior toward women under certain conditions. To the academic researcher, policy advisor, industry executive, or the general public, one question that often arises from these debates is the implications of the research for legislative and political change. A great deal of new social science research has been conducted in the years since the president's Commission on Obscenity and Pornography as we have seen from this book. Yet what impact, if any, will this new research have? Will it have acceptance in the legal community? Can the research be used to implement changes in the legal system that do not interfere with basic constitutional rights? What are the steps for the legal expert, social scientist, and public to take to make better use of this new research on pornography? These and other issues are the major concerns of the two chapters in this section.

In the first chapter, "Using Psychological Research on Violent Pornography

PORNOGRAPHY AND
SEXUAL AGGRESSION

to Inform Legal Change,'' Penrod and Linz first give us a historical overview of current American law on the regulation of pornography and obscenity, noting major court cases and the treatment of First Amendment free speech rights. The authors then contrast how British law has responded to many of the same issues the U.S. courts have addressed and note how the British differ in their definition of the notion of obscenity.

The largely unsuccessful usage of social science research in legal proceedings in these countries is then discussed, and the authors examine the newer research on pornography (that presented in this book) and how it can be incorporated into current law on pornography. The authors conclude that judicial change must be preceded by a show of public support for regulation; they then explore the quasi-legal solution to censorship of films in Britain and the United States.

The focus shifts from constitutional law in Chapter 10 to civil, or tort, law in Chapter 11, ''Bases of Liability for Injuries Produced by Media Portrayals of Violent Pornography,'' by Linz, Turner, Hesse, and Penrod. Is it possible that an individual or a company could be held liable for harm to another following the showing of certain pornographic materials? In order to answer this question, the authors first give us a background of tort law, pointing out cases dealing with the effects of TV violence and subsequent injury. We are then taken through the procedure of a civil suit and examine how current psychological research on violent pornography can be used in such a trial. While this is somewhat hypothetical, the authors note a number of recent cases in which this type of research has been employed. For the reader, however, it is an interesting examination of how materials presented in the preceding parts of this book can be utilized in a practical manner.

10

Using Psychological Research on Violent Pornography to Inform Legal Change*

STEVEN PENROD
DANIEL LINZ

STATE OF THE LAW

Suppose that in the next decade psychologists were able to demonstrate conclusively that exposure to certain types of stimuli—let us say, images of explicit
heterosexual activity paired with aggression or violence directed by the male
against the female—produces harmful consequences. Among these harms are (1)
a small, but detectable, increase in the likelihood that some male viewers will
actually commit a sexual assault (sometimes directly imitating what they have
seen); (2) the fostering of enduring calloused attitudes towards women—including an increased endorsement of rape mythology such as the belief that women
secretly desire to be raped; (3) substantial increases in males' belief that they
would commit a sexual assault if they knew they would escape punishment; (4) a
well-established tendency to aggress against females in a laboratory setting; and
(5) aggressive behavior by males against females after exposure in field settings.
Would these harms be a sufficient basis for state legislation—or even federal

*Preparation of this chapter was partially supported by National Science Foundation grant number
BNS826772 and National Institute of Justice grant number 80-IJ-CX-0034 to Steven Penrod.

legislation—proscribing the production, distribution, and sale of such materials? In this chapter we consider the relationship between psychological research and the law and speculate on the ways in which the research findings on violent pornography might be used to inform legal change.

In the first section of this chapter we consider the current status of American law concerning the regulation of speech generally and obscenity in particular. We then compare contemporary U.S. law with the British approaches to the regulation of obscene materials. We compare the British and American approaches for two reasons. First, as we shall see, much of the case law applicable to the regulation of pornography and obscenity in the United States stems directly from British law. Second, we feel it is useful to compare the treatment of pornographic and obscene materials in two very similar socio–legal systems. The reader may be surprised at the differences in the treatment of these materials in ostensibly similar societies. Our discussion of the interface between social science and the law in the U.S. includes uses by the legal community of the scientific findings of the U.S. Commission on Pornography and Obscenity and the possible uses of the current scientific findings on violent pornography. In the final section we consider a variety of quasi-legal responses to violent pornography, including the film industry's attempt to regulate itself in America and Great Britain and the activities of concerned citizens interested in curtailing the distribution of this material.

Status of American Law

SPEECH AND THE FIRST AMENDMENT

Throughout most of the history of American law, there has been no clear standard for addressing the problem of pornography and obscenity. The First Amendment to the Constitution of the United States is extremely broad in its protections concerning free speech: "Congress shall make no law respecting an establishment of religion or prohibiting the free exercise thereof; or abridging the freedom of speech or of the press; or the right of the people peaceably to assemble, and to petition the Government for redress of grievances." Although enacted in 1791, it was not until the middle of the twentieth century that the U.S. Supreme Court finally began to provide clear guidance on the application of First Amendment protections to obscenity and pornography. Our consideration of the Court's treatment of obscene materials and some of our thinking about the possible directions for the future development of First Amendment law can best be understood by examining some of the other exceptions the Court has made to the First Amendment protection of free speech.

Legal commentators (e.g., Krattenmaker & Powe, 1978), who examined First Amendment law with regard to portrayals of violence on television and whose analysis we follow in this section, note that at least four types of speech have been deemed exceptions to First Amendment protections by the Court: advocacy of violence, the uttering of fighting words, libelous speech, and commercial speech. We argue that in each instance these exceptions have been built around the Court's perception that the speech in question posed a significant possibility of harm that merited the withdrawal of First Amendment protections.

Advocacy of Violence. In *Schenck* v. *United States* (1919)—one of a series of cases arising from prosecution of public speeches advocating opposition to U.S. participation in World War I—Justice Holmes proclaimed that "the question in every case is whether the words used are used in such circumstances and are of such a nature as to create a clear and present danger that they will bring about the substantive evils that congress has a right to prevent" (p. 52). This has been referred to as the clear and present danger test. In the 1928 subversion case of *Whitney* v. *California,* Justice Brandeis articulated a fairly narrow interpretation of the clear and present danger test, which required a showing "either that immediate serious violence was to be expected or was advocated, or that the past conduct furnished reason to believe that such advocacy was then contemplated" (p. 376). The same basic theme was sounded in the 1969 case *Brandenburg* v. *Ohio* in which the Court ruled that advocacy of subversive action fell outside First Amendment protection only if the speech was "directed to inciting or producing imminent lawless action and is likely to incite or produce such action" (p. 447). Similar language can be found in nonsubversion cases. In the 1941 labor dispute case *Bridges* v. *California,* Justice Black declared that the clear and present danger "must be serious and the degree of imminence extremely high before utterances can be punished" (p. 263). Clearly this language is aimed at speech posing an immediate threat of harm.

The Uttering of Fighting Words and Libelous Speech. The notion that the speech must pose an immediate danger also pervades the reasoning behind the "fighting words" exception to the First Amendment. In *Chaplinsky* v. *New Hampshire* (1942) the defendant had been convicted under a state statute that proscribed words likely to provoke a fight (the defendant had called a police officer a "damned Fascist" and "a Goddamned racketeer"). The Court upheld the conviction unanimously and wrote in language also relevant to obscene speech:

> There are certain well-defined and narrowly limited classes of speech, the prevention and punishment of which have never been thought to raise any Constitutional problem. These include the lewd and obscene, the profane, and libelous, and the insulting or fighting words—those which by their very utterance inflict injury or tend to incite an immediate breach of the peace. It has been well observed that such utterances are no essential part of an exposition of ideas, and are of such slight social value as a step to the truth that any benefit that may be derived from them is clearly outweighed by the social interest in order and morality. (pp. 571–572)

The Court implied both that such forms of speech conveyed an instant form of harm and lacked sufficient social value to merit protection.

With regard to fighting words and libel, the Court in later cases retreated somewhat from the view that they fell outside First Amendment protection. In *Cohen* v. *California* (1971) the Court upheld the defendant's right to wear a jacket inscribed with the slogan "Fuck the Draft" and minimized the state's "moral" interest in protecting citizens from such language. They further required that the speech be directed to a particular individual. The 1964 case *New York Times Co.* v. *Sullivan* brought libel under First Amendment scrutiny, and a series of later cases has focused on issues of harm to the defamed party. Thus, if libelous statements are true, the speaker is fully protected. If a plaintiff can prove actual harm, he or she may recover if the libel has been uttered negligently— unless the plaintiff is a public figure in which case the plaintiff must demonstrate actual malice.

Commercial Speech. In the series of cases discussed above the Court seems to be concerned with identifiable and specific harms that might flow from the speech. The *Brandenburg* requirement of likely and imminent lawless action seems to be the acid test of whether speech falls outside First Amendment protection. The test is somewhat less stringent when it comes to commercial speech—that is, advertising for gain. In the area of commercial speech the Court has extended a "limited measure of protection, commensurate with its subordinate position in the scale of First Amendment values" (*Brandenburg,* 1969, p. 1918). In striking down laws prohibiting advertisements of legal services (*Bates* v. *State Bar,* 1977) and prescription drugs (*Virginia State Board of Pharmacy* v. *Virginia Citizens Consumer Council,* 1976), the Court was careful to note that their decisions in no way reduced the power of states to prohibit false advertising or advertising for illegal commercial transactions. Only solicitations or activities motivated by ideological considerations merit protection (*In re Primus,* 1978).

Krattenmaker and Powe (1978) made several observations about the relationship between demonstrations of harm arising from speech and Court-approved First Amendment exceptions. With regard to the regulation of fraudulent advertising and advertising for illegal transactions, they stated:

> Where the Court has indicated regulation is permissible, it plainly assumed that the advertisement in question would increase substantially the likelihood that consumers would enter into a transaction that would be to their detriment and would disrupt the allocative efficiency of the market. This assumption is significant in two ways. First, the mere publication of the advertisement provides no gurantee that it will be answered and therefore cause a consumer to make an inefficient purchase. Rather the existence of the advertisement itself justifies its regulation. Second, because the existence of the advertisement only makes the harmful transaction more likely, rather than certain, to occur, we cannot know who will answer the advertisement, enter into the transaction, and suffer the injury, or when the injury will occur. Thus with commercial speech the Court seems willing to presume clear and imminent harm instead of requiring stringent proof. (pp. 1189–1190)

Of those forms of speech that were deemed to fall entirely outside First Amendment protection by the Court in *Chaplinsky* in 1942, only obscene speech has failed to achieve some measure of protection from the Court. In order to understand the Court's treatment of obscenity, it will be helpful to consider the historiccal context from which their opinions have emerged.

A HISTORY OF THE LEGAL TREATMENT OF OBSCENE
AND PORNOGRAPHIC MATERIALS AND IMPORTANT
COURT DECISIONS

Both within and outside the law there has been a blurring and confusion of obscenity and pornography. Webster's (1965) dictionary suggests that the term *obscene* is derived from the Latin *ob,* which means "to" or "before" and *caenum,* which means filth. In his review of the origins and use of the term, Richards (1974–1975) reported that another source for the term might be the Latin *scena,* which refers to "what takes place offstage," and he noted that many ancient playwrights had acts of violence and acts of moral or sexual perversion take place offstage. Richards noted that *obscene* has traditionally referred to filthy and disgusting acts or depictions that offended people's sense of decency. Obscenity has frequently been associated with feelings of shame and moral corruption, and there is also the familiar notion of obscenities or verbal epithets associated with excretory and sexual behavior. It is Richard's view that the notion captures a sense of abuse or unnatural exercise of bodily function, and he reported that different societies are offended by different forms of behaviors (e.g., La Barre's 1955, observation that Tahitians, at least at one point in time, were offended by eating in public but not by public sexual intercourse).

Webster's (1965) reports that *pornography* is derived from the Greek *porngraphos,* which means "writing of harlots" or descriptions of acts of prostitutes. Richards (1974–1975) emphasized that pornography is linked to graphic and explicit depictions of sexual intercourse and genitalia and argued that pornography traditionally was not viewed as obscene in the sense of filth and shame. Rather, Catholic canon law initiated a confusion of the two notions, Victorian morality reinforced it, and the U.S. Supreme Court has, as we shall see, essentially blurred the distinction in its decisions.

Barber (1972), in his discussion of the history of censorship, noted that the Greeks were largely unconcerned with pornography although both Socrates and Plato raised questions about its effect on children. Obscene and pornographic materials apparently flourished during Roman times, and even the development of Christian morality did not spell the end of pornography, for condemnation of sexual vices was low on the church's agenda. The church was more concerned at the time with political attacks on its sovereignty.

In England, where the crown had undertaken to censor publications as early as 1538 (about 60 years after printing had been introduced), printers had to obtain a license from agents of both the state and church to print their works. The targets

of censorship were largely political. Pornographic materials were readily licensed while "serious" works were given much closer and prolonged scrutiny.
These licensing laws prevailed until near the end of the seventeenth century by
which time they were largely ineffective. Barber noted that in 1708 an unsuccessful effort was made to prosecute (under the common law of libel) a pornographic work, but two decades later the publisher of *Venus in the Cloister* (cited
in Barber, 1972)—a volume concerning sexual debauchery in a convent—was
successfully prosecuted under a new notion of "obscene libel."

With the growth of Victorian morality, prosecutions became more common
during the nineteenth century. Private societies with the avowed purpose of
suppressing vice were formed at the end of the eighteenth century and proceeded,
for the next 150 years, to institute private prosecution of pornography publishers.
Although these private associations were able to initiate their own suits under
English law, they were also active advocates of legislative action. For example,
in 1857 Lord Campbell initiated an Obscene Publication Act in Parliament that
has historically borne his name and that allowed magistrates to order destruction
of works "corrupting the morals of youth and of a nature calculated to shock the
common feelings of decency" (Barber, 1972, p. 29). Campbell's act introduced
the notion of corruption as a defining characteristic and Lord Cockburn enshrined
it in Anglo-American law when he articulated, in 1868, the following test of
obscenity in the case of *Queen* v. *Hicklin* (1868): "The test of obscenity is
whether the tendency of the matter charged as obscenity is to deprave and corrupt
those whose minds are open to such immoral influences and into whose hands a
publication of this sort may fall" (p. 370).

Although, in the United States, the state of Massachusetts had passed an act in
1712 that paralleled contemporary English concerns and forbade obscene mock-
eries of religion, Alschuler noted that the statute appears not to have been used. It
can be argued that all important American legal developments arose after the
passage of the Bill of Rights in 1791 (Alschuler, 1971; Clor, 1969; Lockhart &
McClure, 1954; Richards 1974–1975; Sobel, 1979). The first American common law obscenity prosecution took place in the early nineteenth century—a
Pennsylvania case, *Commonwealth* v. *Sharpless* (1815), in which the defendant
was charged with showing a picture of a man and woman in an indecent posture.
Connecticut enacted an obscenity statute in 1821, and a federal customs law of
1842 and a postal act of 1865 were directed at trade in pornographic materials.
Another mail act was passed in 1873 due to pressures from Anthony Comstock's
Society for the Suppression of Vice, and the act took his name. The Comstock
statute was upheld without interpretation by the Supreme Court in *Ex Parte
Jackson* (1878; cited in Clor, 1969), and a court of appeals case in 1879 (*United
States* v. *Bennett*) approved the trial court's adoption of the definition established
in the British case *Queen* v. *Hicklin* (1868). Under this definition a work is
obscene in "any substantial part" as gauged by its effects on the "most suscepti-

ble persons.'' In fact most state courts of this era adopted the *Hicklin* definitions of obscenity, which amounted to obscene material as that which depraves and corrupts those minds that are open to immoral influences.

Outside the courts, crusaders such as Comstock continued to mount pressures against the abundant vices they detected in society. One of their targets was the post–World War I movie industry, which had introduced increasingly explicit violence and sex into their products. Under the pressure of many state bills proposing censorship of the industry, Hollywood enlisted the aid of Postmaster Will Hays to help it exercise self-censorship. The proposed legislation was withdrawn but new pressures mounted in the late 1920s when sound pictures appeared. In 1930 the industry adopted a code. Interestingly, much of the concern at the time was with portrayals of crime and violence. Krattenmaker and Powe (1978) noted that in 1933 a number of empirical (interveiw) studies of the influence of violence on children were initiated. Under pressure from the Catholic church's Legion of Decency and in response to the film code, violence and crime in films waned. Fifteen years later popular action against the content of another medium began. Spurred on by the writings of psychiatrist Frederic Wertham (1948, 1954), pressure was mounted against post–World War II horror comic books, which depicted sadistic violence, sex crimes, and the use of deadly weapons. Although several state statutes were passed to curtail the sale of these comics, the statutes were struck down by the courts (one such case is discussed below).

Important Supreme Court Cases on Obscenity. Looking back with a considerable amount of hindsight at the legal developments concerning pornography and obscenity in the United States, we see that the Court was striving to answer three essential questions: (1) What is a workable objective definition of pornography? (2) Who should decide what is pornographic or obscene? and (3) Who is most likely to be corrupted or adversely affected by these materials?

As early as 1896 in *Swearingen* v. *United States,* the Supreme Court was defining obscenity in terms of ''sexual impurity,'' and this emphasis on the sexual or pornographic aspects of the materials brought before the Supreme Court still permeates the defnitions. While the *Hicklin* test survived in some states until the 1950s, the decision by federal Judge Woolsey in the 1933 case of *United States* v. *One Book* called *''Ulysses''* began the process of reworking certain portions of Lord Cockburns's definition. Woolsey (with the approval of a majority of the appeals court led by Judge Augustus Hand) insisted that the intent of a work should be considered ''in its entirety'' (or, in Hand's words, its ''dominant effect'') rather than on the basis of isolated passage and that an ''average man'' standard ought to be employed rather than examining effects on the most susceptible persons. The *Ulysses* standard thus called for a balance between scientific and literary value (without which a work loses First Amendment protection) and a work's tendency to lead to lustful thoughts or stir sexual impulses.

The 1948 case of *Winters* v. *New York* merits mention at this point, primarily because it is one case in which the Supreme Court has dealt directly with the issue of violence in the media and secondarily because it illustrates the fate of a state statute directed at publications (such as the comics noted earlier) "devoted . . . to criminal news, police reports, or accounts of criminal deeds, or pictures, or stories of deeds of bloodshed, lust or crime" (*Winters*, 1948, p. 508). Krattenmaker and Powe (1978) noted that the case must have been a difficult one, for it was argued three times before the Supreme Court before the Court overturned the statute for vagueness. Although the lower New York Court of Appeals had approved the legislative finding that massed collections of criminal deeds and bloodshed could incite "violent and depraved crimes against the person" (*People* v. *Winters*, 1945, p. 100), the Supreme Court (Justice Reed) thought the magazine in question (*Headquarters Detective*, cited in *Winters*, 1948) merited First Amendment protection because it was not "lewd, indecent, obscene or profane" (p. 510).

It was not until the 1957 *Roth* v. *United States* case that the Supreme Court rendered its first authoritative decision on pornography–obscenity. Justice Brennan, writing for the majority, largely followed *Ulysses* in formulating his test: "Whether to the average person, applying contemporary community standards, the dominant theme of the material taken as a whole appeals to prurient interests" (p. 489). The definition of "prurient interest" was somewhat ambiguous—in one part of Brennan's opinion, emphasis was placed on "on the tendency to incite lustful thoughts" while elsewhere he approved of the definition of the American Law Institute's Model Penal Code—which, while it used the term "prurient interest", went to great lengths to downplay erotic elements and emphasize "exacerbated, morbid, or perverted interest" in sex, nudity, or excretion. Brennan did not make note of these qualifications.

In *Roth* the Court explicitly placed obscenity outside the area protected by the First Amendment, arguing that obscene materials had traditionally been regarded as utterly without redeeming social value. In 1966 the Court in a plurality opinion (Brennan, Warren, and Fortas) in the case of *A Book Called "John Cleland's Memoirs of a Woman of Pleasure"* v. *Attorney General of Massachusetts* (the so-called *Fanny Hill* case) incorporated the "utterly without redeeming social value" test into the *Roth* standard.

The impact of the *Roth* decision and the problems of interpretation and application to which it gave rise are discussed at length by Clor (1969). One impact was an increase in appellate litigation. Many cases were decided by the Supreme Court in its efforts to refine the *Roth* standards—including *Jacobellis* v. *Ohio* (1964) in which Justice Stewart acknowledged that while he might have trouble specifying an intelligible criterion for pornography, "I know it when I see it" (p. 197).

Roth was the dominant obscenity case for nearly two decades; however, the contemporary standards governing obscene and pornographic materials arise from several 1973 obscenity cases, the most important being: *Miller* v. *State of California* and *Paris Adult Theatre I* v. *Slaton*. In *Miller* Chief Justice Burger,writing for the five-member majority, announced a new and stricter obscenity test:

> The basic guideline for the trier of fact must be: a) whether "the average person, applying contemporary community standards" would find that the work, taken as a whole, appeals to the prurient interest . . . ; b) whether the work depicts or describes, in a patently offensive way, sexual conduct specifically defined by the applicable state law; and c) whether the work, taken as a whole lack serious literary, artistic, political, or scientific value (p. 24).

Miller reaffirmed the notion that obscenity falls outside First Amendment protection, and it tightened the *Roth* standards. *Miller* moved the test standard from a national basis to a local basis and replaced the "utterly without redeeming social value" test with a standard requiring "serious" value. In *Slaton,* also a five–four decision, Burger provided some insights into the majority's reasoning. The Court reasoned:

> The States have the power to make a morally neutral judgment that public exhibition of obscene material, or commerce in such material, has a tendency to injure the community as a whole, to *endanger the public safety* [emphasis added], or to jeopardize, in Mr. Chief Justice Warren's words, the States' "right . . . to maintain a decent society" (p. 69).

The Court seemed prepared to conclude in an unusually sweeping manner that pornographic materials could pose sufficient threat (a clear and present danger?) to a community or even the nation that it might be banned entirely.

To bolster the language concerning possible harms further, Burger cited the 1970 Minority Report of the Commission on Obscenity and Pornography as an indication that "there is at least an arguable correlation between obscene material and crime" (*Slaton,* 1973, p. 58). Although the Court's willingness to turn to empirical research is (in our view) laudable, the Court did ignore a Majority Report (Commission on Obscenity and Pornography, 1971a) caution that they could find "no evidence to date that exposure to explicit sexual materials plays a significant role in the causation of delinquent of criminal behavior among youth or adults" (p. 32).

There are three other Supreme Court opinions that merit mention here. The first is *Young* v. *American Mini Theatres* (1976), a plurality decision in which the Court, with Justice Stevens (joined by Burger, White, and Rehnquist) writing, upheld a Detroit zoning law that limited the locations for motion picture theaters that featured sexually explicit movies or depicted specific anatomical areas. Although the plurality opinion acknowledged that the films might not be obscene, it nonetheless noted that the city's efforts to maintain the quality of the inner city and reduce crime and decay represented interests that outweigh the value of sexually explicit speech.

In *FCC* v. *Pacifica Foundation* (1978) the Court in a five–four decision upheld the power of the Federal Communications Commission to regulate the use of indecent speech on radio broadcasts. (The speech in question was a spicy monologue by comedian George Carlin). The Court rejected an argument that indecent speech should be judged by the standards of obscenity. Instead, the Court acknowledged that indecent speech would merit First Amendment protection in some contexts, but not in public broadcasting where it is difficult for radio users and children to avoid the offense of shocking and vulgar words. Justice Stevens argued that suppressing indecent speech in a public medium did not mean that ideas with social value would be suppressed—only that they would be presented in a different form.

A final case that provides some insight into the Court's thinking about the First Amendment is *New York* v. *Ferber* (No. 81-55, decided July 2, 1982) in which the Court (with all Justices concurring in the judgment) upheld a New York statute prohibiting the distribution of materials showing sexual performances by children under age 16. Justice White cited five bases for the result: (1) the state legislature could reasonably conclude that children could be physiologically, emotionally, and mentally harmed when used as subjects in such portrayals; (2) the social value of such depictions is *de minimus;* (3) child pornography, like other obscenity, is unprotected by the First Amendment; (4) because of harms noted in (1), the test for these portrayals need not even appeal to prurient interests, need not be patently offensive, nor do they have to be considered as a whole; (5) suppressing distribution of such materials will discourage their production.

Prohibition of obscenity in the United States has developed as an exception to an otherwise constitutionally guaranteed freedom—the freedom of speech. The 1957 Supreme Court case *Roth* v. *United States* was the first case that explicitly stated that obscene material fell outside of the protection of the First Amendment. Later cases, in particular. *Miller* v. *State of California* (1973) reaffirmed the notion put forth in *Roth* that obscenity falls outside the protection of the First Amendment, but placed the burden of judging the nature and social value of obscene materials on local communities. This is where the law stands today. The basic question that must be answered by juries defining obscenity are (1) Would the average person applying community standards find that this material, as a whole, appeals to prurient interest? (2) Does the material offensively depict sexual conduct defined by state law? and (3) Does the work lack literary, artistic, political, or scientific value?

As an interesting point of comparison, it is useful to examine contemporary legal developments in Great Britain concerning obscenity and pornography. The British experience with obscenity has lead to slightly different patterns of prosecutions than in the United States. The British have taken a more strident approach to defining obscenity by including depictions of violence. Current notions about what is considered obscene in British material may provide us with guidance for possible changes in American law—particularly as the law relates to violent pornography.

The British Experience

As a starting point, it should be noted that England has no formal constitution and thus the development of obscenity laws has proceeded largely through legislative action. Lord Campbell's Obscene Publications Act of 1857 was merely the first in a series of parliamentary acts designed to regulate obscene materials. Probably the most enduring contribution by the English courts was the *Queen* v. *Hicklin* definition of 1868 discussed earlier, which has governed private actions into modern times and has significantly influenced definitions of obscenity contained in parliamentary acts. As the reader will recall, under *Queen* v. *Hicklin,* the test of obscenity is the tendency for the material in question to "deprave and corrupt" those who come into contact with it.

The influence of *Hicklin* on the definition of obscenity can be seen in the Obscene Publications Act of 1959 as amended by the Obscene Publications Act of 1964 (Davidow & O'Boyle, 1977): "Material is regarded as obscene under these statutes if it is, taken as a whole, such as to tend to deprave and corrupt persons who are likely, having regard to all relevant circumstances, to read, see or hear the matter contained or embodied in it" (p. 254). The terms "to deprave and corrupt" were subsequently defined in a trial in which the book *Lady Chatterley's Lover* by D. H. Lawrence was examined (*Queen* v. *Penguin Books, Ltd.,* 1961). In this case Justice Byrne defined "to deprave" as "to make morally bad, to pervert, to debase, or corrupt morally"; and "to corrupt" as "to render morally unsound or rotten, to destroy the moral purity or chastity of, to pervert, to ruin a good quality, to debase, to defile."

In contrast to U.S. Supreme Court definitions, in Britain the term "obscenity" does not only refer to sexual materials. Under British law, depravity and corruption are thought not only to result from material's tendency to induce erotic desires or sexual perversions, but are also thought to arise from exposure to depictions of drug-taking or brutal violence. In the case of *Director of Public Prosecution* v. *A. & B. C. Chewing Gum Ltd.* (1968), for example, the Obscene Publications Act of 1959 was used to prosecute a bubble gum card maker who manufactured cards for sale depicting scenes of violence (Battle Cards). In the case of *The Queen* v. *Calder & Boyars Ltd.* (1969) portions of the book *Escape From Brooklyn* were deemed objectionable under the Obscene Publications Act because of explicit references to drug abuse.

Other materials that would probably not be considered objectionable in the United States under the *Miller* standards, but that may be found offensive in Great Britain, include those that advocate ideas or views about sexual behavior that may be contrary to accepted moral standards. In the case of *Queen* v. *Handyside* (1971; cited in Davidow & O'Boyle, 1977), for example, the British courts found a book titled *Little Red School Book* objectionable because it tended to undermine respect for marriage as a social institution, contained no injunction about exerting restraint in sexual matters, and also contained evidence, according to the courts, of an antiauthoritarian stance and a hostile attitude toward the teacher–child relationship. Although the same material may be considered offensive and even immoral by people in the United States, it would nevertheless probably not be considered obscene under the *Miller* standard and would be protected under the First Amendment. In practice, however, prosecutions such as this one are extremely rare in Great Britain (Davidow & O'Boyle, 1977).

There are several procedural differences between the United States and Great Britain that also may result in a greater number of obscenity prosecutions under British law. First, the burden of proof rests with the defendant. This means that, in an obscenity case, the defendant must prove to the jury that the evidence shows that the publication is for the public good and that the material has scientific, literary, or artistic merit. In the United States, the prosecution is charged with the responsibility of demonstrating that the material lacks these attributes—a seemingly more difficult task. Second, there is no double jeapordy protection in Great Britain. A defendant may be tried for a crime a second time if the prosecution decides to appeal to a higher court. This means the prosecution in an obscenity case need not rest with an acquittal at the local level; the case can be pressed in a higher court until a conviction is secured. Finally, the defendant in an obscenity trial in Great Britain is often not permitted to bring an expert witness into court on his or her behalf (Davidow & O'Boyle, 1977). These procedural differences obviously put the prosecution in a somewhat better position to obtain convictions in Great Britain.

Probably the most significant similarity between Great Britain and the United States lies in what the obscenity laws do *not* say. Both countries are plagued with the problem of vagueness. In the United States, the Supreme Court has not reached a consensual definition, and even the definition for obscenity articulated in *Miller* v. *State of California* does not meet with the various opinions of differing segments of American society. Justice Douglas's dissent in *Paris Adult Theatre I* v. *Slaton* is an excellent expression of the problem in the United States:

> Art and literature reflect tastes; and tastes, like musical appreciation, are hardly reducible to precise definitions. That is one reason I have always felt that ''obscenity'' was not an exception to the First Amendment. For matters of taste, like matters of belief, turn on the idiosyncracies of individuals. They are too personal to define and too emotional and vague to apply. (p. 70)

The British face a similar dilemma in attempting to describe those materials that have a tendency to deprave and corrupt—a task that the jury may find particularly difficult in light of the specific ban on testimony concerning psychological, sociological, or medical opinion. In fact, as Davidow and O'Boyle (1977) pointed out, the obscenity laws face serious problems: "The 1959 and 1964 English Acts are not reducing the amount of obscene material available. The police refrain from prosecuting because under the 'deprave and corrupt' formula there is no assurance of conviction, and attempts at prosecution either fail or result in slight penalties" (p. 285).

Past Efforts to Integrate Social Science and the Law in Great Britain and the United States

In 1967, the U.S. Congress established an advisory commission to conduct "a thorough study . . . of the causal relationship of (obscene and pornographic) materials to anti-social behavior." The Commission on Obscenity and Pornography (1971b) was organized into four working panels in investigating (1) trafficking and distribution, (2) legal standards, (3) behavioral effects, and (4) positive approaches to the problem of obscenity and pornography.

The working panel on behavioral effects considered several types of empirical research: (1) surveys of national probability samples, (2) experimental research, and (3) studies of the rate of sex offenses in the United States and Denmark.

Surveys of national probability samples of adults and young persons revealed that

> Between 40 percent and 60 percent believe that sexual materials provide information about sex, provide entertainment, lead to moral breakdown, improve sexual relationships of married couples, lead people to commit rape, produce boredom with sexual materials, encourage innovation in marital sexual technique and lead people to lose respect for women. Some of these presumed effects are obviously socially undesirable, while others may be regarded as socially neutral or desirable. When questioned about effects, persons were more likely to report having personally experienced desirable than undesirable ones. (1971b, p. 218)

Experimental research shows short-lived increases in sexual behavior and sexual fantasies following exposure to erotic materials but no significant changes in established patterns of sexual behavior. Exposure to erotic stimuli results in a tendency toward greater tolerance for sexually explicit materials, but individual subject's judgments about whether those materials were obscene differed widely. One experiment shows diminished sexual arousal with repeated exposure over a 3-year period with a recovery period of 3 months.

The commission discovered no detectable relationship between availability of pornography and increase in sex crimes in the United States, while there was some evidence that availability was associated with lowered sex-crime rates in Denmark (but see Court's contention in Chapter 5 that the rape rate in Denmark actually increased).

In general, the commission concluded that

> In sum, empirical research designed to clarify the question has found no evidence to date
> that exposure to explicit sexual materials plays a significant role in the causation of
> delinquent or criminal behavior among youth or adults. The Commission cannot con-
> clude that exposure to erotic materials is a factor in the causation of sex crime or sex
> delinquency. (1971b p. 223)

Even before the commission report was released, the Nixon administration
rejected their findings. Soon after the report was released, President Nixon
remarked that the conclusions of the commission's majority were ''morally
bankrupt'' and refused to advocate relaxation of the nation's obscenity laws. In
the *Miller* case (1973), the Supreme Court also rejected the findings of the
commission's majority report and, in fact, favorably cited the minority report for
the proposition that there is at least an arguable association between exposure to
obscene material and crime.

In Great Britain a similar effort to reformulate the law, at least partially in light
of existing social science research, was undertaken several years later. In 1977 a
special task force—the Williams Committee—was set up to undertake a fundamental review of the laws relating to obscenity. In 1979 the committee (Williams
Committee Report, 1979, November) recommended that Great Britain fomulate
one new statute to replace the existing collection of obscenity laws. One of the
committee's major criticisms was that the deprave and corrupt test was ambiguous and tended, in fact, to be ignored by jurors in deciding obscenity cases. On a
more general level, the committee came to the conclusion that any new comprehensive legislation should be based on considerations of the harms that could
stem from exposure to obscene material. In other words, the committee felt that
unless it could be shown that specific harms arose from exposure to obscene
materials the law had no right to suppress such material. The definition of harm
that was chosen was a very narrow one. Before the law can intervene, the
committee recommended, it must be demonstrated that pornography is likely to
have some effect on human behavior, in particular, that it caused the commission
of sexual crimes.

Three types of evidence were considered by the committee in evaluating the
potential harms caused by exposure to pornography: (1) evidence from particular
court cases, (2) statistical trends in crime as a function of the availability of
pornographic materials, and (3) experimental social psychological evidence.
With respect to the first type of evidence, the committee considered infamous
British cases such as the Moors Murders and the Cambridge Rapist, where
pornographic materials, supposedly found in the possession of the defendants,
were claimed to be instigations to crime. As the committee noted, it is exceed-
ingly difficult to prove that these crimes would not have been committed had the
defendants not been exposed to pornographic material. Consequently, the committee rejected this type of evidence as inconclusive. Second, the committee

reviewed conflicting research on the relationship between the availability of pornography in Denmark in the 1970s and reports of rape and attempted rape during the same period. The committee concluded that the research in this area conducted by Kutchinsky (including some research presented to the U.S. commission) was comprehensive, detailed, and scrupulously careful, and was viewed as indicating no relationship between greater availability of pornography and the commission of sex-related crimes (but see a response by Court, 1980, whose related research was considered but rejected by the committee). The committee also rejected the notion that rising trends in sexual assault in Great Britain in the 1960s and 1970s were the result of greater availability of pornographic materials. Finally, the committee considered the experimental research that had been undertaken up to about 1976 (see Court, 1980, for a report on the studies the committee reviewed and his opinions concerning the studies the committee failed to review—many of which are contrary to the notion that viewing pornographic stimuli does not produce harmful consequences). The committee concluded that, since there was much disagreement among experimenters as to the effects of pornography on behavior, the committee could not recommend further suppression of such material.

OBSCENITY AND THE LAW IN THE 1980s

A "New Breed" of Pornography

Since the time of the presidential commission's report on pornography, and even since the Williams Committee convened in 1977, three substantial changes have occurred. First, the nature of the materials themselves has changed. Second, public concern with these materials has increased. Finally, a new body of social science research, particularly experimental social psychological research, on the effects of aggressive, sexually explicit materials has been produced.

By the latter part of the 1970s many persons were becoming concerned at what they felt was both an increase in violence and changes in the nature of pornographic materials. Feminists warned that images of male–female relationships were becoming explicitly perverse in the widespread pornography trade. According to Morgan (1978, November: "Today's [1978] pornography is in fact escalating its misogyny, promuelgating rape, mutilation, and even murder as average sexual acts, depicting the 'normal' man as a sadist and the 'healthy' woman as a willing victim" (p. 55). Stanmeyer (1977–1978) described the contents of one of the "new breed" of pornographic films:

> One of the many New York exploitation film theaters just off Times Square featured a
> movie called *The Morbid Snatch*. Two men conceive and execute a plan to capture a
> young girl, imprison her, and compel her to submit to sexual acts of various sorts. The

girl is drugged, confined in a basement, stripped naked, and subjected to sexual intercourse, first with one of the men, then with a lesbian, and then with both the man and the
lesbian simultaneously. Periodically, the camera focuses very closely upon the sexual
organs of all participants. Periodically also the girl (whose age is, perhaps by intention,
difficult to determine; she could be as young as sixteen or as old as twenty-five) is
represented as responding erotically to these acts. The sexual scenes, and preparation for
them, constitute practically the sole content and surely the sole interest of this film. (p.
657)

Social scientists, too (Malamuth & Spinner, 1980), have documented this increase in the coupling of sex and violence in men's magazines.

Pairings of sex and violence has also become increasingly prominent in more
popular, mass media depictions. Feminists pointed to the upsurge in what they
termed "brutality chic"—soft-core violent pornographic images finding their
way into high-fashion magazines, onto record covers, and into department store
windows (Morgan, 1978, November). Popular films such as *The Getaway* and
Swept Away depicted women, raped by men, as appreciating the experience and
rewarding the male aggressor by falling in love with him.

In 1970, when the U.S. commission conducted its inquiries, virtually none of
the studies undertaken examined the effects of aggressive pornography on behavior. Since 1970 these materials have appeared much more frequently (Malamuth
& Donnerstein, 1982; Malamuth & Spinner, 1980), and empirical studies have
shown that in contrast to stimuli that are only sexual, aggressive erotica may
affect both subject attitudes and behavior. The research has revealed that even in
a nonrapist population there can be relatively high sexual arousal to media-
presented images of rape, in which the female shows signs of pleasure and
arousal, the theme most commonly presented in pornography (Malamuth, 1981;
Malamuth & Donnerstein, 1982; Malamuth, Heim, & Feshbach, 1980). There
are also data that suggest that exposure to a sexually explicit rape scene in which
the victim shows a "positive" reaction tends to produce a lessened sensitivity to
rape (Malamuth & Donnerstein, 1982) and an increased acceptance of rape
myths and interpersonal violence against women (Malamuth & Check, 1981).
Research on aggressive pornography and aggressive *behavior* toward women has
found that exposure to aggressive pornography increases aggression against
women in a laboratory context (Donnerstein, 1980; Donnerstein & Berkowitz,
1981). There have also been a few investigations that suggest that exposure to
images of violence against women in mass media (R-rated films, advertisements,
etc.) can negatively influence both attitudes and aggressive behavior toward
women (Malamuth & Check, 1981; Malamuth & Donnerstein, 1982).

The scientific evidence to date indicates that the pairing of sex and aggression
in hard-core, soft-core, and mass media portrayals may be harmful. For those
who perceive these findings as revealing a serious social problem, the obvious
question is, What role can the law play in controlling the availability and content
of these materials?

Prosecution of Hard-Core Pornography under Existing Law

Hard-core violent pornography can be prosecuted under existing law. While the hard-core and soft-core materials, described earlier in this section, resemble one another insofar as they combine aggressive and erotic images, when considered from a legal regulation point of view, a distinction can be made between materials that pair aggression with explicit sexual portrayals and those with less explicit sexual portrayals.

Hard-core depictions of sex and violence can theoretically be handled through existing state obscenity statutes. Under the *Miller* standards, if a constitutionally adequate state statute prohibiting the distribution of obscene materials is used as the basis for a prosecution and the local jury is prepared in light of community standards to judge the seized materials as obscene and to convict the defendant, it is plausible that a community can stem the flow of such materials to their citizenry. However, such scenarios may require the presence of highly assertive district attorneys and juries. One example of this combination of an aggressive prosecutor and supportive juries can be found in Atlanta, Georgia, where the prosecutor has successfully closed nearly all X-rated movie houses and adult bookstores (Beck & Smith, 1981). Nonetheless, the Atlanta experience appears to be relatively unusual.

One post-*Miller* survey of prosecutors (Leventhal, 1977) found that fewer jurisdictions were prosecuting for obscenity after *Miller,* and overall the total number of prosecutions had declined. At the same time the majority of prosecutors (57%) reported that obscene materials were increasingly available in their communities (with 22% reporting decreased availability). Although most of Leventhal's respondents indicated that the shift to community standards would increase the likelihood of conviction, this perception was not directly translated into a greater willingness to prosecute. Furthermore, this unwillingness to prosecute has continued despite fewer appeals. Riggs (1981) reports the number of appeals from obscenity convictions in lower courts fell off after 1973—though it is not clear whether this decline can be attributed to fewer prosecutions or a greater reluctance to challenge convictions under the tighter standards of *Miller.* Thus, while it would be possible under *Miller* standards to curtail the availability of aggressive-pornographic materials, it appears that *Miller* has not precipitated an increase in general prosecutions of obscenity, despite the fact that conviction rates have been stable and the rate of higher court reversals may have declined (Leventhal, 1977).

Soft-Core Violent Pornography and Harm

Given the apparent unwillingness or inability to prosecute hard-core obscene materials under existing statutes, the possibility of prosecuting soft-core materials is even more remote. The Supreme Court's emphasis on explicit portrayals of sexual behavior as the basis for judging obscenity does not exclude soft-core depictions from First Amendment protection. But we may ask whether some soft-core depictions of sexual violence might pose dangers that would exclude them from First Amendment protection. As we noted before, research by Malamuth and Check (1981) and Malamuth and Donnerstein (1982) strongly suggests that exposure to R-rated, soft-core pornographic materials results in negative changes in both attitudes and behaviors toward women. Feminists such as Brownmiller (1975) prior to, and in light of studies such as these, have expressed concern that portrayals of sexual violence against women increases cultural acceptance of such violence, promotes actual assaults, and diminishes a society's willingness to punish the perpetrators of these assaults.

However, even with our current state of scientific knowledge, these harms may not achieve the necessary degree of imminent and indentifiable danger required under current advocacy law, the fighting words test, and libel cases. As other commentators (Krattenmaker & Powe, 1978) have noted, it is unlikely that empirical research *can* precisely establish the circumstances under which a particular person is likely to commit a crime after viewing a particular depiction of sexual violence. While a demonstration of specific harmful consequences seems to underlie the prohibition of some forms of advocacy of immediate violence and the use of fighting words, it must be pointed out that the Court *has* been willing to prohibit such speech *without* the benefit of empirical demonstrations. For example, to take a popularly cited example of speech that seems to pose imminent danger (and therefore falls outside the First Amendment), we really do not know how often—if at all—a theater audience would panic at the shout of "fire."

On the other hand, there are other reasons to think the Supreme Court might be somewhat sympathetic to demonstrations of less direct forms of harm of the type that can be provided through empirical research. As noted earlier, part of Chief Justice Burger's rationale in the *Miller* decision was first an acceptance of the minority view (from the pornography commission) that there could be a link between exposure to obscene materials and antisocial behavior and, second, that, in light of pornography's threat to public morality, states have a right to regulate obscene materials in order to maintain a decent society. Clearly Burger was talking about explicit sexual materials in *Miller,* and not soft-core mass media depictions of sexual violence against women. The point, however, is that Burger partially based the Court's *Miller* decision on notions of social harm of a nature that social science research might establish in the domain of violent sexual depictions.

We have already discussed some of the links between exposure to aggressive erotica and changes in (1) attitudes toward rape and toward women, (2) self-reported willingness to commit a rape, and (3) laboratory aggression against women established by existing research. If further research confirms and extends the causal links between exposure to violent sexual images and undesirable changes in attitudes, behavioral intentions, and actual behavior, social scientists may ultimately mount a case against both hard-core and soft-core aggressive erotica depictions that rivals or exceeds that case against children's exposure to violence and aggression in the mass media (National Institute of Mental Health, 1982). Even then, unfortunately, it would be impossible to predict what impact strong social science findings about the adverse consequences of exposure to soft-core aggressive erotica might have on the Supreme Court's view of the First Amendment protections merited by such depictions. Current research findings do not allow anyone to predict that a particular person will act in a particular way after viewing a particular stimulus. But, even though the research is very far from such specific predictions, in First Amendment cases the court has clearly not felt constrained by the presence or absence of either conclusive or inconclusive empirical evidence.

Nonetheless, Burger's concern with general social harms may create a vehicle for using social science findings of social harm as the basis for arguing that some portrayals of sexual violence might not merit First Amendment protection. In *Pacifica* a distinction was made between the form and content of communications and it might be argued that certain portrayals of sexual violence against women—even those without explicit sex—are a form of communication that could be discarded without sacrifice of socially valued ideas.

How Can Current Research be Improved to Demonstrate Harm More Effectively?

Does existing social science research demonstrate that available aggressive erotica produces significant social harm? Most of the existing research has been conducted in laboratory settings, using explicit sexual materials, undergraduate subjects, and relatively short periods of exposure. While the changes in behavior and attitudes that occur in such settings is alarming, it is unlikely that many legislators, First Amendment advocates, or the Supreme Court would be persuaded that the findings are sufficient grounds for removing First Amendment protections for aggressive erotica. The external validity of existing research findings is, however, an empirical question, and studies should be designed that attempt to replicate and extend the laboratory findings.

Current research needs to be extended in several directions. First, researchers need to examine the behavioral and attitudinal effects of exposure to varying forms of aggressive erotica, ranging from graphic portrayals of violence against women in erotic, but not explicit, contexts, to nongraphic portrayals such as those found in some commercially released R-rated films. This would provide the courts with a more specific knowledge of exactly what types of materials are more or less harmful. Second, the research should examine the cumulative effects of exposure to such materials over an extended period of time—periods of months rather than the periods of 1 day or several days. It may be the case, for example, that long-term exposure to violent erotica has a significantly different impact on subjects than short-term exposure and that only long-term exposure results in violent behavior outside the laboratory. Third, all research should use a broad range of dependent variables. It is not enough to demonstrate that exposure to these materials results in more shocks administered to a female confederate of the experimenter. Changes in levels of sensitization to violence against women, perhaps measured physiologically, changes in a wide range of attitudes from a specific willingness to rape to a more general insensitivity to violence against women and a greater tendency to aggress against women well after exposure to violent erotica all need to be included in a list of useful dependent measures. It is very difficult for an experimental researcher to detect behavioral effects outside the laboratory (indeed, it may be unethical for an investigator to conduct research if it seems likely that procedures will produce antisocial behaviors that would harm innocent people), and it also seems unlikely that the base rates of such behaviors would ever be high enough to detect. Nonetheless, changes in attitudes toward sexual assault, personal willingness to commit such assaults, and general attitudes toward women are among the harms alluded to by critics who have challenged the widespread use of images of aggression against women. Finally, the external validity of current research findings would be strengthened by greater use of nonundergraduate subject populations.

As the volume and quality of research on all the variants of aggressive erotica grows, the public, legislators, and the courts will obviously be better equipped to make judgments about the magnitude of harm associated with such materials and formulate appropriate legal and societal responses. But this would only be the first step. Even if the members of the Supreme Court were convinced that aggressive erotica did have significant harmful effects that justified the withdrawal of First Amendment protections, such a decision could not be made on the Court's own initiative. It would be necessary to build enough public support for restrictions that state legislators would pass appropriate legislation. That legislation would, in turn, have to serve as the basis for prosecutions. Only if appeals from successful prosecutions reached the Supreme Court would the Court have an opportunity to pass on the constitutional merits of such legislation (and, possibly, the empirical demonstrations of harm that might serve as one basis for the legislation). Clearly many steps—some of them rather implausible at present—are required in the process of establishing a meaningful precedent of the nature outlined above.

The most straightforward solution to the problem of violent pornography in the United States would be to sidestep court decisions completely and toughen the definition of obscenity to include violence. As we noted in the previous section, this has already been accomplished in Great Britain, and there have been at-tempts at broadening the definition in the United States. In 1973 the Nixon administration submitted to Congress, as part of a larger package of legislation to revise the entire U.S. criminal code, a bill that would have defined obscene material as explicit detailing of sexual intercourse, violence involving sadomasochistic sex, or a close-up view of human genitalia (Sobel, 1979). Modified versions of this proposal could be considered today either through an executive proposal, or through congressional legislation. Such a recommenda-tion could take the form of a comprehensive national obscenity law that would specifically prohibit violent pornography. The statute could list the specific violent depictions that would be considered illegal and any film producer or magazine publisher suspected of depicting one of these illegal acts would be subject to prosecution.

It is unlikely that such a law would be introduced either by the president or a member of Congress unless there was a perception of grass-roots support of such a law. Such public support, in turn, is usually the result of the efforts of special interest or political action groups in the community or across the state. In the case of violent pornography, interested groups such as the National Parent–Teacher Association (PTA), the National Council of Churches, or the American Medical Association (AMA) on the national level, and local churches, PTAs, and wom-en's organizations on the local level could begin to change public sentiment or organize an already concerned public to petition their congressional represen-tatives. There is also the possibility that the motion picture and publishing industries can be persuaded to regulate themselves through pressure from con-cerned groups. We should note that the efforts by groups such as these have proven to be unsuccessful in persuading American TV networks to curb televised violence. TV violence as measured by researchers for the National Coalition on Television Violence (NCTV, 1982) was found to be at an alltime high in 1982 despite the efforts of concerned citizen groups. In the following sections we discuss the film industry's attempts to regulate itself in the United States and Great Britain and attempts by feminists and other private groups to put pressure on those that produce pornographic and violent pornographic materials.

QUASI-LEGAL SOLUTIONS

So far we have discussed the possible legal solutions to the control of violent pornography and the criteria social scientists will have to meet in order clearly to demonstrate harm and to help reformulate laws relating to the specific harms that may arise from exposure to violent pornography. There are many organizations, both in Great Britain and in the United States, who are already convinced that exposure to pornography, particularly violent pornography, will result in aggressive behavior toward women. In this section we briefly describe some of the quasi-legal organizations founded specifically to censor pornographic materials and organizations formed in reaction to increasing numbers of violent-pornographic movies and magazines. In this section we describe the history and function of a well-established film censoring organization, the British Board of Film Censors (BBFC), and the less powerful Motion Picture Association of America (MPAA), as well as less formally organized political action groups such as Women Against Violence Against Women (WAVAW). What each of these diverse groups have in common is either their societally recognized, or heartfelt right, to determine which materials (usually movies or portions of movies) are harmful and which are not.

Film Industry Attempts to Regulate Itself:
British and American Film Boards

In 1909 the British Parliament passed the first Cinematograph Act to help ensure the safety of audiences present at a new form of public entertainment—the cinema. The act stipulated that before a film could be shown it must be licensed by authorities in county councils or county boroughs. This arrangement was originally intended as a safety precaution (film manufactured in the early 1900s was highly flammable). Since the county governments were already responsible for licensing public drinking houses and dance halls it seemed appropriate to have them also license cinemas (Harlech, 1982, March). Local authorities, however, almost immediately began to use their authority to prohibit the exhibition of films of which they disapproved. Further, in 1914 the British court supported the right of local governments to refuse licensing on the basis of offense to public morals. Fearing a myriad of conflicting standards across Great Britain, the film industry urged the government to institute a national censorship policy. The government refused, and instead the industry and the government created a voluntary and unofficial organization, BBFC. In 1923 the government recommended to local authorities that they allow no film to be shown unless it had been certified by the BBFC.

Lord Harlech, the president of the BBFC, has provided an interesting oral account of the board's history. In the early 1950s, according to Harlech, the board introduced an X-rating for adult films that were considered unacceptable for children. Acceptance of the board's rating is purely voluntary. When the board was formed, public sentiment was against an unofficial body having the last word on what could or could not be shown in the cinema; hence democratically elected local authorities are free to revise any decision of the board—either banning films that have already been certified by the BBFC or permitting film the board has refused to certify. Throughout most of the 1950s and early 1960s the board was primarily concerned with censorship of nudity and premarital or extramarital sex. In 1967 the board passed its first film containing pubic hair, and by 1970 the board had developed an informal checklist of acceptable sexual positions and genital displays. By the middle of the 1970s, the board shifted its attention from nudity and display of genitalia to the increasing levels of violence of films from America, Italy, and Hong Kong. According to Harlech (1982, March):

> The combination of sex and violence was a new and alarming trend in films made merely as sensational entertainment for the young male audience of 16–24 who were beginning to dominate the box office. . . . Some film-makers no longer treated rape as a reprehensible crime, but were turning it into an erotic spectacle. (pp. 9–10)

During the 1970s the BBFC's focus of concern shifted from explicit sex to concern for the combination of sex and violence. In 1974, according to Harlech, the board cut a small number of scenes from the French film *Emmanuelle* in order that the film comply with the current checklist of acceptable displays and positions. At that time the board was not concerned with what Harlech maintains might now be considered the "extraordinarily distorted morality" (because of its causal treatment of rape) of the last segment of the film. According to Harlech (1982, March):

> This French money-spinner represented the apotheosis of the male chauvinist view that women are not subjects, but objects for the sexual gratification of men. . . . the Board in 1979 called in the film *Emmanuelle* and required the cutting of the whole of the violent rape which takes place in an opium den in the cast reel.
>
> The reason for cutting this scene had nothing to do with its visual explicitness. The Board had passed rape scenes far more detailed than this one, and has done so since. It was the *intention* of this scene which was unacceptable, since its aim was to persuade the audience that the rape of this woman, despite her resistance, was sexually beneficial rather than harmful. . . .
>
> Everyone knows that murder is wrong, but a strange myth has grown up, and been seized on by film-makers, that rape is really not so bad, that it may even be a form of liberation for the victim, who may be getting what she secretly desires—and perhaps needs—with no harm done. . . . Film-makers in recent years have used rape as an exciting and titillating spectacle in pornographic film, which are nearly always designed to appeal to men. And this, we believe, is a deeply corrupting process. (pp. 10–14)

Clearly, from Harlech's remarks we can conclude that one of the primary concerns within the BBFC in recent years has been the proliferation of films containing scenes that pair sex and violence. The implicit concern, here, is that viewing such films may make the audience (particularly men) more callous in their attitudes to the degradation of women and perhaps more likely to engage in behavior harmful to women. For the board these possibilities constitute the primary justification for censorship:

> We believe . . . that films can influence people's behavior, and that some people may be influenced more than others. For that reason, we believe that society has the right to set some limits. . . . In recent years, many have seen the cinema as the vehicle for

promoting and normalising the use of violent solutions to problems which we as a people have attempted to solve through other means. It is right that we should be concerned about such trends, just as we think it is right to be concerned about the degradation of women for male enjoyment and other activities which can desensitise and brutalise our society. (Harlech, 1982, March, pp.16,19).

In the United States there also exists a voluntary film rating board—the MPAA. The MPAA was formed in 1930 to regulate the content of films produced by major companies in the United States. Originally the code specifically prohibit "lustful kissing" and any depiction that "stimulates the baser emotions." Originally the MPAA had two film classifications: films recommended for general viewing and films recommended for mature audiences (Sobel, 1979). By 1966 the association had adopted a new code that was aimed primarily at restraining portrayals of the taking of life and "detailed and protracted acts of brutality, cruelty, physical violence, torture and abuse." This code proved inefficient and in 1968 the classification categories were introduced: G, suggested for general audiences; M, for adults and mature young people; R, restricted to those 16 or older unless accompanied by parent or gaurdian; and X, those under 16 not admitted. This classification system was revised again in 1970. The M category was dropped and replaced by PG (parental guidance suggested, all ages admitted), and the age limits for R- and X-rated categories were raised from 16 to 17 years.

In contrast to the BBFC, however, there does not seem to be the same explicit concern about the effects of viewing either violent films or films that combine violence with pornography. Many of the criticisms of the MPAA rating system have to do with the industry's tendency to be excessively concerned with judgments concerning nudity and profanity while virtually ignoring other serious antisocial aspects of films. In 1971 Reverend Patrick J. Sullivan, Director of the National Catholic Office for Motion Pictures and at first a supporter of the rating system, complained that the industry's rating system was overly concerned with overt visual sex but showed little concern with "the implicit exploitation of sex and the overall impact of violence and other antisocial aspects of the film" (quoted in Sobel, 1971, p. 44). More recently, the NCTV (1982) has stridently claimed that "allowing the motion picture industry to regulate itself has proven an abysmal failure." Concerned primarily with TV and movie violence, NCTV has also voiced concern over modern film critics' tendency to favorably review mainstream films which pair violence and erotica: "Of *Dressed to Kill*—which opens with Angie Dickinson masturbating in the shower [with frequent cuts to a rape scene] and ends with a transvestite killer slitting Nancy Allen's throat, Kael [Pauline Kael, film critic for the *New Yorker* magazine] says 'One of the most sheerly enjoyable films,' . . . and Canby [Vincent Canby of the *New York Times*] ——'witty, romantic, psychological horror film'" (NCTV, 1982, p. 9).

Fueled primarily by similar concerns, other groups have also begun to confront the motion picture industry as well as that of book and magazine publishing. In the next section we briefly discuss a few of these efforts.

Consumer Action and Civil Disobedience

Largely due to what is perceived as the failure of the American mass media industries to effectively censor themselves, political actions groups have, since about 1976, been involved in trying to alert the American public to the possibility of harm arising from exposure to soft-core as well as hard-core material. In Rochester, New York, for example, WAVAW was involved in picketing the movie *Snuff*, a hard-core violent pornographic film; women have also demonstrated against such soft-core films as *Looking For Mr. Goodbar*. In most factions of the feminist community, there is little doubt as to the relationship between viewing such material and antisocial behavior:

> Practically all pornography is made, sold, and bought by men—and the standard themes are focused against the female. Given the current marketing of cruelty, one can only conclude that pornography is indeed the "theory" and battery, rape, molestation, and other increasing crimes of sexual violence are not so coincidentally the "practice." (Morgan, 1978, November, p. 55)

Given this belief in the implicit link between viewing these materials and subsequent behavior, feminists have advocated a number of quasi-legal tactics for attacking the pornography industry. According to Morgan (1978, November), concerned citizens can, among other things

1. refuse to support publishers and film-makers who profit from pornography by not buying products that advertised in ways that demean women;
2. picket porn shops, confronting porn customers, or even photograph porn customers;
3. urge magazines and newspapers not to include pornographic advertising;
4. attempt to expose those who profit from pornography by naming their sources of financial backing;
5. insist that our public officials cease their jovial collaboration with the New Pornocracy—no more Presidential and diplomatic-level interviews boosting sales of magazines which debase half the electorate . . . ;
6. If necessary . . . resort to civil disobedience again. (p. 80)

Tactics such as these have been employed. Feminist author Susan Brownmiller, one of the organizers of Women Against Pornography (WAP), began in 1979, for example, to lead a weekly tour through Manhattan's Times Square pornography district ("Women's War on Porn," 1979). Other groups, such as WAVAW, campaigned against Paramount Pictures in 1979 to remove ads from the film *Bloodline*. WAVAW also threatened to organize a national boycott against Warner Communications, who was responsible for a billboard on Sunset

Strip in Los Angeles portraying a woman bound and bruised with the caption "I'm Black and Blue from the Rolling Stones—and I Love It." Warner Communications removed the billboard immediately and agreed to stop using images of violence against women in their advertisements (Thompson, 1982, March). Women Against Violence in Pornography and Media (WAVPM), a San Francisco-based group, organized the first national feminist protest against media violence involving concerned citizens in New York, Boston, and Los Angeles to picket the film *Dressed to Kill* (Thompson, 1982, March).

Not only have the feminist groups expressed concern about the number of violent-pornographic images of women in the media, but other groups, less vocal, but presumably no less concerned about violence (including violent erotic depictions of rape and sexual abuse), are the National PTA Action Center, the AMA, the NCTV, Ralph Nader's National Citizen's Committee for Broadcasting, the American Association for Marriage and Family Therapy, and the Menninger Foundation.

SUMMARY AND CONCLUSIONS

In this chapter we have attempted to give the reader an overview of the historical development of exceptions to the First Amendment protection of free speech and particularly of obscenity exceptions in the United States. We contrasted American notions of obscenity with the broader definition found in Great Britain, which includes violence as well as graphic sexual depictions. We then described largely unsuccessful attempts by both the British and U.S. legal systems to incorporate empirical social science research into decision making about the harmful effects of pornography on the viewer's behavior. We also discussed the possibility of framing legislation on the basis of social science findings in this area in the future. Our conclusions are that while sexually explicit violent materials could theoretically be handled under the existing statues in most states (patterned after *Miller,* 1973), this is unlikely to occur in the face of the general trend toward declining prosecutions in recent years. Second, we noted that softcore, R-rated films and other depictions, as well as the more hard-core depictions, could possibly be controlled through a focus on the harm such materials produce if the viewer's attitudes toward women were adversely affected or if the viewer showed a greater tendency to behave antisocially after viewing. Here, social scientific evidence demonstrating such harms would clearly be useful, but the Supreme Court and lesser courts seldom feel compelled to rely on scientific evidence in their decision making, or when such evidence is used it is often not thoroughly or objectively considered (the use of the minority report of the presidential commission report being the best example of this selective use of social science data). Nevertheless, social scientists and the law may still benefit from efforts to assess the robustness of laboratory findings on the effects of violent pornography empirically in field settings. If the evidence is compelling enough, perhaps courts and legislators cannot ignore it. In any case, many quasi-legal organizations are convinced of the link between violent pornography and aggression and have taken substantial steps toward curbing its growth. Particularly active has been the BBFC, whose concern in the 1970s and 1980s has been with scenes whose intent is to depict rape or other violence against women as sexually liberating. Feminist groups and less vocal organizations have also been instrumental in pressuring distributors to curtail poduction of some of the more objectionable of these materials. Ultimately, efforts such as these may mobilize large portions of the citizenry whose support would greatly facilitate anti-pornographic legislation.

REFERENCES

Alschuler, M. (1971). Origins of the law of obscenity. In *United States Commission on Obscenity and Pornography,* 2 Technical Report 65. Washington, DC: Government Printing Office.

Barber, D. F. (1972). *Pornography and society.* London: Charles Skilton.

Bates v. State Bar, 433 U.S. 350 (1977).

Beck, M., & Smith, V. E. (1981, May 25). How to make it hot for porn. *Newsweek,* A Book Called "John Cleland's Memoirs of a Woman of Pleasure" v. Attorney General of Massachusetts, 383 U.S. 413 (1966) p. 46.

Brandenburg v. Ohio, 395 U.S. 444 (1969).

Bridges v. California, 314 U.S. 252 (1941).

Brownmiller, S. (1975). *Against our will: Men, women and rape.* New York: Simon & Schuster.

Chaplinsky v. New Hampshire, 315 U.S. 568 (1942).

Clor, H. M. (1969). *Obscenity and public morality: Censorship in liberal society.* Chicago: University of Chicago Press.

Cohen v. California, 403 U.S. 15 (1971).

Commission on Obscenity and Pornography. (1971a). *Presidential Commission on Obscenity and Pornography.* Washington, DC: Government Printing Office.

Commission on Obscenity and Pornography. (1971b). Technical Report of the Commission on Obscenity and Pornography: Legal Analysis (Vol. 2). Washington, DC: Government Printing Office.

Commonwealth v. Sharpless, 2 S. & R. (Pa. 1815).

Court, J. H. (1980). *Pornography and the harm condition.* The Flinders University of South Australia: J. H. Court.

Davidow, R. P., & O'Boyle, M. (1977). Obscenity laws in England and the United States: A comparative analysis. *Nebraska Law Review, 56,* 249–288.

Director of Public Prosecution v. A. & B. C. Chewing Gum Ltd. (1968) I Q.B. 159.

Donnerstein, E. (1980). Pornography and violence against women. *Annals of the New York Academy of Sciences, 347,* 277–288.

Donnerstein, E., & Berkowitz, L. (1981). Victim reactions in aggressive erotic films as a factor in violence against women. *Journal of Personality and Social Psychology, 41,* 710–724.

FCC v. Pacifica Foundation, 438 U.S. 726, 742–748 (1978).

Harlech, Rt Hon The Lord. (1982, March). *Film censorship in Britain—Past, present and future.* Presentation given at International Conference, London.

In re Primus, 98 S. Ct. 1983, 1904 (1978).

Jacobellis v. Ohio, 378 U.S. 184 (1964).

Krattenmaker, T. G., & Powe. L. A., Jr. (1978). Televised violence: First Amendment principles and social science theory. *Virginia Law Review, 64,* 1123–1297.

La Barre (1955). Obscenity: An anthropological appraisal. *Law and Contemporary Problems, 20,* 533.

Leventhal, H. (1977). An empirical inquiry into the effect of *Miller v. California* on the control of obscenity. *New York Law Review, 52,* 810–935.

Lockhart, W. B., & McClure, R. C. (1954). Literature, the law of obscenity, and the constitution. *Minnesota Law Review, 38,* 295.

Malamuth, N. M. (1981). Rape proclivity among males. *Journal of Social Issues, 37,* 138–157.

Malamuth, N. M., & Check, J. V. P. (1980). Penile tumescence and perceptual responses to rape as a function of victim's perceived reactions. *Journal of Applied Social Psychology, 10,* 528–547.

Malamuth, N. M., & Check, J. V. P. (1981). The effects of mass media exposure on acceptance of violence against women: A field experiment. *Journal of Research in Personality, 15,* 436–446.

Malamuth, N. M., & Donnerstein, E. (1982). The effects of aggressive–pornographic mass media stimuli. In L. Berkowitz (Ed.), *Advances in experimental social psychology* (Vol. 15). New York: Academic Press.

Malamuth, N. M., Heim, M., & Feshbach, S. (1980). Inhibitory and disinhibitory effects. *Journal of Personality and Social Psychology, 38,* 399–408.

Malamuth, N. M., & Spinner, B. (1980). A longitudinal content analysis of sexual violence in the best-selling erotica magazines. *Journal of Sex Research, 16,* 226–237.

Miller v. State of California, 413 U.S. 15 (1973).

Morgan, R. (1978, November). How to run pornographers out of town and preserve the First Amendment. *Ms,* pp. 55, 78–80.

National Institute of Mental Health (1982). *Television and behavior: Ten years of scientific progress and implications for the eighties* (Vol. 1, Summary Report). Rockville, MD: National Institute of Mental Health.

NCTV (National Coalition on Television Violence). (1982). Sexual violence. *NCTV News, 3,* (2–3), 10–11.

New York v. Ferber, No. 81–55, decided July 2, 1982.

New York Times Co. v. Sullivan, 376 U.S. 254 (1964).

Paris Adult Theatre I v. Slaton, 413 U.S. 49 (1973).

People v. Winters, 63 N.E. 2d 98, (1945).

Queen v. Calder & Boyers Ltd. (1969) 1 Q.B. 151, 172 (C.A. 1968).

Queen v. Hicklin, L.R. 3 Q.B. 360 (1868).

Queen v. Penguin Books Ltd. (1961), The trial of *Lady Chatterley.*

Richards, D. A. J. (1974–1975). Free speech and obscenity law: Toward a moral theory of the First Amendment. *University of Pennsylvania Law Review, 123,* 45–91.

Riggs, R. E. (1981). *Miller v. California* revisited: An empirical note. *Brigham Young University Law Review, 2,* 247–273.

Roth v. United States, 354 U.S. 476 (1957).

Schenck v. United States, 249 U.S. 47 (1919).

Sobel, L. A. (Ed.). (1979). *Pornography, obscenity and the law.* New York: Facts On File.

Stanmeyer, W. A. (1977–1978). Obscene evils v. obscure truths: Some notes on first principles. *Capital University Law Review, 7.* 647–682.

Swearingen v. United States, 161 U.S. 446(1896).

Thompson, A. (1982, March). *Media incited violence and crime: Who can control it?* Paper presented at the meeting of the Academy of Criminal Justice Sciences, Louisville. KY.

United States v. Bennett, 16 Blatchford 338 (N.Y. S.D., 1879).

United States v. One Book Called "Ulysses." 5 F. Supp. 182 (S.D. N.Y., 1933).
Virginia State Board of Pharmacy v. Virginia Citizens Consumer Council, 425 U.S. 748 (1976).
Webster's Third New International Dictionary (1965). Springfield, MA: G. & C. Merriam.
Wertham, F. (1948, May 24). The comics . . . very funny! *Saturday Review of Literature,* p. 6.
Wertham, F. (1954, May). Comic books—blueprints for delinquency, p. 24.
Whitney v. California, 274 U.S. 357 (1927).
Williams Committee Report. (1979, November). (The Report of the Departmental Committee on Obscenity and Film Censorship.) Cmnd 7772.
Winters v. New York, 333 U.S. 507 (1948).
Women's War on Porn. (1979, August 27). *Time, pp.*
Young v. American Mini Theatres, 427 U.S. 50, 66 (1976).

11

Bases of Liability for Injuries Produced by Media Portrayals of Violent Pornography*

DANIEL LINZ
CHARLES W. TURNER
BRADFORD W. HESSE
STEVEN D. PENROD

CIVIL LIABILITY AND THE CONSTITUTION

A 1978 court case raised a number of important questions about the legal responsibilities for the harm caused by media portrayals of sexual violence. In *Olivia N. v. National Broadcasting Company, Inc.,* a minor brought a civil suit against a broadcast company claiming that a TV drama program, *Born Innocent,* had stimulated certain juveniles to inflict injury on her by an "artificial" rape with a bottle. The suit alleged that the juveniles had viewed a similar artificial rape scene in the television drama and the scene had caused them to decide to perform a similar act against the minor girl. The case also alleged that the producers or distributors of media products portraying sexual violence should be held legally responsible for a victim's injury if the media product stimulated a consumer of the product to inflict injury on an innocent victim. The plaintiff in the case attempted to establish a legal precedent for holding media corporations legally responsible for the harm caused by their products. These products include books,

*Preparation of this chapter was partially supported by National Science Foundation grant number BNS8216772 and National Institute of Justice grant number 80-IJ-CX-0034 to Steven Penrod

277

magazines, films, or TV programs. As shown later in this chapter, the plaintiff in the *Olivia* case was not able to recover damages because of constitutional barriers. However, as we shall see, while the First Amendment may be a viable barrier to the practice of holding media corporations liable for violent assault, it is arguable that "the First Amendment cannot be a shield from civic responsibility for foreseeable consequences of harmful acts" (California Medical Association cited in Levering, 1978, p. 6). Also, as attorney for the plaintiff in the *Olivia* case, Marvin Lewis argued that the intent of the First Amendment was probably not to protect the graphic portrayal of rape (Liebert, Sprafkin, & Davidson, 1982). In this chapter we argue that empirical research on the effects of exposure to violent pornography and aggressive erotica can be used by the plaintiff in a civil suit to help establish whether or not media portrayals of sexual violence represent acts of foreseeable or predictable harm.

It is important to note at the outset that individuals harmed by media products are more likely to recover damages from the media corporation than from the audience member (consumer) who directly produced the harm. That is, an audience member who harms someone may be charged with a criminal offense and may be incarcerated. Although the audience member is unlikely to have substantial resources, in contrast, the media corporations often make large profits from portrayals of sexual (or other) violence. Some of the corporation's profits could be used to compensate victims (Spak, 1981).

Criminal versus Civil Liability

Media corporations might be held either criminally or civilly responsible for harm to innocent victims that results from media portrayals of violent material. In Chapter 10 Penrod and Linz examined contemporary scientific research and the major principles of criminal and constitutional law that might determine whether an individual would be held criminally liable for portrayals of obscenity and pornography. This chapter relates the scientific evidence to the legal principles of civil (tort) law that would determine whether an individual or corporation could be held civilly liable for injuries following media portrayals of sexual violence.

In a criminal case, the state charges an individual (the defendant) with violation of laws. If the charges are sustained, the defendant may serve a jail term or be compelled to pay a fine to the state. When a defendant harms someone by his or her actions, the criminal law usually does not establish a basis for the injured party to recover damages for injuries. In a civil action based upon tort law, the injured party (the plaintiff) alleges that the wrongful or negligent conduct of the defendant has resulted in harm to the plaintiff's person or property. The courts evaluate the circumstances of the alleged action to determine whether (and how) the defendant should be made to compensate the plaintiff for injuries.

Three separate bodies of knowledge must be evaluated to determine whether the media corporations would be civilly liable for an audience member's actions. First, the principles of tort law provide guidelines for determining liability. Second, the injured party may cite current scientific research to demonstrate that specific types of material portraying sexual violence could stimulate audience members to commit violent acts of the type inflicted upon the victim. However, the causal inferences made in scientific research must be evaluated against the requirements of tort law for establishing the *legal* principles of causality. Third, the distributors, producers, and consumers of media materials have certain rights guaranteed by the First Amendment of the U.S. Constitution. These First Amendment rights may limit the possibilities of recovery.

Principles of Tort Law Concerning Product Liability

Tort law describes the circumstances under which one person (the defendant) is required to compensate another (the plaintiff) because the defendant's wrongful or negligent conduct resulted in harm to the plaintiff's person or property (Epstein, 1978; Wade, 1973). A manufacturer or distributor of a commercial product (e.g., a media product) could be held liable if wrongful or negligent conduct caused harm to the defendant.

Within tort law, the responsibility for injury (as in the *Olivia* v. *NBC* case) could be assigned to one (or more) of four causes: (1) the conduct of the defendant, (i.e., NBC); (2) the conduct of the plaintiff (i.e., Olivia); (3) the conduct of some third party (i.e., neither the defendant nor the plaintiff) such as the parents of the juveniles who committed the assault; and/or (4) some natural force or event (sometimes described as an "act of God"). The defendant usually is not held responsible for injury due to a natural event or the actions of a third party. This principle implies that NBC would not be responsible for Olivia's injuries since the actual injury was produced by a third party (i.e., the juveniles). However, tort law describes some circumstances in which a defendant is liable even though a third party actually produced the injury. That is, if the film *Born Innocent* was a *concurrent* cause of the injury, then NBC could be held financially liable for the injuries to Olivia.

To establish a case to recover damages, the plaintiff would have to demonstrate that the manufacturer's product was a concurrent cause of the injury. For example, the manufacturer of a bus in which the brakes failed might be liable for injuries to a passenger resulting from an accident. The manufacturer could be liable even though the person driving the bus did not work for the manufacturer (a third party) and the roadway was slippery due to a snowstorm (natural event).

The defendant would be held liable for injuries if his or her behavior was causally *dominant* in the case (i.e., the defendant's conduct was a necessary precondition for the injury). This condition is frequently phrased as follows:

"But for the action of the defendant, the injury would not have occurred." In the *Born Innocent* case, this legal test would imply that except for the portrayal of the artificial rape scene in the televised drama, the juveniles would not have committed the crime.

The defendant in a tort case might attempt to avoid liability by asserting that the ultimate injury occurred because the plaintiff or a third party used a product in a manner other than the purpose intended by the manufacturer or the distributor. In the *Olivia* v. *NBC* case, the media corporation might have claimed that the film product was designed solely for entertainment, and it was not intended to be used as it was by the juvenile assaulters. Hence, the third-party purchasers or consumers of the product should have been solely liable for the injury.

The courts have provided some guidelines to determine when a manufacturer or distributor would be liable even though the product was mishandled or misused. In *Escola* v. *Coca Cola Bottling Co.* (1944), the courts ruled that a manufacturer or distributor was liable if a product defect created or brought about the harm. However, the consumer of a product implicitly accepts some of the risk of injury caused by a product if the product exhibits an open and obvious risk of danger. For example, a sharp knife provides some danger of misuse by the consumer, but the typical consumer can reasonably evaluate the risks associated with purchasing and using the knife. Hence, the purchaser implicitly accepts some of the risks involved in using the product. If the danger associated with misuse of the product is not obvious, then the manufacturer may be required to limit distribution to those individuals who have adequate training in using the product or the manufacturer may be required in some other way to ensure the proper use of the product.

Media materials portraying sexually violent behavior may increase the risk of imitation by some audience members (consumers of the product). Suppose current research indicated that teenagers were most likely to imitate the violent behavior in the film. Then, to avoid liability, NBC might be required to reduce the likelihood of imitation by procedures such as the following: (1) prevent distribution of the film *Born Innocent* to these potential violence-imitating consumers, (2) provide warning labels to counteract the potential risk of imitation, (3) provide training in the appropriate use of the product, or (4) modify the design of the product to eliminate the potential harm-producing aspects of the film. To satisfy the last condition, NBC might have removed the artificial rape scene from the *Born Innocent* drama. Alternatively, NBC might have presented the drama in a way to reduce the risk of imitation.

The theory of strict liability from product defects has been extended to the third-party injury of bystanders in *Elmore* v. *American Motors* (1969, 70 Cal. 2d 278). According to the court, "Absent his own misconduct, the bystander's case for recovery is in truth stronger than that of a product user as there is no possibility that the bystander assumed, even by implication, the risk of latent defects in a product that others had chosen to use'' (p. 652). Suppose that a sexually violent film stimulated an audience member to commit a rape against a bystander. Both the rape victim and the rapist might sue the filmmaker. However, the rape victim would have a better chance of recovering than the rapist since the rapist implicitly accepted some risk in using the product but the victim could not have tacitly agreed to any risks associated with the media product.

Tort law provides three sets of criteria for evaluating possible manufacturing problems. Two of these criteria are particularly relevant to the production of media material containing sexual violence. First, a manufacturer may be liable for construction defects in a product. For example, a restaurant may be liable for selling contaminated foods and a machine maker may be liable if an engine fails to satisfy design requirements. This criterion probably would not be relevant to cases of sexual violence.

Second, the manufacturer is liable for design defects in which the material does not perform in accordance with its own performance standards when put to ordinary use. For example, a manufacturer might use a supporting brace for a platform but the brace may not possess sufficient strength to provide the intended support. Since the brace was not designed properly, the manufacturer could be liable for injuries resulting from a collapse of the supporting brace. In a media product, the material could be inadvertantly designed in a way that results in injury to an innocent party. As we argue extensively in an upcoming section, by portraying scenes in a particular fashion, the material may cause injury by stimulating audience members to imitate the product. Hence, the product may be considered to have a defective design. If the plaintiff can show that it is possible to redesign the product so that the defect can be removed, then the manufacturer would be liable. In the *Born Innocent* show, the plaintiff could have argued that removing or redesigning the artificial rape scene might have been sufficient to prevent the injury to Olivia.

Third, the manufacturer may not have used adequate labels to warn the user of nonobvious dangers. For example, labels are included on medicines to warn the user of nonobvious danger in using the product. The manufacturer of a media product could use labels to provide warning of potential harm that could be caused by the product. For example, the film *Born Innocent* might contain a warning label to audience members of the potential effects of the film (and the probable consequences of imitating the film). We talk about the use of warning labels specifically designed to counter the effects of violent pornography more extensively in the next section.

To summarize, the current status of tort law concerning strict product liability can be applied to media corporations portraying sexual (or other) violence. The manufacturer of media products might be liable for injury if it was demonstrated that the media product was a dominant cause of the plaintiff's injury. That is, the plaintiff would have to show that the injury would not have occurred except for the portrayal of sexual violence in media products. The plaintiff also might try to show that the manufacturer had not made an effort to limit distribution of the media product to individuals who might be particularly likely to misuse the product (e.g., young teenagers who may not be able to evaluate the potentially harmful effects of the film). The plaintiff might further present evidence that adequate warning labels about use of the product were not included. That is, parents may not be adequately warned of the potentially harmful effects of the film on their children's behavior. Finally, the plaintiff would want to show that the media product could be redesigned so that the risk of the plaintiff's injury would be prevented. If the plaintiff could provide evidence establishing each of these parts, then the courts could rule that the manufacturer's media product should be evaluated by tort principles of strict product liability.

Constitutional Barriers to Civil Actions

Before pornography can be successfully tackled under tort law, it will be necessary to balance the possible harmful censoring effects that civil suits could have on the media against the benefits of compensating individual victims. As Hilker (1979) pointed out, imposition of strict liability on broadcasters of acts executed by third parties may serve to "chill" broadcasters' freedom of speech. The constitutional aspects of criminally prosecuting obscenity and pornography were extensively discussed in Chapter 10 by Penrod and Linz. As these authors note, the courts, while deeming certain types of speech as falling outside the protection of the Constitution, have proceeded rather cautiously, preferring to err on the side of less regulation of speech. As with criminal prosecutions, the chilling effect of civil suits against the media may be seen as so menacing by the courts that they will repeatedly go out of their way in order to tip the balance in favor of First Amendment safeguards.

It is important to note that although First Amendment rights are paramount in any civil deliberation, they are not always absolute. In *Weirum* v. *RKO General Inc.* (1975), for example, a California appeals court found the Southern California radio station KHJ civilly negligent when a contest in which contestants were to be awarded prize money upon being first to locate the DJ's traveling van resulted in the death of an innocent nonparticipant. The widow of the accident victim sued the radio station and won on the grounds that "the First Amendment does not sanction the infliction of physical injury merely because it is achieved by word rather than act" (p. 472).

There are several major classifications of speech that are not protected by the First Amendment. These are (1) obscenity, (2) libel, (3) speech that presents clear and present danger or that incites lawless action. Since Penrod and Linz (Chapter 10) discuss the development of obscenity and libel as exceptions to First

Amendment protection, we limit ourselves to only the briefest comments on these exceptions, concentrating instead on the notion of clear and present danger and incitement to lawless action as they have been applied in civil cases.

OBSCENITY

There is some evidence (Leventhal, 1977) that fewer jurisdictions were actually prosecuting obscenity cases after the 1973 Supreme Court decision *Miller* v. *State of California*. *Miller* defined obscenity as that which patently offends community standards as applicable by state law and which "taken as a whole, does not have serious literary, artistic, political, or scientific value." These standards are apparently difficult to actually apply, and prosecutions have continued to decline despite fewer higher court appeals. In fact, it may be the case, as Berns (1975) has suggested, that the courts have ignored the dilemma posed by pornography and obscenity rather than confronting it. Berns has stated that "the law has resigned in favor of the free mass market" (p. 55). Following this train of thought, Berns's comments present an interesting perspective. If it is true that the courts, rather than tangle with the issue of obscenity, have relegated pornography to the domain of free enterprise, then it may be appropriate to ascribe the same limitations to obscene materials as to any other potentially dangerous product. Perhaps in this way it would be possible to create a sense of social responsibility with respect to violent pornography where presently none exists. In this sense, tort law may gain greater legal responsiveness than criminal litigation. We have suggested in the previous section that producers and distributors of these materials may, on the basis of currently available research, be able to predict with reasonable certainty that harmful acts are likely to arise from widespread exposure to such material. As Spak (1981) and others have noted, there are two alternatives for controlling the dangers resulting from predictable harm presentations. One recourse would be to censor such materials before they ever reach the public. To a certain degree this is already done with all types of pornography. Age restrictions and limitations of locale tend to prevent portions of the general population from viewing disapproved material. But prior restraint, in any other form, has resulted in many constitutional problems. This may make a second alternative more practical and generally acceptable: ensuring compensation for harm after the fact through tort law—"a free society prefers to punish the few who abuse the right of speech after they break the law then to throttle them and all others beforehand" (*Southeastern Promotions Ltd*, v. *Conrad*, 1975 p. 559). However, even the second alternative raises constitutional questions.

A good example of the confrontation between civil and constitutional law and harms arising from media exposure is *Walt Disney Productions Inc.* v. *Shannon* (1981). Here the plaintiff sued the producers of the Mickey Mouse Club show, claiming eye injury arising from the imitation of a method for creating sound effects involving placing a BB pellet inside of a balloon. The plaintiff maintained that those responsible for producing the Mickey Mouse Club show had "invited [the plaintiff] to do something posing a foreseeable risk of injury" (p. 582).

The *Shannon* case was reviewed first by a Georgia trial court, which granted the defendant's motion for summary judgment on the grounds that the First Amendment was an absolute defense in the action. The case was then carried to the Georgia Court of Appeals where the decision was reversed, but an appeal to the Georgia Supreme Court upheld the lower court's judgment. Using the clear and present danger test, the Georgia Supreme Court could not find the TV actor's instructions as causitive of any substantial evil insidious enough to warrant impingement of First Amendment rights.

Even though it was ultimately unsuccessful, Moody (1981) recognized the significance of *Shannon* case. *Shannon* demonstrates that certain types of speech are potentially addressable by tort law. But the case also demonstrates the overshadowing power of constitutional protections. As Moody puts it, "It does not matter whether speech is penalized under criminal or tort law. The fear of civil damage awards could inhibit freedom of speech as effectively as fear of criminal prosecution" (p. 428).

CLEAR AND PRESENT DANGER

One of the oldest judicial guidelines of protected speech is the "clear and present danger" test delivered by Justice Oliver Wendell Holmes in the landmark case of *Schenck* v. *United States* (1919). Schenck was charged with violating the Federal Espionage Act of 1917 when he allegedly interfered with military recruitment by distributing antiwar leaflets to potential enlistees. Essentially, the test asserts that freedom of speech should not be curtailed unless it presents a clear and present danger to society. A colloquial example is the often-cited situation in which someone falsely shouts "fire" in a crowded theater.

The clear and present danger test has been reviewed and modified a number of times since its original conception. One variation of the guideline, called the "fighting words" test, declares that some speech is unprotected by the Constitution because "by their utterance [they] inflict injury or tend to incite an immediate breach of the peace" (*Chaplinsky* v. *State of New Hampshire*, 1942, pp. 571–572). The prohibition of fighting words added a new ingredient to judicial determination of unprotected speech—incitement.

In the late 1960s, Brandenburg, a leader of the Ku Klux Klan in southern Ohio, was indicted for "advocating" lawless action at a KKK political rally. Brandenburg was convicted under the Ohio Criminal Syndicalism statute for publicly endorsing violent insurrection. He consequently appealed the case to the Supreme Court, which reversed the Ohio court's decision. Mere advocacy "not distinguished from incitement to imminent lawless action" (p. 447) was not seen as sufficient cause to relinquish First Amendment protection. The Court's effort to distinguish advocacy of a certain belief from incitement to lawless action has become known as the Brandenburg test (*Brandenburg* v. *Ohio,* 1968).

The Brandenburg test is an appropriate standard for examining cases of violent pornography, since it embodies the best of two extremely useful lines of constitutional analysis: the clear and present danger test and the incitement test.

The primary question is: At what point does violent pornography cease to become mere advocacy entitled to the same protections of the spoken word (*Kingsley International Pictures Corp.* v. *Regents of the University of the State of New York,* 1959) and assume the qualities of an incitement to lawless action? The answer obviously lies in how one defines incitement. The test of incitement was first proposed by Judge Learned Hand (*Masses Publishing Co.* v. *Patten,* 1917) as a standard in which the very utterance of a word would undoubtedly lead to the commission of a crime. From its beginnings it connoted an element of action. In its original formulation it was based primarily upon the written and spoken word. The question arises as to whether this language-bound test would be applicable to modern depictions of violence. In answer, it must be remembered that Judge Hand's original statements were delivered in 1917, well before motion pictures and television became popular. Taking the spirit of the incitement test into consideration, we might describe violent pornography as a communication that could motivate a viewer to illegal behavior through graphic visual representations of that action and implicit instructions on how to commit the illegal actions. Described in this way, violent pornography may not merit the protection of the First Amendment to the extent that it is considered a communication that creates a clear and present danger or incites lawless action. There is little guarantee that the courts will accept this definition of violent pornography and limit the First Amendment rights of film producers or television broadcasters. In *Olivia* v. *NBC* violation of First Amendment rights was the major argument of the defense lawyers for NBC. The defense argued that, while it was true that speech directed to inciting or producing imminent lawless action was not protected by the First Amendment, the television broadcast of a rape scene was not speech of this type. NBC did not, according to their lawyers, advocate rape or intend to incite rape through its broadcast (Liebart *et al.,* 1982). In 1978, when the case went to court in San Francisco, it was dismissed because the plaintiff could not prove that the network intended its viewers to imitate the violent rape.

As we emphasize in the remainder of this chapter, the question of whether or not certain materials may incite the viewer to imminent lawlessness may be an empirical one answerable through social scientific inquiry. The courts' acceptance of this form of evidence has been inconsistent at best, with the courts accepting those findings that appear to justify their prior conceptions and ignoring contradictory findings. (See Penrod & Linz, Chapter 10 of this volume, for an example of the courts' use of the findings of the Commission on Obscenity and Pornography.) Nevertheless, the courts have at times relied on social science data. The data collected to date on the effects of violent pornography may be quite effective in establishing the incitement effects of violent pornographic material in a civil case.

USING SOCIAL SCIENCE DATA ON THE EFFECTS OF VIOLENT PORNOGRAPHY IN A CIVIL SUIT

In this section we apply the general principles of strict product liability that we have just outlined to the specific problem of establishing liability for injury arising from portrayals of sexual violence. First, we very briefly discuss the role of the social psychologist as expert witness in a civil trial and describe some of the prerequisite legal hurdles that may need to be leaped before social psychological evidence concerning the impact of violent pornography could even be presented to a judge or jury. Second, we review the empirical findings to date on the effects of exposure to violent pornography and point out how they may help inform a judge or jury about the possible risks contained in these materials. In particular, we concentrate on two questions that must be answered in a civil suit involving these materials: (1) Was the media product the dominant cause of the plaintiff's injury, or more specifically, did exposure to violent pornography lead to incitement and/or instructional effects that were instrumental in injury to a victim? and (2) Is there sufficient social psychological evidence to conclude that the creators, producers, or distributors of these materials could have reasonably foreseen the danger they pose to innocent victims? Finally, we discuss what the psychological evidence to date can tell us about the creator's or producer's ability to eliminate or at least modify the unsafe character of violent pornographic materials.

A Prototypical Case and Some Legal Hurdles

For the purpose of illustrating the possibilities for using some of the social psychological research presented in this volume in civil litigation, we will use a case scenario similar to that in the *Olivia* case. Let us say that a woman has been sexually assaulted, and the attacker has been apprehended, tried in criminal court, and convicted. During the criminal trial, evidence is presented that implies that the rapist was "inspired" by his continuous viewing of a collection of violent pornographic videotapes. After the criminal trial the victim decides that she wishes to name the producers, directors, and distributors of the violent pornographic materials as defendants in a civil suit.

Establishing That a Harm Has Been Done

First the victim or plaintiff, as she will now be called, must establish that a harm or injury has occurred (Hilker, 1979; Wade, 1973). This is not a significant problem because there has been a criminal trial in which it was proved that the victim was raped and the defendant was found guilty. Presumably, this is a harm that society wishes to redress. It should be noted that the victim could press a civil suit *without* prior involvement in a criminal trial in which a defendant has been found guilty of the crime. It would be more difficult, however, to establish that the victim had indeed been harmed without the benefit of a criminal conviction. In order to simplify matters we have chosen a scenario in which establishing that a harm has been done is not problematic, so that we may devote our attention to the possibility of using social psychological research to establish a causal link between exposure and harm.

Naming a Defendant

Next, a defendant must be named. The first question is: What do we do about the rapist himself? Films do not rape women, men rape women. While it would be possible to name the rapist himself as a defendant in a civil suit, to simplify matters we will, for two reasons, assume that the victim does not name the rapist in the suit. First, as we mentioned at the beginning of the chapter, the defendant in many cases will be "judgment proof." That is to say that the convicted and incarcerated rapist will probably be unable to pay damages even if the suit were successful. Second. it may even be useful to call the convicted rapist to the witness stand to testify on behalf of the victim's case. It would be very helpful, for example, for the rapist to testify that he had indeed been exposed to violent pornography before committing the crime. The primary defendants or tort-feasors in the suit then could be the creators, producers, and distributors of the films. Having established that a harm has been done and a defendant named, we want first to consider the possibility that the victim could call a social psychologist to the stand to report findings from studies reported in this volume.

The Social Psychologist as Expert Witness

Under Federal Rule of Evidence 702, an expert witness may be called by either party in civil or criminal trials "if scientific, technical or other specialized knowledge will assist the trier of fact to understand the evidence or determine a fact in issue." The expert witness may be permitted to do two things during the course of a trial that the nonexpert is usually not allowed to do. First, the expert witness may be permitted to give testimony in the form of an opinion. Second, the expert may be allowed to answer hypothetical questions if he or she does not have first-hand knowledge of some or all of the facts to support an opinion. The courts have generally believed that a psychologist with an accredited degree qualifies as an expert and may be useful in telling the judge or jury something that they do not already know.

Traditionally, psychologists as courtroom experts have been associated with the insanity defense, but psychologists have testified in criminal courts concerning eyewitness reliability, for postsentencing dispositions, on community standards in obscenity, on the effects of prejudicial pretrial information, and on change-of-venue motions. In the civil area, psychologists have testified in accident disability cases, on questions of degree of neurological impairment, on matters such as degree of mental retardation, and on the acceptability of certain psychological treatments or therapies. It is still rare, but social psychologists have been called upon to testify as to the causal factors underlying the commission of a harmful act committed by a particular person.

The criminal case *State of Indiana* vs. *Schiro,* 1980 (Wathen, 1981, September 12) is an example of the use of social psychological testimony on the effects of violent pornography being used by the courts. Schiro, who was charged with sexually assaulting and killing a 28-year-old woman, had been exposed at the age of 6 or 7 years to a stag film called *Bed Time* that his father had hidden in the house. The film, which was admitted as evidence and shown to the jury, "showed a woman's face as if she were in pain and, at the same time, showed her body as if she were enjoying her sexual encounter" (p. 11). As a result of continually viewing this film, according to the testimony of two psychologists, "Schiro has formed the opinion that women enjoy pain and enjoy being raped and their pain arouses him. . . . Schiro finds that sadism, masochism and rape are just part of sex and [he] enjoys modeling what he has seen in movies and on television" (p. 11).

A second case, *State of Minnesota* v. *Marhoun,* 1982 (Clifford, personal communication, January 4, 1983), also provides evidence of a specific instance in which violent pornography seemed to play a causal role in facilitating predictable aggressive acts. In this case the defendant was eventually convicted of first-degree murder and criminal sexual conduct. According to the prosecuting attorney in this case, pretrial testimony by a psychologist convinced the trial judge that the subject of the defendant's possession of sexually explicit bondage and discipline magazines was relevant and should be admitted.

In both of these cases we do not know exactly what impact the expert testimony of the psychologists had on the jury. In the first case the actual materials used by the rapist and psychological testimony that the defendant believed that women enjoyed being raped perhaps as a result of exposure to violent pornography were admitted to evidence for the jury's consideration. In the second case, while the jury did not hear the testimony from the psychologist, they were allowed to hear testimony from others on the pornographic materials used by the defendant because the judge was apparently convinced of the validity of the pretrial evidence presented to him by a psychologist. The fact that the testimony was admitted in both cases, and in one case the materials themselves admitted into evidence, provides some measure of the degree to which trial authorities are willing to accept the premises specified in the social scientific theories and empirical research.

Demonstrating Incitement Effects and Instructional Effects

Due to the nature of the data that social psychologists have collected on the effects of exposure to violent pornography, the expert social psychologist witness may have difficulty making definitive statements about the individual case. This point is important for establishing a legal context within which to view the social psychological findings reported in this volume (in particular, Chapter 1 by Malamuth, Chapter 2 by Donnerstein, and Chapter 4 by Zillman and Bryant). Social psychological research, as we have seen in these chapters, has almost exclusively relied upon comparisons of the behaviors of one *group* versus another *group*. The social psychologist can only assert, for instance, that there is a tendency on the *average* for members of the group exposed to violent pornography to behave more aggressively than a control group. In a tort action against a media defendant for alleged acts of harm to a particular victim, it is first necessary to provide the existence of a causal link in the *specific* case at hand—perhaps even a constitutionally acceptable incitement to illegal action.

Any tort suit requires that the plaintiff demonstrate to the jury that there is a causal connection between an ''individual instance [depiction] of damage and an individual instance of damage-causing behavior'' (Hilker, 1979, p. 531). For our particular case it is necessary to demonstrate that there is a relationship between a particular message, portrayal, movie scene or scenes, and the harm done to the victim. It is not sufficient merely to assert that since these materials are widely available in the culture, or that because the rapist had access to a wide range of these materials that an aggressive tendency is built up in people in general and that the rapist's act was a reflection of this process. This would imply that all or at least an unmanageable number of film producers, directors, etc., are liable. Instead, tort liability is most reasonably established where an identifiable message or messages can be located in a particular film or films and where the specific film and persons associated with these materials be named in the suit (Prosser & Wade, 1971).

It is doubtful that the social psychological research or the expert social psychologist witness can be very useful in helping establish the relationship between a specific movie or scene and a specific harm. One alternative is for the plaintiff to establish general causal links between media exposures and behavior and demonstrate specific causation in the particular case by satisfying the jury that the harm suffered by the victim closely resembled in severity and detail specific acts portrayed in the film presentation. In other words, it may be necessary (and sufficient) for the plaintiff to demonstrate that the injury resembled in some unique detail a similar rape enacted in the materials to which the rapist has been exposed. This is admittedly a difficult task, but as Spak (1981) has noted, the uniqueness of the act is probably the pivotal point for establishing media liability. In Spak's words, "a relatively commonplace punch in the nose—a generally violent act" (p. 672) can never be directly traced to a specific media presentation. But rare of uncommon acts may be traceable. For example, "murder by means of a 'magnum' gun rather than an ordinary gun, assault with a karate blow rather than a more useful fisted punch, a stabbing with a machete instead of a more mundane knife" (p. 672) may all be violent acts traceable to a specific media event. (The most dramatic example of this form of traceable act is perhaps an incident in which Boston youths doused a woman with gasoline and set her on fire two days after the presentation of the TV movie *Fuzz* which contained a scene involving a wino who suffered a similar fate [*New York Times,* 1973, October 4]). Analogously, asserting that a rape which contained no unusual characteristics or peculiarities traceable to a specific film presentation was, in fact, caused by these film depictions, could be a significantly more difficult task.

claiming a particular harmful act can be traced to a particular media depiction can be thought of as a demonstration of an instructional effect. The claim would be that the rapist learned his particular method from certain film materials. The victim might, however, also claim a more general incitement effect. It could be asserted that the rapist was compelled or motivated by the materials more or less to reenact what he has learned. Hilker has noted that it may be difficult to prove an incitement effect without first proving an instructional effect. In any event, it would probably be very difficult to convince a jury that a rapist derived his provocation to commit a rape from viewing certain materials unless the rape resembled in some unique way the rape portrayed in the film materials.

The Role of the Social Psychologist in Determining the Risk of an Incitement Effect for Violent Pornography

The social psychologist could be called to the stand on behalf of the plaintiff to help demonstrate an instructional effect, an incitement effect, or both, provided that there is some causal groundwork laid by the attorney that leads the jury to believe that the harmful act and the film depiction were ostensibly related to one another. Of the two effects, however, the social psychologist is probably best able to assist the jury in determining if an incitement effect was present. This is so because none of the data collected to date on the effects of violent pornography have directly demonstrated that exposure to these materials results in observers learning or mimicking the specific behaviors portrayed in films (as have early studies on childhood modeling of aggression conducted by Bandura and his associates [e.g., Bandura, 1977]). Obviously these studies cannot be done for ethical reasons. What the research to date has shown, and shown convincingly, is that exposure to these materials may instill in the exposed individual sufficient degree of motivation to aggress against women in a more general way, and the material may provide the viewer with sufficient psychological means of justification of such aggression.

What Type of Materials Pose the Greatest Risk?

Research conducted by Malamuth and his colleagues (Malamuth, Heim, & Feshbach, 1980; Malamuth & Check, 1980a, 1980b) and by Donnerstein and Berkowitz (1981) have examined the effects of the victim's response in the rape depiction and males' sexual arousal, acceptance of violence against women, and actual violent behavior. Malamuth et al. (1980), for example, found that if the victim was portrayed as becoming involuntarily sexually aroused by the assault, male subjects' own sexual arousal, as indexed by both self-reports and penile tumescence measures, becomes as high as, and is sometimes higher than sexual arousal resulting from mutually consenting depictions. In other studies (Malamuth, Haber, & Feshbach, 1980; Malamuth & Check, 1980a, 1980b; Malamuth & Check, 1981a), males who watched or listened to rape depictions that supposedly had positive consequences for the victim thought the victim had suffered less, and they believed that a larger percentage of women in general would find forced sex or rape pleasurable compared to males exposed to materials depicting a negative consequence for the victim. Even exposure to mass media films such as *Swept Away* and *The Getaway,* which have segments depicting women as victims of sexual violence (who later fall in love with their assailants), was found to increase acceptance of interpersonal violence against women by men (Malamuth & Check, 1981b).

Studies by Donnerstein and Berkowitz (1981) have provided evidence that a positive victim response will facilitate aggressive behavior against females by male laboratory subjects. These researchers have found that, if subjects are first angered, rape depictions involving *both* positive and negative reactions by the victim result in higher levels of aggression by men against women (indexed by shocks delivered to a female confederate of the experimenter by male subjects). More importantly, however, when male subjects were *not* angered, only the positive-outcome aggressive–pornographic film significantly increased aggression against females. These results are only obtained when the target of aggression is a female. When the experimenters' confederate is a male, male subjects shock the confederate significantly less in both positive and negative outcome conditions than when the target is a female.

From these research findings we can begin to construct a profile of what may constitute the most "risky" set of materials—that is, the type of film or magazine portrayal that may inspire or instigate an imitation effect. First, the materials that are most likely to pose a risk for an incitement effect for the average or nonrapist male population are *portrayals of rapes or other forms of sexual assault that show the female victim becoming involuntarily aroused or otherwise responding positively to sexual aggression.* Second. there is some indication that the film or other materials need not necessarily be hard-core explicitly detailed portrayals. There is some evidence that mass media portrayals of sexual aggression against women have, at least, an impact on male attitudes about aggression against women. The effects of these materials on behavior have not yet been adequately empirically assessed. Because behavioral effects have only been demonstrated for material that is both rather sexually explicit and rather explicitly violent, it may be best to limit our definition of what is most risky to materials that contain more explicit sex and violence. It is possible, however, that future research will allow us to extend our definition of risky material to less explicit sexually aggressive imagery.

WHO IS MOST LIKELY TO BE INFLUENCED BY THESE MATERIALS?

The commonplace assumption, and indeed a likely argument to be advanced by the producers of violent pornography, is that there will always be certain sick, immoral, imbalanced individuals who will be *both* especially drawn to this material *and* likely to commit a violent sexual assault. To hold the film or publishing industry responsible for the actions of these imbalanced few is unreasonable. The experimental evidence collected to date does, in fact, lend credence to the view that rapists differ in their patterns of sexual arousal from other males. Rapists appear to become sexually aroused by material that stresses the rape victim's abhorrence (Abel, Barlow, Blanchard, & Guild, 1977; Barbaree, Marshall, & Lanthier, 1979). Normal males, on the other hand, experience significantly lower levels of sexual arousal to portrayals that depict the victim as abhorring the experience, compared to mutually consenting themes (Malamuth, Heim, & Feshbach, 1980; Malamuth & Check, 1980a, 1980b). But, as noted in the previous section, males selected from nonrapist populations become just as aroused to a rape depiction as to a mutually consenting one if the victim is portrayed as somehow deriving pleasure from the experience. Furthermore, the potential claim by film producers and distributors that only an extremely small minority of individuals will be unduly affected by violent pornography may only be true for certain types of materials—specifically, that material that portrays the victim as abhorring the experience of being sexually assaulted. For a sizeable portion of the normal male population (which might be identified via instruments such as the likelihood of raping scale [LR] devised by Malamuth and Check, 1980a), depictions of rape in which the victim experiences abhorrence as well as depictions where the victim seems to experience a positive outcome are sexually arousing. There are also data to suggest that men who score relatively high on psychological scales measuring power as a motivation for sexual acts, men who report lower levels of actual sexual experience, and men who score relatively low on love and affection as a motivation for sex are likely to perceive an ambiguous rape experience as having a positive outcome for the victim and to become more accepting of rape myths as a result of exposure to aggressive pornography. (Malamuth and Check, 1981). On the basis of current research, then, distributors and producers may be justified in asserting that only some members of the population may be incited by these materials (e.g., persons who score relatively high on power motivation for sex, etc.). This does not imply by any means that distributors and producers are justified in asserting that only an extremely small and very deviate minority of males may be affected by these materials.

Film distributors and producers could conceivably make the additional claim that only individuals that are predisposed to aggression or that are somehow angered or stimulated by circumstances other than violent pornographic materials will be likely to aggress against women. In other words, the materials alone are not sufficient to produce an incitement effect. As we have seen in this volume, the work of Donnerstein and Berkowitz calls this into question. These researchers have demonstrated that, as film producers may assert, males are more likely to aggress against females after exposure to violent pornography *when they have been angered first* (Donnerstein & Berkowitz, 1981). This effect is obtained when subjects are exposed to material in which the victim abhors the rape *and* to material in which the victim expresses a positive reaction. When subjects are not angered, however, *only* the films depicting a positive outcome for the victim result in increased aggression against females by males. These findings lead the researchers to conclude that while depictions which emphasize the pain and suffering of the victim have their effect only with male subjects who are predisposed toward aggression, the more 'common' story line in aggressive pornography of a willing and positive reacting victim influences *all* subjects. Thus, as with the prior assertion by the producers and distributors that these materials only affect a deviant few, the assertion that only those who are first predisposed to aggression will be affected also appears untenable.

WHO IS MOST LIKELY TO BE THE VICTIM
OF THE INDIVIDUAL INCITED BY THESE MATERIALS?

The research presented in this volume can also help us answer the question of who is most at risk as a victim of a violent assault incited by these materials. Donnerstein (1980), for example, conducted an experiment in which subjects viewed either neutral, pornographic, or aggressive–pornographic materials. Afterwards subjects were given the opportunity to aggress against either a male or a female target. The exposure to the aggressive–pornographic materials resulted in no increase in aggression against a male target. Exposure to the aggressive–pornographic material did increase male aggression against a female target, however, and this effect occurred regardless of whether the males were angered or not angered before exposure. Thus, we can conclude that the most obvious targets of aggression incited by these materials will be females. An interesting question not addressed by the research conducted to date is the impact of materials depicting homosexual rape on aggression against *male* victims. The effect of positive versus negative male victim reactions on subsequent aggressive behavior toward males by males is unknown. It may be that exposure to these materials results in a pattern of responses similar to male–female rape with victim depictions resulting in greater male–male aggressiveness. Defining this risk must await further empirical research.

Estimating the Likelihood of Injury

The question that may arise in the juror's mind and, indeed, one of the primary elements of establishing product liability (Prosser & Wade, 1971) is the perception of how likely, or how probable, is the occurrence of an injury to a victim given the current condition of the product. One could imagine the juror saying to him or herself, ''I have heard the testimony from the social psychologist who has told me that when you expose a male to certain types of violent pornography, this results in aggressive behavior against women in the laboratory. Does this mean that every man exposed to this material reacts aggressively in all settings? Also. how *much more* aggressively do men expose to this material behave compared to men who are not exposed?'' In more technical terms, the juror may be concerned with the magnitude of the relationship between exposure and aggression or the size of the effect that exposure has on behavior. Judging by the mean differences between control group subjects and experimental subjects in most of the research cited in this volume, the effect sizes (Cohen & Cohen, 1975), if one were to compute them, would generally fall within the small-to-lower-medium range typical for research in the social sciences.

These minimal effects for exposure to aggressive–pornography may lead the plaintiff in our case, as they have sometimes led social scientists themselves, to conclude that the social psychological evidence is not compelling enough to build a case around. There are two reasons why this concern should not deter the plaintiff. First, it may not be necessary for the social psychologist to take the witness stand and say with absolute certainty that exposure will lead to aggression in all or even most cases, because that is not what needs to be proven in a liability case. The plaintiff must demonstrate to the jury that exposure resulted in aggression against a third part in this particular case. Presumably, the plaintiff will be significantly aided in proving this connection if a high degree of similarity between the materials viewed by the assailant and details of the assault can be shown (an instructional effect). The social psychologist can be instrumental in bolstering this claim by asserting that the empirical research, regardless of the small effect sizes, indicates that the probability is definitely increased (if only to a small extent) that an individual will be motivated to reenact what he has seen depicted in a film (an incitement effect). Second, the plaintiff should be encouraged by prior attempts to press other types of civil suits based on scientific evidence from other disciplines that may be even less compelling than the type of evidence social scientists have accumulated.

The products-liability cases arising from injury to daughters of women who were exposed to diethylstilbestrol (DES) provide a good example of the level of causation provided by other scientific inquires being considered compelling enough that plaintiffs were willing to bring suit against drug manufacturers (*Georgia Law Review,* 1981). During the 1940s and 1950s the synthetic estrogen DES was prescribed to millions of pregnant women to prevent miscarriages. Recently (Downey & Gulley, 1983), several hundred daughters of mothers who used DES have brought civil suits against the drug companies that have produced the drug. The plaintiffs contended that at the time they marketed the drug the manufacturers should have known that it was carcinogenic and that the manufacturers should have relied on tests conducted by other drug manufacturers that indicated that DES was potentially unsafe. Medical research has revealed a "highly significant association between the treatment of mothers with estrogen diethylstilbestrol during pregnancy and the subsequent development of adenocarcinoma of the vagina in the daughters" (Herbst, Ulfelder, & Poskanzer, 1971, p. 879). The "highly significant association" in many of the studies is obtained by first identifying those young women who have contracted cancer of the vagina (a rare occurrence in women under the age of 50) and comparing these patients with a control group of young women who do not have cancer matched on birth date or other characteristics (Herbst *et al.,* 1971; Greenwald, Barlow, Nasca, & 8urnett, 1971). In these studies it has been found that in nearly every case (but not in *all* cases) mothers of young women with cancer of the vagina had been exposed to DES while matched control mothers had not been exposed.

At first glance this appears to be quite compelling—nearly every young woman with cancer had a mother who took DES. But it is not so compelling when you ask the question, Of all those mothers who took DES, how many daughters contracted cancer? As we mentioned before, DES was administered to millions of women, but only a very small minority of daughters have actually contracted cancer. One doctor noted for his DES research estimated that incidence of adenocarcinoma in DES-exposed daughters might be as low as 1 in 10,000 (*Wall Street Journal,* 1977, May 17). We are not implying that these cancer victims do not deserve compensation from the drug manufacturer because so few daughters contracted cancer. In fact we believe just the opposite. The point is that major civil liability suits are being brought to the bar backed by epidemiological evidence that may be no more compelling than the social science evidence on the effects of exposure to violent pornography. A cause-and-effect relationship does not necessarily follow from the statistical relationship medical scientists have found in their DES research. The causation of cancer could only be determined through an understanding of the specific mechanism or process whereby the introduction of a carcinogen into the body creates a tumor. This is not understood in the case of DES. For that matter, it is not well understood in any instances of environmentally caused cancer. Nevertheless, courts have found liability in other cases of environmentally induced cancer (e.g., *Karjala* v. *Jolins-Manville Products Corporation,* 1975), and many attorneys estimate that it should not be difficult for a court to find a legal causal relationship between DES and cancer (Sheiner, 1978).

We could imagine a study done in which the social scientist selected the 100 worst cases of unusual and sadistic rape in the United States during 1 year and through the use of survey techniques determined whether or not the rapist had been exposed to violent pornographic materials.[1] We would probably not be surprised if many of the defendants had had some history of exposure in one form or another to violent pornographic materials. The incidence would probably be especially high if the convicted rapists were compared to a group of controls matched on characteristics other than exposure to pornography. Such a study, of course, would be dissatisfying to the social psychologist, especially for two reasons. First, interview techniques are neither informative or reliable enough to enable the researcher to determine the type and frequency of exposure or whether the respondent was telling the truth. Second, and most importantly, such data help us little in determining what percentage of the population upon being exposed to these materials will actually commit a violent rape. In other words, we would only have established, as have researchers examining DES cases, that exposure increases the risk of a particular outcome. But this level of proof may be compelling enough for the jury deciding the case.

From a practical standpoint—that is, from the standpoint of extracting damages from film producers and directors—the plaintiff's attorney and social scientists themselves should not feel that the scientific evidence they have to present at such a trial would be unconvincing to a jury. There is no abstract standard of proof deemed necessary to try a civil case. A medical expert testifying in DES case cannot inform a jury with any certainty (at least at this time) as to the exact probability associated with mothers being exposed to DES and vaginal cancer among daughters. Yet, hundreds of plaintiffs have been willing to press suit with the aid of the limited information medical experts can provide. Social psychologists have information that may be just as compelling (or even more

---

[1]For examples of such cases see *State of Minnesota* v. *Marhoun,* 1983 and *Indiana* v. *Schiro,* *1981.*

compelling considering the experimental nature of the data collected to date) to jurors in establishing the likelihood of injury from a given set of materials. In summary, the lack of precision in the social scientific evidence linking exposure to violent pornography to violent behavior need not stand in the way of tort action against film producers, directors, and distributors. Existing data may be just as compelling as that brought forth in other large-scale damage suits.

Foreseeability or Predictable Harm

So far we have suggested ways in which social science data could be used to establish that violent pornographic materials pose a risk to innocent victims who may be harmed by a third party who is incited by these materials. Another important question in establishing the liability of manufacturers and distributors of these materials is the determination of the degree to which the harmful or violent act could have been foreseen. As we mentioned in the beginning of the chapter, it is assumed, under modern tort law theory, that the product supplier is responsible for anticipating how consumers will use a particular product. This includes anticipating that the consumer will use the product as it is intended to be used by the manufacturer or distributor and anticipating possible misuses or uses that are unintended (Turley, 1983).

Spak (1981) has argued that under certain conditions TV and movie producers should be able to predict with relative certainty that a violent act will result from showing a unique act of violence. Spak reaches his conclusion from a consideration of single documented cases as well as sociological and psychological evidence gained by researchers studying the responses of individuals exposed to televised violence (i.e., Berkowtiz, 1964, February; Bandura, Ross, & Ross, 1963; Lovass, 1961; Report to the Surgeon General, 1972). Earlier we mentioned Spak's argument about the merits of linking a specific act or harm with a specific depiction in order to establish an instructional effect. He also argues that this specificity may serve as one of the criteria for determining that a harmful effect can be predicted—only those acts that are unique acts of violence constitute acts of predictable harm.

To this notion of uniqueness Spak adds two more factors that may help to determine whether a producer or director could be expected to predict that a media-depicted act will result in harm: (1) the degree to which the act is glamorized when performed by the charismatic leading character and (2) the detail with which the violent acts are presented. A violent act committed by Clint Eastwood or Charles Bronson enacted in slow motion or using close-ups or repetitions, for example, might have the net effect, argues Spak, of reinforcing the act in the viewer's mind and "directly increasing the likelihood of reproduction of real life" (Spak, 1981, p. 672).

Although Spak's own analysis is limited to televised and movie violence and does not address subject of pornography, one can easily extend this basic notion of foreseeability based on empirical research to the area of violent pornography. We have already discussed the empirical research in the previous sections. We suggest that this evidence in combination with a theoretical account of the findings would provide a reasonably sound basis for establishing foreseeability. Further, as Spak notes, scientific theory and evidence in conjunction with actual, documented, well-publicized cases of sexual–aggressive acts (such as *Indiana* v. *Schiro,* which we discussed in a previous section) apparently resulting from exposure to violence may create a very sound basis for establishing foreseeability.

Two complementary theoretical approaches parsimoniously account for many of the empirical findings presented by Malamuth and his colleagues and Donnerstein and his research associates (Malamuth & Donnerstein, 1982). The first theory, proposed by Berkowitz (1970, 1974), emphasizes stimulus–response (S–R) associations. In this formulation, media presentations activate a wide range of responses in the individual that he or she is predisposed to make in that setting. It is presumed that repeated pairing of sex and violence, for example, could result in the viewer "automatically" equating the two under certain conditions. Later, when confronted with a stimulus person that resembles those encountered when viewing violent pornography (the stimulus need not necessarily be any more restricted than the general category: young woman vs. young man), the viewer responds with aggressive ideas and feelings and perhaps even aggressive behaviors. As Malamuth and Donnerstein (1982) point out, the empirical studies that found increased aggression against female but not male targets after exposure to depictions of sexual aggression against women (i.e., Donnerstein & Berkowitz, 1981) support this theoretical notion. Likewise, the finding that negative-outcome aggressive–pornographic depictions result in increased aggression when the individual is predisposed to attack someone because he is angry (Donnerstein & Berkowitz, 1981) supports this theory.

A modeling process may operate in conjunction with these S–R associations. It has been well established (Bandura, 1977) that the observation of the rewarding and punishing consequences accompanying a model's behavior can result in either inhibition or disinhibition effects. Observing a model being rewarded or punished for a particular behavior results in the viewer vicariously learning about the consequences of enacting a given behavior and serves to strengthen or weaken restraints on similar behavior in the observer. In the case of exposure to violent pornography (or even less explicit depictions of sexual aggression) in which the victim is portrayed as deriving some pleasure or positive outcome the observer presumably learns that "aggressive acts do not result in negative and may even lead to positive consequences. [Thus] this explanation would predict, as indicated by the data, that exposure to aggressive–pornographic depictions with a positive outcome would result in increased aggression" (Malamuth &

Donnerstein, 1982, p. 125). It is not immediately apparent, however, how this disinhibition theory would account for increased aggression against females among angered males who are exposed to materials depicting a negative outcome for the victim.

From these theoretical accounts, particularly the disinhibition–modeling theory, and the supporting empirical data, we could reasonably assert that under some circumstances the mere showing of certain films or the distribution of certain materials will increase the probability that violent acts will be reproduced in real life. Specifically, we can, on the basis of evidence collected to date and on the theoretical interpretation of this evidence, assert that the depiction of rape or other sexual violence against women in such a manner as to emphasize the positive reactions of the victim to this aggression increases the probability that the depicted harm will be reproduced in real life. Thus, the movie producers, directors, etc., or magazine publishers responsible for these depictions may be held liable because of the foreseeability of an actual harm arising from exposure to these materials.

Producer's Ability to Eliminate the Unsafe Character of Violent Pornography

Another factor in the determination of negligence is the ability of the manufacturer to eliminate the unsafe character of the product without either making it too expensive or reducing its utility (Wade, 1973). Are there ways in which the producers and publishers of violent pornography can make their product safer (i.e., reduce the probability that these depictions will motivate or incite the viewer to reenact what he has seen)? There have been several investigations of the effectiveness of debriefing procedures given to subjects after they have participated in experiments in which they have been exposed to violent pornography that suggests ways to improve the safety of this material. It could be argued that producers and publishers could easily incorporate the messages developed for experimental debriefings in the form of either viewer warnings or film epilogues at little cost to themselves and the failure to have done so is an indication of negligence.

Malamuth and Donnerstein and their colleagues (Check & Malamuth, 1981, August; Donnerstein & Berkowitz, 1981; Malamuth & Check, in press) have assessed the effectiveness of debriefing procedures that have emphasized that the idea women enjoy or secretly desire sexual assault is purely a myth. The results of these assessments have consistently yielded the finding that participation in the research and receipt of the debriefing results in a significant reduction of subjects' belief in rape myths. In fact, the combination of exposure to violent pornography and debriefing results in a greater reduction of belief in rape myths than simply receiving the debriefing alone (Check & Malamuth, 1981, August; Malamuth & Donnerstein, 1982).

The content of these debriefings might be directly inserted into violent pornographic films themselves, placed on the front of videocassettes, included in catalog advertisements of videotapes or even placed on magazine racks that contain violent pornographic materials. Borrowing heavily from a debriefing actually used by Malamuth and Check (in press) and Burt's (1980) Rape Myth Acceptance Scale, the following warning might be included on these materials:

> The movie you have just seen has depicted a rape. In reality, rape is a terrible crime and punishable by many years in prison. Rape victims suffer severe psychological damage as well as the more obvious physical effects on the assault. Unfortunately, many people still believe a number of falsehoods or myths about rape. One totally unfounded myth is that most women secretly desire to be raped or actually enjoy being forced to submit to violence. A second falsehood is that any woman could resist a rape if she really wanted to. These are in fact just myths and are totally unfounded.

The effectiveness of a disclaimer such as this one may be limited. It is unlikely, for example, that children who might be exposed to violent pornography through home videotapes would be adequately protected from these materials through the use of warning labels or epilogues. Further, even for adults the effectiveness of warning labels for other products deemed hazardous is estimated to be extremely low (Kanouse & Hayes-Roth, 1980). Winkler, Kanouse, Berry, Hayes-Roth, and Rogers (1981), however, provide some evidence that pamphlets included with prescription drugs may be somewhat more effective. Still, the results of the studies cited above do indicate that at least among college student subjects, debriefing may be quite effective in changing attitudes about rape and violence against women. These debriefings might provide guidance on steps that movie producers and magazine publishers could take in order to reduce the dangers of their products.

Loss Spreading of Liability to the Consumer

This chapter has been devoted to exploring the possibility of holding manufacturers and distributors responsible for potentially dangerous media products. There is, however, another possibility for allocating responsibility for the harms arising from media products. We offer this possibility in the interest of thoroughness and to encourage the reader to think about who is responsible for the effects of the proliferation of these materials in our society.

Turley (1983) has noted that the recent developments in tort theory actually reflect a shift away from holding the manufacturer liable for injuries; instead the law holds the *product* liable for the injuries. The consumers who create a market for a potentially dangerous product such as violent pornography are the ones who actually create a risk to some innocent bystanders. If the potentially dangerous product cannot be redesigned to reduce the risk of injury, the profits from the product could be used to compensate for injuries produced by the product.

Ultimately, these costs could be spread among consumers who created the market for the product. If the product produces frequent or severe injuries, then the cost of compensating injured parties could substantially inflate the price of the product. Hence, the resulting price of the product may be so high the product would no longer be marketed. In short, the utility of the product to the consumers would be weighed against the costs of compensation for any injury. If these consumers are unwilling to absorb the costs of compensating for injuries resulting from the product, then the product would no longer be marketed and the risk of injury would be removed.

SUMMARY AND CONCLUSIONS

In this chapter we have attempted to do several things, First, we have provided an overview of some of the major principles of product liability and constitutional law. Second, we have applied the tort principles to the case in which a plaintiff claims injury through a third party as a result of exposure to violent pornography. The social psychological evidence collected to date may greatly assist the plaintiff in claiming that violent pornography was a causal factor in the victim injury. Specifically, the plaintiff is able, through reference to the scientific literature, to define what type of materials may be most dangerous, determine who is likely to be influenced by violent pornography, to show who is likely to be victimized by a third party exposed to these materials, and to verify that these injuries were both foreseeable by the distributors and producers of these materials and could have potentially been prevented through certain product modifications.

As more scientific evidence is accumulated on the impact of exposure to violent–pornographic material on behavior, it is likely that we shall witness greater reliance by the courts on experts familiar with this research. Expert testimony by social psychologists in this research area has already been used in several criminal cases. The impact of this type of evidence in civil litigation remains untested up to now. But this may soon change, particularly as researchers in the area of violent pornography begin to extend their efforts toward the development of more externally valid studies involving, in particular, longer exposure times rather than the one-exposure experimental sessions used in most research. A plaintiff coming to court with findings such as those in this volume, as well as more externally valid research findings (should they support the initial work), may fair quite well before the jury.

It is also possible that by winning a civil suit the plaintiff could be indirectly responsible for the limitation of these materials throughout our society in general. A ''ripple effect'' could occur whereby producers and distributors, afraid of being sued in similar cases, refrain from depicting violent sexual scenes that could potentially bring them to court. The case we used to open this chapter, *Olivia* v. *NBC,* is interesting in this regard. As the reader will recall, the case was eventually dismissed on constitutional grounds. In the meantime NBC offered to settle out of court immediately after the suit was filed. More importantly, NBC aired *Born Innocent* a second time after the suit had been filed. This time, however, it was shown at 11:30 P.M. and most of the offensive rape scene had been edited out (Liebert *et al.,* 1982).

REFERENCES

Abel, G. G., Barlow, D. H., Blanchard, E., & Guild, D. (1977). The components of rapists' sexual arousal. *Archives of General Psychiatry, 34,* 395–403.

Bandura, A. (1977). *Social learning theory.* Englewood Cliffs, NJ: Prentice-Hall.

Bandura, A., Ross, D., & Ross, S. A. (1963). Imitation of film-media aggression models. *Journal of Abnormal and Social Psychology, 66,* 3–11.

Barbaree, H. E., Marshall, W. L., & Lanthier, R. D. (1979). Deviant sexual arousal in rapists. *Behavior research and therapy, 17,* 215–222.

Berkowitz, L. (1964, February). The effects of observing violence. *Scientific American,* 35–41.

Berkowitz, L. (1970). The contagion of violence: An S–R mediational analysis of some effects of observed aggression. In W. J. Arnold & M. M. Page (Eds.), *Nebraska symposium on motivation* (Vol. 18). Lincoln, NE: University of Nebraska Press.

Berkowitz, L. (1974). Some determinants of impulsive aggression: The role of mediated associations with reinforcements for aggression. *Psychological Review, 81,* 165–176.

Bern, W. (1975). Beyond the (garbage) pale, or democracy, censorship and the arts. In R. C. Rist (Ed.), *The pornography controversy.* New Brunswick, NJ: Transaction Books.

Brandenburg v. Ohio, 1968. *United States Supreme Court Reports, 395,* 444–457.

Burt, M. R. (1980). Cultural myths and supports for rape. *Journal of Personality and Social Psychology, 38,* 217–230.

Chaplinsky v. State of New Hampshire, 315 U.S. 568 (1942).

Check, J. V. P., & Malamuth, N. (1981, August). *Can exposure to pornography have positive effects?* Paper presented at the annual meeting of the American Psychological Association, Los Angeles.

Cohen, J., & Cohen, P. (1975). *Applied multiple regression/correlation analysis for the behavioral sciences.* Hillsdale, NJ: Erlbaum.

Donnerstein, E. (1980). Pornography and violence against women. *Annals of the New York Academy of Sciences, 347,* 277–288.

Donnerstein, E., & Berkowitz, L. (1981). Victim reactions in aggressive erotic films as a factor in violence against women. *Journal of Personality and Social Psychology, 41,* 710–724.

Downey, A. H., & Kenneth, G. G. (1983) Theories of Recovery for DES Damage: Is Tort liability the answer? *The Journal of Legal Medicine.* (Vol. 4), *2.*

Elmore v. American Motors. *California Reporter,* 1969, *70,* 578.

Epstein, R. A. (1978). Products liability: The search for the middle ground. *North Carolina Law Review, 56,* 643–662.

Escola v. Coca Cola Bottling Co. *California Reporter,* 1944, *24,* 453.

Georgia Law Review. (1981). Industry-wide liability and market share allocation of damages. *15,* 423–450.

Greenwald, P., Barlow, J. J., Nasca, P. C., & Burnett, W. S. (1971). Vaginal cancer after maternal treatment with synthetic estrogens. *New England Journal of Medicine, 284,* 390–392.

Herbst, A. L., Ulfelder, H., & Poskanzer, D. C. (1971). Adenocarcinoma of the vagina: Association of maternal stilbestrol therapy with tumor appearance in young women. *New England Journal of Medicine, 284,* 878–881.

Hilker, A. K. (1979). Tort liability of the media for audience act of violence: A constitutional analysis. *Southern California Law Review, 52,* 529–571.

Kanouse, D. E., & Hayes-Roth, B. (1980). Cognitive considerations in the design of product warnings. In L. A. Morris, M. Mazis & I. Barofsky (Eds.), *Banbury report 6: Product labeling and health risks.* Cold Spring Harbor, NY: Cold Spring Harbor Laboratory.

Karjala v. Jolins-Manville Products Corporation, 523 F. 2nd 155 (8th Cir. 1975).

Kingsley International Pictures Corp. v. Regents of the University of the State of New York, 1959.

Leventhal, H. (1977) An empirical inquiry into the effect of *Miller* v. *California* on the control of obscenity. *New York Law Review, 52,* 810–935.

Levering, R. (1978, August 3) TV on trial, *San Francisco Bay Guardian,* 5.

Liebert, R. M., Sprafkin, J. N., & Davidson, E. S. (1982). *The early window: Effects of television on children and youth.* New York: Pergamon Press.

Lovass. (1961). Effect of exposure to symbolic aggression on aggressive behavior. *Child Development, 32,* 37–44.

Masses Publishing Co. v. Patten, 1917 *244* F. 535 (S.D.N.Y.).

Malamuth, N. M., & Check, J. V. P. (1980a). Penile tumescence and perceptual responses to rape as a function of victim's perceived reactions. *Journal of Applied Social Psychology, 10,* 528–547.

Malamuth, N. M., & Check, J. V. P. (1980b). Sexual arousal to rape and consenting depictions: The importance of the woman's arousal. *Journal of Abnormal Psychology, 89,* 763–766.

Malamuth, N. M., & Check, J. V. P. (1981a). *The effects of exposure to aggressive-pornography: Rape proclivity, sexual arousal and beliefs in rape myth.* Paper presented at the Annual Meetings of the American Psychological Association, Los Angeles.

Malamuth, N. M., & Check, J. V. P. (1981b). The effects of mass media exposure on acceptance of violence against women: A field experiment. *Journal of Research in Personality, 15,* 436–446.

Malamuth, N. M., & Check, J. V. P. (in press). Debriefing effectiveness following exposure to pornographic rape depictions. *Journal of Sex Research.*

Malamuth, N. M., & Donnerstein, E. (1982). The effects of aggressive–pornographic mass media stimuli. In L. Berkowitz (Ed.), *Advances in experimental social psychology* (Vol. 15). New York: Academic Press.

Malamuth, N., Haber, S., & Feshbach, S. (1980). Testing hypotheses regarding rape: Exposure to sexual violence, sex differences, and the "normality" of rape. *Journal of Research in Personality, 14,* 121–137.

Malamuth, N. M., Heim, M., & Feshbach, S. (1980). Inhibitory and disinhibitory effects. *Journal of Personality and Social Psychology, 38,* 399–408.

Michelson, P. (1975). The pleasures of commodity, or how to make the world safe for pornography. In R. C. Rist (Ed.), *The pornography controversy.* New Brunswick, NJ: Transaction Books.

Mill, J. S. (1943). *On liberty.* New York: Appleton-Century Crofts.

Miller v. State of California, 413 U.S. 15 (1973).

Moody, G. R.(1981). Broadcast negligence and the First Amendment: Even Mickey Mouse has rights. *Mercer Law Review, 33,* 423–432.

New York Times, (1973, October 4). at 1, col. 2.

Olivia N. v. National Broadcasting Co., Inc. *California Reporter,* 1978, *141,* 511–515.

Prosser, W., & Wade, J. W. (1971). *Cases and materials on torts* (5th ed.). Mineola, N.Y.: Foundation Press.

Report to the Surgeon General. (1972). *Television and growing up: Impact of televised violence.* Washington, DC: Government Printing Office.

Rist, R. C. (Ed.). (1975). *The pornography controversy.* New Brunswick, NJ: Transaction Books.

Schenck v. United States, 249 U.S. 47 (1919).

Sheiner, N. (1978). DES and a proposed theory of enterprise liability. *Fordham, 46,* 963.

Shiners. (1982). Offensive personal product advertising on the broadcast media. *Federal Communication Law Journal, 33,* 74–85.

Southeastern Promotions Ltd. v. Conrad, 1975.

Spak, M. (1981). Predictable harm: Should the media be liable? *Ohio State Law Journal, 42,* 671–687.

State of Minnesota, Appellant, v. William Edward Marhoun, Respondent, No. 82-611 Supreme Court of Minnesota 323 N.W. 2d 729, August 24, 1982; Rehearing Denied October 5, 1982. Thomas N. Schiro, Defendant–Appellant, v. State of Indiana, Plaintiff–Appellee, No. 1181 S 329, Supreme Court of Indiana, 451 N.E. 2d 1047, August 5, 1983, filed.

Turley, W. (1983). Manufacturers' and suppliers' liability to handgun victims. *Northern Kentucky Law Review.*

Wade, J. W. (1973). On the nature of strict tort liability for products. *Mississippi Law Journal, 44,* 825–851.

Wall Street Journal. (1977, May 17). at 13, col. 1.

Walt Disney Productions Inc. v. Shannon, 1981.

Warren, E. J. (1975). Obscenity laws—A shift to reality. In R. C. Rist (Ed.), *The pornography controversy.* New Brunswick, NJ: Transaction Books.

Wathen, P. W. (1981, September 12). Schiro's sexual behavior linked to pornography. *The Evansville Courier,* p. 11.

Weirum v. RKO General Inc. 15 Cal. 3d 40, 539 P.2d 36, 123 Cal. Rptr. 468 (1975).

Winkler, J. D., Kanouse, D. E., Berry, S. H., Hayes-Roth, B., & Rogers, W. H. (1981). *Informing patients about drugs: Analysis of alternative designs for erythromycin leaflets.* Santa Monica, CA: Rand.

Young v. American Minitheaters, Inc. *United States Supreme Court Reports,* 1976, *427,* 66–67.

Afterword

Sex, Violence, and the Media: Where Do We Stand Now?

H. J. Eysenck

PROBLEMS WITH EXPLORING PORNOGRAPHY

Obscenity and pornography have been with us since recorded history began and so has the debate about the possible consequences of portrayals of explicit sex, aggression, and, in particular, the explosive combination of the two. To the social psychologist the problems in this field are of considerable interest because they are common to all attempts to use scientific psychological investigations in the solution of social problems. It has always been the hope of social psychologists (and perhaps psychologists as a whole) that our science could be of use in suggesting answers of a factual kind to social problems, and the issues here raised are perhaps crucial in deciding to what extent such hopes may be justified.

Thouless's Principle

Let us note, first of all, that in most fields in which a social psychologist would want to inject factual information, there are already in existence violently antagonistic groups of people believing that they know the true answer to the question and do not need scientific evidence. This view has been incorporated in one of the most important laws of social psychology, Thouless's (1935) *principle of certainty*. Thouless formulated this principle in relation to religious beliefs, and I

PORNOGRAPHY AND
SEXUAL AGGRESSION

extended it (Eysenck, 1954) to a great variety of different social beliefs. This is Thouless's principle: "When, in a group of persons, there are influences acting both in the direction of acceptance and rejection of the belief, the result is not to make the majority adopt a lower degree of conviction, but to make some hold the belief with a high degree of conviction, while others reject it also with a high degree of conviction" (p. 16).

True to this law in relation to pornography, we have in society two groups with differing views. One proclaims loudly that pornography and obscenity in the media are not responsible for such phenomena as rape, greater callousness of males in their relationship with females, and general coarsening of sexual attitudes. The other group is equally convinced of the opposite and lays a great deal of blame for these evils on the portrayals of sex and violence in the media. The former group is often called (or considers itself) progressive or permissive, while the latter group prefers denominations related to ethics, religion, or social responsibility. Both groups are equally impervious to factual demonstration; they seem to have adopted the famous wartime slogan, "Don't confuse me with facts, my mind is made up!"

The irrationality of the debate is illustrated in a report by Fisher (1983) in which she points out that at the American Psychiatric Association Convention in New York in 1983, two teams arguing the question, "Do we exaggerate the impact of television violence?" agreed mainly that extremism was rampant on the other side.

Fisher (1983) also pointed out that at the same time a similar exchange was going on between a television network and a group of federal officials and behavioral scientists. The topic of this debate was a 32-page booklet issued by the American Broadcasting Company that took issue with portions of a report on Television and Behavior released in 1982 by the National Institute of Mental Health. The report by Fisher on these verbal and written exchanges must be read to indicate the depth to which presumably rational and scientifically informed people can sink when emotional prejudices take over; Thouless could not have wished for a better example to illustrate his principle!

Governmental Investigations

In debates in which social action becomes the issue, governments tend to shun responsibility and call upon specially set up commissions or committees to look at the facts of the case and make recommendations. Traditionally such committees (e.g., the Williams committee in Great Britain or the Commission on Obscenity and Pornography in the United States) contain few if any experts in the field, and their judgments are not usually determined by the actual facts of the case. Having given evidence to the Williams committee, I can testify to the absence of psychologists on that committee and the obsessional tendency of members of the committee to protect themselves from any contamination or contact with scientific laws relevant to the topic. In this, of course, the Williams committee was not exceptional, but true to type; having also testified before Senate and House of Representatives committees in the United States (on other issues), I have come to know the form reasonably well, and it is not one that would lead me to put much credence in the findings of such commissions or committees.

The psychologist, therefore, is put from the beginning in an invidious position. For thousands of years people have debated with much passion the issues on which psychologists are invited to contribute factual evidence. Many of the minds they address are completely closed and wish to hear only evidence in favor of their views; evidence against their position is immediately dismissed on all sorts of specious and irrelevant grounds. Committees are chosen deliberately to represent nonscientific interests and outlooks and are often (as in the case of the Commission of Obscenity and Pornography) influenced strongly by commercial interests that may have a veto on the choice of scientific witnesses (Eysenck & Nias, 1978). Little financial support is available for the necessary scientific studies, and even when results are available and reported, they are often misinterpreted or disregarded by the committee or commission in question. Not in this way are correct conclusions likely to be reached! It is not surprising that both the Williams committee and the Commission on Obscenity and Pornography came to vacuous conclusions, pretending that no evidence really existed to suggest any effects of the portrayal of sex and violence in the media on human behavior, and dismissing contrary evidence on grounds owing more to prejudice than to sound scientific reasoning. Cline (1974) has exposed some of the errors committed by the Commission on Obscenity and Pornography; it would be a task of supererogation to do the same for the Williams committee.

The Rejection of Laboratory Findings

It must be said that psychologists working in this field, and attempting to furnish relevant evidence, have often played into the hands of those who wish to use their results for partisan purposes. They have also often failed to follow the dictates of the scientific method and have laid themselves open to criticism that could easily have been avoided. I will give two examples to substantiate these points.

The first point relates to the allegation (repeatedly found in the reports of the Williams committee and the Commission on Obscenity and Pornography) that experimental laboratory studies are in some way untrustworthy and unlikely to give correct information on human reactions. When Eysenck and Nias (1978) published their book *Sex, Violence and the Media* and formulated the conclusion that there was good evidence to show that human conduct was indeed affected by the portrayal of sex and violence in films and on television, many critics rejected this conclusion on the grounds that the firmest evidence (although not the only evidence) for this conclusion was derived from experimental laboratory studies. Such studies, it was emphatically declared, can throw no light on the natural behavior of human beings in nonlaboratory situations. No evidence was furnished for this belief; it was pronounced as a self-evident truth that did not require any support. Yet, as we shall see, this belief is entirely false and rests on another assumption, equally false, but unfortunately often supported by psychologists in their work, particularly in relation to the topic under discussion.

Let us consider for a moment the argument of the critics. Essentially what they say is this: You, the experimentalist, carry out research in the laboratory in which certain stimuli, usually of an explicit sexual and aggressive character, are followed by certain consequences, such as greater aggression against females, greater callousness in relation to females, and a greater belief in certain sexual myths. But because this happens in the laboratory, it does not follow that it must happen in real life. Because it happens after short-term exposure in the laboratory, it may not happen after long-term exposure. In other words, the induction is faulty and has to be rejected; we cannot form any conclusions at all about what would happen in everyday life situations from knowing what happens under very restricted laboratory conditions.

This argument, as far as it goes, is perfectly true. It is the age-old philosophical argument against the sufficiency of Baconian induction, almost universally accepted among philosophers (even though it does not do justice to Bacon's actual writings, which are much more sophisticated than most of his critics seem to realize). And insofar as experimentalists argue along inductive lines, the criticism cannot be dismissed. However, and here we now come to the second great issue, science in general, and psychology as one of the sciences, does *not* proceed along purely inductive lines. It lays down quite general theories, tests those theories experimentally, and phrases generalization in terms of the theory, provided it is supported by the experimental evidence. In other words, the generalization is not from one laboratory experiment (or a series of laboratory experiments) to everyday life events. Starting with a theory that usually unifies a number of quite diverse empirical findings, the laboratory study is undertaken to test crucial deductions from the theory. If these deductions are supported, then the theory is sustained and may be used to make generalizations and predictions. It is because the theory applies *both* to laboratory investigations *and* to everyday life circumstances that we consider the experimental investigations important and relevant. No direct induction is intended or would be justified. Hence the criticism falls to the ground.

It is this interplay of theory and experiment that is not readily understood by the layman, and when I tried to explain it to the Williams committee, the lack of any scientific expertise on that committee made it a hopeless and uphill task.

Much the same may be said of the Commission on Obscenity and Pornography; what they have to say in their report shows little understanding of scientific methodology as portrayed by modern philosophers of science (Suppe, 1974). For most scientists in the hard sciences, a good theory can be far more influential than a number of doubtful facts. Let us consider, as an example, the shape of the planets.

The man in the street (and no doubt Professor Williams and the other members of the various committees and commissions I have been criticizing) would consider that our belief that any newly discovered planet would be ball-shaped was due to the fact that all previously discovered planets have this shape. This is a simple example of induction and completely unacceptable to physicists and astronomers. Newton's theory demands that all planets greater than a certain mass are ball-shaped, and the existing planets simply verify and illustrate this law. Our predictions, then, are based on that law, not on simple induction, and of course the law itself is based on a huge number of experimental studies embracing many more and different types of investigation, experiment, etc.

What makes Newton's theory all the more attractive to scientists, of course, is that it predicts not simply that planets will be round in shape, but it also predicts lawful deviations from this rule, for example, that planets will form a bulge around the equator because of the rotary movement of the planet around its axis. This prediction also well illustrates the comparative faith of scientists in theory and empirical investigation. Several expeditions were set up to investigate the actual shape of the earth, with results that were sometimes negative, sometimes positive; it was only relatively recently that measurement was sufficiently accurate to give convincing results. Nevertheless, scientists universally accepted Newton's precise predictions, and negative results were laughed out of court.

Another example of the superiority of theory-based prediction over induction is that Newton could also predict that asteroids would *not* show the typical planetary shape, as indeed they do not. Simple induction from planets to asteroids would have made the wrong prediction. This is but one example out of many that could be given; as Lewin was fond of saying: "There is nothing more practical than a good theory!"

Perhaps an example from my colleagues' and my work will illustrate the difference between the Baconian inductivism approach and the modern type of scientific approach. In one of our studies, E. Nelson (unpublished) carried out an experiment in which four groups of males, high and low respectively on the personality traits of extraversion–introversion and neuroticism–stability, were shown a series of very explicit pornographic films. These were put together from a large number of films made available to us by the British Customs and Excise Department; they were cut up into short scenes and joined together so that each 4-minute film portrayed much the same type of sexual activity, for example, cunnilingus, fellatio, missionary position intercourse, and intercourse a tergo.

There were nine films in all, and each subject was shown three films on any given day, with 4-minute intervals between films on that day. Films were shown on 3 consecutive days, and the order was randomized. There were 40 subjects in all, 10 in each group.

The effect of the film was monitored by means of a penis plethysmograph, and the outcome was very clear-cut. There was little difference relating to the neuroticism–stability dimension, but extraverts showed significantly greater habituation–extinction within films, between films on the same day, and between days. Overall, from the first to the ninth film, there was a very large degree of habituation–extinction for the extraverts but relatively little for the introverts.

From the standpoint of Baconian induction, very little could be inferred from these results. They could not necessarily be generalized to other groups of subjects (ours were not students but members of the general public paid for their services), nonlaboratory situations, or different types of stimuli. But that, of course, was not the purpose of the experiment. It was set up to test a number of theories, for each of which there was a considerable amount of a priori evidence already available. Thus my theory of extraversion–introversion posits that extraverts should show greater habituation–extinction (Eysenck, 1967; Stelmack, 1981), while neuroticism–stability is not related to this reaction. What was predicted, and found, was that this particular theory would apply just as much to sexual reactions as other types of physiological reactions that had been tested previously.

From another point of view, the experiment was an extension of earlier work on the relationship between sexual behavior and personality (Eysenck, 1976). In these studies, it had been shown that extraverts tend to be much more variable than introverts in their sexual behavior, and the theory was put forward that this was due to quicker habituation–extinction in extraverts. Last but not least, there was in existence a general theory relating Pavlovian extinction to human behavior, in the laboratory, in everyday life situations, and in the clinic (Eysenck, 1982, 1983). This is a general theory of habituation–extinction in humans and animals, applied to neuroses and their treatment in particular, but clearly also extending to such behavior as was investigated in the experiment.

What I have been trying to indicate is that a particular experiment is part of a *nomological network*; it does not stand alone. We do not make generalizations from the findings of a single experiment, but from general and well-supported theories. The purpose of the experiment is to test the theory in new and stringent ways; it is not to provide a foundation for generalization in and by itself. It is this function of the experiment that Williams and his committee found so difficult to understand and that the Commission on Obscenity and Pornography seemed to disregard completely. It is easy to dismiss, in addressing a popular and nonscientific audience, the contribution of experimental psychology by furthering this fundamental misunderstanding of the purpose and function of an experiment. It is unfortunate that many psychologists have followed this popular prejudice in their presentation and have failed to indicate the importance of general theories and their relevance to social action.

GENERAL THEORY ON SEX, VIOLENCE, AND THE MEDIA

What then is this general theory that underlies predictions in this general field of sex, violence, and the media? As Eysenck and Nias (1978) have pointed out, rules against intraspecies aggression, cruelty, and violence, whether against women or men, are firmly established in society. In part, as sociobiology teaches us, there is probably a genetic basis for these rules, due to the better chances of longevity and hence child production offered by societies operating under these rules. In part these rules are impressed on children through a process of Pavlovian conditioning (Eysenck, 1977). And in part, no doubt, Seligman's notion of preparedness (1971) plays an important part. This is the view that certain responses are more readily conditioned because of a genetic predisposition to form such conditioned responses more speedily, more strongly, and even in situations where the relations of the conditioned stimulus (CS) and unconditioned stimulus (UCS) are degraded; that is, where there is a long interval between CS and UCS (Seligman, 1971). Such responses are subject to *habituation,* if unconditioned, or to *extinction,* if conditioned; there is a very extensive literature on these processes, particularly in relation to neurotic disorders, embracing both animal and human subjects, in a great variety of different situations. Much of this work has gone under the heading of "desensitization" (Wolpe, 1958, 1973), but other methods of therapy, such as "flooding" (Rachman & Hodgson, 1980) have also recently been widely used for the purpose of extinguishing neurotic fears.

The general laws and rules discovered in relation to the experimental study of extinction, and the clinical work on behavior therapy, particularly desensitization, clearly apply to the exposure of human beings to the portrayal of explicit sex and violence in the media. (Note that the theory asserts that the kind of conditioning involved here is Pavlovian B, not Pavlovian A type conditioning, as Eysenck [1982, 1983] has argued; criticisms involving the latter type of conditioning do not apply to the former.) Indeed, in 1961, that is, long before adequate experimental studies were carried out in this field, I predicted very much what empirical research has since found, on the basis of this particular theory (Eysenck, 1961). Thus we should view the empirical studies summarized by Eysenck and Nias (1978), or the more recent ones described in this volume, as verifying the theory of desensitization rather than as a simple basis for Baconian induction.

The theory may also be useful in explaining such apparent paradoxes as that of

Japan, where apparently, as indicated in Chapter 6 by Abrahamson and Hayashi, rape is relatively rare, even though it is widely portrayed in the media. Their explanation is in terms of shame, and this explanation would seem to find support in the theory that conscience (which may be equated with shame here) is in fact a product of long-continued Pavlovian conditioning (Eysenck, 1977). Such a hypothesis could easily be tested by questioning Japanese males about the likelihood that they might rape if detection was impossible. The personalities of those with high scores could then be compared with those who indicated they would not rape under any circumstances.

ROBUSTNESS OF EXPERIMENTAL SUPPORT FOR THE GENERAL THEORY

When looking at the empirical infrastructure, it is most impressive that so much of it has in fact given experimental support to the desensitization theory. There are many reasons why one might have expected inconclusive results, and the fact that results have on the contrary been very supportive in itself suggests the strength of the causal factors involved. The reasons why one might have been rightly pessimistic in anticipating positive results from these studies will be fairly obvious, but they may perhaps with some advantage be listed.

In the first place, and most importantly, one would not expect effects to be very strong after a single exposure to the stimuli in question, or even after exposure to a small number of such stimuli. Desensitization is a lengthy process, and even on commonsense grounds one might expect that long-term, repeated exposure to explicit scenes of sex and violence would have a greater effect than single exposures, or even a small number of exposures. This is often stated as a criticism of the experimental studies showing effects even of small-scale exposure; one would think that this is not a reasonable criticism, because it would be expected that long-term and repeated exposure would have stronger effects than single or small-scale exposure! However that may be, effects would be expected to be minimal in the typical research design that has been used in this field and might, in fact, be almost undetectable. The fact that they have proved highly significant in many instances is an indication of the strength of the effects produced and their comparative robustness.

The second point to be considered is that, in behavior therapy, effects are very dependent on a fairly precise design of the sequence of stimuli administered. In desensitization, graded stimuli ranging from those provoking little anxiety to those provoking extreme anxiety are presented in ascending order, constituting a hierarchy such that desensitization to a less anxiety-provoking element is required before proceeding to a higher level of anxiety-provoking stimuli. If this rule is broken, and too much anxiety is provoked, the extinction process breaks down, and it may be necessary to begin at the beginning. Flooding procedures start with high anxiety-provoking stimuli, but these have to be presented for a very lengthy period of time, because otherwise what I have called incubation of anxiety sets in, that is, an incrementation of the conditioned response (Eysenck, 1982, 1983). Thus in either case success is contingent on precise planning and execution of a program of stimulus presentations. Little attention has been paid to these refinements in research on the effects of sex and violence, and if stimuli are presented in an atheoretical and haphazard fashion they might have positive or negative effects, which might, in some cases, cancel out.

A third problem is related to the ever-present existence of individual differences. Identical procedures will not have identical effects on different people, and indeed may have opposite effects. Thus exposure to explicit sexual material may lead to such responses as disgust and avoidance in some people, but to a greater liking for such material and a coarsening of attitudes toward the opposite sex in others. These reactions to pornography by differing personalities are probably related to the method of presentation, so that we might expect the graded hierarchy involved in desensitization to be more effective with people who are very antagonistic to pornography in the first instance, while flooding procedures might be more effective with people already somewhat accustomed to pornography, or in any case not hostile to it. Personality differences are only just beginning to be appreciated by workers in this field, as shown by the Malamuth research summarized in Chapter 2. When different people react oppositely to identical stimuli, most of the main effects of an experiment will go into the "error" part of the variance unless specific hypotheses relating to personality differences are made part of the research plan and tested explicitly. In most of the work in this field this has unfortunately not been done (Eysenck & Nias, 1978).

DEFECTS OF EXPERIMENTAL LITERATURE

Personality effects should of course be studied not by firing random shots from a blunderbuss of multiphasic personality trait questionnaires, but by carefully setting up appropriate theoretical concepts and then relating these in a predictive fashion to the experimental elements involved. Of particular relevance to the topic of this book is of course the personality dimension of psychoticism (Eysenck & Eysenck, 1976). As Barnes, Malamuth, and Check (1984) have found, "High P (psychoticism) scorers were characterised by more favourable attitudes and enjoyment of force and unconventional sexual activities" (p. 159). This is as predicted and should be seen in relation to the general findings by Malamuth and others in this book that it is precisely such people who react more strongly to scenes of rape in pornography, and acknowledge a greater likelihood of committing such a crime when it is likely to be undetected. Eysenck (1976) has also shown quite close relationships between personality dimensions of extraversion and neuroticism, on the one hand, and sexual attitudes and behavior on the other; these were found to be genetically determined to a powerful extent and are certainly relevant to any discussion of the effects of sex and violence in the media.

One particular defect of the experimental literature is that it has almost completely eschewed the desensitization paradigm, and has concentrated almost entirely on the flooding paradigm, whereas in real life it is much more likely that people graduate through a series of slightly erotic to more erotic to pornographic to hard-core pornography presentations, becoming desensitized more and more at each stage. Flooding, on the other hand, requires more long-term exposure, and when duration of exposure is too short, this may produce what in the case of anxiety I have called incubation of anxiety, and what in this case might be called incubation of shame, that is, an *incrementation* in the shame reaction to exposure to explicit sexual and aggressive material (Eysenck, 1982, 1983). Theory predicts that such reaction would be linked not only to duration of exposure but also to personality, and quite specific predictions can be made in this field. Little attention has been paid to the theoretical considerations, and hence it might be considered that very strong effects would be required in order to produce statistically significant results in experiments not designed to take these factors into account.

Another problem, this time of an ethical nature, appears to produce great difficulties in the way of obtaining positive results in relation to a possible increase in the desire to use force against women (in a sexual sense) after viewing depictions of rape and other instances of the use by males of force against females. To test the effects, most writers have used the Buss paradigm (Buss, 1961), in which the putative delivery of aversive stimuli (e.g., electric shock, noise) to the confederate of the experimenter constitutes the operational definition of aggression. But this a rather remote way in which a person might discharge his sexual aggression; much more likely ways would be to slap the woman, beat her, or punch her, combining aggressive with sexual motives. The finding that even with this very much watered-down response very clear results can be achieved again testifies to the robustness of the findings. It is unrealistic to criticize such experiments as being laboratory situations as opposed to real-life situations; the limitations are ethical and apply just as much in real-life studies as in laboratory studies. Nevertheless, the limitations do exist and should be taken into account. Many males, sexually aroused by films and made angry by experimental manipulation, while not very interested in the Buss-type vicarious response, might vent their sexual aggressiveness on the experimental victim if this could be done in a suitable sex-related fashion.

A third problem, frequently disregarded in the earlier part of research, is the mood of the subject. In typical experimental situations, the mood is "flat," cautious, and reticent. With subjects in this mood, it is difficult to register any kind of emotional reaction, as extensive research on emotion has amply demonstrated. Recent work has used experimental designs in which the subject is angered before the experiment proper begins, and it has been amply demonstrated, as in the relevant chapters in this volume, that this makes a considerable degree of difference in the outcome of the experiment. The use of such stratagems incidentally demonstrates the power of the laboratory experiment, which apparently can incorporate elements that the critics would have thought could only be found in real-life situations. This is by no means so, and ingenuity will usually find a way round the fairly obvious difficulties that confront the path of the experimenter at every stage. These findings should make us cautious in evaluating the earlier work that did not incorporate the evocation of emotion prior to the experiment in the paradigm. Negative results of this kind are due to an insufficient theoretical analysis of the situation, not to the absence of the hypothesized effects.

A final difficulty, which is almost unavoidable, is that, like all people, social scientists tend to take certain things as given, when in actual fact there is little evidence for them. Thus we often talk about rape myths—such as that women approve of, or may enjoy, the use by males of force in sexual encounters. Is this really a myth? There is at least the possibility that some women (certainly not all, and probably only a minority) may indeed see the use of force on the part of the male as a good excuse for overcoming their puritanical reactions; they would be able to say to themselves, "I didn't really consent; he forced me into it!" This might then be balm to their conscience and reconcile them to finally taking part in a voluntary manner in sexual activities they might otherwise have felt impelled to reject. Chapter 9 by Goodchilds and Zellman suggests that this kind of rationalization may be operating in the relationships of adolescents. I am not suggesting that this is an established fact; I am merely suggesting that we should be careful about labeling as a myth something that, at least in some contexts and for some people, may not be a myth at all. Much research could profitably be devoted to this problem.

It is widely recognized that only 1 rape victim in 10 (if that) actually reports the crime to the police, and of course in these reported cases it is very likely that the reaction of the female was indeed one of revulsion and rejection to the male. However, clearly there is a continuum from the extreme of violent rape—cruel, invasive, and completely against the wishes of the female—to lesser uses of force, and it is this of course that makes the definition of rape so difficult. Research among females who had some degree of force employed in producing conformity to the wishes of the male, but who have not gone to the police to complain of rape, might unearth interesting reactions, probably related to personality and degree of force exerted, as well as the degree of prior knowledge of the male involved, which would throw new light on these myths. This should not be read as presenting any kind of endorsement of the use of force by males against females or of rape; I merely suggest that the study by Goodchilds and Zellman seems to indicate that the definition of rape is much more complex than it seems at first and that simple-minded statements can be very far off the mark.

An additional argument, though not an unconnected one, relates to the prevalence of masochism. There is much clinical evidence for the association of sexual satisfaction with undergoing certain types of physical pain and degradation, an association perhaps more frequently observed in females than males, although clearly not absent in the latter either, as illustrated by the widespread activities of *dominatrixes,* (prostitutes willing to abuse, punish, and beat males wishing to pay for these services). It would be easy to suggest that masochists present a group completely separate from normal persons and qualitatively different from them, but such a categorical view is quite untenable; what we find is a continuum or dimension with many intermediate types. The popularity of sadomasochism is illustrated by the many advertisements found in such American magazines as *Screw,* British magazines such as *Forum,* or any of the many contact magazines; clearly the sexual satisfaction in inflicting pain of the sadist is reciprocated by the sexual satisfaction of the person receiving the painful stimuli, and thus the possibility can never be ruled out that for certain persons (possibly constituting a far from small minority), the myth considered as such may not in fact be a myth at all.

These are some of the reasons why one might have expected experiments such as those described in this volume to fail, or at best to give indecisive results; the fact that they do in fact give results that not only are highly significant, but that also agree very much and in detail with prediction from theory, must indicate the strength and robustness of the correlations involved. This was the conclusion of the Eysenck and Nias (1978) review of the literature, and it is powerfully reinforced by the studies reported in this volume. What are the possible social applications of these findings?

Here we must realize, first of all, that empirical findings and social actions are two quite different things, the former not necessarily entailing the latter in any way. Social action is determined by a large number of factors, including ethical considerations, political ideals, and feasibility estimates; factual considerations are only one factor influencing a final decision. Thus religious people might favor extensive censorship of films and television presentations including nudity and violence, regardless of an absence of evidence concerning socially undesirable consequences, simply because they regard such presentations as immoral, degrading, and generally undesirable. In a similar vein, libertarians might jib at censorship even if it could be proved that evil social consequences followed from the presentation of explicit sex and violence, particularly in combination, simply because they value freedom of speech more highly than the prevention of the antisocial activities in question. Social action is always determined by values that are independent of factual evidence, but of course for the majority of citizens, who are not members of either group, factual evidence does have some value. A clear-cut demonstration of socially undesirable consequences of the presentation of such material would have some power in helping them decide if something ought to be done in order to reduce the output and influence of such material.

The complexities and difficulties of dealing along legal and other lines with the problem of violent pornography are well discussed by Penrod and Linz in Chapter 10 and by Linz, Turner, Hesse, and Penrod in Chapter 11. Unfortunately, as Penrod and Linz discuss, the courts have not accepted much of the research by psychologists and other social scientists as evidence. Another problem is that legal language is not only unintelligible to the general public but also of necessity not precise in definition, thus making enforcement much more difficult. I have attempted to show elsewhere how one could make definitions more meaningful and realistic (Eysenck, 1972), but the law being what it is, it seems unlikely that such recommendations will ever be implemented!

CONCLUSION

In a sense this whole field is a testing ground for social science. We have been challenged by government and the legal profession to contribute factual clarification in a field in which confusion has been made worse, confounded by partisan attitudes of various persuasions. After a shaky start, I think it may be said that psychology has come up with the goods. Psychologists have shown considerable ingenuity in setting up experimental laboratory situations, in quantifying real-life situations, and in combining the two in ingenious research paradigms that have given meaningful answers to important social questions. There is now, I think, very little doubt (1) that the portrayal of sex and violence in the media does have important effects on at least some people; (2) that it is possible to formulate general theories that explain the findings, and that indeed have predicted most of them; and (3) that these results present problems for society that go far beyond the realm of social psychology and involve sociologists, philosophers, law-givers and politicians in general, as well of course as the community at large, whose voices cannot in this context be disregarded. We must be careful, on the one hand, to avoid the foolishness of prohibition, and on the other hand, we must avoid the sins of the three monkeys—see no evil, hear no evil, speak no evil! What is the best way of dealing with evil is a more difficult question that social scientists are not capable of answering by themselves; their task is to present society with the facts. It is up to society to take the facts seriously and to debate how best to deal with them.

REFERENCES

Barnes, G., Malamuth, N. & Check, J. (1984). Personality and sexuality. *Personality and Individual Differences, 5,* 159–172.

Buss. A. (1961). *The psychology of aggression.* New York: Wiley.

Cline, V. B. (Ed.) (1974). *Where do you draw the line?* Provo, Utah: Brigham Young University Press.

Eysenck, H. J. (1954). *The psychology of politics.* London: Routledge and Kegan Paul.

Eysenck, H. J. (1961). Television and the problem of violence. *New Scientist, 12,* 606–607.

Eysenck, H. J. (1967). *The biological basis of personality.* Springfield: C. C. Thomas.

Eysenck, H. J. (1972). The uses and abuses of pornography. In H. J. Eysenck, *Psychology is about people* (pp. 230–286). London: Allen Lane, The Penguin Press.

Eysenck, H. J. (1976). *Sex and personality.* London: Open Books.

Eysenck, H. J. (1977). *Crime and personality.* Boston: Routledge and Kegan Paul.

Eysenck, H. J. (1982). Neobehavioristic (S–R) theory. In G. T. Wilson and C. M. Franks (Eds.), *Contemporary behaviour therapy.* New York: Guilford Press.

Eysenck, H. J. (1983). Classical conditioning and extinction: The general model for the treatment of neurotic disorders. In M. Rosenbaum, C. M. Franks, & Y. Jaffe (Eds.), *Perspectives on behavior therapy in the eighties* (Vol. 9). New York: Springer.

Eysenck, H. J., & Eysenck, S. B. G. (1976). *Psychoticism as a dimension of personality.* London: Hodder & Stoughton.

Eysenck, H. J., & Nias, D. K. B. (1978). *Sex, violence and the media.* London: Maurice Temple Smith.

Fisher, K. (1983). Nobody's giving in on debate over impact of violence on T.V. *A.P.A. Monitor, 14* (7), 7.

Rachman, S., & Hodgson, R. (1980). *Obsessions and compulsions.* Englewood Cliffs, NJ: Prentice-Hall.

Seligman, M. (1971). Phobias and preparedness. *Behavior Therapy, 2,* 307–320.

Stelmack, R. M. (1981). The psychophysiology of extroversion and neuroticism. In H. J. Eysenck (Ed.), *A model for personality.* London & New York: Springer.

Suppe, F. (Ed.) (i974). *The structure of scientific theories.* London: University of Illinois Press.

Thouless, R. H. (1935). The tendency to certainty in religious beliefs. *British Journal of Psychology, 26,* 16–31.

Wolpe, J. (1958). *Psychotherapy by reciprocal inhibition.* Stanford: Stanford University Press.

Wolpe, J. (1973). *The practice of behavior therapy.* Oxford: Pergamon Press.

Author Index

Subject Index